PRAISE FOR APPALACHIAN RECKONING

———

"In this illuminating and wide-ranging collection, the authors do more than just debunk the simplistic portrayal of white poverty found in *Hillbilly Elegy*. They profoundly engage with the class, racial, and political reasons behind a Silicon Valley millionaire's sudden triumph as the most popular spokesman for what one contributor cleverly calls 'Trumpalachia.' This book is a powerful corrective to the imperfect stories told of the white working class, rural life, mountain folk, and the elusive American Dream."

—Nancy Isenberg,
author of *White Trash: The 400-Year Untold History of Class in America*

"So often the song of this place has been reduced to a single off-key voice out of tune and out of touch. *Appalachian Reckoning* is the sound of the choir, pitch perfect in its capturing of these mountains and their people. This book is not only beautiful, but needed."

—David Joy, author of *The Line That Held Us*

"This edited volume continues the rich Appalachian studies tradition of pushing back against one-sided caricatures of Appalachian people. The essays, poems, and photo-essays in this book demonstrate the diversity of Appalachian perspectives on the serious problems facing our nation as well as the role that myths about Appalachia continue to play in US policy debates. This is a must-read for everyone who read (or refused to read) J. D. Vance's deeply flawed, best-selling memoir, *Hillbilly Elegy*."

—Shaunna Scott, University of Kentucky

APPALACHIAN RECKONING

A Region Responds
to *Hillbilly Elegy*

Edited by

ANTHONY HARKINS

AND

MEREDITH McCARROLL

WEST VIRGINIA UNIVERSITY PRESS

MORGANTOWN 2019

First edition published 2019 by West Virginia University Press
Printed in the United States of America

ISBN:
Cloth 978-1-946684-78-3
Paper 978-1-946684-79-0
Ebook 978-1-946684-80-6

Library of Congress Cataloging-in-Publication Data
is available from the Library of Congress

Book and cover design by Than Saffel / WVU Press
Cover image: A dirt road fades into a heavy fog rolling off Wayah Bald,
Macon County, North Carolina, May 26, 2015.
Photograph by Nathan Armes.

CONTENTS

CONTENTS

CONTENTS

ACKNOWLEDGMENTS

WE ARE DELIGHTED to express our appreciation to the many people who helped this project come to fruition over the past year. We thank the original participants (all of whom are also contributors to this volume) to the roundtable discussion of reflections on *Hillbilly Elegy* at the 2017 Appalachian Studies Association conference in Blacksburg, which marks one of the launching points of the project. Special thanks to Emily Satterwhite for her support for the roundtable, her abiding friendship, and her bringing the editors together at a memorable dinner in Blacksburg. Little did we know then that our professional lives would become so entwined in such a rewarding way! We also thank all the contributors to this book, with a special shout out to Theresa Burriss, who offered essential feedback at several steps in the project's journey and was instrumental in selecting and organizing many of the poets and photographers in the book. Thanks to Roger May, who helped give voice to our desire to see the book as a project of bridge building, and who had a ready resource in Looking at Appalachia for soliciting images of and from the region. We gratefully acknowledge financial support from the history department at Western Kentucky University and the dean of academic affairs at Bowdoin College that made possible our participation in the 2017 ASA conference. Finally, we offer our deep appreciation to our current and former editors at West Virginia University Press, Derek Krissoff and Andrew Berzanskis. Andrew offered enthusiastic support for our work in its earliest manifestations and strongly encouraged and facilitated our collaboration. This act of listening, finding common ground, and imagining the possibilities beyond either of our individual perspectives is what we hope the book will do for its readers.

WHY THIS BOOK?

ANTHONY HARKINS AND MEREDITH McCARROLL

THIS IS A BOOK born out of frustration. This is a book born out of hope. It attempts to speak for no one and to give voice to many. This is a book that could have emerged without *Hillbilly Elegy*, but it was also created in the explicit context of a postelection, post–*Hillbilly Elegy* moment. It therefore attempts to respond to those who have felt they understand Appalachia "now that they have read *Hillbilly Elegy*" and to push back against and complicate those understandings. It is meant to open a conversation about why that book struck such a deep nerve with many in the region, but it is not meant to demonize J. D. Vance. Instead, the contributors to this book prioritize focusing on the region, reclaiming some of the talk about Appalachia, and offering ideas through the voices of many who have deep, if varied, lived experiences in and of Appalachia.

Either explicitly or implicitly, begrudgingly acknowledged, directly repudiated, or partially welcomed, the shadow of *Hillbilly Elegy* hangs over this book. Not since Harry Caudill's *Night Comes to the Cumberlands* (1963) has a nonfiction book on Appalachia attracted such widespread national acclaim and success as J. D. Vance's 2016 account, controversially subtitled *A Memoir of a Family and Culture in Crisis*. As of February 2018, the book had been on the *New York Times* best-seller list for a remarkable seventy-three weeks in a row and had sold in all formats combined well over a million copies. It ranked first in the combined E-book and nonfiction list for six weeks in 2017 and was the top selling nonfiction iBook of the year.[1] It has also received broad critical attention, and has been reviewed across a wide swath of the national media landscape from the *National Review* and the *Wall Street Journal* to *All Things Considered*, *Fresh Air*, and *Slate*. In book reviews and on-air interview programs, it has been routinely described as "riveting" and "starkly honest." "The most important book about America," pronounced the *Economist*. David Brooks called it "essential reading." Although such rave reviews have since somewhat abated, Vance himself continues in early 2018 to be a common presence on television and radio interview shows and as a guest speaker, and he was even for a time courted as a potential Republican Senate candidate in Ohio.[2]

Clearly Vance's account of growing up in Middletown, Ohio, and visiting eastern Kentucky as a member of a multigenerational family scarred by drug abuse and alcoholism has resonated with many readers, including some Appalachians. Yet, just as obviously, *Hillbilly Elegy* and Vance have been criticized by many within the Appalachian region and beyond as anti-intellectual, overly anecdotal, and attempting to revitalize widely discredited "culture of poverty" explanations for persistent inequities in the region. Regardless of their particular perspective on Vance, though, all the voices in this book stress that Appalachia is a far more diverse and complex place and identity than *Hillbilly Elegy* and the media's interpretation of it imply or that the president tweets about. The people and region belie simplistic definitions or characterizations of a monolithic and predeterminative "hillbilly culture," as Vance labels it. All of its inhabitants and experiences are not simply an extension of Vance's individual family and life story, nor should the notion of a "memoir of a culture" (as Vance's subtitle constructs it) go unchallenged. There is not a single "truth" about Appalachia and its people, and the essays, narratives, and artistic expressions in this book, integrated in the best tradition of Appalachian studies, collectively break up this too solid image of the place simply by speaking multiple truths about multiple experiences. In so doing, they challenge the idea that any single book, including this one, can sum up the entirety of Appalachia and what it means to be Appalachian.

This book provides a platform for reactions to and insights about Vance's book and its reception but also for writings that reach well beyond *Hillbilly Elegy* to consider the many ways that Appalachians experience their Appalachianness. As citizens and scholars, Appalachians have been fighting against gross simplifications and stereotypes since at least the early nineteenth century, and this work should be considered only the latest effort to challenge such views.[3] Some contributors emphasize the need to challenge distorting and debilitating stereotypes; some stress the need to face the region's problems forthrightly and squarely. Some are quiet and contemplative; others are angry. Yet despite what the majority of our contributors find to be *Hillbilly Elegy*'s flaws and even damages, they share the sense that the broader public "rediscovery" of the region that *Hillbilly Elegy* and the conceptual construction of "Trumpalachia" (in the neologism of contributor Dwight Billings) have engendered should also be seen as an opportunity—a chance to reclaim Appalachia and to help those unfamiliar with the region to recognize its complexities and its diversities.

In this spirit, the contributors address from a range of perspectives an array of pressing questions the *Hillbilly Elegy* phenomenon raises: What about Vance and his book accounts for the explosion of interest in Appalachia and its people in this historical moment of national political turmoil? Why have the ideas in *Hillbilly Elegy* caused such a firestorm in the region? What can we learn about both actual Appalachia and the way it is perceived from these reactions and debates? What does it mean in the twenty-first century to be Appalachian? Perhaps most significantly, as poet Jeff Mann explicitly asks here in his poem "Social Capital," what other Appalachian voices have been drowned out in the flood of attention that Vance and his book have garnered? And how can these voices be heard?

To bring some conceptual structure to this wide range of topics, *Appalachian Reckoning* is organized broadly into two parts. Part I, "Considering *Hillbilly Elegy*," features texts directly assessing or commenting on the words and impact of Vance's influential work. It is further divided into two sections: a collection of primarily scholarly essays (although also shaped by the authors' mountain backgrounds and experiences) that carefully consider *Hillbilly Elegy* through various social and political prisms, and a section of personal and autobiographical reflections on the book (although also informed by scholarly analysis). Interspersed throughout part I are poems and photographs that provide artistic responses to Vance's book.

Part II, "Beyond *Hillbilly Elegy*," features narratives and images that together provide a snapshot of a place that is at once progressive, haunted, depressed, beautiful, and culturally and spiritually rich. These stories are difficult to categorize because of their range in voice, focus, perspective, and plot. They are at turns heartbreaking, humorous, contemplative, and defiant. In their broad outlines, they are stories that anyone could tell. But they are stories told by Appalachians, grounded in the specific. The sound of a vowel, the feel of a tool, the recipe for corn pone, the name of a school. There is no singular focal point to part II other than the shared idea that there is no consensus about Appalachia.

———

Let us further elaborate on each part of the book, starting with some general thoughts on *Hillbilly Elegy* and the public persona of J. D. Vance. It is important to recognize the often-stated point that *Hillbilly Elegy*'s surprising and sustained success is largely a product of the presidential campaign and election of Donald Trump. As others have noted, Vance's sensational book would most likely have found an audience anyway, since Appalachia is "(re) discovered" cyclically. This political earthquake was the latest shock again bringing Appalachia and some of its people and issues to the forefront of media attention and through that attention to the broader public across the country (and indeed the world).[4] The Trump campaign and postelection media coverage have framed one version of Appalachia defined almost exclusively through the prism of the white male coal miner, depressed towns, and rampant opioid addiction. This has served as the perfect signifier of white working-class "forgotten Americans." In turn, it has led to a partial reconceptualization of the region less as an exotic exception to the rest of America (the "strange land and peculiar people" mindset that has so characterized views of the region since at least the nineteenth century) and instead more as an intensified signifier of the hazily defined conceptual category of "the white working class"—regardless of both the concept's and the region's actual geographic, demographic, and cultural diversity.[5]

There is also appeal for many in Vance's ability to transcend his early childhood traumas and in his simple and personalized account of that transcendence. Vance's story, largely devoid of analyses of broader socioeconomic and historical dynamics, is compelling—the quintessential "up from your bootstraps" "American Dream," as he often notes. He describes growing up in an unstable, nontraditional, lower middle-class household and experiencing harrowing moments navigating childhood and early adulthood with a drug-dependent, dysfunctional mother. Overcoming a long string of ineffectual and uncommitted stepfathers and his mom's boyfriends and an extended family prone to violence, he is cared for by his strong and loving, if "crazy hillbilly," maternal grandmother and generally hardworking maternal grandfather. Vance barely avoids becoming a high school dropout, joins the Marines upon graduation to get his life in order, and graduates early and summa cum laude from Ohio State University. A degree from Yale Law School and marriage to a classmate complete his transformation into the upper class. Vance's story of transformation may not be over, since *Hillbilly Elegy*'s phenomenal success has launched him into the role of pundit and potential national politician. As some of our contributors stress, this end result is crucial to both the book's appeal and his claims to hillbilly authenticity. Despite his hardscrabble beginnings, only his later success in the world of law and politics and the valuable personal connections he has made (with the likes of billionaire businessman and investor Peter Thiel and Yale University "tiger mom" Amy Chua) make him seem a legitimate "spokesperson for the white working class." In other words, only in distancing himself from Appalachia and what he dubs "greater Appalachia" has Vance come to be seen as the "authentic" and "credible" voice of the region and the white working class.

This is not meant to blithely dismiss the obvious appeal of the book for so many as simply a form of "false consciousness." Nor is it meant to discount the legitimacy of the issues his book and life story bring to the foreground, including the devastating impact of drug abuse and addiction, particularly in rural America and Appalachia; the economic and social debilitation brought on by the collapse of the old industrial economy and the jobs so many relied upon; the sustaining power of intergenerational bonds and the importance of positive role models and social stabilizers; and the deep sense of cynicism, pessimism, and resignation felt by many, especially older white men in non-coastal America. But it is important to also consider what it is about the story he tells that makes it such an appealing vision to many Americans of a variety of political stripes who so desperately want to believe that the "American Dream" (a term that Vance repeatedly uses but never really defines) is still possible—especially because they also fully recognize how the country is characterized by deep economic and political inequities and injustices.

The ideas and contradictions introduced above are explored and elaborated on in part I of the book. The essays in the first section, "Interrogating," assess the accuracy of Vance's so-called memoir of a culture and seek to illuminate the ways *Hillbilly Elegy* and its social impact are tied to powerful political ideologies and institutions active in America today. Historian T. R. C. Hutton begins by critiquing the book as an unrealistic modern-day Horatio Alger tale of advancement over economic and familial obstacles through "luck and pluck" that rejuvenates long-discredited "culture of poverty" arguments to explain the hardships the region faces. He argues this approach erases larger socioeconomic factors, relies falsely on ethnic determinism, and essentializes working-class society. Sociologist Dwight Billings reflects critically on the way the book has been embraced, in the wake of the election of 2016 and the Trump presidency, by neoliberals in both major political parties and contributed to the idea of a mythical realm he dubs "Trumpalachia." However, Billings argues that the region, rather than being inherently "the reddest of red state America," is potentially far more politically progressive than the media and both political parties have acknowledged or Vance's book implies. Next, public historian and writer Elizabeth Catte considers the causes and implications of the book being featured as the selection of a campus or community-wide "one read" book program by many colleges and universities. She concludes that one effect is to too narrowly define who and what Appalachia is and, more problematically, is not. Urban migration scholar Roger Guy then considers the accuracy of the book's portrayal of the urban Appalachian migrant experience, comparing Vance's account and experience with those of twentieth-century Appalachian migrants to Chicago and other Midwestern cities. He explores multigenerational patterns of work and life for Appalachian out-migrant and shuttle-migrant communities, concluding that Vance's story of familial violence and degradation contrasts with the experiences of most first- and second-generation migrants.

The remaining essays under "Interrogating" consider the messages of the book through the prisms of race and racial ideology and drug addiction and criminality. Although she empathizes with Vance's emotional journey and appreciates his attention to place, class, and culture, legal scholar Lisa Pruitt ultimately sees the book as more of a distortion than an illumination of white socioeconomic disadvantage. She argues that by understating the positive role of the state in his own life trajectory (especially the military and public higher education), erasing the concept of white privilege, and presenting the idea of "hillbilly" as strictly a cultural and not a racial identity and construction, Vance promotes the myth of a society based on true meritocracy so dear to white elites largely ignorant of the reality of systemic working-class inequity. Travis Linnemann and Corina Medley, analysts of media representations of justice, focus instead on the portrayal of the drug abuse and addiction that is so central to *Hillbilly Elegy* as well as to the ways Appalachia has come to be perceived as ground zero of this nationwide epidemic. While in no way discounting the seriousness of this crisis, these authors argue that by erasing broader social and historical forces and explanations, *Hillbilly Elegy* offers a form of victim blaming in which drug abuse becomes nearly the sole explanation for familial and social ill fortunes rather than a symptom of larger debilitating forces of neoliberal capitalism.

"Responding," the second section of part I, offers the individual reactions of five very different Appalachians who see the book as resonating with, or more often diverging from, their own personal and familial experiences. Ivy Brashear, Michael Maloney, Kelli Haywood, Allen Johnson, and William Turner offer eloquent and heartfelt responses to Vance's portrayal of growing up in Appalachia and southern Ohio. Community activist Brashear forcefully condemns the book for distorting the complexity of the region, erasing the history of "oppressive systems of extraction," and leaving the impression that all Appalachian families share the same dysfunction as Vance's own. She reveals this destructive history through sharing her own family's generations-long experiences of resisting exploitation and supporting one another emotionally. Brashear further challenges Vance's narrative by telling her own story of a typical American childhood in Perry County, Kentucky, building forts, playing Nintendo, and going to prom. Michael Maloney's narrative is grounded in his own geographically similar history to that of Vance, having grown up just outside of Jackson, Kentucky (where Vance spent many of his summers with his grandparents), and later in the southern Ohio towns around Cincinnati near Middletown where Vance was raised. Maloney also draws on his decades of work assisting urban migrant communities to explore the ways Appalachian migrants have dealt with the hardships of economic relocation and eventual deindustrialization. Although he acknowledges the problems with Vance's understating of systemic causes, he also sees much truth and value in Vance's story and ends with a call to embrace Vance as a means to achieve better public policy in Appalachia and Appalachian migrant communities in the wake of deindustrialization, globalization, and automation.

Kelli Haywood largely defends the book as a powerful and honest personal account of the harsh realities of the lives of many living in the mountains. She argues that though Vance's portrait is at times simplistic, it nonetheless brings uncomfortable truths to the foreground and highlights a litany of negative statistics—a reality that must be faced squarely if the region as a whole is to advance. Allen Johnson offers yet a different take from his perspective as a rural West Virginian with decades of experience in social services, ministry, environmental stewardship, and raising a family. Although he does not personally share Vance's rough origin story, Johnson praises the book as a window into and model of the central role of what he calls "transcenders"— individuals who are able to overcome adverse childhood experiences to become successful and fulfilled adults. Finally, sociologist and researcher William Turner offers his unique perspective as both an African American who grew up in the coalfields of southeastern Kentucky and a leading scholar of the history of blacks in Appalachia and out-migration communities. Drawing on his own remarkable achievements and those of so many of his classmates from Lynch (Kentucky) Colored School and others in the self-named "Eastern Kentucky Social Club," Turner stresses the total absence of African Americans from Vance's book and from national views of the hardships of the people of the region. These conceptions exist, he argues, despite the fact that blue-collar black migrants collectively both have disproportionately suffered more than blue-collar whites from deindustrialization and have proven more resilient in the face of these difficulties.

Scholarly essays and personal narratives are not the only ways Appalachians have grappled with *Hillbilly Elegy* and its regional and national reception. Part I therefore also includes a selection of poems and photographs that reveal other ways of envisioning what Vance gets right and wrong about the region. Jeff Mann's poem "Social Capital" captures the ways Vance simultaneously illuminates and erases this elusive if powerful idea, whereas Ricardo Nazario y Colón's "Panning for Gold" frames the book as the latest contribution to the "politics of poverty" show. Crystal Good's "HE Said/SHE Said" rejects Vance as representative of her Appalachian experience; Dana Wildsmith's "Elegies" sympathetically ties Vance to an earlier Appalachian voice of cultural celebration and lamentation. The photographs and explanatory notes of Theresa Burriss, Lou Murrey, and Danielle Dulken offer yet other ways to consider a region shaped by the dignity of hard work and devastating environmental degradation, diversity and activism, and countless stories of the joys and sorrows of everyday people.

———

When the War on Poverty came to Appalachia in the early 1960s, many felt that the region's story was being told by the wrong voices. Or at least too few voices. After President Johnson traveled to Appalachia in 1964 to bring media attention to its needs as part of his launch of this massive economic support program, many filmmakers and documentary crews followed those well-rutted dirt roads into the same hollows. Charles Kuralt's *Christmas in Appalachia* (CBS, 1965) had the broadest reach, but other filmmakers swept in to capture familiar images and tell familiar stories about a complex place.[6] One response to this wave of cinematic depictions of Appalachia was the desire to empower residents of those places to tell their own stories and make their own films. The result was Appalshop, a nonprofit cultural arts organization that opened its doors in 1969, funded by the Office of Economic Opportunity along with the American Film Institute. The War on Poverty that paved the path for simplistic representations of Appalachia, therefore, also helped launch an organization dedicated to countering and complicating those narratives and to giving voice to more people living in the region—to allow them to tell their own stories.[7]

In the same way, the collection of personal narratives that make up part II of this book, "Beyond *Hillbilly Elegy*," was imagined partly in response to the noise surrounding Vance's book and took as its inspiration other recent collections of astute and powerful Appalachian writers.[8] A good way to quiet one voice is to add other voices to it. Simply put, that is the aim of this collection of stories and reflections on Appalachia. Casting a wide net, the narratives collected here give voice to a broad range of Appalachian writers who, just by sharing their stories, complicate the narrow story often told about this place. These stories defy the limited Appalachia that Vance sells in his book. They hail from different parts of the region; they boast different racial identities and sexual orientations and represent diverse life stories. Young as well as seasoned, they are educators, activists, poets, photographers, mothers, fathers, brothers, and sisters. And they come from a long Appalachian tradition of speaking up and talking back.[9] These personal narratives range in content and context widely but are all grounded in specific Appalachian experiences. Many focus on capturing movement into and out of Appalachia from a new generation's perspective. Some writers grapple with what it means to be Appalachian as they leave the region and understand how others have framed it for them. When a place is defined for them, they ask, how much power do they have to define it themselves? Other writers and poets ask similar questions but from within the region. Seeing a changing landscape and culture, they work to maintain connections to traditions of their elders, and to pass those along to a new generation. Some strive to escape parts of their inheritances while celebrating others. Part II deals with the way others have seen us (as snake handlers, as mountain men, as *Deliverance* extras) and the more complex ways that we try to see ourselves. And like people from anywhere, no one marker of identity suffices. But unlike people from some places, all these Appalachians feel a strong need to define themselves in opposition to the (mis)defining that others are doing on our behalf. The contributors are all reclaiming Appalachia in their own ways.

Part II begins with three poems from Jesse Graves, each an expression of a bodily connection to place—generations deep, yet never stagnant. Meredith McCarroll laments the ways that she shifted her accent as she spent more time in academia, and celebrates the opportunity to reclaim and integrate layers of identity. A photograph from Rebecca Kiger, the first of four featured here from Looking at Appalachia, the crowd-sourced photography project launched by Roger May, challenges negative perceptions of downtrodden Appalachians and shows them instead as strong, vital, and joyous. In "Kentucky, Coming and Going," Kirstin Squint wrestles with family legacies and lore, asking what it means to be from a place, to leave a place, and to claim a place as your own. Poet Richard Hague defiantly celebrates Appalachia in his poem "Resistance, or Our Most Worthy Habits." Jeremy B. Jones recalls being called a mountain man and reflects on the multiplicity of being a ninth-generation mountaineer, but he also thinks about Ernest T. Bass and *The Andy Griffith Show* and the legacy of labels we inherit without claim. Edward Karshner, too, remembers the sting of being characterized as a "hillbilly," and later comes to revel in the stories that he passes down to his own children—complicated by his rich knowledge of language and its implications in Appalachia and what he calls the "Off." Luke Travis's photograph, set in Pittsburgh, reminds him that the small-town values he knew from childhood make their way into the city. In "The Mower—1933," Robert Morgan crafts a tangible description of work as he both conquers and communes with the land that he knows so well. Chelsea Jack's story of leaving and finding home is tied to her mother's labor, her family's mobility, and her ability to bring with her that which was left behind.

Robert Gipe traces his own path through Appalachia, enabled by his mother's humor and sense of voice, which allows him to work, through storytelling, with his community in Harlan County. Roger May's photograph "Aunt Rita along the King Coal Highway, Mingo County, West Virginia" defies elegy and celebrates home. Poet Keith S. Wilson's series "Holler" explores travel and migration, belonging and not belonging—both inside and outside of Appalachia. Through close readings and reflections empowered both by theory and experiences of class migration, Rachel Wise writes about the tension of finding one's place in the out-of-place. Inspired by antebellum texts and imaginings of new freedom, Kelly Norman Ellis contributes two poems that situate the black female body squarely in the mountains of the American South. In the form of a recipe, Jim Minick reflects on homesteading, cornbread, migration, and home. In "Tonglen for My Mother," Linda Parsons reflects on suffering, compassion, and peace. Meg Wilson's photograph "Olivia at the Intersection" captures a small moment on a Friday night when community fills the streets in its own Appalachian celebration. Jodie Childers's vivid recollection of caretaking winds us through her own comings and goings in and out of Appalachia, in and out of her familial role. In "Canary Dirge," Dale Marie Prenatt directly and bitterly calls on America to see itself in Appalachia. Finally, Elizabeth Hadaway writes about her experiences being stereotyped, both in academia and in the ministry—where she learned, at last, how to handle the snakes that surrounded her.

Collectively, the scholarship, personal reflections, poetry, and photography in this book offer a rejoinder to the national reportage on Appalachia that is rooted in the *Hillbilly Elegy* phenomenon and that defines the region monochromatically and almost completely in terms of backwardness, ignorance, isolation, violence, dependency, and passivity—ultimately as a place of social, economic, and cultural death. This book instead presents a very different Appalachia and Appalachians as a place and people with undeniable problems but also intellectual vitality, diversity (in terms of ideology, gender and sexuality, race and ethnicity), and a powerful resilience. It is these characteristics that are lost in imagining *Hillbilly Elegy* as the sole window into the Appalachian experience.

———

On the closing day of the 2018 Appalachian Studies Association conference in Cincinnati, J. D. Vance was an invited panelist alongside ethnographer and journalist Wendy Welch on the topic of poverty and the opioid epidemic. The presence of Vance was deeply upsetting and disruptive to many engaged in the work around Appalachia. In response, The STAY Project (Stay Together Appalachian Youth) organized a protest of Vance, turning their chairs and bodies to the back of the room when he spoke, periodically booing and talking back to him, and singing "Which Side Are You On?," a protest song written in 1931 by Florence Reece during the Harlan County Mine Wars. Many supported this demonstration of anger and frustration, but others tried to quiet the protesters. The aftermath of Vance's presence at ASA has exposed a problematic generational divide within the organization as well as calls by

STAY and Y'ALL (Young Appalachian Leaders and Learners) for reforms to the process of organizing and convening panels at the national conference.

Painful as this experience has been for many, we also see it as offering opportunities for greater understanding and dialogue that we hope this book can help fulfill. At a time in which policy making too often takes the form of 140-character tweets, Russian bots decipher our online profiles in order to influence the way that we vote by creating extreme division, and differences among us seem to create insurmountable chasms, we desperately need a space to open up, listen, make room, and disagree with respectful candor. This does not mean treating all sides and all forces as equally valid. When Florence Reece wrote and performed "Which Side Are You On?," it functioned as a moral rallying cry to wake people in and beyond the region and to align them with the workers around them rather than the company that exploited them. We do not need to smooth out our differences or silence protestors or shout down those with whom we disagree, or shame someone who has a story to tell. Rather, we need to magnify the ways we are unique, give voice to all who want to contribute a verse, and acknowledge the full range of experiences that constitute Appalachia.

Postelection America has made it strange to be from Appalachia. Many of us have not liked the way that *Hillbilly Elegy* has been used as a shorthand way to explain the Trump phenomenon. While it is frustrating to have one person speak for a place, it is worse to have so many people listen to that one person and assume that he's right and representative of all of Appalachia. Contributor Elizabeth Catte recently recalled in her blog the way she addressed the question of audience at a talk at West Virginia University, writing, "I think self-definition is power and if I tell you what or who you are I have taken some power from you and I do not want to do that."[10] So when coworkers in Maine or in-laws in Florida or even college friends in western Kentucky say that they now understand Appalachia because they have read *Hillbilly Elegy*, it strikes a nerve. We've been defined by so many journalists and filmmakers over the years who've briefly dropped in only to confirm what they already suspected, and we're sick of it.

So we're passing the microphone. We're making room for scholars who have spent careers thinking about poverty and family and race and labor and addiction to share what they know about some of the topics that Vance touches on in *Hillbilly Elegy*. We are carving out space for more people to tell their family stories, their Appalachian memories, their lived experiences, and their views of future Appalachias. Inspired by Looking at Appalachia, we are featuring powerful and poignant images that resonate with the writings and offer a perhaps unexpected window into what it means to be Appalachian.[11] May this collection of scholarship, poetry, photography, and personal narrative remind us all that there is and always has been space to differ, to disagree, to protest, to rage, to reimagine, to commemorate, and to learn. There is space for all of us to reclaim Appalachia as it is for us. And there is a desperate need for the fierce hope embedded in these grounded critiques, humorous anecdotes, and captured moments. Let this book inspire a fierce hope for Appalachia.

NOTES

1. "Combined Print and E-Book Nonfiction," *New York Times*, February 11, 2018, https://nyti.ms/2BjQKkv; Jim Milliot, "Print Units through September Up 2%: Sales of Popular Backlist Books Offset the Lack of New Blockbuster," *Publishers Weekly*, October 6, 2017, https://www.publishersweekly.com/pw/by-topic/industry-news/bookselling/article/75012-print-units-through-september-up-2.html.

2. For a sampling of such reactions, see https://www.harpercollins.com/9780062300546/hillbilly-elegy. On Vance's Senate decision, see Kevin Robillard, "J. D. Vance Passes on Senate Run in Ohio," *Politico*, January 19, 2018, https://www.politico.com/story/2018/01/19/jd-vance-no-senate-run-ohio-349970.

3. For an overview of some of these important efforts, see Stephen L. Fisher, *Fighting Back in Appalachia: Traditions of Resistance and Change* (Philadelphia: Temple University Press, 1993); Dwight Billings, Gurney Norman, and Katherine Ledford, eds., *Back Talk from Appalachia: Confronting Stereotypes* (Lexington: University Press of Kentucky, 1999); Stephen L. Fisher and Barbara Ellen Smith, eds., *Transforming Places: Lessons from Appalachia* (Champaign: University of Illinois Press, 2012); and, most recently, Elizabeth Catte, *What You Are Getting Wrong about Appalachia* (Cleveland: Belt, 2017).

4. The idea that the book would have found an audience is from Joshua Rothman, "The Lives of Poor White People," *New Yorker*, September 12, 2016, https://www.newyorker.com/culture/cultural-comment/the-lives-of-poor-white-people. On the continual "rediscovery" of Appalachia, see Catte, *What You Are Getting Wrong*, especially pt. II; Allen W. Batteau, *The Invention of Appalachia* (Tucson: University of Arizona Press, 1990); Henry D. Shapiro, *Appalachia on Our Mind: The Southern Mountains and Mountaineers in the American Consciousness, 1870–1920* (Chapel Hill: University of North Carolina Press, 1978); Emily Satterwhite, *Dear Appalachia: Readers, Identity,*

and Popular Fiction since 1878 (Lexington: University Press of Kentucky, 2011); and Billings, Norman, and Ledford, *Back Talk from Appalachia*.

5. The phrase "Strange Land and a Peculiar People" comes from an 1873 article by Will Wallace Harney. On this tradition, see Anthony Harkins, *Hillbilly: A Culture History of an American Icon* (New York: Oxford University Press, 2003), 29–45.

6. See Harkins, *Hillbilly*, 184–86; Batteau, *Invention of Appalachia*, chaps. 8–9; Ron Eller, *Uneven Ground: Appalachia since 1945* (Lexington: University Press of Kentucky, 2013), 80–82, 102–3; Meredith McCarroll, *Unwhite: Appalachia, Race, and Film* (Athens: University of Georgia Press, 2018), chap. 4.

7. Appalshop, https://www.appalshop.org/about-us/our-story/; Stephen P. Hanna, "Appalshop," in *Encyclopedia of Appalachia* (Knoxville: University of Tennessee Press, 2006), 1693–94, and "Three Decades of Appalshop Films: Representations, Strategies, and Regional Politics," *Appalachian Journal* 25, no. 4 (Summer 1998).

8. Adrian Blevins and Karen Salyer McElmurray, eds., *Walk Till the Dogs Get Mean: Meditations on the Forbidden from Contemporary Appalachia* (Athens: Ohio University Press, 2015); Charles Dodd White and Larry Smith, eds., *Appalachia Now: Short Stories of Contemporary Appalachia* (Huron, OH: Bottom Dog Press, 2015).

9. Thanks to Theresa Burriss for helping us appreciate this spectrum and put it into words.

10. Elizabeth Catte, "A Message to the Future of Appalachia," https://elizabethcatte.com/2018/04/16/future/.

11. Looking at Appalachia, http://lookingatappalachia.org/.

PART I

Considering
Hillbilly Elegy

INTERROGATING

HILLBILLY ELITISM

T. R. C. HUTTON

> *Let not Ambition mock their useful toil,*
> *Their homely joys, and destiny obscure;*
> *Nor Grandeur hear with a disdainful smile*
> *The short and simple annals of the poor.*
> *The boast of heraldry, the pomp of pow'r,*
> *And all that beauty, all that wealth e'er gave,*
> *Awaits alike th' inevitable hour:*
> *The paths of glory lead but to the grave.*

> —Thomas Gray, "Elegy Written in a Country Churchyard"

> *Ain't nothing scarier than poor white people.*

> —Chris Rock

IT IS A COMMON REFRAIN among Appalachia's writers and defenders that the region has rarely been allowed to speak for itself. Since the 1870s, the region has been incessantly "discovered" and then "rediscovered" by a long series of novelists, journalists, social scientists, satirists, and documentarians, most—if not all—inspired by the irony of Appalachian Otherness. How can a region defined by the Euro-American frontier myth be so different, so *far behind*, the perceived American mainstream? "'Inequality,'" liberal polemicist Thomas Frank wrote in 2016, "is a euphemism for the Appalachification of our world."[1] Frank's intended analogy, and his invented noun-verb, would be meaningless without the prior work of William Wallace Harney, William Frost, John Fox Jr., Paul Webb, Horace Kephart, Harry Caudill, and many other writers who established the permanent American assumption of innate Appalachian depravity and poverty. The previous authors first established Appalachia not only as a region unlike the American mainstream, but also as a place with crippled access to the commonly assumed entitlements of Americanness. Now, Frank is suggesting that the country at large is learning to temper its expectations just like Appalachia has been doing since it was first "discovered."

J. D. Vance's *Hillbilly Elegy: A Memoir of a Family and Culture in Crisis* (2016) is the latest book-length attempt to explain Appalachia to the "outside world," and a special plea for why it needs explaining, given this new era of lowered expectations. *Hillbilly Elegy* is also the most recent book-length attempt to come highly recommended: *National Review* executive editor Reihan Salam, Silicon Valley scion Peter Thiel, and "tiger mother" Amy Chua all wrote glowing jacket blurbs. Positive reviews appeared across the conservative press, in Salam's *National Review* (where Vance regularly contributes), the *American Conservative*, and the *Weekly Standard*. Center-right columnist David Brooks hailed *Hillbilly Elegy* in a 2016 *New York Times* op-ed that called for a "better form of nationalism." "When I lived in Brussels," Brooks wrote, recalling his time in Belgium, "this sort of intense personal patriotism was simply not felt by the people who ran the EU, but it was felt by a lot of people in the member states. This honor code has been decimated lately. Conservatives argue that it has been decimated by cosmopolitan cultural elites who look down on rural rubes. There's some truth to this, as the reactions of smug elites to the Brexit vote demonstrate. But the honor code has also been decimated by the culture of the modern meritocracy, which awards status to the individual who works with his mind, and devalues the class of people who work with their hands."[2] Throughout the summer of 2016, Brooks's praise was duly repeated among liberal commentators as well, especially those looking for a relatively simple explanation for the relative success of the Donald Trump presidential campaign. Around the time of Trump's election, Vance was roundly referred to as a "Trump whisperer."[3] At the time of the book's greatest hype, Vance came across on the CNN screen as a sort of technocratic center-right figure not unlike Brooks or Thomas Friedman, the sort of briefcase Republican who in 2016 seemed like Kevin Bacon's character at the end of *Animal House* screaming to a panicked crowd to "remain calm, all is well!" despite the chaos and nonsense that pervaded the airwaves in light of the unprecedented presidential campaign.

The outpouring of right-leaning support shouldn't be surprising, especially from Brooks, who has since spent many a column rending his proverbial garments over the changing face of American conservatism. But Vance's broader appeal is not limited to Brooks's technocratic vision of a trickle down world. It is far more general, and melds old political modes with newer ones. Vance, after all, is personally acquainted with most of them (Chua was his professor at Yale Law School), and *Hillbilly Elegy* staunchly defends the up-by-your-own-bootstraps fairy tale that capitalism has always used to win support from the underclasses. The white working class is a group Brooks can legitimately claim as conservative, even if his and Chua's brand of conservatism is not the same as what seems to make Trump appealing.

But of course, the book is aimed not at that underclass (few books are), but rather at a middle- and upper-class readership more than happy to learn that white American poverty has nothing to do with them or with any structural problems in American economy and society and everything to do with poor white folks' inherent vices. On cable news channels like CNN, Vance comes across as a voice of moderation, and a scold to his fellow technocrats for misunderstanding the white middle class that produced him. At the same time, Vance's professional associations with openly antidemocratic conservatives like Charles Murray and Peter Thiel, as well as his later courtship with the Heritage Foundation, have also raised eyebrows. Even though Vance presented himself in 2016 as an anti-Trump Republican and a Silicon Valley centrist (for instance, he criticized Republican attacks on the Affordable Care Act for their lack of a viable alternative plan), his professional trajectory previous to the publishing of *Elegy* suggests a politics probably defined by Reagan era conservatism (in contrast to Trump era nationalism). At its heart, *Hillbilly Elegy* might be seen simply as an antistatist screed about the failures of the Great Society. But a close reading suggests there is far more than that behind his story, particularly a forced obfuscation of class and region summarized by the word "hillbilly."

In describing his meteoric rise from poverty, Vance paints a picture of generations-old depravity in his ancestral home in Kentucky, and his childhood home in Ohio. The poor are, as the English told themselves in Dickens's day, poor because of who they are, not because of their circumstances. Although Vance is more subtle than a Herbert Spencer or a William Graham Sumner, that is the chief takeaway from this book. Vance spells out his thesis in the introduction: conditions beyond their control brought economic hard times to white Americans in a particular part of America, but their preexistent "hillbilly culture" dictates that they react to "bad circumstances in the worst way possible" (7). It is a point he makes over and over again, using his parents, grandparents, and any number of kin and acquaintances as examples. Many of the stories are sad, while many others reflect the "old Southwest" humor tradition that dates back at least as far as Samuel Clemens's (later known as Mark Twain) "The Dandy Frightening the Squatter" (1852). Vance deems himself a bit of a dandy, but from a family of squatters, and he finds them both hilarious and pathetic; even his relatively heroic portrayal of his grandmother has embellishments reminiscent of Al Capp's Mammy Yokum. And when he wrote this book, he knew a significant segment of the middle-brow reading public would agree or, at least, respond positively. As far as media portrayals of Appalachia and the working class go, *Hillbilly Elegy* is nothing new under the sun. But its first-person narration by a regional "insider" who is now a bona fide member of the elite is a rarity indeed.

This is important. Vance differs from Sumner et al. by crafting his critique of working-class Appalachia as both memoir and nonfiction *bildungsroman*. His story follows the Horatio Alger template, extolling the virtues of "hillbilly culture" while simultaneously scolding it for its flaws. Vance exploits what Christopher Lasch once called the "confessional style" of writing, but for the opposite effect. Lasch lambasted the confessionalist for seeking "not to provide an objective account of a representative piece of reality but to seduce others into giving him their attention, acclaim, or sympathy."[4] In contrast, Vance asserts not only that he objectively recounts his own biography, but also that it epitomizes the white working-class experience. If faced with empirical evidence that suggests his experience is more exception than rule, he can always fall back on the position that *Hillbilly Elegy* is simply his own personal "journey"—a brilliant, infuriating paradox for anyone looking to criticize him for what he or she might interpret as his arguments about "hillbillies" as a group. Read *Hillbilly Elegy* and you will find that "American Dream" is one of Vance's favorite phrases, although it is rarely explained and readers are left to decide for themselves what the term entails. Vance's publisher calls the book a "multi-generational journey from Appalachia to Yale Law School—two worlds that couldn't be farther apart" (back cover; a remarkable statement considering both, at least, exist in the same nation-state). By highlighting the distance between the two, Vance can better advance the book's thesis: that his accomplishments came from hard work and the traditional values instilled in him by a relatively normative family situation provided by his "hillbilly" grandparents (in contrast to his dissolute, substance-abusing parents). Vance's personal story permits him to claim the term "hillbilly," then scold his fellow hillbillies for their cultural and moral failings.

The timing of Vance's book is interesting, considering that it appeared on the heels of the *National Review*'s recent attacks on impoverished whites in central Appalachia. Kevin Williamson's 2014 exploration of poverty (and excess soft drink consumption) in Owsley County, Kentucky—which sits next to Breathitt County, Vance's familial hearth and one of *Hillbilly Elegy*'s primary settings—was a kind of coming out of the closet for the magazine's disdain for this class and its supposed self-imposed degradation.[5] The magazine's sudden viciousness toward a population once cheered as the "Reagan Democrats" comes after the white working class flocked (or so it would appear) to Donald Trump's revanchist sado-nationalism in apparent rejection of the "establishment" conservatism established in the days of Nixon and Reagan. Remarkable even for a fan of laissez-faire neoliberalism, Williamson refuses to acknowledge that the poverty of Owsley County might be due to any extraneous factors beyond its inhabitants' individual or collective control.

Nothing happened to them. There wasn't some awful disaster. There wasn't a war or a famine or a plague or a foreign occupation. Even the economic changes of the past few decades do very little to explain the

> dysfunction and negligence—and the incomprehensible malice—of poor white America. So the gypsum business in Garbutt ain't what it used to be. There is more to life in the 21st century than wallboard and cheap sentimentality about how the Man closed the factories down.
>
> The truth about these dysfunctional, downscale communities is that they deserve to die. Economically, they are negative assets. Morally, they are indefensible. (emphasis original)

With or without Trump, *National Review* conservatives have decided to display their previously hidden disgust for retrograde whites.

Observers like *New Republic* editor Jeet Heer have clearly linked the *National Review*'s disdain for/toward the white poor to their fear that Donald Trump is taking over American conservatism, a development they were none too pleased about during the 2015–16 election cycle. "The magazine was founded as the organ of a distinctively aristocratic conservatism, one that in the early days never concealed its scorn for ordinary people," Heer writes. "In recent decades, that aristocratic conservatism has sometimes been obscured by a populist mask, but under the pressure of Trumpism, *National Review* is showing its true face."[6] As a figure originating among "ordinary people" (although Vance makes them seem quite extraordinary in a sense) but accepted among allegedly "aristocratic" conservatives, Vance was pressed into service, doing the rounds of radio and television trying to explain Trump's appeal to "hillbilly" Americans like himself. Most of his observations have dealt with his own experience and that of his family.

On its face, *Elegy*'s portrait starkly contrasts with Williamson's overtly vicious attack. Vance does acknowledge that his family suffered from the ravages of an indifferent globalized economy and the withering away of the New Deal political coalition. But Vance shares with Williamson the view that poor whites are bound by their regressive culture. How, then, can the hillbilly be simultaneously praised and scorned, praised for her toughness and dedication to family yet scorned for her inability to escape the bonds of poverty? Vance's balancing act is nothing new, and in fact has roots in nineteenth-century discourse on the growing chasm between the American countryside and its cities. His wielding of the term "hillbilly" is perhaps the most obvious common denominator between his book and past literature on Appalachia. Vance's ancestors were first identified as a people apart from the white mainstream in the two or three decades immediately following the Civil War, a time of rapid urban growth and chaotic economic change that laid bare the vast barrier between the rich and poor. The yeomanry once praised by Thomas Jefferson were overtaken by industrialists once and for all, and a large segment of the former became known as hillbillies. "Hillbilly" ultimately saw more literary mileage in the twentieth century, but its etymology is an undeniable product of the Gilded Age; it is notable that Twain and his coauthor Charles Dudley Warner began their novel *The Gilded Age: A Tale of Today* (1873) in the mountains of eastern Tennessee, a place Americans would later come to associate with the label. In *Hillbilly: A Cultural History of an American Icon*, historian Anthony Harkins explains that hillbilly is just one of "dozens of similar labels . . . and ideological and graphic constructs of poor and working-class southern whites coined by middle- and upper-class commentators, northern and southern." Epithets like this allowed a "non-rural, middle-class, white, American audience" to "imagine a romanticized past, while simultaneously enabling the same audience to . . . caricatur[e] the negative aspects of premodern, uncivilized society." Later, well into the twentieth century, white rural people "reappropriated" the term and others like it (e.g., redneck, brush ape, poor white trash, cracker) "as badges of class and racial identity and pride." The term's popularity survived the era of multiculturalism, Harkins explains, because "the hillbilly's whiteness . . . allowed the image to serve as a seemingly apolitical site" where "[white] producers could portray images of poverty, ignorance, and backwardness without raising cries of bigotry and racism from civil rights advocates and the black and minority communities."[7]

Like many labels of disapprobation, "hillbilly" is used by both the observer and the observed; it is a word some people apply to others, as well as one some apply to themselves, depending upon their rhetorical purposes. In Vance's case, he seems to be distancing himself from an Other while also reappropriating depending on what part of the narrative he happens to be in. There is also some question as to whether Vance is using the term to describe a taxonomy of humanity (as his open admiration for Charles Murray suggests) or as a means to an end to describing place—namely the postindustrial limbo overlapping eastern Kentucky and southern Ohio. "There is a lack of agency here [in the 'Rust Belt']," Vance writes, "a feeling that you have little control over your life and a willingness to blame everyone but yourself" (7). Vance and his family call themselves hillbillies by virtue of their residency in "Greater Appalachia"—a term he borrows, without attribution, from Colin Woodard's "Eleven Nations" theory (though he does support his point with a quote from Hank Williams Jr.).[8] However, the story he tells is not necessarily one exceptional to Appalachia but is probably familiar to any number of locales where poverty with a white face is rampant.

Hillbilly Elegy is inadvertently a book about race, more so than region or class. In his introduction, Vance attempts to deny it, but overstates his case: "I do hope that readers of this book will be able to take from it an appreciation of how class and family affect the poor without filtering their views through a racial prism" (7–8). He also mentions that he has known quite a few "welfare queens" in his time but, assuming the reader associates this Reaganesque term with blackness, he offers assurance that they were all white, as are virtually all of the people mentioned in the book (8). *Hillbilly Elegy* is about whiteness, and the failure of American capitalism to give whiteness the natural purchase it once promised, but Vance seems to think that "white" is not a race, but rather the absence of race. This is something to consider in understanding how he utilizes "hillbilly," a term with no explicit racial association *but* an age-old gnomic interchangeability with whiteness. Vance uses "hillbilly" uncritically to describe the people in Jackson, Kentucky, and Middletown, Ohio, and—as did Woodard—takes the whiteness of his subjects as a given; ethnic heritage seems to be one of the main factors that makes Vance's hillbillies do what they do. For over a century, "hillbilly" has been used liberally but has very rarely been applied to a nonwhite person. It not only denotes whiteness, but also implicitly acknowledges an intraracial hierarchy in which, it goes without saying, hillbillies are on the bottom, thanks to their rejection of bourgeois modes of behavior.

Vance establishes early on that "hillbilly culture" is a product of its residents' "Scots-Irish" ethnicity, a strain for whom "poverty is the family tradition" and the "intense sense of loyalty" and "a fierce dedication to family and country" are leavened with xenophobia and a proclivity toward fighting (3). Within this relatively brief discussion of ethnic stock, Appalachia as a place gets momentarily lost, although it is assumed that the place and the people are basically interchangeable. Vance sets aside the region's centuries of economic trials and tribulations—to say nothing of Indian wars or slavery—arguing that the Scots and Irish fundamentally shaped the area. This piece of Vance's analysis smacks of racial determinism, even if "culture" replaces biology in his account. He cites a 2012 *Discover* article for his grossly ahistorical description of Scots-Irish tendencies, but his general assessment echoes former Virginia senator Jim Webb's *Born Fighting*, as well as the work of David Hackett Fischer, Forrest McDonald, and Grady McWhiney, three historians beloved by conservatives (McWhiney is regarded as the intellectual vanguard of the neo-Confederate movement) because they favor continuity over contingency. The latter two each served as directors of the white nationalist League of the South, an organization that continues to embrace the "Celtic thesis" of white southern society, the somewhat popular contention that the permanent cultural blueprint of the American South was drawn by Scottish and Irish Protestant drovers in the seventeenth and eighteenth centuries. Vance's argument regarding folkways falls prey to the same circular logic of the League of the South and the theory's other proponents, namely the neo-Confederate community. In their contribution to *Neo-Confederacy: A Critical Introduction*, Euan Hague and Edward Sebesta describe Celtic (or Scots-Irish) culture as a packet of elements "available for reinterpretation and appropriation based on whatever meaning is useful." They continue, "Elements that do not meet the required vision of a Celtic culture can be omitted, whereas others—such as the propensity for violence—can be heralded. That a certain behavior (e.g., violence) is taken as evidence of an individual acting on their Celtic culture thus becomes self-fulfilling: a person exhibiting Celtic behavior is Celtic because the behavior they are exhibiting is Celtic. Not only does this assume a homogenous Celtic culture, but it also suggests that individuals are beholden to their culture when acting in the world."[9] What is culture (actually, that is a good question left to itself: what is "culture"?) other than a set of modes or habits that are subject to human choice and change over time? In Vance's imagining, however, people are bound not by a culture imposed upon them by market forces, as Christopher Lasch warned, but instead by a preexistent "code of the hills" (to borrow a phrase once used by Jed Clampett) that has made them ill adjusted to market forces.

Unless they go to college—the one contingency that Vance seems to think that only he, among hillbillies, is capable of experiencing. Vance worked for years in Silicon Valley, where neo-Confederate sympathies are considered gauche and countless ethnicities mingle, so it's unlikely that this explanation accounts for his unacknowledged use of Webb, McDonald, and McWhiney. Rather, "Scots-Irish," "hillbilly," and even the term "culture" itself serve as shorthand that make for a much simpler story than one that explores the multiple contingencies of Appalachian poverty. The descendants of Scottish and Irish immigrants live all over the United States; they have married descendants of other nationalities; they are as likely to be rich as they are to be poor. In eastern Kentucky, however, locals of all ethnicities are subject to a continuity of poverty that goes back to the nineteenth century. The problem of poverty may be partially geographical, but Vance would will it to be ethnic, or perhaps even racial. "Hillbilly," a word with racial specificity that no one associates with race, is his fig leaf.

Even if Vance truly believes that Appalachian poverty is somehow a product of ancestry, he ignores the wealth of scholarship on the subject. Sociologists Dwight Billings and Kathleen Blee's meticulously researched longitudinal study of Clay County, Kentucky, *The Road to Poverty: The Making of Wealth and Hardship in Appalachia*, demonstrates that elite families dominated local industry and politics, laying the groundwork for a permanent low-wage economy before the Civil War. Likewise, historian John R. Burch's *Owsley County, Kentucky, and the Perpetuation of Poverty* comes to similar conclusions about the very county Williamson lampooned. (No great defender of the welfare state himself, Burch also shows how local elites used New Deal and Great Society programs for their own venal purposes.)[10] Unlike in *Hillbilly Elegy*, in these two books concrete human action—particularly wealthy whites' mastery over local politics—explains the grinding poverty that is universally associated with eastern Kentucky. In turn, the "hillbillies" suffer under hegemonic and market conditions beyond their control, not the diktats of ancestral origin. Of course neither Williamson nor Vance considers these authors, perhaps because to do so would be to accept their argument that eastern Kentucky residents' greatest mistake isn't wallowing in poverty but following the lead of economic elites.

Instead, *Hillbilly Elegy* invites us to return to the "culture of poverty" theory popularized by Michael Harrington, Oscar Lewis, and, most famously, Daniel Patrick Moynihan in the 1950s and 1960s. Moynihan, especially, was accused of crafting his proposals around innately racist preconceptions about black families involving single mothers, child abandonment, drug use, and other forms of wantonness that Vance also details in his personal narrative.[11] By virtue of their whiteness, the images of hydrocodone-addicted "rednecks" become, in the words of Harkins, "a seemingly apolitical site for often highly charged political struggles over the definition of race, class, gender norms and roles, as well as the nature of mass culture."[12] Like all other Americans, Vance's subjects are categorized primarily by their (in this case, lack of) productivity as workers.

Vance's is an argument that conservatives like Kevin Williamson, their differences in tone notwithstanding, can get behind because capitalism requires its mudsill. Liberals might also embrace it since they don't consider "hillbillies" their political allies and, in cities like Knoxville, Tennessee, they do not properly clean up their yards when academics move to their neighborhood (or so I have been told by more than one liberal colleague).

Not surprisingly, Vance's solutions reflect his somewhat milquetoast right-center political commitments. He recommends school vouchers "administered in a way that doesn't segregate the poor into little enclaves," so that poor kids can learn to imitate their wealthier classmates. Citing the "outsize role" the extended hillbilly family plays, he also proposes that social services loosen regulations on foster parentage so that grandparents, aunts, and uncles can help endangered children. "Our country's social services weren't made for hillbilly families," he writes (243). This is a somewhat eccentric but fairly harmless idea, although it begs an annoying question: are "hillbilly" families the only ones in the United States with extended families who are ready, willing, and able to raise nieces, nephews, cousins, and grandchildren? This is another case of Vance describing a problem as specific to his setting when it is arguably universal to the American experience—especially during the process of "Appalachification" of the country. At no point does Vance suggest that Kentucky and Ohio residents might benefit from higher wages, better health care, or a renewed labor movement. That would run in the face of his bootstraps thesis.

Such concepts would interfere with Vance's aims in writing *Hillbilly Elegy*, for the book is primarily a work of self-congratulation—a literary victory lap— and a vindication of a minimalist safety net. Little surprise then that David Brooks is such a fan. Condescension overpowers the love Vance expresses for his family and the "crazy hillbillies" back home. His book ultimately illustrates the oxymoron capitalism and its defenders require: any hardworking individual can rise to the top, but, at any given time, far more individuals must remain on the bottom. This is a narrative for which many, if not most, of the American reading public has shown affection, just as they have always shown Appalachia a sort of patronizing affection. The bipartisan popularity of *Hillbilly Elegy*, at a time when bipartisanship is in short supply, suggests that the American reading public still wants to hear about an Appalachia and, by extension, a white working class that is uniform, tractable, and easy to understand. The public appetite for complexity today is perhaps lower than usual whether we are talking cable news or social media. The fact that a Silicon Valley millionaire is now the most popular source for understanding twenty-first-century rural poverty is nothing more than a product of the marketplace. Up against a politics of extremism we now see in control of the federal government, soft-spoken simplicities like Vance's are going to seem all the more attractive to the otherwise well-meaning American center. Unfortunately, when the politics of hatred is the only apparent alternative, many Americans will turn instead to the politics of condescension.

Hillbilly Elegy is misnamed. Elegies are poems dedicated to the dead. The American hillbilly (assuming we can use that word for the white working class) isn't dead; she is just poor. She is not going to fade away like nineteenth-century white Americans expected Native Americans would. Like everyone living under capitalism, she is defined by her ability to do work and, in this specific case, her apparent inability to make said work turn a livable profit. And even when there is work, it is becoming less worth attempting because the value of surplus labor has gone down precipitously in the last four decades. But that does not seem to be Vance's concern. He seems to be giving his people a (mostly) gently worded lecture on their lack of willingness to work even when it appears almost pointless to do so. For that reason, the book should have been titled *Hillbilly Reprimand*, because Vance doesn't want to mourn his hillbilly family—he wants to make them good proletarians like they allegedly were in the twentieth century. But until workers in the postindustrial economy are shown a sufficient cause for work, this is not likely to happen. As long as this is the case, the dissolute poor will continue to be America's favorite native scapegoat.

NOTES

1. Thomas Frank, *Listen, Liberal: or, What Ever Happened to the Party of the People?* (New York: Macmillan, 2016), 7.

2. David Brooks, "Revolt of the Masses," *New York Times*, June 28, 2016.

3. "Trump Whisperer J. D. Vance's Turning Point," *Columbus Monthly*, November 3, 2016.

4. Christopher Lasch, *The Culture of Narcissism: American Life in an Age of Diminishing Expectations* (New York: Norton, 1979), 47–61, 55.

5. Kevin Williamson, "The White Ghetto," *National Review*, January 9, 2014, http://www.nationalreview.com/article/367903/white-ghetto-kevin-d-williamson.

6. Jeet Heer, "*National Review*'s Revolt Against the Masses," *New Republic*, March 15, 2016.

7. Anthony Harkins, *Hillbilly: A Culture History of an American Icon* (New York: Oxford University Press, 2003), 5–7.

8. Colin Woodard, *American Nations: A History of the Eleven Rival Regional Cultures of North America* (New York: Penguin, 2012), chap. 9.

9. Euan Hague and Edward Sebesta, "Neo-Confederacy, Culture, and Ethnicity: A White Anglo-Celtic Southern People," in *Neo-Confederacy: A Critical Introduction*, ed. Heidi Beirich, Euan Hague, and Edward Sebesta (Austin: University of Texas Press, 2008), 113.

10. Dwight Billings and Kathleen Blee, *The Road to Poverty: The Making of Wealth and Hardship in Appalachia* (Cambridge University Press, 2000); John R. Burch, *Owsley County, Kentucky, and the Perpetuation of Poverty* (West Jefferson, NC: McFarland, 2007).

11. See, for instance, James T. Patterson, *Freedom Is Not Enough: The Moynihan Report and America's Struggle over Black Family Life—From LBJ to Obama* (New York: Basic Books, 2010); Susan D. Greenbaum, *Blaming the Poor: The Long Shadow of the Moynihan Report on Cruel Images about Poverty* (New Brunswick, NJ: Rutgers University Press, 2015).

12. Harkins, *Hillbilly*, 8.

SOCIAL CAPITAL

JEFF MANN

Social capital is all around us. Those who tap into it and use it prosper. Those who don't are running life's race with a major handicap. This is a serious problem for kids like me.

—J. D. Vance, *Hillbilly Elegy*

Social capital, it's a spotlight's hot glory,
a bag of bullion, the whitewater
of applause, dawn breaking through
New River fog, the gift of being
forgiven anything, "the inner workings

of a system that lay hidden to most
of my kind." It's filet mignon, a magnum
of champagne, a silvery mess of confusing
cutlery and arcane etiquette, the sugar
tit of praise and frenzied adulation.

This scruffy Summers County kid
picking potato beetles and hoeing corn,

he doesn't have it. Neither does
this mountain boy struggling through
WVU, his education only afforded

because his daddy's poverty decades
back embraced the GI Bill. Watching
snowmelt running down the street
past Boreman Hall, he's scarfing lemon
bars his mother baked and mailed

and feeling damned grateful. He has
no idea that "networks of people
and institutions around us have real
economic value. They connect us to
the right people, ensure that we have

opportunities, and impart valuable
information. Without them, we're
going it alone," not unlike the same
young hillbilly hunched in the corner
of a scroungy gay bar, drinking simple

tonic water—florescent blue under
the black lights—crunching ice
to make one drink last all evening.
He's too poor to afford gin, a phone, a car,
and often enough his home-cooked

dinner's prime peasant food,
the unofficial West Virginia
state meal: pinto beans, fried cabbage,
and cornbread. He knows no more
of networking than the shamefaced poet

who sets out a contribution hat
before his reading, and, afterwards,
flushed with humiliation and greed,
counts the tossed bills and coins,
dreaming of pricy Cheddarwurst,

or hot dogs with kraut from the local
convenience store. Without that hidden
system, his poems are not published, or,
if published, not read, not reviewed,
sluicing down the shit-chute of oblivion.

Who has it, capital sufficient to cast
a corona around a face, a body, a life?
The vivid few. Among them
the fulvous fool in the Oval Office, waxen
vacuities mounting Hollywood. Sleek,

furry, and fuckable, those goateed singers
on the radio, on the Grand Ole Opry stage.
The mainstream author's lengthy bio
on Wikipedia, complete with enviably
chunky endnotes. Vaunted poets

in vaunted poetry anthologies used
in university classrooms, their lives
listing Harvard, Stanford, Yale,
Vanderbilt, Princeton, Iowa, far from
WVU. Finally, the young Republican's

elegiac memoir—solid content,
unremarkable style—published by
HarperCollins, glory-maker

nesting there in the Great Yankee
Cultural Capital. The handsome hardback's

prominently displayed in bookstore
windows, reviewed across the nation
in venues both print and online,
regarded as the voice of Appalachia,
the last and latest word summing up

its people, a book so acclaimed,
cussed, and discussed that conference
panels focus on it, a book—this book—
is published about that book, and
meanwhile the works of a myriad

mountain authors (Irene McKinney,
Maggie Anderson, Victor Depta,
doris davenport, Julia Watts,
Richard Hague, Okey Napier, et al.,
et al., et al.) languish with little notice.

ONCE UPON A TIME IN "TRUMPALACHIA": *HILLBILLY ELEGY*, PERSONAL CHOICE, AND THE BLAME GAME

DWIGHT B. BILLINGS

ONCE UPON A TIME, there was "a strange land and peculiar people." It was a mythical place known as "Trumpalachia."[1] J. D. Vance, author of the best-selling book *Hillbilly Elegy: A Memoir of a Family and Culture in Crisis*, has been widely acclaimed as its foremost explorer, mapmaker, interpreter, and critic. Countless readers have turned to his book to understand the appeal of Donald Trump to white working-class voters. But *Hillbilly Elegy* is not a "Trump for Dummies," nor is it an elegy for Appalachia. It's an advertisement for capitalist neoliberalism and personal choice. I did not choose to write about this book; it chose me.

J. D. Vance, a political conservative and self-described "Scots-Irish hillbilly," was a thirty-one-year-old graduate of Yale Law School and a principal in a Silicon Valley investment firm when he wrote *Hillbilly Elegy*. Vance was haphazardly raised by an unstable and abusive, drug- and alcohol-addicted single mother in Middletown, Ohio, a once-thriving but now Rust Belt town he describes as "hemorrhaging jobs and hope." His childhood was full of emotional trauma and economic insecurity. Vance says he wrote *Hillbilly Elegy* to explain how he overcame the obstacles of his childhood and the surrounding despair of his community. He attributes his success to his severe but loving hillbilly grandparents who preached the value of hard work and the American Dream of upward mobility as well as to an empowering stint in the Marine Corps. His other purpose for writing in these troubling economic times is to deliver a jeremiad to the white working class, especially those of Scots-Irish descent with ties to Appalachia. Here he speaks like the stern but loving father figure he never had. "I knew that better days were ahead," he explained after completing the book, "because I lived in a country that allowed me to make the good choices that others in my neighborhood hadn't." It is one thing to write a personal memoir extolling the wisdom of one's personal choices but quite something else—something extraordinarily audacious—to presume to write the "memoir" of a culture.[2]

A nostalgic image of an Appalachian barn on the side of a gravel road is on the book's front cover. But Vance knows very little about contemporary Appalachia—certainly not the region's vibrant grassroots struggles to build a post-coal economy, nor its past and ongoing struggles for economic, labor, environmental, and social justice.[3] He has only visited family members in eastern Kentucky or attended funerals there. His inventory of pathological Appalachian traits—drug addiction, teen pregnancy and illegitimacy, violence, fatalism, the lack of a work ethic, "learned helplessness," poverty as a "family tradition," the inability to face the truth about one's self, and so on—reads like a catalog of stereotypes Appalachian scholars have worked so long to dispel.[4] Vance's Appalachia is refracted through the distorted lens of his own dysfunctional family experience. It makes as much sense as generalizing about Italian Americans from the fictional Tony Soprano.

The real focus of *Hillbilly Elegy*, however, is not Appalachia but the experience of Appalachian out-migrants. This topic has been expertly documented by Appalachian scholars, but their research does not inform this book.[5] Vance claims his authority to speak to and about this regional group on the basis of being a Scots-Irish descendant of Appalachia whose maternal grandparents migrated from the Kentucky mountains to the Midwest for industrial work. They were rough, foul-mouthed, and violent. Vance describes his beloved grandmother—his "Mamaw"—as a "pistol-packing lunatic" who "came from a family that would shoot at you rather than argue with you" (6). He claims that one of his Vance ancestors set off the Hatfield and McCoy feud, and he seems to relish telling how his Mamaw once tried to kill his grandfather by setting him on fire after he had passed out drunk. Nonetheless, his grandfather made a good living as a steelworker, and he and his wife provided the "love and stability" Vance's mother could never offer. Vance contends that their demands for hard work, discipline, and a love of America as the greatest country on earth enabled him to become, in my words, a veritable Puff'n Toot, the little engine that could.

I tell my students in Appalachian studies courses to beware two intellectual tendencies in writings about any group—essentialism ("this is the essence of what they are like") and universalism ("everyone in the group is like this"). Vance heaps on both. I also warn them not to ontologize their neuroses. I picked up this advice from Arthur Mitzman's psychoanalytical study of the great sociologist Max Weber, which contended that Weber was guilty of trying to reconcile his childhood angst about the irreconcilable family conflict between his pietistic Protestant mother and his capitalist businessman father by writing *The Protestant Ethic and the Spirit of Capitalism* in an attempt to show how those seemingly antithetical cultural orientations were, in Weber's view, mutually supportive.[6] Weber was largely correct. Nonetheless, not ontologizing one's personal and family neuroses by projecting them onto a culture or regional group is good advice unless one is as brilliant a cultural analyst as Max Weber. J. D. Vance is no Max Weber.

Vance's main argument in *Hillbilly Elegy* is that Appalachians and their descendants in the Rust Belt have been "reacting to [economic decline] in the worst possible way." He notes that "Nobel-winning economists worry about the decline of the industrial Midwest and the hollowing out of the economic core of working whites," but more important, he contends, is "what goes on in the lives of real people when the economy goes south." There is nothing wrong with that question of course, but Vance's answer points in the wrong direction. In his opinion, the problem boils down simply to the bad personal choices individuals make in the face of economic decline—not to the corporate capitalist economy that creates immense profits by casting off much of its workforce or the failure of governments to respond to this ongoing crisis. The real problem, he says, is "about a culture that increasingly encourages social decay instead of counteracting it" (7).

Vance's bottom line is this: "Public policy can help, but there is no government that can fix these problems for us. . . . These problems were not created by governments or corporations or anyone else. We created them, and only we can fix them" (255–56). Vance's fix, the usual neoliberal fix, is fix thyself. There is of course nothing new here in Vance's recycling of worn-out culture of poverty theory. *Hillbilly Elegy* is the pejorative 1960s Moynihan report on the pathology of the black family in white face and a rehash of Charles Murray's more recent *Coming Apart: The State of White America, 1960–2010.*[7]

Although some readers in Appalachia and the Midwest (including some in this volume) have identified positively with the book, most Appalachian commentators have written trenchant critiques of *Hillbilly Elegy* and the Vance phenomenon.[8] So too have some national writers. Robert Kuttner, for instance, claimed that *Hillbilly Elegy* is nothing more than "a conservative infomercial, disguised as an affectionate memoir," and another described it as "a vicious little book, a litany of well-worn complaints against the intemperate and shiftless poor disguised as a hardscrabble personal narrative." Describing Vance as "the liberal media's favorite white trash-splainer," Sarah Jones called him "the false prophet of blue America." Writing more personally, Betsy Rader, currently a Democratic candidate for Congress in Ohio, described herself in the *Washington Post* as "an older, female version of Vance"—a single mother born in poverty in Appalachia and raised in Ohio who, like Vance, graduated from Ohio State and Yale Law School. Nonetheless, she took great exception to Vance's argument that, in her words, "his family and peers are trapped in poverty due to their own poor choices and negative attitudes." Cutting right to the heart of Vance's politics, she wrote, "With lines like 'We choose not to work when we should be looking for jobs,' Vance's sweeping stereotypes are shark bait for conservative policymakers. They feed into the mythology that the undeserving poor make bad choices and are to blame for their own poverty, so tax payer money should not be wasted in programs to help lift people out of poverty."[9]

But many national commentators were not as discerning as these writers. In a *New York Times* review, Jennifer Senior described Vance's "tough love analysis of the poor who back Trump" as "a compassionate, sociological analysis," and in the same newspaper David Brooks hailed *Hillbilly Elegy* as "essential reading for this moment in history."[10] Conservative commentator Rod Dreher went even further, stating that "for Americans who care about politics and the future of our country, *Hillbilly Elegy* is the most important book of 2016." Writers at the *Economist* must have agreed, suggesting, "You will not read a more important book about America this year."[11] Even Larry Summers got into the act, calling *Hillbilly Elegy* "the most important book for understanding American inequality."[12] (Summers should know about inequality since he contributed greatly to it in his role as Bill Clinton's secretary of the treasury and chief economic advisor to President Obama.) With such accolades, Vance soon became the darling of the corporate media. He was hailed as a spokesman for the white working class, the hillbilly guru, the Trump whisperer, the foremost interpreter of the Trump phenomena, the Rust Belt anger translator, and even the poor whites' Ta-Nehisi Coates. His omnipresence on television and radio—CBS, NBC, ABC, MSNBC, NPR, CNN, Fox News, and *Fresh Air*—and in the print media was remarkable. *Hillbilly Elegy*, according to one source, is said to have sold more than one million copies by October 2017. Sadly, no book about Appalachia has ever been this widely read. Attesting to its popularity and its assignment as required college student reading, Amazonbooks.com offers no fewer than six short published summaries of the book for lazy readers and a film version of the book is said to be in the works.

How can we make sense of *Hillbilly Elegy*'s popularity? There are undoubtedly many reasons for its success. For one thing, it is a good read, a very personal, compelling, compassionate, and at times heartrending memoir that confronts painful issues such as economic insecurity, abuse, and drug dependency that threaten many people's lives well beyond Appalachia and the Rust Belt—issues that Appalachian activists are addressing in more community-based ways than the self-help approach Vance points toward. Beyond this immediate level, I believe there are three other reasons for the book's success: its initial sponsorship by very influential right-wing endorsers; the alignment of its simplistic message about white working-class pathology with the ideology of neoliberalism; and readers' expectation that it might provide a key to understanding the voters who, to many readers unfathomably, sent Donald Trump to the White House.

It's often said that you can't judge a book by its cover, but in this case you can. One of the reasons that *Hillbilly Elegy* burst onto the publishing scene with such unimaginable force can be learned from the initial endorsements listed on the back cover: Reihan Salam, Peter Thiel, and Amy Chua. Salam is the widely known executive editor of the right-wing publication *National Review* who is said to be "Literary Brooklyn's Favorite Conservative."[13] Thiel is the libertarian venture capitalist, hedge fund manager, and cofounder of PayPal who endorsed Donald Trump at the Republican National Convention (he was Vance's boss in a venture capital firm when *Hillbilly Elegy* was published). Amy Chua, Vance's mentor in law school, is the author of *Battle Hymn of the Tiger Mother*, a best-selling but highly controversial book advocating harsh child-rearing practices to instill a hunger for success among children. With her husband Jed Rubenfeld, Chua also wrote *The Triple Package*, which purports to explain why some ethnic/cultural groups such as Jews and Asians are more successful than others, namely, because of their internalized sense of superiority and strong impulse control, which enables them to respond positively to highly motivating levels of status insecurity. (Vance's hillbilly losers would appear to be the opposite of Chua and Rubenfeld's winners.)[14] Having backers like these—along with conservative columnists like David Brooks—helps to explain, at least in part, the extraordinary but undeserved attention Vance's book has been getting. Its endorsements by well-placed and highly respected intellectuals on the right may also help to explain why a book publisher like HarperCollins would give serious attention to the manuscript of an unknown author and why conservative business-oriented newspapers like the *Wall Street Journal* would signal its importance.

When the *Wall Street Journal* endorsed *Hillbilly Elegy*, it commended the book for its stress on the values of "religion, discipline, and family," but chiefly lauded the fact that "most of all [Vance] wants people to hold themselves responsible for their own conduct and choices."[15] This stress on personal choice and accountability is a central theme in the ideology of neoliberalism. *Hillbilly Elegy*'s alignment with it is surely another reason for the book's sales success. Capitalist neoliberalism encompasses a broad range of ideas, practices, and policies. Its diverse economic, political, and cultural projects promote, among other things, deregulation, privatization, the outsourcing of public services, fiscal austerity, global trade liberalization, supply-side monetarism rather than demand-side stimulation, financialization, marketization, antiunionism, and massive tax cuts for the superrich and corporations. At the individual level, however, it stresses above all personal responsibility for one's own well-being.[16]

Procorporate and antidemocratic policies are hardly new in American politics.[17] Beginning in the 1930s and extending through the 1980s, however, hostility toward the New Deal and later Keynesianism, welfare state liberalism, and the Great Society was given new impetus by right-wing intellectuals such as Friedrich von Hayek, Ludwig von Mises, James Buchanan, and Milton Friedman, whose once marginal thought slowly gained acceptability in economics and politics. Their thinking has been heavily subsidized and promoted by vastly wealthy right-wing capitalists such as the Koch brothers and other extreme libertarians.[18] Margaret Thatcher and Ronald Reagan were neoliberalism's first democratically elected national leaders, and their policies were soon implemented throughout the world.[19] Since then, American presidencies have followed suit, representing right-wing (two Bushes), centrist (Clinton), and so-called "progressive" versions of neoliberal politics (Obama).[20] Despite their differences, throughout all these administrations, corporations and the rich have been the winners, the rest of us the losers.

Ronald Reagan famously said that government is the problem, not the solution, but apostles of neoliberalism do not oppose state action per se. In the United States its leaders are willing to spend billions of dollars on policing and prisons and, since 9/11, $5.6 trillion on war. Nor do they oppose the billions of dollars the federal government spends to subsidize fossil fuels. What neoliberalism does oppose is public spending on social welfare, health care (including Medicare and Medicaid), public education and housing, labor and environmental protections, and other public goods, that is, tax dollars for ordinary people's needs. That's why neoliberalism emphasizes personal responsibility.

The stress on personal responsibility is of particular relevance for understanding why *Hillbilly Elegy* fits so comfortably into this ideological milieu. When wages decline and jobs disappear, unions are crushed, and public safety nets become frayed or removed, individuals are left to fend for themselves. Personal responsibility becomes enshrined in the language of neoliberal laws such as President Clinton's 1996 Personal Responsibility and Work Opportunity Reconciliation Act, which eliminated welfare as a right of citizenship and further shifted national policy from the War on Poverty to a war on the poor.[21] The problem is not a "culture of poverty" but, as Henry Giroux contends, "a culture of cruelty":

> Underlying this form of neoliberal authoritarianism and its attendant culture of cruelty is a powerfully oppressive ideology that insists that the only unit of agency that matters is the isolated individual. Hence, mutual trust and shared visions of equality, freedom and justice give way to fears and self-blame reinforced by the neoliberal notion that individuals are solely responsible for their political, economic, and social misfortunes. Consequently, a hardening of the culture is buttressed by the force of state-sanctioned cultural apparatuses that enshrine privatization in the discourse of self-reliance, unchecked self-interest, untrammeled individualism and deep distrust of anything remotely called the common good. Once again, freedom of choice becomes code for defining responsibility solely as an individual task, reinforced by a shameful appeal to character.[22]

Wendy Brown refers to this ideology as a new "normative order of reason, a new governing rationality" that constantly cajoles all persons, not just the poor, to police, reinvent, and perfect themselves, to be adept and flexible enough to make the right personal choices that hopefully will protect them against harsh and unpredictable vicissitudes of economic turmoil they can't control.[23]

The piper we are being asked to dance to is corporate capitalism. Currently fashionable language in the social sciences unreflectively but aptly captures our intellectual subjection to capitalism when we begin to think of—and invest in—our friends and acquaintances as "social capital," the art and music we love as "cultural capital," our environment as "natural capital," and, ultimately, ourselves as readily deployable units of "human capital." In a neoliberal capitalist order that imagines us to be little more than isolated and competitive entrepreneurial selves, who better to give us hard advice about how to live and what to choose than an investment broker like J. D. Vance?

But wait. Things get a little more complicated. Vance isn't saying that his hillbillies are perfect neoliberal subjects—just that they should become so. To get ahead, they must fix themselves, but what holds them back is a dysfunctional ethno-regional, Scots-Irish culture. Here is where the two tracks of *Hillbilly Elegy*, Vance's personal memoir and his cultural one, come together, or perhaps tensely collide. On the personal level, *Hillbilly Elegy* is about the good choices Vance made that he believes allowed him to escape poverty. On the cultural level it is about good choices that "others in [his] neighborhood hadn't" made because of their ethnic heritage. Never mind that the book's premise about what constitutes Scots-Irish culture in Appalachia or elsewhere is based on stereotypes that have long been refuted, or that its demographic claim that the Scots-Irish ever constituted a majority of the Appalachian population is simply not true. *Hillbilly Elegy* is at once an advertisement for the neoliberal promised land of zombie-like entrepreneurial souls and an elegy for a dying but not yet dead enough Scots-Irish regional culture that doesn't really exist.

If Vance's hillbillies are not yet fully realized neoliberal subjects, however, some of his readers seem to be. Like the solitary neoliberal subjects that are imagined to live in social vacuums, authors are viewed as solitary figures whose writings reflect only personal choices and thus must be defended as such. I have examined many blog entries from *Hillbilly Elegy* fans who are vexed by criticisms of the book. Such readers don't seem to understand that narratives always exist in wider discursive contexts, that all books have intellectual debts, ideological commitments, and genealogies. They are annoyed by critique. For example, here are some reader responses to Ivy Brashear's powerful takedown of *Hillbilly Elegy*:

- He is just telling his story and I found it enlightening.
- Just one guy's story. I liked it.
- His experience was not everyone's experience but it is the experience he had and he has a right to write about it.
- The book was what he saw thru his own eyes. No pretense.

- JD is entitled to his experience, his point of view, and the expression thereof. It is not a treatise on everyone's experience, only his.

Or consider these responses to R. Mike Burr, a self-described "Appalachian liberal ex-pat" who also wrote a highly critical essay about *Hillbilly Elegy*:

- I just finished reading *Hillbilly Elegy* and I'm wondering what book most of the rest of you read . . . I read an autobiography. . . . Want to hear a different story? Write your own.
- This is what he wrote. Why should he write what you suggest. He writes what his experience was. . . .
- You are all full of crap! It's his life and his story and you cannot dispute his story as you did not live his life.

One of Brashear's readers pushed the personal choice trope the farthest when she wrote simply, "I do not understand why you *chose* to be offended" (emphasis added).[24]

If neoliberalism's new order of reason, as Brown aptly calls it, produces readers who cannot see beyond the personal choices of authors to the cultural, intellectual, and political contexts that help to shape their books, the same can be said of many writers in the mainstream corporate media when they turn to electoral politics. Structural and institutional factors in elections, even when they are acknowledged, are eclipsed by myopic attention to voter choices. The exclusive focus on voting behavior is like focusing on drug use in Appalachia without examining the pharmaceutical industry that pushed its painkillers by the millions on the region, the doctors and pain centers that promoted them, the DEA that refused to police this, and the politicians who fail to provide money for treatment and rehabilitation.[25]

Undoubtedly, efforts to understand voters' choice for Donald Trump led many readers and much of the mass media to *Hillbilly Elegy*, probably the single factor that most directly contributed to the book's phenomenal sales. (The *New York Times* hailed it as one of the most important books to read for understanding the election.) Despite its ultra conservative slant—Senate majority leader Mitch McConnell recommended it as his favorite book of 2016—many of its readers were political liberals according to an analysis in the *Economist* based on Amazon book sales. Readers of *Hillbilly Elegy* were far more likely to buy books like Mark Lilla's *Once and Future Liberal*, Nancy Isenberg's *White Trash*, and Arlie Russell Hochschild's *Strangers in Their Own Land* rather than right-wing books such as Ann Coulter's *In Trump We Trust*, Eric Bolling's *The Swamp*, or Mark Levin's *Rediscovering Americanism*.[26] One hundred fifty years of stereotypes about Appalachia and elitist stereotypes about poor people as "white trash" (shown by Isenberg to date back to the early colonial era) help to explain why liberal readers might find J. D. Vance to be a plausible guide to the current political scene as well as an analgesic for any qualms over inequality and injustice in the United States.

Analysts will undoubtedly be trying to unravel Donald Trump's bewildering victory over Hillary Clinton for some time to come. Left-leaning writers point to a wide array of structural and institutional factors that benefited Trump, including mass media election coverage; the massive increase in right-wing "dark money" in political campaigns since passage of *Citizens United* that has enabled the Republican Party to gerrymander electoral districts and pass voter-suppression laws in many states; the ideological use of racism to thwart class identity; the decline of unions and with it their potential to divert voters from socially divisive issues; the reality of real economic decline—especially in rural communities; and a corporate-friendly Democratic Party that failed to advance policies benefiting these areas, marginalized its progressive wing, and ran an ineffective presidential campaign in traditionally Democratic ("blue wall") Rust Belt states that were taken for granted by the Clinton campaign.[27]

On the other hand, writers in the corporate media have tended to overemphasize voter attitudes, beliefs, and preferences, that is, personal choices, as factors explaining Trump's victory.[28] As if following J. D. Vance's advice to liberals to "stop pretending that every problem is a structural problem" and instead "to deal with the poor as moral agents,"[29] they stressed voters' vulnerability and despair, sensitivity to perceived disdain by elites, and corresponding feelings of envy and shame, coupled with nativism, xenophobia, Islamophobia, anti-immigrant sentiments, racism and fear of the loss of white privilege, sexism, homophobia, right-wing evangelical religious beliefs, and antiabortion politics.

All of these forces—structural, institutional, and individual—undoubtedly had their effects in Appalachia and the rest of the country, but the 2016 election results are the overdetermined outcome of a myriad of complex factors. How these factors are sorted out and weighed is a matter of theory, methods, and ideological frames.[30] Mainstream media, however, honed in on one particular statistical category of voters—rural, non-college-educated whites—and especially those living in one particular place—Appalachia—as the key reason for Trump's victory.

The aggregation of non-college-educated whites—a category that, it should be noted, includes the superrich Bill Gates and Mark Zuckerberg—does not a class or real group make, but the media treated it as such before and after the 2016 election. It conjured up this pure abstraction and gave it life, attributing cultural and psychological attributes to a nonbeing. To learn more about it, hit-and-run journalists descended upon Appalachia, now dubbed "the heart of Trump country," to scrutinize the region's imaginary geography and culture as they have done so often before. Although one media analyst complained that *Hillbilly Elegy* is "the closest most journalists have gotten to that region," some reporters did in fact visit West Virginia and eastern Kentucky, but often the results weren't pretty.[31] At the worst, their dispatches read like the hillbilly horror movies that depict Appalachians as inbred, mutant, deformed, and murderous villains who savagely prey upon innocent urban travelers who accidently get lost or are detained in the "monstrous rural."[32]

Most extreme was Kevin D. Williamson's 2016 report in the *National Review*, which focused on "welfare dependency, drug and alcohol addiction, [and] family anarchy" in places like eastern Kentucky where he writes, "Even the economic changes of the past few decades do little to explain the dysfunction and negligence—and the incomprehensible *malice*—of poor white America" (emphasis original). Williamson had earlier described Appalachia as America's "white ghetto"—"a slowly dissipating nebula of poverty and misery with its heart in eastern Kentucky, the last redoubt of the Scots-Irish working class." "Welfare," he wrote, "has made Appalachia into a big and sparsely populated housing project."[33] His 2016 rendition of hillbilly porn went even further: "The truth about these dysfunctional, downscale communities is that they deserve to die. Economically, they are negative assets. Morally, they are indefensible.... The white American underclass is in thrall to a vicious, selfish culture whose main products are misery and used heroin needles. Donald Trump's speeches make them feel good. So does OxyContin. What they need isn't analgesics, literal or political. They need real opportunity, which means that they need real change, which means that they need U-Haul."[34]

Not all reporters were as harsh or cunning as Williamson. Even when they discussed the very real economic plight of coal mining communities and even, more rarely, when they interviewed minority groups in the region, they nonetheless framed Appalachia as America's unique "other." One journalist admitted that entering McDowell County, West Virginia, "felt a bit like crossing a national border." A writer for the *New Republic* visiting the same county after the election complained that West Virginia had "let itself be reduced" to "almost feudal destitution." He added, "The people of Trump Country, like so much of white America, long for a past that never was, and a future that cannot be." (Ironically, he was covering a Bernie Sanders postelection rally in McDowell County for universal health care that was met with thunderous applause from a large audience.) In a particularly lame effort after the election, a *Vox* writer asked why people would vote for a presidential candidate who campaigned on taking away their health insurance but interviewed only one person, a woman who said she didn't think Trump would do that and wasn't sure the law could be changed anyway. (Fact check: Trump promised to do away with "Obamacare" but still provide better health care coverage.) Coal miners in particular were interviewed about why they hoped that Trump might bring back jobs to the industry as he had promised, though the prospects were dim. One national journalist who interviewed prominent activists reported finding "some incredible, intelligent and warm Appalachians" who were "working tirelessly to rebuild their communities, protect their environment and preserve their cultures." This seemed to come as a surprise. She confessed that before going there, "when we thought of Appalachia, we saw poverty, Trump, and cultural caricatures," the "reductive images and tropes we, ourselves, had been exposed to." Such self-reflection among liberal journalists, however, was rare.[35]

Without it, Appalachia became what I call "Trumpalachia," a media-constructed mythological realm, backward and homogenous. Appalachians were still "yesterday's people" as they were described in the 1960s, but now it seems they had grown bitter, resentful, right-wing, and racist. Appalachia's supposed "cultural issues with racism, sexism, and homophobia" took center stage in liberals' diagnosis of its pathology. "A perfect storm of economics, creeping conservatism and outright racism" was said to have spawned its turn to the right after decades in the Democratic column. Hillbillies were said to be in despair over their "perceived and real loss of the social and economic advantages of being white." *The Guardian* described them as part of "a backlash from white, working-class voters frustrated by their relative decline in status in America— symbolized, in part, of course, by its first black president." "America is no longer white enough" for these voters wrote a *New York Times*' columnist. "To these people, Trump's 'Make America Great Again' is not the empty rhetoric of a media-savvy con artist from Queens but a last-ditch rallying cry for the soul of a changing land where minorities will be the majority by the middle of the century."[36] Another stated, "Let's put this clearly, the stressor at work here is the perceived and real loss of the social and economic advantages of being white." Above all, white Appalachia came to be represented as "a tinderbox of resentment that ignited national politics."[37]

Resentment is not necessarily bad. Although resentment is often portrayed as a dark and sinister emotion, it a common moral sentiment in response to feeling wronged. At issue is how resentment is directed, sometimes by politics.[38] In *Hillbilly Elegy* J. D. Vance expressed the resentment he once felt toward a drug-addicted Ohio neighbor on welfare who purchased T-bone steaks when Vance could not afford them. "I could never understand why our lives felt like a struggle while those living off government largess enjoyed trinkets that I only dreamed about" (139). Elsewhere, exposing the racial subtext of his thinking, he explained the resentment he believes hillbillies and other white working-class Americans feel toward President Obama for being "everything that American meritocracy values" when it "doesn't value very much about us at all."[39]

Speaking of blame and resentment, Republican politicians in Appalachia, in conjunction with the coal industry's Astroturf "War on Coal" campaign, did a masterful job of diverting coal miners' resentment over massive job loss away from the Appalachian industry's inability to compete with cheaper fuels and more productive regions in the West and directing it solely toward Obama's environmental regulations. Corporate neoliberals in the Democratic Party and the mainstream media, in contrast, directed their resentment at Trump's presidential victory toward Trumpalachia.

There was no more outrageous expression of the election blame game than one published in the *Daily Kos*, an unofficial voice of the Democratic Party. Implausibly, it defined Appalachia as a "large cultural region" and then drew an imaginary map of the United States that depicted Appalachia as if it were a single state with twenty-three Electoral College votes. This creative bit of fiction allowed its writers to claim dramatically that "Donald Trump only won the Electoral College thanks to Appalachia." It "impos[ed] its will on the rest of the U.S. . . . to elect a president the rest of the country disagreed with."[40] What an amazing metamorphosis. First Appalachia, composed of portions of twelve states and millions of people, became a unitary cultural region, then a state, and then the single cause of a national political disaster. Wow!

There are lots of ways to play the blame game about the last election besides blaming it all on Trumpalachia or the white working class. Liberals like to blame Appalachia (along with Russia). I like to blame liberals.[41] One could blame Trump on the Democrats, as West Virginia novelist Denise Giardina has done, for running a procorporate, neoliberal candidate (Hillary Clinton) who campaigned on more of the same policies that have neglected Appalachia, rural and Rust Belt communities, and the working class for many years.[42] The Democrats could also be blamed for simply failing to defend their home court ("blue wall") advantage in traditional party strongholds like Pennsylvania, Michigan, and Wisconsin with ineffective on-the-ground campaigns that failed to get the turnout of previous elections. Alternatively, one might blame the Republican Party's voter-suppression tactics in those same states where, by some estimates, Clinton's Electoral College victory would otherwise have been ensured. Just don't lay the blame on the working class as a whole when, by one tally, perhaps no more than a few hundred thousand former Obama voters in a score of Midwestern counties with recent plant closings and heightened foreign immigration defected to Trump. Also, don't blame poor people; many of them didn't vote, and besides that, data from the primaries show that Trump supporters' yearly income averaged $72,000, well above the national average and above those of Clinton and Sanders supporters. The typical Trump voter was not a poor hillbilly. And please, don't blame Trumpalachia.[43]

Appalachian voters did of course resoundingly support Donald Trump in 2016, and like non-metropolitan voters elsewhere, for a variety of reasons.[44] For many, Hillary Clinton's stupid remark that she would put "a lot of coal miners and coal companies out of work" was decisive.[45] But there is more to the story than this. When asked to explain why Trump was so popular in Appalachia, J. D. Vance explained, "The simple answer is that these people—my people—are really struggling, and there hasn't been a single political candidate who speaks to those struggles in a long time. Donald Trump at least tries."[46] But that's not true. Bernie Sanders did, and he beat Hillary Clinton in every county in West Virginia and almost all the counties in Appalachian Kentucky including all its coal counties in the presidential primaries, yet the national media gave this almost no attention at all. McDowell County, West Virginia, probably got more media attention than any other place because while Obama had won a majority of votes there in 2008, Trump won by 74 percent in 2016. Significantly, however, Sanders won twice as many votes as Trump in the primary election there. When he was not on the ballot, however, 73 percent of McDowell's registered voters simply stayed home and did not vote at all. This strong support for Sanders suggests to me that a significant number of voters in the coalfields and the wider region were prepared to vote for a more progressive candidate in the general election had one not indebted to Wall Street been available.[47] The media neglected to report Sanders's success in Appalachia, however, just as it failed to report on the thousands of people from across the region who marched in protest of Trump soon after his inauguration.

Be that as it may, the construction of Trumpalachia resulted in what Elizabeth Catte has aptly termed the "liberal shaming of Appalachia."[48] In his now famous article, "No Sympathy for the Hillbilly," Frank Rich advocated letting those voters "reap the consequences for voting against their own interests." Charles Pierce promised he would "never sympathize with regretful Trump voters" because "they brought this disaster on themselves." "I try to be charitable," Paul Krugman wrote, "but when you read about Trump voters now worried about losing Obamacare it's kind of hard." Not to be outdone, the editor of *Daily Kos* advised, "Be happy for coal miners losing their health insurance. They're getting exactly what they voted for." Finally, Scott Galindez added, "I'm going to say it: West Virginia might as well still be in the Confederacy."[49] (Fact check: it never was.)

National columnists were not alone in their disdain. Letters to editors and readers responding to blogs registered their disgust as well. Here is just one instance. When Appalachian novelist Ron Rash wrote an op-ed piece in the *New York Times* one week after the presidential election that linked Flint, Michigan's, water crisis to the poisoning of Appalachia's drinking water by the coal industry, it was met with considerable hostility. Two examples among many will have to suffice. A New York reader wrote, "Appalachian voters cast their ballots overwhelmingly and decisively for Donald Trump. I don't think now is a good time for an Appalachian complaint," and one from Nashville stated, "Yeah, you get the government you vote for. Appalachia voted to remain a colony that poisons itself. No pity. No excuses."[50]

In the meantime, J. D. Vance has gone on to shore up his right-wing credentials. He has been discussed as a candidate for high political office and has established a nonprofit organization in Ohio to fight "opiate abuse, save families, and create a pathway to the middle class."[51] Recently, he wrote the preface to the Heritage Foundation's "2017 Index of Culture and Opportunity," a Koch-funded reiteration of the culture of poverty thesis. In line with the Koch brothers, who put their vast money behind down-ticket Republican candidates rather than Donald Trump, Vance reports that he loved but was terrified by Trump and voted for a conservative write-in candidate instead.[52] Nevertheless, he was promoted by alt-right extremist Steve Bannon as a candidate for head of the Heritage Foundation. To be clear, Vance is misguided, but he is no Steve Bannon. Given his depiction of hillbillies as a distinct race of disadvantaged white ethnics, however, it's perhaps not surprising that Bannon, who called *Hillbilly Elegy* "a magnificent book," would try to recruit him as a potential "ally."[53]

The top echelon of the superrich in America has never been wealthier, while the income of deeply indebted American wage earners has been stagnant for decades. Millions of people in the United States are forced to live in poverty, and millions more suffer from economic insecurity and severe hardship.[54]

Now is no time for identity politics and shibboleths about self-sufficiency and personal choice. In "The Afterlife of a Memoir," Aminatta Forna advises, "Write a memoir but only if you are sure you want to live with the consequences every day for the rest of your life."[55] The great danger and ultimate tragedy of *Hillbilly Elegy* is not simply that it perpetuates Appalachian stereotypes. It is that it promotes toxic politics that will only further oppress the hillbillies that J. D. Vance professes to love and speak for.

NOTES

I am grateful to Jeremy Popkin, Herb Reid, David Ruccio, and Karen Tice for their assistance and encouragement of this chapter. I have also benefited from Randy Ihara's insightful comments before and after the 2016 election.

1. Appalachian readers will be familiar with the phrase "strange land and peculiar people" as an early instance of the "othering" of Appalachia. See Henry D. Shapiro, *Appalachia on Our Mind: The Southern Mountains and Mountaineers in the American Consciousness, 1870–1920* (Chapel Hill: University of North Carolina Press, 1978).
2. J. D. Vance, *Hillbilly Elegy: A Memoir of a Family and Culture in Crisis* (New York: HarperCollins, 2016), 3, 1; Vance, "How the White Working Class Lost Its Patriotism," *Charleston (WV) Gazette-Mail*, July 30, 2016.
3. For recent examples of activism, see Stephen L. Fisher and Barbara Ellen Smith, *Transforming Places: Lessons from Appalachia* (Champaign: University of Illinois Press, 2012); on efforts to build a post-coal economy, see "A Green New Deal for Appalachia, parts 1 and 2," *Journal of Appalachian Studies*, Spring 2017 and Winter 2017, by B. Taylor, M. Hufford, and K. Bilbrey and L. Tarus, M. Hufford, and B. Taylor, respectively.
4. For instance, Dwight Billings, Gurney Norman, and Katherine Ledford, eds., *Back Talk from Appalachia: Confronting Stereotypes* (Lexington: University Press of Kentucky, 1999); Anthony Harkins, *Hillbilly: A Culture History of an American Icon* (New York: Oxford University Press, 2003).
5. Chad Berry, *Southern Migrants, Northern Exiles* (Champaign: University of Illinois Press, 2000); Phillip J. Obermiller, Thomas E. Wagner, and E. Bruce Tucker, eds., *Appalachian Odyssey: Historical Perspectives on the Great Migration* (Westport, CT: Praeger, 2000). A classic study is Harry Schwarzweller, James Brown, and Walter Mangalam, *Mountain Families in Transition* (University Park: Pennsylvania State University Press, 1971).
6. Arthur Mitzman, *The Iron Cage* (New York: Knopf, 1969).
7. Daniel P. Moynihan, "The Negro Family: The Case for National Action" (Washington, DC: Office of Policy Planning and Research, US Department of Labor, 1965); Charles Murray, *Coming Apart: The State of White America, 1960–2010* (New York: Crown Forum, 2012).
8. Besides the contributors to this volume, see James Branscome, "Lamenting 'Hillbilly

Elegy,'" *Daily Yonder*, August 3, 2016; Herbert Reid, posted at http://www
.recoveringthecommons.org/single-post/2016/11/22/Hiding-American-Injuries-
under-the-hillbilly-hat; and Bill Turner, "Another Take on 'Hillbilly Elegy,'" *Daily Yonder*, August 16, 2016.

9. Robert Kuttner, "The Hidden Injuries of Class, Race, and Culture," *American Prospect*, October 3, 2016; Chris Maisano, "The New 'Culture of Poverty,'" *Catalyst* 1, no. 2 (Spring 2017); Sarah Jones, "J. D. Vance, the False Prophet of Blue America," *New Republic*, November 17, 2016; Betsy Rader, "I Was Born in Appalachia. 'Hillbilly Elegy' Doesn't Speak for Me," *Washington Post*, September 1, 2017.

10. Jennifer Senior, "In 'Hillbilly Elegy,' a Tough Love Analysis of the Poor Who Back Trump," *New York Times*, August 10, 2016; and David Brooks, "Revolt of the Masses," *New York Times*, June 28, 2016.

11. Rod Dreher, "Trump: Tribune of Poor White People," *American Conservative*, July 22, 2016. The *Economist*'s endorsement is quoted on the Amazon book web page for *Hillbilly Elegy*.

12. Summers is quoted in Paul Lewis, "*Hillbilly Elegy* Author JD Vance on Barack Obama: 'We Dislike the Things We Envy,'" *Guardian*, January 25, 2017.

13. See https://wikipedia.org/wiki/Reihan_Salam.

14. In his "Acknowledgments" to *Hillbilly Elegy*, Vance writes that, besides his agent, Chua "deserves the most credit for this book's existence," noting that she "convinced me that both my life and the conclusions I drew from it were worth putting down on paper" (259).

15. Alexandra Wolfe, "J. D. Vance and the Anger of the White Working Class," *Wall Street Journal*, July 29, 2016. A writer in the *Washington Post* concurred: "Perhaps Vance's key to success is a simple one: that he just powered through his difficulties instead of giving up or blaming someone else." See Amanda Erickson, "A Hillbilly's Plea to the White Working Class," *Washington Post*, August 4, 2016.

16. For a brief overview of neoliberalism and its effects, see George Monbiot, "Neoliberalism—The Ideology at the Root of All Our Problems," *Guardian*, April 15, 2016. For more extensive discussions, see David Harvey, *A Brief History of Neoliberalism* (Oxford: Oxford University Press, 2005); Kean Birch and Vlad Mykhnenko, eds., *The Rise and Fall of Neo-liberalism* (London: Zed Books, 2010); and Wendy Brown, *Undoing the Demos: Neoliberalism's Stealth Revolution* (Brooklyn: Zone Books, 2015).

17. For the first era of robber barons, see R. Jeffrey Lustig, *Corporate Liberalism: The Origins of Modern American Political Theory, 1890–1929* (Berkeley: University of California Press, 1982); for the 1960s and 1970s, see Bertram Gross, *Friendly Fascism: The New Face of Power in America* (New York: M. Evans, 1980).

18. Jane Mayer, *Dark Money* (New York: Anchor Books, 2017); Nancy MacLean, *Democracy in Chains* (New York: Penguin, 2017).

19. Some would see Jimmy Carter's monetary policies as a first inroad of neoliberalism. Augusto Pinochet's violent dictatorship that overthrew the socialist government of Salvador Allende preceded Thatcher and Reagan by more than half a decade. Under the guidance of US market fundamentalists such as Milton Friedman and Jeremy Sachs, Chile provided a testing ground for the authoritarian imposition of neoliberalism. See Naomi Klein, *The Shock Doctrine: The Rise of Disaster Capitalism* (New York: Picador, 2007).

20. It is possible that Trump will represent a nationalist rather than international version of neoliberalism, as Sasha Breger Bush suggests in "Trump and National Neoliberalism," *Dollars and Sense*, December 24, 2016.

21. Premilla Nadasen, "How a Democrat Killed Welfare Reform," *Jacobin*, February 9, 2016. Also see the earlier classic book by Francis Fox Piven and Richard Cloward, *Regulating the Poor: The Functions of Public Welfare* (New York: Vintage, 1993).

22. Henry A. Giroux, "The Culture of Cruelty in Trump's America," *Truthdig*, March 22, 2017.

23. Brown, *Undoing the Demos*.

24. For reader responses, see "Response to 'Hillbilly Elegy,'" *Young Kentuckian*, April 3, 2017, and http://tropicsofmeta.wordpress.com/2017/02/27/the-self-serving-hustile-of-hillbilly-elegy.

25. Eric Eyre, "Drug Firms Poured 750m Painkillers into WV amid Rise of Overdoses," *Charleston Gazette Mail*, December 17, 2016.

26. "Political Books, Purple Blues," *Economist*, September 30, 2017.

27. Two good examples are Connor Kilpatrick, "This Didn't Have to Happen," *Jacobin*, October 27, 2016, and Mike Davis at https://catalyst-journal.com/v011/n01/great-god-trump-davis.

28. One of the most comprehensive studies of voting behavior in the 2016 election is by the Democracy Fund Voter Study Group, a research group that spanned the political spectrum and included two dozen commentators, issued in 2017. See www.voterstudygroup.org.

29. Quoted in Dreher, "Trump."

30. In responding to Nate Silver's comment that the 2012 election was "overdetermined," David Ruccio points out that overdetermination is the epistemological position that every event can be both a cause and an effect, i.e., that social events including elections cannot be reduced to a single or essential explanation. See Ruccio, "Overdetermined Election," *Occasional Links and Commentary*, November 5, 2012.

31. Michael Massing, "Journalism in Trump's America," *Nation*, February 6/13, 2017.

32. In an astute analysis of viewer responses to these films, Emily Satterwhite has shown that even when anti-capitalist messages are encoded, such as blaming industrial toxins for Appalachians' mutations, viewers tend to focus only on the hillbillies' monstrous qualities. See Satterwhite, "The Politics of Hillbilly Horror," in *Navigating Souths: Transdisciplinary Explorations of a U.S. Region*, ed. Michele Grigsby Coffey and Jodi Skipper (Athens: University of Georgia Press, 2017), 227–45.

33. Kevin D. Williamson, "The White Ghetto: In Appalachia the Country Is Beautiful and the Society Is Broken," *National Review*, January 9, 2014.

34. Kevin D. Williamson, "Chaos in the Family, Chaos in the State: The White Working Class's Dysfunction," *National Review*, March 17, 2016. Also see David French, "Working-Class Whites Have Moral Responsibilities—In Defense of Kevin Williamson," *National Review*, March 14, 2016. Some analysts interpret Williamson's condemnation of the working class as a return to the *National Review*'s intellectual genealogy of aristocratic conservatism that sees the "poor as beyond saving, and all that is left to do is shower them with contempt." See Jeet Neer, "National Review's Revolt Against the Masses," *New Republic*, March 15, 2016.

35. See, in order, Lauren Gurley, "West Virginia, 'Identity Decline' and Why Democrats Must Not Look Away from the Rural Poor," *In these Times*, December 15, 2016; Kevin Baker, "The Eternal Sunshine of the Spotless White Mind," *New Republic*, March 18, 2017; Sarah Kliff and Byrd Pinkerton, "This Trump Voter Doesn't Think Trump Was Serious about Repealing Her Health Insurance," *Vox*, December 13, 2016; Sheryl Gay Stolberg, "Trump's Promises Will Be Hard to Keep, but Coal Country Has Faith," *New York Times*, November 28, 2016; Gregory S. Schneider, "Deep in Virginia's Craggy Coal Country, They Saw Trump as Their Only Hope," *Washington Post*, November 12, 2016; and Sana Saeed, "Appalachia—Without the Classism and Caricatures," *Medium*, February 6, 2017, http://medium.com/aj-story/Appalachia-without-the-classism-and-caracatures-c1a71d9b271.

36. Jack Jenkins, "Appalachia Used to Be a Democratic Stronghold: Here's How to Make It One Again," *ThinkProgress*, May 25, 2016, https://thinkprogress.org/appalachia-used-to-be-a-democratic-stronghold; Roger Cohen, "We Need 'Somebody Spectacular': Views from Trump Country," *New York Times*, September 9, 2016.

37. Karen Heller, "'Hillbilly Elegy' Made J. D. Vance the Voice of the Rust Belt. But Does He Want the Job?," *Washington Post*, February 6, 2017.

38. See Jürgen Habermas, *Moral Consciousness and Communicative Action* (Cambridge, MA: MIT Press, 1990), esp. 45–50; also Elizabeth Morelli, "Ressentiment and Rationality," https://www.bu.edu/wcp/Papers/Anth/AnthMore.htm.

39. Quoted in Paul Lewis, "Hillbilly Elegy Author JD Vance on Barack Obama: 'We Dislike the Things We Envy,'" *Guardian*, January 25, 2017. For further discussion of the resentment that "surfaces again and again in his book," see Alec Macgillis and Propublica, "The Original Underclass," *Atlantic*, September 9, 2016.

40. https://www.dailykos.com/stories/2017/1/4/1613126/-Forget-imperial-California-Donald-Trump-only-won-the-Electoral-College-thanks-to-Appalachia.

41. So does Thomas Frank in his important book *Listen, Liberal* (New York: Metropolitan Books, 2016).

42. Denise Giardina, "Dems Deserve Share of Blame for Trump's Rise," *Charleston (WV) Gazette-Mail*, July 30, 2016.

43. On Obama-turned-Trump voters, see the excellent article by Mike Davis, "The Great God Trump and the White Working Class," *Catalyst* 1, no. 1 (Spring 2017). On the effects of voter suppression on the 2016 presidential election, see Jeffrey Toobin, "The Real Voting Scandal of 2016," *New Yorker*, December 17, 2016, and Bob Fitrakis and Harvey Wasserman, "How the GOP Flipped and Stripped Yet Another American Election," *Reader Supported News*, November 20, 2016. Also, on the more recent congressional election in Georgia, see Bob Fitrakis and Harvey Wasserman, "Jim Crow GOP Steals Another Election as Brain Dead Democrats and Media Say Nothing," *Reader Supported News*, June 21, 2017; Nate Silver, "The Mythology of Trump's 'Working Class' Support: His Voters Are Better Off Economically Compared with Most Americans," *FiveThirtyEight*, May 3, 2016.

44. Alexander Zaitchik, "A Conversation with a Trump Supporter That Will Surprise You," *Alternet*, August 22, 2016. The Democracy Fund Voter Study Group (cited above) identified five distinct types of Trump supporters with sharply differentiated views.

45. Coral Davenport, "Coal Country Is Wary of Hillary Clinton's Pledge to Help," *New*

York Times, August 28, 2016. Clinton made this quip while promising a multibillion-dollar program to rehabilitate coal communities and workers, but that is not what got remembered during the campaign.

46. Quoted in Amanda Erickson, "A Hillbilly's Plea to the White Working Class," *Washington Post*, August 4, 2016.

47. On McDowell County, see Kilpatrick, "This Didn't Have to Happen," and Elizabeth Catte, "The Mythical Whiteness of Trump Country," *Boston Review*, November 7, 2017. On the lack of turnout nationally in 2016, see David Leonhardt, "The Democrats' Real Turnout Problem," *New York Times*, November 17, 2016.

48. Elizabeth Catte, "Liberal Shaming of Appalachia: Inside the Media Elite's Obsession with the 'Hillbilly Problem,'" *Salon*, March 21, 2017.

49. Frank Rich, "No Sympathy for the Hillbilly," *New York Magazine*, March 21, 2017; Charles Pierce, "Why I'll Never Sympathize with Regretful Voters," *Esquire*, March 2, 2017; *Daily Kos* and Krugman quoted in Clio Chang, "Ending the Empathy Gap," *Jacobin*, March 21, 2017; and Scott Galindez, "Shocking News," *Reader Supported News*, August 8, 2017.

50. Ron Rash, "Appalachia's Sacrifice," *New York Times*, November 18, 2016.

51. See http://ourohiorenewable.org.

52. Reported in Dreher, "Trump."

53. Robert Costa et al., "Heritage Foundation Considers . . . ," *Washington Post*, October 17, 2017.

54. For a comprehensive analysis of inequality in the United States, see David F. Ruccio, "Class and Trumponomics," *Real-World Economics Review*, no. 78 (2017).

55. Aminatta Forna, "The Afterlife of a Memoir," NYR Daily, *New York Review of Books*, November 13, 2017, http://www.nybooks.com/daily/2017/11/13/the-afterlife-of-a-memoir/.

STEREOTYPES ON THE SYLLABUS: EXPLORING *HILLBILLY ELEGY*'S USE AS AN INSTRUCTIONAL TEXT AT COLLEGES AND UNIVERSITIES

ELIZABETH CATTE

IN FEBRUARY 2017, five students from Rosemary Choate Hall, an elite college-preparatory boarding school in Connecticut, traveled to Yale University to hear its alumnus J. D. Vance speak. Vance drew deeply from his memoir during a thirty-minute lecture—he repeated, for example, his often-used anecdote about the bewilderment of fine dining as a hillbilly—but he also shared his trademark political insight as well. Vance's enthusiasm for diagnosing current political shifts and the rise of Donald Trump through the lens of his harrowing childhood in Ohio has made the former venture capitalist an accessible and popular public figure since his memoir's release. On this occasion, his remarks drew mixed reactions from attendees interviewed by the *Yale Daily News* after the event.[1] The experience left the Choate students in attendance, however, deeply impressed. Choate's campus newspaper ran a warm review of the field trip—"Choate Students Learn about 'Hillbilly Culture'"—and one senior shared that she now had "a new perspective and appreciation for 'hillbillies' ... there's this whole population of lower class white people in this country that feel left behind by college educated liberals and felt that Trump gave them a voice."[2]

60

The Choate review ignited a small and brief firestorm on social media. One reader from Appalachia, for example, invited us to imagine a world in which "hillbillies" became curious students of elite boarding school culture. This cynical and humorous imagined reversal was, in many ways, a perfect encapsulation of a distinct type of fatigue felt by many in Appalachia and the Rust Belt, often confused and ever-expanding sister geographies, since the 2016 presidential election. The deep historical antecedents of various "hillbillies-as-objects-of-study" tropes will, no doubt, inform many of the essays collected in this volume, and many will also, no doubt, concur that our current political moment has inspired their resurrections. Cleveland-based writer Alex Baca recently commented, "It's zeitgeisty, still, nearly a year after Donald Trump's ascension, to talk about poor, mostly rural white people as if they hold the key to the political hellscape in which we've found ourselves."[3]

If the fault of some pundits and political observers is using the wrong key in perhaps the right lock, then what can be said of Vance's straight-in-with-bolt-cutters approach to working-class analysis? The most obvious answer, and the one that gives this essay its subject, is that it is incredibly popular and lucrative, not just among a broad public but also among educators seeking contemporary instructional texts, to "start a conversation," in higher education administration speak, about our troubled times. *Hillbilly Elegy* is currently experiencing a second wave of popularity and sales courtesy of colleges and universities across the country, and institutions of these types have also featured prominently in Vance's ambitious and ongoing speaking tour. "In this timely talk," the University of Arkansas shared in publicity materials announcing an invited lecture, "Vance sheds light on an often forgotten corner of the country, offering not just a powerful picture of how upward mobility really feels, but also the loss of the modern-day American dream."

As universities prepare both their institutions and their students for life under the Trump administration, many are turning to *Hillbilly Elegy* to explore themes considered relevant to our current political moment, a facet of the memoir's reach that has yet to receive analysis. This essay offers an opportunity to "start a conversation" about the conversations that have been started about Appalachia at institutions of learning since *Hillbilly Elegy*'s release.

Hillbilly Elegy is most typically assigned through common reading experiences, popularized by university administrators as campus culture-building events in which a single text, often mandatory reading for college freshmen, becomes the basis for a year of related programing and knowledge exchange. They exist at the intersection of aggressive publishing industry marketing, current events, and learning outcomes, and it is not surprising that *Hillbilly Elegy*, a fixture on best-seller lists since its release, has fared well in this market.

It is difficult to assess the full impact of *Hillbilly Elegy*'s placement in such programs because many directed readings are still in progress at the time of this writing. Nonetheless, it is vital to begin considering the risks or rewards that might follow in what has become a moment of almost unprecedented national interest in Appalachia. This consideration raises many questions. Does criticism of the memoir or belief in its utility become more pronounced when its readership is captive and more likely to reflect a younger audience? Are universities assigning *Hillbilly Elegy* well placed or receptive to offering additional context about the region's history? What about *Hillbilly Elegy* excites university administrators and common reading selection committees? Can we learn something from the ways in which faculty, students, and recent graduates embrace or reject Vance's expertise? What does it feel like to read and engage with *Hillbilly Elegy* as an instructor or student from Appalachia?

It is productive to start with the question of why *Hillbilly Elegy* and build from there, looking first at the intention behind common reading programs. According to the National Resource Center for the First-Year Experience and Students in Transition (FYE) at the University of South Carolina, approximately 40 percent of colleges with orientation programs sponsor a common reading event.[4] Although common reading experiences can inspire campus-wide events, their intended audience is most often first-year students. Many universities include delivery of the assigned text during first-year orientation festivities over the summer, with the expectation that students dedicate a modest portion of their remaining freedom to reading. The common reading text gives students experiencing a significant life transition at least one thing in common with their new classmates during a time that some find isolating. From there, universities might use the reading in a variety of programing, from public lectures to course assignments for freshman classes.

University administrators link common reading programs to the development of a number of skills and learning outcomes among transitioning students such as critical thinking and civic engagement. Common reading texts and universities' approaches to these texts intend to signal that students are now liberated from their tight intellectual collar, fastened in high school by standardized tests and state requirements. University administrators use common reading programs to underscore that students are now of the world and that it is right and expected of them to form opinions about serious topics and important books. And at a time when STEM fields are more popular than the humanities at many universities, common reading programs offer the chance to inject something of the liberal arts into the curriculum of students on a different path.

Data collected by FYE allow us to generalize about recent trends in college reading programs.[5] Most common reading programs are found at four-year universities, and public institutions are slightly more likely than private universities to host a program. The majority of common reading program selections are books published since 2010, and nonfiction set within the United States is the most popular genre. Within that, the top five subject areas are science and technology, women and gender, history, psychology and self-help, and race and race relations. The least popular subject is LGBT issues. *Hillbilly Elegy* obviously fits well within these categories. It is a recently published nonfiction memoir set within the modern United States that overlaps categories of history, self-help, and even race relations in its emphasis on the cultural decline of the white working class.

I began tracking the use of *Hillbilly Elegy* as an instructional text after I learned that my PhD alma mater, Middle Tennessee State University, had selected the memoir for its 2017–18 common reading experience. *Hillbilly Elegy* is also featured as the selection for common reading programs nationwide. It has been or will be read at Augustana College, Bowling Green State University, Flagler College, Indiana University Southeast, Malone

University, Miami University, Ohio University, Somerset Community College, University of Denver, University of Wisconsin–Madison, and Wake Forest University. It was shortlisted among reading selections at other universities including Auburn and West Virginia University, and its influence will doubtless appear through Vance's continuing college speaking tour featuring universities like Boston College, Denison University, Marietta College, Morningside College, Pepperdine, Sinclair College, University of Cincinnati, Xavier, and Yale. This list, which is just a sample of the institutions that appear in popular search results for Vance's university speaking engagements, undoubtedly will have grown by the time this volume is published.

Beyond FYE, the most thorough cataloguing of common reading program selections and analysis comes via conservative organizations that monitor higher education. This fact hints at a broad tension embedded in common reading programs and, much more obviously, the state of higher education itself that further explains *Hillbilly Elegy*'s widespread adoption. In our ongoing and never-ending campus culture wars, reading selections are not just useful or popular texts but perceived tools of political and cultural indoctrination. In 2014, for example, a South Carolina legislative committee condemned the use of two common reading texts with LGBT themes, Alison Bechdel's *Fun Home*, used at the College of Charleston, and the *Out Loud: The Best of Rainbow Radio* anthology selected by Carolina Upstate. Republican committee member Gary Smith called the selections "promotion of a lifestyle without academic debate."[6]

Universities often link common reading programs to institutional missions that promote diversity, but this tendency also inserts common reading programs into the larger debate about how diversity is construed on college campuses.[7] One of the most common definitions of diversity is the promotion of students and faculty from historically underrepresented groups into full participation in campus life and governance. University administrators often signal the inclusiveness of their campus culture by choosing selections authored by individuals from marginalized backgrounds that are reflective of themes relevant to these backgrounds, such as immigration, racial discrimination, and overcoming adversity. Believing conservative voices to be growing ever more scarce on liberal college campuses, however, many right-leaning organizations are more concerned with what these groups often call diversity of thought. By framing conservative texts and ideas imperiled or neglected by university administrators and faculty, such organizations co-opt the language of diversity by arguing that intervention is necessary to correct prejudice and restore intellectual balance within curriculums.

The National Association of Scholars (NAS), a conservative nonprofit organization, has been particularly vocal about what it perceives as the political uses of common reading programs to further a liberal agenda on college campuses. The NAS has labeled common reading experiences a "bureaucratic exercise" designed to "forward progressive dogma" by obscuring the inherently liberal politicization of college campuses.[8] The organization, for example, objected strongly to the inclusion of Ta-Nehisi Coates's *Between the World and Me* and Bryan Stevenson's *Just Mercy: A Story of Justice and Redemption* on the common reading roster at several universities for promoting liberal politics in the guise of honoring diversity. Conservative publication the *National Review* concurred with the NAS's sentiments and in June 2017 criticized common reading programs for "embracing a historical narrative of oppression and victimhood that molds a false identity for them [students] based on tribal classifications of skin color, class, and gender." The *National Review* concluded, "That way lies the death of the individual, of culture, and of civilization itself."[9]

Tellingly, though, these organizations and cultural monitors have had nothing as yet to say about the popularity of *Hillbilly Elegy* as a common reading selection, despite the fact that a frequently used secondary criticism of such programs is the promotion of contemporary "buzz-worthy" texts at the expense of the classics.[10] Noting an absence of criticism from the right brings us closer to understanding the appeal of *Hillbilly Elegy* as a common reading selection. It is a text authored by a conservative white individual that projects a powerful illusion of political neutrality, and it both honors and subverts our usual definitions of diversity. While Vance's background as a first-generation college student is enough to place him in the category of persons underrepresented on college campuses, *Hillbilly Elegy* goes a step beyond. The world created by *Hillbilly Elegy* is one populated by marginalized white individuals intended to challenge what Vance perceives as an overuse of white privilege or advantage as a social organizing logic.

The *New York Times* has written that *Hillbilly Elegy* is a natural choice for universities wishing to buck liberal trends, but the popularity of *Hillbilly Elegy* among liberal readers is a well-noted phenomenon.[11] The *Economist* recently identified *Hillbilly Elegy* as a book that spanned political divides, placing it in the same category as Arlie Russell Hochschild's *Strangers in Their Own Land* and Susan Bordo's *The Destruction of Hillary Clinton*.[12] Despite Vance's conservative credentials, the *Economist* found, using data supplied by online retailer Amazon, that *Hillbilly Elegy*'s readership was actually more left-leaning than right. The scope and tone of media coverage that has contributed to Vance's meteoric rise to fame confirms his popularity among liberal readers, and Hillary Clinton recently endorsed Vance's insight about cultural decline in her memoir *What Happened*.

The malleability of *Hillbilly Elegy*'s political logic is, in my view, both sinister and clever. *Hillbilly Elegy* blankets fundamentally right-wing observations and diagnostics in a compelling personal story intended to present those insights as hard-earned, authentic, and politically neutral. Despite graduating from Yale University, boasting a circle of mentors that include Charles Murray, Peter Thiel, Amy Chua, and Steve Bannon, and commanding a sphere of influence than stretches from Silicon Valley to Washington, Vance nonetheless consistently projects himself as a sort of "hillbilly" everyman still growing out of his naivety, and is frequently received as such, with praise, by both liberals and conservatives alike.

Acknowledging the broad appeal of *Hillbilly Elegy* to those on both the left and the right and the utility of this gift to college administrators is an important facet in understanding the book's transformation from popular memoir to educational text. This phenomenon also suggests that our institutions of learning might have an Appalachia-sized blind spot in their worldview, one in which simplistic narratives and monolithic representations flourish without the scrutiny normally demanded by higher education. To discuss this phenomenon, and to gauge how prepared universities are to add nuance to Vance's arguments about Appalachia, I offer the case of my alma mater, Middle Tennessee State University (MTSU), a university on the periphery of Appalachia, just outside of Nashville, and particularly its decision to offer a unique tie-in to the common reading selection of *Hillbilly Elegy*—a photographic exhibit and public lecture exploring Appalachian poverty using the images of Shelby Lee Adams, a prolific and controversial photographer of destitute communities in eastern Kentucky.

In November 2016, MTSU announced that it had received a significant donation of photographic materials—enough to create a special archive—from Adams. A close friend of Adams and a photography professor at MTSU facilitated the donation. The donation's deed of gift included a provision that allows MTSU to benefit financially from the archive by selling reproduced images, and Adams stated his intention to donate a portion of his own proceeds to the subjects of his photographs.

Adams's relationships to his subjects and the power dynamics these relationships reflect are a source of controversy within Appalachia. Adams, from Hazard, Kentucky, and trained at the Cleveland Institute of Art, most often photographs individuals experiencing extreme poverty, some with profound disabilities, and frequently blurs the line between fine art creator and objective documentarian when challenged about his goals and process. Appalachian studies scholar Chelsea Brislin writes, "As a contemporary artist, Adams consciously and consistently uses sensationalism and morbidity to create a product that differentiates his goals from that of a traditional documentary photographer; viewers see a warped representation of reality which prioritizes appeal to a contemporary art market over an obligation to truth or authenticity."[13]

This appeal relies on the gleeful curiosity of audiences who are happy to visually consume a version of Appalachia that, in many ways, fits well-worn regional stereotypes. According to scholar Katherine Ledford, Adams traffics in images of "men's gunshot-scarred bodies, of grossly swollen limbs after religious-associated snakebite, of rattlesnakes resting on Bibles, of eviscerated hogs, of naked, dirty, and sick children."[14] The inclusion of a hog in Ledford's roll call of visual tropes nods at one of Adams's most controversial images, "The Hog Killing," from 1990. For that image, Adams bought a hog carcass and delivered it to a poor family in eastern Kentucky, then photographed them as they continued the slaughter, a practice the family had not engaged in for many years. Critics often cite this image as evidence of Adams's willingness to manipulate his subjects, while Adams insisted this and similar arrangements reflected an "honest exchange" between artist and collaborator-subjects.[15]

Despite such controversy, MTSU president Sidney McPhee announced that "an artist of the magnitude of Shelby Lee Adams will raise the stature of the Baldwin gallery [the university's art space] and raise the consciousness of students and scholars looking to understand the conditions and quality of life in Appalachia." Adams concurred, and added that he also hoped that the location of his archive in Middle Tennessee would encourage "people in the mountains of Eastern Kentucky" to travel to Murfreesboro (a nine-hour round-trip drive from Hazard) to view their images on display. Adams christened the new archive and resulting exhibition with a public lecture. *Nashville Arts*, a magazine devoted to local culture, wrote of the exhibit, "It can be hard to believe the photographs are real. They depict scenes that appear lost in time if not from a different reality all together. Crowds of children missing shirts and shoes stare ominously in the lens. Adults with weathered skin pose in front of ramshackle buildings and cluttered rooms."[16] Viewers' detachment from the images is so strong that they have difficulty placing themselves and the subject in the same reality, a concerning reaction that challenges MTSU's promotion of the exhibit as a consciousness-raising experience.

MTSU encouraged faculty and students to visit the Adams exhibition prior to reading *Hillbilly Elegy* as a preview of coming attractions. University administrators even dubbed Adams's archive the "photographic analog of J. D. Vance's book *Hillbilly Elegy*" and insisted that "the author and the photographer tell corresponding stories through different means" while emphasizing the "rare opportunity" of matching a photographic exhibition with a summer reading selection.[17]

The promotional material did not elaborate on what these corresponding stories are, but let me do so here and highlight the similarities between J. D. Vance and Shelby Lee Adams as I see them. Rather than affirm Vance and Adams as MTSU intended, as twinned experts whose contributions are attached to rare educational potential, these connections complicate an authority often uncritically granted to popular creators. In this way, these corresponding stories are about not only people but also power and the way this power is asserted to control a narrative about Appalachia that first and foremost suits commercial purposes.

Both men's processes exploit their closeness to vulnerable subjects and a region believed to be "forgotten" with a goal of extracting and selling stereotypes to a commercial audience. Both men are resistant to and dismissive of criticisms of this exploitation, and both find more acclaim outside of than within Appalachia, a reality that does not often receive the weight that it should. As cultural interventionists—individuals who adopt a position of explaining or introducing a "misunderstood" culture to wide audiences—both men embrace the role of regional "authority" and benefit financially from a claim of ownership and expertise not just of their personal histories and relationships but of all Appalachian lives.

Many students assigned the reading and encouraged to view the exhibit will have had limited formal opportunities to study Appalachia and would need guidance to recognize this exploitation. Like most universities using *Hillbilly Elegy* as a common reading selection, MTSU does not offer regular courses in Appalachian studies or history. Of course, the modest reach of Appalachian studies as an academic discipline might be all the more reason to conduct knowledge exchange about the region through auxiliary programing like common reading experiences. But much like MTSU, a number of universities are using tie-ins that endorse or affirm rather than complicate Vance's insights and his vision of and for Appalachia.

In some cases, universities have consciously or unconsciously endorsed Vance's insight by recommending authors who share similar beliefs about other population groups. For example, Bowling Green State University (BGSU), just outside of Toledo, Ohio, hosted J. D. Vance alongside Clarence

Page, an African American journalist who got his start at the Middletown High School newspaper in Vance's hometown. On the common reading experience page of BGSU's website, administrators encourage students to read an older op-ed written by Page titled "Tough Love to Poor Whites as Well as Inner-City Blacks." Page writes, "Go out and preach the value of hard work, good schooling and saying no to meth and addictive painkillers to poor rural Appalachians. . . . Go and preach tough love to unemployed blue-collar white males and unmarried mothers in the devastated factory towns studied by Charles Murray."[18] One of the more alarming side effects of *Hillbilly Elegy* is the reintroduction of Charles Murray, discredited in the academic social science community but often cited by Vance, as a contemporary expert on race and poverty to audiences that might not normally be on guard for the racial and class bias reflected in the larger body of his work.

In the process of conducting this research, I have thought often about what it might be like to spend a year locked into the promotional frenzy for *Hillbilly Elegy* alongside students at MTSU, where I taught undergraduate courses. While I have no doubt I would enjoy the absolute freedom to criticize the book and its tie-ins at will, I would also be assuming a burden to support my conclusions with a wide complement of evidence outside my personal experiences, something often rejected by Vance. In other words, as an instructor, it would not be appropriate for me to comment on the observational material presented by one very specific person without bringing the weight of my training and credentials to bear on my comments. This style of pedagogy would dictate that students take a similar approach by supporting their reactions to Vance's arguments with additional research and the insight of other scholars. While textual engagement of this sort appears anodyne, it also risks further devaluing and degrading the personal experiences of the reader while granting enormous privilege to the experiences of the author. The transformation of *Hillbilly Elegy* from memoir to educational text makes it difficult to critique or debate the book in the most powerful and accessible way, by simply articulating a personal experience with poverty that is different.

There is a noticeable disconnect between the way that university administrators intend the book to be received and its reception by students, and the selection of *Hillbilly Elegy* as a common reading text has provoked strong reactions from students, particularly among students from Appalachia and the Rust Belt. While university administrators highlight the text's big ideas and debatable conclusions, many students have used a variety of platforms—from social media to local and campus newspapers—to question the appropriateness of debating stereotypical and widely refuted representations of their regions.

The University of Wisconsin–Madison, which selected *Hillbilly Elegy* as its Go Big Read text, said on its website that it hoped its selection would "generate a lively conversation about a set of important issues, about which people can agree or disagree." Chancellor Rebecca Blank commented, "We hope this will generate a conversation of that sort, which leads people to think more about the social and political issues raised in the book." Miami University called the selection a strong look at "the struggle to include all members in a diverse population in a dynamic society," and a way to encourage students to examine "broad themes that can be viewed in many contexts." These innocuous statements suggest that *Hillbilly Elegy* can serve as something of a blank slate on which individuals may project a variety of thoughts about the people who live in Appalachia. Although this utility might be a boon to university administrators, it takes on very different dimensions for those connected to the region or experiencing circumstances like poverty or addiction.

In some contexts, university administrators have even joined Vance in his diagnostics of Appalachia. Gary Houchens, writing for his personal website but in his capacity as a professor of education administration for Western Kentucky University, stated that he was "pleased that a number of educators have also noticed the book and its troubling implications for how we address the needs of 'hillbilly' children and their families."[19] He explained, much like Vance does, that "hillbilly culture" is one that exhibits "self-defeating close-mindedness, defensiveness, and even violence." Houchens conceded that naming the problem did not bring him any closer to solutions, but he affirmed the utility of Thomas B. Fordham Fellow Ian Rowe's controversial "success sequence," which stipulates that the government should reorganize tax policy and federal assistance programs to incentivize marriage to break the cycle of poverty within economically disadvantaged families.

For some academics and administrators, the usefulness of *Hillbilly Elegy* to understanding student populations does not stop at "hillbillies." Robert Maranto, from the Department of Education Reform at the University of Arkansas, wrote in an essay for *Inside Higher Ed* that *Hillbilly Elegy* is useful for understanding the anger of black college students at elite universities. After describing the alienation of rural white voters, he writes, "Ironically, a similar alienation may explain why privileged college students of color at places like Yale seize any opportunity to express outrage."[20] Maranto insists that although he is writing as "a right-leaning white man," he has "African American friends and collaborators." The larger purpose of his essay is to criticize what he feels is an unproductive emphasis on diversity among liberal college administrators, which results in policies that he argues "wall off" students of color from campus life.

By contrast, many students have offered opinions about *Hillbilly Elegy* that in some cases have challenged its utility to higher education. Audrey Ash, a recent graduate of Centre College in Danville, Kentucky, wrote to the *Courier-Journal* about her objections to the honorary degree the college bestowed on Vance and his selection as the May 2017 commencement speaker. Calling Centre College's actions "insensitive to Appalachia," Ash writes, "Vance's placement into Centre's alumni was unapologetically dismissive of the student population and Appalachian community on campus. The insensitivity in choosing J. D. Vance lies in the school's insensitivity to the region of Appalachia, placing on a pedestal the champion for hard earned success and passive avoidance of structural problems that will persist without political action."[21] For Ash, it is inappropriate and dangerous for institutions with a significant population of Appalachian students to endorse a narrative that strongly suggests leaving the region is an unfortunate but necessary step on the path to success. Writing of Vance's yet-to-unfold commencement address, Ash suggests that "given his current solution for Appalachia, I assume it will be an echo-chamber for elitist success, including a pat on the back for all those who have made it out."

Jonathan Isaac, a graduate student at the University of Wisconsin–Madison, also published an essay condemning *Hillbilly Elegy* as the selection for his university's Go Big Read program. Centering his remarks on a socialist critique of Vance's ideas, Isaac expresses alarm that a flawed memoir has occupied so much space as a primer on our political moment. "The idea that individuals' bad choices are to blame for their own poverty isn't a new narrative, but in the wake of Donald Trump's election, it's enjoying a resurgence," he writes.[22] Much like Ash, Isaac finds it disingenuous to read *Hillbilly Elegy* as a political-neutral text, noting that a willingness to avoid engaging with structural problems that exacerbate the conditions of poverty in the United States is itself a political position. My own experiences echo Isaac's criticism. Reviewers often identify me as a writer on the left simply because I acknowledge the structural and political roots of inequality, while Vance is touted as a moderate conservative who has set politics aside in order to speak and write about poverty and social mobility from the heart.

When Vance made his third appearance of the academic year at Ohio State University (OSU), the campus Appalachian Studies Network—an interdisciplinary group of students and faculty—distributed at his lecture handouts that highlighted other resources about the region, including work by Appalshop and West Virginia Public Radio's Inside Appalachia program. The Appalachian Studies Network invited me to speak to their group in November 2017 shortly after Vance's talk, and I was eager to know if their outreach was successful. Members spoke of positive interactions and their enjoyment of preparing and distributing their list of resources, but also wished they knew how to make their activities have greater impact both on campus and within the larger conversations about Appalachia occurring in the age of *Hillbilly Elegy*. This is, in essence, the million-dollar question among many of us who work in or adjacent to Appalachian studies.

On the surface, engagement and reactions of the sort offered above might be taken as evidence that reading *Hillbilly Elegy* on campuses has generated the type of debate intended by university administrators, but it is also important to consider terms of the debate before judging success. Returning to the case of the Appalachian Studies Network at OSU, it is particularly telling that a university so apparently fixated on the people and problems of Appalachia that it has hosted multiple campus-wide discussions of *Hillbilly Elegy* has not taken steps to transfer even a fraction of that interest to an organization on its own campus that studies the same topic. Although many campus communities have framed conversations about *Hillbilly Elegy* as an opportunity to debate controversial ideas, care is usually taken in a debate to ensure that each position is given equal space. Acknowledging the resources invested in promoting *Hillbilly Elegy*—from aggressive marketing by its publisher to using institutional or donor funding for Vance's speaking fees or attaching his ideas to related programing like the Adams exhibit at MTSU—proves this is obviously not the case. Rather, these "lively conversations," in the words of one university president, appear to be one-sided in both the endorsement of views held and authority granted. This is not to say that the book has not created or cannot produce productive classroom conversations, but we should disabuse ourselves of the notion that there is an even playing field—in the market and within these campus conversations—for divergent views about Appalachia in this context.

So what to do instead? In a July 2017 essay on *Hillbilly Elegy* for the literary website the *Millions*, bookseller Douglas Koziol asked, "What can you do when a customer wants a book that you not only find objectionable but also believe actually dangerous in the lessons it portends amidst such a politically precarious time?"[23] The context of his essay comes from his experience selling *Hillbilly Elegy* to the "largely liberal, well-meaning, and well-educated" customers of his independent book store in Boston, a base that has much in common with many university instructors and students nationwide. The solution that Koziol lands on is also not incompatible with higher education. He developed a recommended reading list for customers insistent on reading *Hillbilly Elegy* that included similar but more nuanced texts such as *Strangers in Their Own Land*. Koziol did not offer a full array of suggestions, but Eric Kerl, the author of *White Bred: Anti-racism and the Boundaries of White Racial Solidarity*, published a fuller syllabus-style reading list in December 2017 designed to challenge *Hillbilly Elegy* as a "touchstone" for discussions about Appalachia.[24]

In a similar vein, crowd-sourced reading lists that contextualize *Hillbilly Elegy*'s insight have been to date the most forceful collective challenge by faculty and scholars to J. D. Vance's popularity on campuses. The author has not always taken such reactions positively. In June 2017, a mild criticism on Twitter about *Hillbilly Elegy*'s limited potential as an instructional text from southern historian Karen L. Cox generated a sharp response from Vance himself: "Congratulations on your appointment as the spokesperson for academia," he replied. Another user then congratulated *him* on his appointment as the "spokesperson for Appalachia." In response to this exchange, Cox, currently at the University of North Carolina at Charlotte, and Emily Senefeld, a PhD candidate at the University of Virginia, started #therealappalachiasyllabus, an attempt to collaboratively with other social media users create a more balanced reading list about Appalachia that included titles such as *Appalachians and Race, Back Talk from Appalachia, Uneven Ground, Power and Powerlessness, Hillbilly: A Cultural History of an American Icon*, and other regionally specific texts.

Crowd-sourced reading lists and hashtag syllabi have been popular on Twitter since the enormous impact of #fergusonsyllabus and #charlestonsyllabus created by African American historians and sociologists—Dr. Marcia Chatelain, and Drs. Chad Williams and Kidada Williams, respectively—in the wake of white supremacist violence in 2014 and 2015 to encourage a broad cross section of users, but particularly instructors, to better contextualize the history of racial violence in the United States. Following this lead, academics have responded to other current events or gaps in university course offerings with a number of crowd-sourced reading lists.

A secondary goal of crowd-sourced reading lists is often to be intentional about the inclusion of a more diverse array of authors, acknowledging that the most cited texts in many disciplines are authored by white men. This imbalance is also true of work about Appalachia, particularly because outside of courses dedicated to Appalachian studies or history, instructors might illustrate Appalachian perspectives with only a single contribution. A popular staple of Appalachian reading lists is, for example, still Harry

Caudill's 1963 work *Night Comes to the Cumberlands*, well over fifty years after its publication. This "one-and-done" approach is certainly not unique to Appalachian studies, but it is fair and useful to acknowledge that in a number of classrooms as well as living rooms our history might well be bookended by *Night Comes to the Cumberlands* on one end and *Hillbilly Elegy* on the other, with little in between.

Hillbilly Elegy is, in many ways, a perfect successor to *Night Comes to the Cumberlands*, and this is not a positive attribute. Like Vance, Caudill appointed himself as an expert on Appalachia, and although he wrote passionately about damage to the region caused by the coal industry, he could be vicious toward Appalachia's poorest residents.[25] Furthermore, the frequency with which he appeared, both in his own time and in the present, as a representative voice from the region is at odds with how little he had in common with his neighbors. Although he shared with them the burden of living in a coal-exploited region and the environmental consequences that followed, he had a comfortable life, a good education, a middle-class profession, and a stable family, and he exhibited resentment toward those lacking the same, particularly after the War on Poverty failed to lift Appalachians out of poverty as intended.

Caudill's career as the spokesperson for Appalachia came courtesy of his prolific body of writing and his outsized media influence, but also from a readership content to not look particularly hard for other voices. It was true in 1963 just as it is true today that the public often finds it difficult to elevate the expertise of more than one member of an underrepresented group at a time. The *American Conservative*, for example, praised *Hillbilly Elegy* for doing "for poor white people what Ta-Nehisi Coates's book did for poor black people: give them a voice and a presence in the public square," a warm comparison from a publication critical of Coates but one that nonetheless demonstrates that, to some, marginalized individuals need but one champion.[26] Because of this tendency, the world I am forced to exist in—as an Appalachian writer and advocate for my region—is a product of the imaginations of a few designed for the consumption of many, and most of these world makers are white men. Some of these men have been rightly honored for their contributions with a wide readership, and some of these men are Harry Caudill and J. D. Vance.

The history of the region suggests that collective action is our most powerful tool in creating sustainable change, and perhaps this also extends to navigating our way beyond *Hillbilly Elegy*. We might use this moment to recommit to supporting each other's work and developing stronger networks, and engage in self-reflection about the relationship we'd like our work to have with the public. It is understandable that some scholars are sensitive to accusations of gatekeeping given the privilege that academic credentials often confer, but viewing collective criticism of Vance as gatekeeping implies there has been a reversal of power of which I find no evidence. Rather, collectively challenging problematic texts and ideas—as many of the essays in this volume do—is a way to comment from within a claim of ownership that a powerful person has made about our lives. That is not gatekeeping; it is struggle.

The older principles of community organizing can serve us well in this by affirming that each of us has a part to play in what happens next. Some of us will continue to tear down stale narratives while others will build new ones, and some of us will bring loud voices to the conversations while others prefer to work in the background. There are a host of individuals omitted from Vance's version of Appalachia—young progressives, LGBT and nonbinary people, Appalachians of color, and individuals who have healed from struggles with addiction, to name just a few—and one of the tasks before us is to ensure those individuals both are reflected in our scholarship and narratives and have the opportunity to produce scholarship themselves.

Offering other suggestions about how universities might resist endorsing exploitative writing about Appalachia while joining pressing conversations about the region requires me to introduce recommendations that should be distressingly obvious. It is important, for example, to read other and better books for balance, and it is fair to give criticism (and praise) from Appalachians special consideration. It might be useful to invite Appalachians of color and white women from the region to campuses to offer their perspectives, an approach that would have, judging from my recent honorariums, the added bonus of costing only about one-eighteenth the amount commanded by J. D. Vance for a thirty-minute lecture. Above all, it is necessary to place Vance's memoir within the context of the region's deep and coherent history of cultural and economic exploitation. Or, failing all other options, universities might simply choose to pass on the book completely as most schools in Appalachia have. The existence of this volume attests to the fact that our region's scholars and activists, even those who find points of agreement with his book, are not content to allow J. D. Vance to have the final word about Appalachia. Institutions that use *Hillbilly Elegy* as an instructional text would do well to follow our example.

NOTES

1. Annie Cheng, "J. D. Vance Talks about the Working Class," *Yale Daily News*, February 2, 2017, http://goo.gl/HcgkwZ.
2. Sophie Mackin, "Choate Students Learn about 'Hillbilly Culture' through J. D. Vance Book and Talk," *Choate News*, February 15, 2017, http://goo.gl/pXZqzr.
3. Alex Baca, "Against Corporate Urbanism in the Heartland," self-published on *Medium*, October 20, 2017, http://goo.gl/EWGHZb.
4. Jennifer R. Keup, "Common Reading Programs as High Impact Practice: Going beyond the Book," digital resource guide created by the National Resource Center for First-Year Experience and Students in Transition, http://goo.gl/4Xi7S5.
5. Ibid.
6. J. Bryan Lowder, "South Carolina Champions Academic Freedom by Punishing Colleges for Assigning Gay Books," *Slate*, February 20, 2014, http://goo.gl/V97nV3.
7. Dana Goldstein, "Summer Reading Books: The Ties That Bind Colleges," *New York Times*, July 1, 2017, https://nyti.ms/2ux1nd5.
8. National Association of Scholars, "Beach Books 2016–2017: What Do Colleges and Universities Want Students to Read Outside Class?," http://goo.gl/TxzcLx.
9. Mark Tapson, "How College Summer-Reading Programs Are Failing Our Students—and Our Culture," *National Review*, June 3, 2017, http://goo.gl/xVUkRt.
10. National Association of Scholars, "Beach Books 2016–2017."
11. Goldstein, "Summer Reading Books."
12. "Daily Chart: Books Aiming to Span America's Political Divide Rarely Succeed," *Economist*, September 28, 2017, http://goo.gl/yVm4Vv.
13. Chelsea Brislin, "Strangers with Cameras: The Consequences of Appalachian Representation in Pop Culture" (PhD diss., University of Kentucky, 2017), 36–37.
14. Katherine Ledford, "'Thanks for Not Shooting Me'—A Review Essay on Shelby Lee Adams's 'Appalachian Lives,'" *Appalachian Journal* 31, nos. 3/4 (Spring/Summer 2004): 390.
15. American Suburb X, "Interview with Shelby Lee Adams," May 27, 2010, http://goo.gl/WeR25C.

16. Peter Chawaga, "Archiving Appalachia," *Nashville Arts*, November 2016, http://goo.gl/gmYdJ1.

17. "2017 Summer Reading—Hillbilly Elegy and the Shelby Lee Adams Exhibit," email from MTSU Academic Affairs to university faculty and staff, December 12, 2016.

18. Clarence Page, "Tough Love to Poor Whites as Well as Inner-City Blacks," *Illinois Daily Journal*, April 8, 2014, http://goo.gl/XMks5q.

19. Gary Houchens, "Educating 'Hillbillies,'" *School Leader: An Education Administration Blog*, January 5, 2017, http://goo.gl/ZKqNmZ.

20. Robert Maranto, "Separate and Unequal," *Inside Higher Ed*, December 19, 2016, http://goo.gl/pvQH8q.

21. Audrey Ash, "Centre Insensitive to Appalachia with J. D. Vance Commencement Address," *Courier-Journal*, May 18, 2017, http://goo.gl/2DSJp9.

22. Jonathan Isaac, "Hillbilly Mythology," *Socialist Worker*, October 9, 2017, http://goo.gl/kX9Xqo.

23. Douglas Koziol, "A Bookseller's Elegy," *Millions*, July 19, 2017, http://goo.gl/cHLqah.

24. See Chitucky Blog, "A Hillbilly Syllabus," December 10, 2017, http://goo.gl/Ums1dC.

25. For general criticism of Caudill's influence, see Dwight Billings's introduction to *Back Talk from Appalachia: Confronting Stereotypes*, ed. Dwight Billings, Gurney Norman, and Katherine Ledford (Lexington: University Press of Kentucky, 1999), 10–12.

26. Rod Dreher, "Trump: Tribune of Poor White People," *American Conservative*, July 22, 2016, http://goo.gl/5TQBfW.

BENHAM, KENTUCKY, COAL MINER / WISE COUNTY, VIRGINIA, LANDSCAPE

TEXT AND PHOTOGRAPHS BY THERESA BURRISS

Despite the setbacks, both of my grandparents had an almost religious faith in hard work and the American Dream. . . . "Never be like these fucking losers who think the deck is stacked against them," my grandma often told me. "You can do anything you want to."

—J. D. Vance, *Hillbilly Elegy*

VANCE'S RELENTLESS INSISTENCE on the "American Dream" woven throughout his self-proclaimed memoir perpetuates, conveniently, this enduring myth. Like many before him who have written about not only Appalachians but also other othered groups, he omits systemic critiques of decades-long oppression and succumbs to easy essentialization. After all, myths persist to serve those in power, regardless of factual evidence to the contrary. As a result, the proverbial deck is indeed stacked against those without power, who are politically and socially disenfranchised due to a variety of reasons, including race, class, gender, and geographic location.

In the fall of 2000 in the coal community of Benham, located in Harlan County, Kentucky, women, many of whom were widows, raised money to erect a six-foot-eight statue of a coal miner to honor those who died in the mines.[1] Holding a pickax and wearing a miner's hardhat, the bronze statue serves as a reminder of the immense sacrifices demanded of miners, who labored in

unsafe work environments willfully ignored by numerous industry owners. Many central Appalachian residents lived (or still live) in communities where profit trumped people and coal executives owned literally everything.

The massive mountaintop removal site in Wise County, Virginia, serves as evidence of the region's designation as a national energy sacrifice zone. Much of the central Appalachian landscape has been decimated to provide steel and electricity to the rest of the nation for over a century, as well as serving international markets more contemporaneously. According to the grassroots environmental protection organization Appalachian Voices, "Southwest Virginia had a disproportionate concentration of at-risk communities on the [mountaintop removal] list (20%), but accounted for only 8% of Central Appalachia's surface mine coal production in 2014."[2] It is yet further evidence that the American Dream is primarily achieved by certain groups living in particular areas, often at the expense of those living in less affluent ones, especially where plentiful natural resources have ironically provided a powerful minority with great wealth.

NOTES

1. Roger Alford, "Miner Statue Offers Solace to Eastern Kentucky Coal Town," *Bowling Green (KY) Daily News*, November 26, 2000, 5A.
2. Appalachian Voices, "New Map Tracks Growing Threat of Mountaintop Removal" (press release, April 28, 2015), http://appvoices.org/2015/04/28/new-map-tracks-growing-threat-of-mountaintop-removal/.

PANNING FOR GOLD
A REFLECTION OF LIFE FROM APPALACHIA

RICARDO NAZARIO Y COLÓN

The truth in the story of a boy from a sunken place is that
the lives of mountain folk are more than just Scots-Irish.
They are a mix of Cherokee defiance and forgotten African
voices. Of thin air rich and sea level poor. Of new accents
thick as southern humidity, who declare their existence.

On election season politicos dawn their timber boots
and red handkerchiefs. Many claim salt of the earth roots
every time they eat a watermelon, but they never bite
the bitterness of the rind. Everyone likes a good show
and the politics of poverty never disappoint.

On the bestsellers' list, you read of the continuous
love affair with the ins-and-outs of "Hollers." Newly
minted shirt-tail cousins and their expert views write
with the intention of a bearded cheekbone, pecking
at the stitching of a handmade quilt.

When the election came to town and kicked over an
anthill of fire ants, the spill of people cried out their

only care. They coughed up lungs, black as the
underground caskets they have hung their hopes upon.
These coal places lay claim to fathers and sons.

Few pay attention to old diseases that gnaw at the souls
of Appalachian folk. America's spine is J. D. Vance's fetish.
"Deplorable" is a prescribed numbness for broken backs
and promises of a better sacrifice. It makes way for mutable
poverty when panning for gold.

Amidst the blue ridge mountains, there are remarkable
expressions of life. Tapestries woven by generations that
are always on trial by those who amputate hope from what
once was native land. Digesting each day, the unpleasant
taste of yesterday's homemade buttermilk.

WILL THE REAL HILLBILLY PLEASE STAND UP? URBAN APPALACHIAN MIGRATION AND CULTURE SEEN THROUGH THE LENS OF *HILLBILLY ELEGY*

ROGER GUY

Everybody was so afraid of the hillbillies. That is what was so wild. They were the safest group in the world. I was more afraid of Chicagoans.

—Raleigh Campbell, August 1995

Mamaw came from a family that would shoot at you rather than argue with you.

—J. D. Vance, *Hillbilly Elegy*

THE FIRST EPIGRAPH is from Raleigh Campbell, a social worker from eastern Kentucky who worked with Appalachian migrants in the 1960s. Unlike Campbell's view of the hillbillies, J. D. Vance's quotation about his admired hillbilly bloodline is strikingly similar to the sensationalized and disparaging accounts in the media about hillbilly culture at the height of Appalachian migration to northern and Midwestern cities. Make no mistake, these quotations refer to the same generation of people. Vance's grandparents were part of the wave of Appalachians with whom Campbell worked, only in a different city. How could there be such a distinctly different perception of this same group? Part of the reason may be that Campbell had sustained contact with Appalachian migrants while Vance has reconstructed an impression from his memory and those of his family members. Therefore, Campbell's quotation probably reflects a more balanced understanding of the millions of Appalachians like Vance's grandparents who left their homes in search of a better life in cities.

Using research focusing on Chicago as well as other Midwestern cities, this essay addresses the degree to which Vance's first-person reflections about migration, settlement, and "hillbilly culture" are congruent with the reality of urban life for Appalachian migrants. I argue that Vance's definition of a single "hillbilly culture" leaves the reader with an erroneous image that does not fit the diversity of migrant origins and experiences that scholars have documented over the years, probably because he extrapolated it from discrete experiences in his own family. Research suggests that Appalachian migrants were a varied lot. While some came from mountain regions of eastern Kentucky, as did his family, others came from farming areas as far flung as Tennessee and Arkansas. Moreover, his superficial cultural template and behavioral references would have been impossible to maintain given the demands and diversity of life in the urban environments in which most Appalachians settled. Considering the nature of work, daily life, participation in local protest, political activism, and the ultimate legacy that urban Appalachians created in their adopted cities, they were far from static, one-dimensional hillbilly caricatures. They were dynamic actors who responded and adapted to the urban milieu.

APPALACHIAN MIGRATION AND *HILLBILLY ELEGY*

The South to North movement of families and individuals from the Appalachian region has been the subject of much scholarly activity and informs some parts of *Hillbilly Elegy*.[1] According to historians, the postwar migration from the upper portions of the South was one of the largest internal migrations in US history, involving some twenty-eight million southerners who left the South in the twentieth century alone.[2] Indeed, the subject of urban Appalachians has been addressed by nearly all disciplines in the humanities and social sciences in some fashion and "discovered" and rediscovered by the media over the years.[3] In some works Appalachians are depicted in stereotypical ways, and in others they are portrayed as sensitive and complex individuals responding to the demands of a new way of life in the city.

Appalachian migration was perhaps most famously portrayed in Harriette Arnow's 1954 novel *The Dollmaker*, about a Kentucky family's tragic struggle to make ends meet in urban Detroit during World War II. ABC made a miniseries of the novel in 1984 starring Jane Fonda and Levon Helm.[4] The book and miniseries provided a glimpse of a family that is vastly different from Vance's impulsively violent family. There are no beatings and maiming in Arnow's original novel, as are so prominent in *Hillbilly Elegy*. A less nuanced portrayal was the 1989 film *Next of Kin*, set in Chicago's Hillbilly Heaven in Uptown—the same neighborhood where social worker Raleigh Campbell worked. The main character, Truman Gates, played by Patrick Swayze, is an Appalachian migrant from the hills of Kentucky who escaped urban poverty to become a Chicago police detective. However, as much as the director John Irvin tried (even to the extent of using Appalachians in Uptown as consultants), he could not escape portraying the folks back home as backward snake handlers with beards and in need of dental work, thus reinforcing preconceived notions of Appalachians. For example, the film's hillbillies insist on "mountain justice" and come to Chicago to avenge the murder of Gates's brother, ending with a violent standoff in a cemetery.[5] The characters from down home appear much like those members of J. D. Vance's family that he describes in *Hillbilly Elegy* as having a "culture" that values violence to settle disputes using extralegal means.

Although *Hillbilly Elegy* contains brief depictions of the mass migration of Appalachians, it generally lacks depth when it comes to the experience of the tens of thousands of families who found themselves trying to adapt to unfamiliar urban surroundings. *Hillbilly Elegy* relies on numerous presumptions that stem mostly from Vance's personal experiences as a third-generation urban Appalachian. As a result, he leaves the impression that all families from the region behave like his or have the cultural attributes he describes. While this approach is acceptable for an autobiographical narrative, his conclusions are superficial and entirely out of sync with the long tradition of scholarly work devoted to urban Appalachian migration beginning with the study of southern migrants to northern cities in the 1930s cited above. Below, I will briefly discuss some of the more notable works on Appalachian migration to flesh out their depth of experience in contrast to Vance's description primarily in chapters 2 and 4 of *Hillbilly Elegy*.

One of the earlier scholarly works on southern white migrants (before they were distinguished from Appalachians) was conducted by sociologist Lewis Killian, who studied white southerners living in the Near West Side neighborhood in Chicago in the immediate postwar years. Killian's exhaustive qualitative study revealed a complex web of social interaction and integration with the community in which they settled.[6] Unlike Vance's implication that nearly all Appalachian migrants tended to be somewhat uneducated and destitute, Killian found that southern migration tended to be selective, leading him to conclude that the region was exporting its better educated and retaining a higher proportion of its less educated, especially during economic downturns. The phenomenon of selective migration has been applied to nineteenth-century European immigrants to US cities as well.[7] Citing an earlier classic study of Appalachian migration, Killian noted that the same applied to Appalachia during the 1950s and 1960s when young, better educated migrants departed, thus lowering the region's overall average level of education.[8] This is the period that Vance's grandparents (both of whom lacked high school diplomas) settled in Ohio. The distinction here suggests that they were in fact not typical of those going to cities at that time. Killian's findings are important to keep in mind given the extremely negative perceptions of Appalachian migrants and culture proffered by the press I will discuss below.

Vance further envisions all migrants as having had a somewhat uniform urban experience when it came to work, for example. He argues correctly that the industrial demand for labor brought men into factory work, but he makes no mention of the essential role of women in contributing to family survival. Oral histories of Appalachians who migrated to Chicago at the same time as Vance's grandparents chose Ohio reveal their varied adaptation and survival strategies, including the common practice of women earning money by managing buildings occupied by their fellow southerners and working in candy factories with other immigrants from Cuba or Mexico.[9] Tennessean Helen Elam, for instance, recalls that her uncle owned a tavern, but women also worked in various light industrial positions after migrating north in the

1960s: "Most of the women I knew worked. Like my mother and two of my aunts all worked at LaSalle Candies. Women worked at different factories like Continental Can. There were sewing machine factories. My aunt found a job two weeks after she got up here at LaSalle Candies as a packer."[10] Unlike the vision of migration that Vance describes, migrants also became neighborhood activists; some spent their lives fighting for the working poor and victims of black lung in legal clinics as paralegals, or in local politics working to elect progressives like alderwoman Helen Shiller and African American mayor Harold Washington.[11] Grassroots organizing among Appalachians also occurred in other cities, most importantly Cincinnati.[12]

Other notable examples indicating that there was no uniform migration experience include Appalachian migrants in Chicago who defied the racist stereotype of being from the South by forming an interracial coalition of the poor in the late 1960s—what has come to be known as the Original Rainbow Coalition.[13] Younger Appalachians formed the Young Patriot Organization (YPO), modeled after the Black Panthers. The YPO joined with other neighborhood residents and Peace Corps volunteers to oppose appalling neighborhood housing, conditions of poverty, and police brutality. They also successfully organized a free medical and dental clinic for the poor in Uptown. Eastern Kentucky migrant Charles "Chuck" Geary formed the Voice of the People and the Uptown Area People's Planning Coalition. Together with architect Rodney Wright and urban planner Sydney Wright, he created Hank Williams Village, a redevelopment project modeled after a southern town meant to resist the neighborhood's displacement due to the development of a community college that now sits in the heart of Uptown's Hillbilly Heaven— an area that contained the largest concentration of Appalachian migrants in Chicago at the time.

Unlike Vance's assessment of the ultimately negative economic consequences of urban migration, research also suggests that the economic opportunities promised by leaving home paid off. Historians have pointed out that by the 1970s the majority of southern migrants (including Appalachians) were reaping the fruits of postwar economic growth in well-paying blue-collar jobs, which not only took them out of cities to suburbs, but solidly established them as members of the middle class.[14] Therefore, Appalachians did relatively well after migrating to cities, and found the economic opportunity and financial stability for which they were searching.[15] Vance confirms that Appalachians were able to leverage their families out of poverty and achieve the American Dream. His grandfather's well-paying position at Armco, for instance, allowed him to purchase a home and succession of new cars. He casts doubt, however, on the long-term benefits of migration. He argues that although the migrant generation (in this case that of his grandparents) left Appalachia so that their children could prosper and take advantage of the "head start" it offered, much as foreign immigrants to the United States had, he concludes, "It didn't quite work out that way" (36). He quotes Kentuckian Dwight Yoakam's lyrics from "Readin', Rightin', Route 23" stressing that migrants found a "world of misery" in their urban destinations. Vance thus implies that the road out of the hills was a disappointing, perhaps even a disastrous, choice for most Appalachian families (37). The problem with this assertion is that it is not logical to assume that such a large and sustained movement of people northward would have continued were migrants not improving their lives. In fact, it was only later, when the entire Rust Belt deindustrialized, that Appalachian migrants along with most other blue-collar workers experienced plant closings and layoffs, which eliminated their well-paying jobs. This economic distress was felt by all workers, not simply southern migrants. And the low-paying, dead-end, minimum-wage jobs that have followed in the wake of Midwestern economic decline do not provide stability and the possibility for advancement.[16]

KIN-CENTERED MIGRATION AND TRIPS BACK HOME

One aspect of the Appalachian migrant story that Vance gets right is that kinship networks were crucial to migration and not only influenced the destination of those who left but also drew those migrants back to their places of origin for family visits. He rightly notes that migrants' settlement in neighborhoods with other kinfolk often provided initial support and connections for employment. Places of employment were also chosen based on kin connections.[17] Migrant J. D. Donnelson related this process to me in an interview in the 1990s: "I came to Chicago because my mother was here. We had lots of relatives here. I had about four aunts and uncles already here, and they had relatives that had migrated years ago. . . . That's why we could migrate because we had other people that we would stay with till we got jobs."[18] The process of migration produced humorous conglomerations, in some cases with entire blocks and buildings in a neighborhood occupied by migrants and their kin from the same county or state. One observer in the 1960s observed, "I was always amused . . . you'd see this block with cars from Tennessee [based on their license plates] and that one with cars from Kentucky and you knew where people were from by that."[19] Because home and family was desperately important to migrants, especially those who first made the trip north, there was a great deal of shuttle migration on weekends and holidays. Vance, like experts on Appalachian migration, points out that Appalachian migrants regularly returned home for visits. Vance, however, attributes this to a feeling that they had "abandoned their families" back home (30). While this is an interesting conception, it has not been born out in research. More likely, migrants returned south so regularly because of their intense attachment to home, and their conception that migration was somehow temporary and that they would eventually return home permanently.[20]

WHO ARE YOUR PEOPLE?

The question of identity is important for any migrant group, including Appalachian migrant descendants like J. D. Vance. The children of the millions of people who moved to northern and Midwestern cities are often conflicted about Appalachian culture and their southern identity.[21] Much like second- and third-generation European immigrants, these Appalachian migrants' offspring like Vance have an option of adopting and emphasizing selective elements of culture in a symbolic manner.[22] In *Hillbilly Elegy*, Vance chose to relate to his hillbilly roots in such a way: "I identify with the millions of working class white Americans of Scots-Irish descent who have no college degree. To these folks, poverty is a family tradition. . . . Americans call them hillbillies, rednecks, and white trash. I call them neighbors, friends, and family" (3). In my research, I found that the children of Appalachian migrants around Vance's age tended to identify as being "southern" rather than being a "hillbilly" because they considered the term inapplicable or derogatory. In their view, hillbillies are an abstract caricature rather than a distinct culture or cultural type. For the children of Appalachian migrants whom I interviewed, having roots in the hills of Appalachia primarily meant an identification and appreciation for unique expressions of art, music, and family, and a sense of deep attachment to the land and home.[23] It is apparent that Vance considers being a hillbilly a source of pride, and that there is some broad community of hillbillies out there.[24] At the same time, he defines that hillbilly culture primarily as a set of negative behavioral attributes that have robbed people of initiative and rotted out their will to succeed or achieve any vestige of the American Dream. In short, it is all that has gone wrong with America (4–7).[25]

While mountaineers made up a modest portion of the ebb and flow of urban migrants from the South, the term "hillbilly" was eventually applied to all southern newcomers, most often in a derogatory manner to distinguish them in sociological terms as an out-group.[26] Time and again research has shown that Appalachians and southern migrants overall resented being labeled hillbillies by others because of the term's negative connotations and because they considered the usage of the word quite specific to a subpopulation of the South rather than, as Vance believes, all working-class whites from the South.[27] Moreover, more educated southerners bristled at being mistaken for hillbillies because of a southern accent. The negative connotation of being a hillbilly followed migrants to most cities, where they were perceived at times as more undesirable than African Americans, immigrants, or even drifters.[28] Most of these perceptions, however, reflected stereotypes of residents rather than the actual characteristics of the bulk of southern white migrants. Much as Vance does, the term "hillbilly" was applied to all working-class white southerners by journalists and residents in cities experiencing an influx of migrants.[29]

SPREADING THE CULTURAL SEED

Migration, according to Vance, resulted in the proliferation of "hillbilly values" in the cities in which Appalachians settled. At one point, he defines these values as "blending a robust sense of honor, devotion to family, and bizarre sexism into a sometimes-explosive mix" (41). And let's not forget the pervasive violence that laces the book and that he apparently at times admires in his kinfolk. He does acknowledge, however, that any migration, including an internal one, involves a process of shedding and adapting values and worldviews as a response to new urban surroundings rather than a wholesale transplanting of "hillbilly values" (if they really exist) to the North. As an example, recall that Appalachian migrants to northern cities encountered a racial order vastly different from the South that sometimes was at odds with their views of race relations. While some southerners maintained their views of white supremacy and southern-style racism, others radically changed their values and perspective on race. After moving to the Midwest, for instance, Helen Elam had an experience that eventually influenced her views of race relations: "I remember going out to this place on Lawrence and seeing blacks and whites out together. Everybody dancing, blacks and whites, everybody getting along good, having a good time. No fights or nothing. I said man you wouldn't find that down South, you wouldn't find that in my home town. Everybody was white."[30] Over time, however, the normality of observing blacks and whites interacting with one another in public places convinced many migrants to alter their views of white superiority, putting them at odds with their family members. Migrant Virginia Bowers related how her more tolerant views of other races caused conflict with her family who remained in the South: "I lost closeness with my family because they were so prejudiced. I am the only one in my family that has black friends, Spanish friends. I'd go home and listen to this [her family members] nigger, nigger, nigger, you know. Then I'd come back to Chicago and just go about my business. When I do go home, I just keep my mouth shut."[31] While not typical, perhaps, Bowers's experience suggests evidence of a shift in cultural values regarding race that directly affected her post-migration life. It is reasonable to assume, therefore, that other hillbilly values (Vance's bizarre sexism perhaps) changed as well. Bowers eventually became a social activist involved in civil rights, through Students for a Democratic Society. Therefore, unlike what Vance implies, hillbilly values were not simply transported to the cities to which Appalachians migrated and remained static. There is little doubt that many Appalachian migrants may have retained racist views that engendered conflict with those like Bowers when she returned for visits. "When I would go back South," she noted, "[I would] see how the blacks were treated. I mean, I would get up in a restaurant . . . to go and help the black person. And I'd have to be drug back down [to her seat by people she was with]. 'Look you're not in Chicago' they would say."[32] While Vance does not acknowledge this, there is evidence of acculturation over time as migrants remained in cities and engaged in close social interaction with other racial and ethnic groups on more equal terms than in the South.[33]

SOUTHERN CULTURE IN NORTHERN CITIES

Moreover, *Hillbilly Elegy* leaves the reader with the false impression that Appalachian migration and hillbilly culture did not have any positive impact on the sociocultural fabric of American life. Indeed, until recently, historians also failed to recognize how the region both shaped and was shaped by Appalachian migrants. Just as individuals like Bowers experienced a personal transition in their views about race relations because of what they experienced in the North, southern cultural expressions such as country music flourished in and transformed the northern urban scene. Historians remind us that even though migrants assimilated in a traditional sense, they retained a *southern* identity and transplanted their culture, especially religion and music, to urban destinations.[34] Chad Berry, for example, has demonstrated the early proliferation of country music that later became institutionalized in the *National Barn Dance* aired from Chicago's WLS studio. In his words, "Migration had helped create a new musical style in the South, and migration northward has refined that new sound."[35] As a result, in some cases the term "hillbilly" took on a more ameliorated connotation. Berry notes that some of the radio announcers referred to themselves as "educated hillbillies" and deliberately aimed their sound at those they considered the more cosmopolitan migrants from Appalachia as well as the broader northern audience that tuned in each week.[36] Vance, in contrast, leaves the reader with the impression that the only things transplanted to urban areas were dysfunctional hillbilly values that represented the very worst that a small segment of migrants had to offer, and that these were a corrupting influence on the towns and cities in which migrants settled, even today. He neglects to consider any other more positive and identifiable elements of culture such as musical forms.

A CULTURE OF DERELICTS?

It is true, however, that in the early period following migration, the numbers of migrants were so large and their needs so great that local officials and social service infrastructures were at times overwhelmed. As a result, many observers initially assumed that migration yielded few positive economic benefits for families or individuals. This was fueled initially by negative reactions to their presence in sensational journalistic accounts that in places appear eerily like some of Vance's descriptions of hillbilly culture.[37] In 1958, for instance, an article appeared in *Harper's*, penned by Albert Votaw, titled "The Hillbillies Invade Chicago." Votaw, an executive director of the Uptown Chicago Commission, a business-dominated group exasperated with the presence of Appalachians, painted a grim picture of these newcomers as a "small army of white Protestant, Early American migrants from the South—who are usually proud, poor, and fast with a knife."[38] As others before and after him, Votaw questioned whether Appalachians were capable of assimilating because of an abhorrent cultural orientation (read "hillbilly culture").

Similar to Votaw, Vance adopts the view that hillbilly culture (which he defines as Scots-Irish-infused white working-class culture) deviates from mainstream values and American cultural norms, which now indirectly hinders their social mobility. This too is not a new idea. It has long been argued that group characteristics of southern mountain folk impede the acquisition of social capital they need to advance. These negative qualities include the lack of a work ethic, willingness to accept and remain on public assistance, and general deviance. Despite abundant scholarship showing that such attitudes and behaviors are the exception rather than the rule, these ideas appeal to much of the general public, conservative and moderate policy makers, and even, in some cases, the poor themselves as when they support policies or political parties one could argue are not in their best interests.[39] As a result of such mistaken beliefs, public policies often center on forcing and coercing the poor out of welfare dependency by establishing work requirements, thereby saving them from their "lack of morality."[40]

Vance blames hillbilly culture for a host of social ills, including young men unwilling to work. In his words, it is a "culture that increasingly encourages social decay instead of counteracting it" (7). In one example, he cites a one-time coworker of his at a tile warehouse as a presumably typical example of the lack of an Appalachian white working-class work ethic. Bob (as he calls him) had a nineteen-year-old pregnant girlfriend, was chronically absent, spent long periods in the bathroom, and generally slacked off until he was fired. Vance had taken the job at the warehouse to save money before departing for law school at Yale and uses the example to illustrate the failure of Bob and those like him to respond to solid job opportunities because of a culture that encourages "social decay" and "young men immune to hard work" (read "lazy") (6–7). Vance's example closely parallels the famous portrait of the fictitious couple of Harold and Phyllis in Charles Murray's *Losing Ground: American Social Policy, 1950–1980*, who also lack a work ethic and whom Murray uses to illustrate how current public policies make it much more logical to remain single parents and collect welfare than to marry and work.[41] The view of the working-class poor as unwilling to work sufficiently hard is also reminiscent of Edward Banfield's approach to understanding the social position of the lower class in his books *The Unheavenly City* and subsequently *The Unheavenly City Revisited*. Banfield stated, "At the present-oriented end of the scale the lower class individual lives from moment to moment. If he has any awareness of the future, it is something fixed, fated, beyond his control: things happen *to* him, he does not *make* them happen. . . . He works only as he must to stay alive and drifts from one unskilled job to another."[42] Banfield argued that the lower class shared a worldview characterized by holding a less future-oriented time horizon than individuals in higher social classes.[43] As a result, they are less likely to value working, preferring instead more immediate pleasures derived from vices like alcohol and drugs. I have no doubt that there are individuals like Bob, but Vance wrongly presents them as representative of an entire culture rather than as individuals who exist at all socioeconomic levels but get less attention because people are already prone to believe the worst about the poor (especially "hillbillies").

VIOLENCE ANYONE?

There are other parallels between Vance and Banfield's views of the working class, particularly their propensity for violence. Banfield argued that lower class individuals place more emphasis on "masculinity and violence," which makes them "extraordinarily violent."[44] Vance's conception of hillbilly culture closely matches these ideas. He cites numerous examples of a destructive, violence-oriented culture in *Elegy*, such as when his grandfather mercilessly smashed a toy in a store because a clerk objected to his son playing with it. During this incident, his grandmother started ransacking the shelves while screaming "kick his fucking ass" and threatening violence (33–34). Indeed, violence, up to and including murder, pervades his account of both sides of his family. He describes his grandmother's family as people who preferred to shoot someone rather than argue with them, and who can "go from zero to murderous in a fucking heartbeat" (25, 40). His uncle Pet's charming personality was a "fierce temper" so extreme that it led him to beat someone unconscious and maim him with an electric saw for merely insulting his mother (14). In fact, the threat or fear of violent retaliation due to a sexual indiscretion was the initial motivation for his grandfather to leave Kentucky for Ohio (25–27, 40). Vance promotes the idea that his family (and by extension, all Appalachian migrants) uprooted this culture of violence and transplanted it wholesale to northern and Midwestern cities.

While Vance certainly has the right to characterize his own family in his autobiography as he chooses, he implies that his family's values and attributes are part of a monolithic Appalachian culture or even the white working-class culture more broadly. Vance correctly notes early in *Hillbilly Elegy* that Appalachia is a vast geographic area, but he nonetheless states that "the culture of greater Appalachia is remarkably cohesive" as if it were some rigid and identifiable set of cultural attributes held by rural folks and urbanites alike (4). He also romanticizes the same culture that he condemns. He showers the reader with stories of his grandmother who is a "pistol-packing lunatic" and subscribed to what he terms "hillbilly justice" (15). Descriptions like this and other passages of his mixed admiration of certain violent family members sound eerily like other much older accounts I have read, especially a series of articles from the 1950s by *Chicago Daily News* reporter Norma Lee Browning. These articles have become standard readings for students and scholars of exaggerated caricatures of Appalachians akin to the horrific images of African Americans in cartoons, art, and cultural artifacts in the twentieth century depicted in the documentary *Ethnic Notions*.[45] Browning described hillbillies as violent, odorous savages and sexually depraved miscreants who do not understand the concept of rape, honor the institution of marriage, or observe wedlock birth and are a plague on the city of Chicago.[46]

It is no exaggeration to state that Browning's descriptions of hillbillies were taken literally by the public and forged powerful and long-lasting images of Appalachians settling in the Windy City and the Midwest in general. In one article, Browning stated that she traveled to Appalachia, in addition to spending considerable time among Chicago's "Jungles of Hillbillies." In truth, she had little contact with her subjects, and relied on misinformed accounts and half-truths.[47] Despite her lack of firsthand knowledge, Browning described migrant homes as places of degradation and filth inhabited by uncaring adults who were bent on satisfying their own pleasure at the expense of their children: "The hillbilly's home and family life experienced investigators say is the most depraved of any they have ever encountered, with no understanding of sanitation and health. Many children do not know who their parents are and nobody cares."[48] She also depicted Appalachia itself as an isolated place that time had forgotten. In one article, sensationally titled "A Trip to Appalachia: Visit to the Middle Ages," Browning warned that the hundreds of thousands of mountaineers who were migrating to Chicago, Cincinnati, Indianapolis, and Dayton uniformly believed that the "earth was flat," espoused neither evolution nor education, spoke a "patois of Elizabethan and Chaucerian" English, and lived by the law of the shotgun.[49] Such views dated at least back to the nineteenth century.[50] Although Vance may be aghast at these absurd characterizations of his culture, they merely occupy a different position along the spectrum of those who wreck a pharmacy and threaten a clerk who objects to his son playing with a toy, or a foul-mouthed grandmother apt to reach for a firearm when angered or willing to set her husband alight with gasoline (43). One wonders whether this is hillbilly culture or mere deviant impulsivity present in certain individuals in any cultural group. If his accounts are accurate and his grandparents were violent (or prone to violence), that does not mean that Appalachian migrants were or that this constituted a unique hillbilly culture. However, Vance implies the latter by conflating a personal biography and a memoir of a "culture in crisis" as the title of his book contends.

CONCLUSION: A COMMON GROUND?

Overall, I do not question Vance's accounts of his family. Instead I oppose the way he suggests that they apply to Appalachian migrants and Appalachian culture in general. Without a doubt, there is much superficiality and many inaccuracies in Vance's understanding of urban Appalachian migration and hillbilly culture. From all scholarly accounts, migration was initially economically beneficial for substantial numbers of Appalachians, as Vance notes with the case of his grandparents. However, it was the subsequent deindustrialization of the original neighborhoods in which migrants settled (including that of Vance's grandparents), *not* the culture of Appalachian migrants, that led to significant economic and social decline. The children of Vance's generation have faced more obstacles and thus limited opportunities to exit their predicament. It is more likely that structural impediments (e.g., high unemployment rates, low-wage jobs, and punitive social policies) rather than cultural values explain this generational difference.

While much scholarship and popular writing have offered alternative and balanced accounts of the region and its people, Vance seems largely unaware of it (or at least does not cite it in his bibliography). To be fair, he admits early on that his book is not attempting to be unbiased scholarship. Nor is there anything wrong with taking pride in one's kinfolk in a memoir. The problem is that *Hillbilly Elegy* also reinforces distorting stereotypes of violent and depraved hillbillies dating back to at least the turn of the twentieth century. *Hillbilly Elegy*'s great acclaim and financial success also reveal how such views still lie just below the surface of popularized contemporary narratives of Appalachians. It is soothing for some to place the blame on "hillbilly culture" for contemporary social problems like unemployment and the opioid epidemic. However, it gets us nowhere when it comes to addressing these problems in a meaningful way.

As for Vance's insistence that hillbillies are impulsive and sometimes violent, there is evidence in earlier media accounts that a small segment of Appalachians and southern whites in cities were involved in violent altercations with one another and law enforcement. However, this has less to do with hillbilly values than the social conditions and influences in which any new urban migrant group find themselves. It is more likely, therefore, that these traits may have just run in his family. His claim that settling disputes using extralegal "mountain justice" involving revenge killings, retaliation, and not reporting crimes was commonplace is also not borne out in research. I have found that although in the immediate post-migration period transplanted Appalachians were sometimes reluctant to report crimes to the police, this had more to do with the chances of them being victims of police brutality than some warped sense of hillbilly justice or a culture of honor. The poor of all colors and cultures have historically displayed an aversion to law enforcement (not without reason) and will likely do so in the future.[51]

Even if we go so far as to acknowledge that a distinctive "hillbilly culture" exists, *Hillbilly Elegy* leaves the impression that that culture is static and does not respond to changing social conditions. Moreover, Vance implies that all that is wrong with contemporary hillbilly values of those he terms the "Scots-Irish Appalachian" and the white working class is somehow a product of having migrated to towns and cities. For Vance, migration wreaked havoc on traditional values of family and the work ethic, making it difficult or impossible for these migrants to take advantage of the American Dream. This has left them particularly vulnerable to contemporary social problems such as drug addiction, welfare dependency, or worse. Yet this probably has less to do with the loss of those virtues of the cultural values of his grandparents than it does the struggle to manage the larger social forces.

Finally, any work that spawns such enthusiastic and spirited public response and debate is noteworthy. As an academic, I am a firm proponent of the free exchange of ideas and oppose any type of censorship or thought police when it comes to creative expression. One of the strengths of *Hillbilly Elegy* is that Vance offers insight about and gives voice to the public disillusionment with abandonment by social, political (*especially political*), and economic institutions felt by many of his generation. The popularity of his book has opened up an opportunity to engage one another about the changes required to address deep and enduring contemporary social problems, and perhaps come to some agreement on their proximate causes, be they cultural or structural. My hope is that, through civil public discourse, we (as Americans) may advance beyond the recurring stereotypes about any migrant group that reinforce and justify the social fissures that seem to have widened in recent years whether they involve travel bans, immigration, or bigotry.

NOTES

1. The works on the topic of southern and Appalachian migration are too numerous to list here. See Lewis Killian, "Southern White Laborers in Chicago's West Side" (PhD diss., University of Chicago, 1949); Chad Berry, *Southern Migrants, Northern Exiles* (Champaign: University of Illinois Press, 2000); Phillip J. Obermiller, Thomas E. Wagner, and E. Bruce Tucker, eds., *Appalachian Odyssey: Historical Perspectives on the Great Migration* (Westport, CT: Praeger, 2000); Roger Guy, *From Diversity to Unity: Southern and Appalachian Migrants in Uptown Chicago, 1950–1970* (Lanham, MD: Lexington, 2007).

2. Berry, *Southern Migrants, Northern Exiles*, 104, and James Gregory, *The Southern Diaspora: How Black and White Southerners Transformed America* (Chapel Hill: University of North Carolina Press, 2005), 18.

3. For earlier examples, see James A. Maxwell, "Down from the Hills and into the Slums," *Reporter*, December 13, 1956; Donald Janson, "The Displaced Southerners Find Chicago an Impersonal Haven," *New York Times*, August 31, 1963; William Braden and Morton Kondracke, "Mountain Folk Adrift in Our City" and "What City Is Doing for Hill Folk," *Chicago Sun-Times*, February 9 and 10, 1964.

4. Harriette Arnow, *The Dollmaker* (New York: Macmillan, 1954); Daniel Petrie, dir., *The Dollmaker* (ABC, 1984).

5. John Irvin, dir., *Next of Kin* (Warner Brothers, 1989).

6. Killian, "Southern White Laborers." See also Killian's *White Southerners* (New York: Random House, 1970).

7. See, for example, John Bodnar, *The Transplanted: A History of Immigrants in Urban America* (Bloomington: Indiana University Press, 1987).

8. Killian, *White Southerners*, 92. See also James S. Brown and George S. Hillery, Jr., "The Great Migration, 1940–1960," in *The Southern and Appalachian Region: A Survey*, ed. Thomas Ford (Lexington: University Press of Kentucky, 1962).

9. Roger Guy, "Of Voices Few and Far Between: White Appalachian Women in Postwar Chicago, 1950–70," *Oral History Review* 37, no. 1 (2010): 54–70. For an account of southern whites owning bars, see Guy, *From Diversity to Unity*, chap. 4.

10. Personal interview by the author with Helen Elam, December 18, 1994.

11. Guy, *From Diversity to Unity*.

12. Thomas Wagner, Phillip Obermiller, Melinda B. Wagner, and Mike Malony, "Fifty Years of Appalachian Advocacy: An Interview with Mike Maloney," *Appalachian Journal* 40, nos. 3/4 (2013): 174–218, http://www.jstor.org/stable/43489086.

13. Amy Sonnie and James Tracy, *Hillbilly Nationalists, Urban Race Rebels, and Black Power: Community Organizing in Radical Times* (Brooklyn: Melville House, 2011).

14. Gregory, *Southern Diaspora* and Berry, *Southern Migrants, Northern Exiles*.

15. Chad Berry cites census data to support this. See "Southern White Migration to the Midwest, an Overview," in Obermiller, Wagner, and Tucker, *Appalachian Odyssey*, 18–20.

16. There is abundant scholarship on this topic. See, for example, Barry Bluestone and Bennet Harrison, *The Deindustrialization of America: Plant Closings, Community Abandonment, and the Dismantling of Basic Industry* (New York: Basic Books, 1984) and *The Great U-Turn: Corporate Restructuring and the Polarizing of America* (New York: Basic Books, 1990).

17. Berry, *Southern Migrants, Northern Exiles*, esp. chap. 5.

18. Personal interview by the author with J. D. Donnelson, March 14, 1994.

19. Personal interview by the author with Raleigh Campbell, August 4, 1995. Campbell was the former director of the Chicago Southern Center, 1965–68. The first epigraph to this chapter is also from this interview with Campbell.

20. Roger Guy, "Down Home: Perception and Reality among Southern Whites in Chicago, 1955–1975," *Oral History Review* 24, no. 2 (1997): 35–52.

21. I have written of the duality of home among first-generation Appalachians in Chicago and their second-generation offspring. See Guy, "Down Home."

22. See Mary Waters, *Ethnic Options: Choosing Identities in America* (Berkeley: University of California Press, 1990).

23. Guy, "Down Home."

24. Vance elaborates on this in the conclusion of his book.

25. This concept is alluded to in other parts of the book, for example, 244–46.

26. Lewis Killian, "The Adjustment of Southern White Migrants to Northern Urban Norms," *Social Forces* 32 (October 1953): 66–69.

27. Killian, "Southern White Laborers," 145–46.

28. Killian, *White Southerners*, 97–101.

29. Ibid.

30. Elam interview.

31. Personal interview by the author with Virginia Bowers, March 18, 1994.

32. Ibid.

33. Bowers was not the only migrant who expressed these views. See Guy, "Of Voices Few and Far Between."

34. James Gregory, *American Exodus: The Dust Bowl Migration and Okie Culture in California* (New York: Oxford University Press, 1989); and Berry, *Southern Migrants, Northern Exiles*, esp. chap. 6.

35. Berry, *Southern Migrants, Northern Exiles*, 156.

36. Ibid., 156–57.

37. While there were numerous stories in local newspapers, an often-cited portrait in a national magazine is Albert Votaw, "The Hillbillies Invade Chicago," *Harper's* 216 (February 1958): 64–67.

38. Votaw, "Hillbillies Invade Chicago," 64.

39. The idea of the deserving and undeserving poor has been explored in numerous works, most notably by Michael Katz in *The Undeserving Poor: From the War on Poverty to the War on Welfare* (New York: Pantheon, 1990).

40. On the motivations of the working poor, see Sharon Hays, *Flat Broke with Children: Women in the Age of Welfare Reform* (Oxford: Oxford University Press, 2003). Jennifer Sherman criticizes the notion that the poor lack morality in *Those Who Work, Those Who Don't: Poverty Morality, and Family in Rural America* (Minneapolis: University of Minnesota Press, 2009).

41. Charles Murray, *Losing Ground: American Social Policy, 1950–1980* (New York: Basic Books, 1994).

42. Edward C. Banfield, *The Unheavenly City Revisited* (Boston: Little, Brown, 1974), 61–62.

43. Edward Banfield, *The Unheavenly City: The Nature and Future of Our Urban Crisis* (Boston: Little, Brown, 1970) and *Unheavenly City Revisited*, chap. 3.
44. Banfield, *Unheavenly City*.
45. Marlon Riggs, dir., *Ethnic Notions* (California Newsreel, 1987).
46. Norma Lee Browning, "New Breed of Migrants City Problem," *Chicago Daily Tribune*, March 4, 1957.
47. Norma Lee Browning, "Girl Reporter Visits Jungles of Hillbillies," *Chicago Daily Tribune*, March 3, 1957, and "New Breed of Migrants City Problem."
48. Browning, "Girl Reporter Visits Jungles of Hillbillies."
49. Norma Lee Browning, "A Trip to Appalachia: Visit to the Middle Ages," *Chicago Daily Tribune*, May 5, 1957.
50. Henry D. Shapiro, *Appalachia on Our Mind: The Southern Mountains and Mountaineers in the American Consciousness, 1870–1920* (Chapel Hill: University of North Carolina Press, 1978).
51. Roger Guy, "The Media, Police, and Southern White Migrant Identity in Chicago, 1955–1970," *Journal of Urban History* 26, no. 2 (2000): 329–49.

WHAT *HILLBILLY ELEGY* REVEALS ABOUT RACE IN TWENTY-FIRST-CENTURY AMERICA

LISA R. PRUITT

MY INITIAL RESPONSE to the publication of *Hillbilly Elegy* and the media hubbub that ensued was something akin to pride.[1] I was pleased that so many readers were engaged by a tale of my people, a community so alien to the milieu in which I now live and work. Like Vance, I'm from hillbilly stock, albeit the Ozarks rather than Appalachia. Reading the early chapters, I laughed out loud—and sometimes cried—at the antics of Vance's grandparents, not least because they reminded me of my childhood and extended, working-class family back in Arkansas. Vance's recollections elicited vivid and poignant memories for me, just as Joe Bageant's *Deer Hunting with Jesus: Dispatches from America's Class War* (2007) and Rick Bragg's *All Over but the Shoutin'* (1997) had in prior decades.

I appreciated Vance's attention not only to place and culture, but to class and some of the cognitive and emotional complications of class migration. I'm a first-generation college graduate, too, and elite academic settings and posh law firms have taken some getting used to. Vance's journey to an intellectual understanding of his family instability and his experience grappling with the resulting demons were familiar territory for me. In short, I empathize with Vance on many fronts.

Yet as I read deeper into *Hillbilly Elegy*, my early enthusiasm for it was seriously dampened by Vance's use of what was ostensibly a memoir to support ill-informed policy prescriptions. Once I got to the part where Vance harshly judges the food stamp recipients he observed while bagging groceries as a high school student, I was annoyed by his highly selective dalliances into the social sciences and public policy. A few more chapters in, Vance was advocating against the regulation of payday lenders, and I began to realize that *Hillbilly Elegy* was a net loss for my people.

Indeed, because so many readers have made Vance authoritative vis-à-vis the white working class, I have come to grips with the fact that *Hillbilly Elegy* represents a regression in our understanding of white socioeconomic disadvantage. And that's saying a lot given the decades—even centuries—of disdain for those often referred to as "white trash."[2] The attention that *Hillbilly Elegy* draws to low-income, low-education whites does not foster understanding or empathy for those Vance left behind; rather, it cultivates judgment.

Vance invites us not to see the white working class in their full complexity but instead to cast all the blame on them for their often dire circumstances. Never mind neoliberal trade policies and the decimation of unions; never mind the rise of Walmart and contingent employment; never mind crummy public education and spatial inequalities with respect to a wide range of services and infrastructure. Never mind the demise of the safety net. According to Vance, "hillbillies" just need to pull themselves together, keep their families intact, go to church, work a little harder, and stop blaming the government for their woes.

In spite of this message—or perhaps because of it—*Hillbilly Elegy* has made J. D. Vance a very rich and famous man. Not only has the book spent dozens of weeks on the *New York Times* best-seller list, Vance has leveraged its commercial success into a gig as a CNN commentator. National media treat him like a celebrity, providing updates on his career and family.[3] The Brookings Institution even gave Vance a quasi-academic platform in late 2017, putting him into conversation with eminent Harvard sociologist William Julius Wilson to opine about "race, class, and culture."[4]

How is it that an unassuming and not especially artful memoir of white class migration—by definition anecdotal—has been elevated to the status of authoritative text? How has Vance parlayed three short decades of life into a small fortune and a career as America's "favorite white trash-splainer,"[5] "the voice of the Rust Belt,"[6] and "the Ta-Nehisi Coates, if you will, of White Lives Matter"?[7] How did Vance go from being just another "hillbilly" (albeit one with an Ivy League degree, two generations removed from the hills) to the man of the hour, his popularity compared to that of a boy band?[8] How did this contemporary Horatio Alger come to be fodder for a forthcoming Ron Howard film?

The sales figures for *Hillbilly Elegy* suggest a wide audience. That the book has been greeted with near universal acclaim in elite media outlets such as the *New York Times* and the *Washington Post* suggests that many highly educated folks are among its readers,[9] as does the fact that Bloomberg News and the *Economist* listed it as one of the most important books of the year.[10] One commentator called the book "all the rage in DC" in the run-up to the 2016 election,[11] and Frank Rich has referred to the book's "NPR-ish" readership,[12] implying that elected officials, policy makers, the professional class, and the professoriate dominate Vance's fawning audience. *Hillbilly Elegy* has become a must-read among those often referred to as the chattering classes, and many college campuses have been on Vance's speaking circuit. Tickets to hear him at my institution, UC Davis, ranged in price from twenty-five to fifty-five dollars. Not a bad day's work for a (former) hillbilly.

In this essay, I argue that elites and our nation more broadly have embraced *Hillbilly Elegy* and given Vance a national platform because, on some level, he confirms a story elites—and arguably Americans more broadly—tell ourselves, a story we want to believe is true. As Vance acknowledges, he is the American Dream personified. His tale—as he curates it—is one of industry and (apparent) meritocracy, a tale that affirms our nation's core values and aspirations.

What Vance does not talk about is *his* privilege—male, whiteish (for I acknowledge that Appalachians are often at the fringe of whiteness,[13] and I return to this issue below), and urbanish—or at least not rural. He also does not talk about the role of the state as a positive force that facilitated his upward trajectory to the Ivy League and beyond. What also goes unacknowledged is that Vance is actually an outlier, the exception to the rule.[14] Upward mobility in the United States has been declining for decades, and indeed, many previously "working class" by some standard or definition (demarcations of socioeconomic class categories are notoriously squishy) are now facing downward mobility,[15] along with attendant despair.[16] Vance is a good role model for the average "hillbilly" child, yes, but the data trends suggest that only the very rare one will be able to achieve a fraction of what Vance has. Further, those children's outcomes will be shaped not only by the presence or absence of lay-about parents and/or inspiring teachers but also by the political economy of regions and of the nation, and by the opportunity structures engineered by government.

While the widespread fascination with Vance and his story in national public discourse—as well as the staying power of both—is a function of many phenomena, I highlight here three that shed light on race, race relations, and racial politics in twenty-first-century America. First, the chattering classes' "shock and awe" response to *Hillbilly Elegy*—(white) people actually live like that?!?—demonstrates apparent widespread ignorance of white socioeconomic disadvantage and the dysfunction it frequently spawns, a feedback loop that, in recent years, has taken on the character of a death spiral.

One reason for such ignorance is that the public face of poverty in America today is almost exclusively Black or Brown.[17] Only in the aftermath of the 2016 election has the media renewed attention to white socioeconomic disadvantage.[18] Second, the widespread praise of *Hillbilly Elegy* suggests that elites across the political spectrum are willing to make scapegoats of poor whites. Progressive folks (among whom I count myself) would vigorously protest Vance's tough-love stance if he were writing about poor people of color, calling them lazy and criticizing them for "bad choices." Most progressives seem unfazed, however, that Vance's assessments and policy proposals throw low-income whites under the proverbial bus. Third, and closely related to the second revelation about race, Vance's tale confirms the way in which white elites, including those on the left, see themselves—as products of a meritocracy that levels the playing field for all, or at least for those with white skin. *Hillbilly Elegy* also confirms the way elite and middle-class whites typically see low-income, low-education whites (when we see them): as defilements of whiteness.

I will return to expand on these points in the pages that follow. First, however, I provide an overview of what Vance says expressly about race, as well as what he arguably implies about it. I then illustrate how so many among the chattering classes have not only consumed Vance's story but also acquiesced uncritically to his regressive policy prescriptions.

WHAT J. D. VANCE SAYS—AND DOESN'T SAY—ABOUT RACE

For the most part, Vance does not highlight race in relation to his story or his politics. Some direct mentions of race in *Hillbilly Elegy* seem incidental, offered in passing. For example, at one point he expresses optimism about the prospects of cross-racial cooperation based on his experience as a Marine, "where I saw that men and women of different social classes and races could work as a team and bond like family" (175).

Scratch the surface, however, and you find a book that is very much about race. First and foremost, Vance is clearly writing about white people—in particular a low-education, socially and economically precarious subset of whites. But Vance's choice of the word "hillbilly"—the term he repeats frequently as shorthand for his "people," including those who moved out of the hills, to metropolitan areas, a generation or two earlier—downplays race. "Hillbilly" gives whiteness a lower profile, though Vance is, in fact, talking about those many would refer to as "white working class," if not the more pejorative, even damning moniker "white trash."[19] Vance's choice of "hillbilly" is therefore an apparent act of identity entrepreneurism,[20] not least because it was his grandparents who grew up in the hills of rural Kentucky, not Vance.

Reflecting the common practice of white default or transparency,[21] and in the fashion of Appalachian studies, Vance elects merely to imply race.[22] Even though that race is "white," the use of the "hillbilly" label permits Vance to suggest a downtrodden minority.[23] This rhetorical maneuver downplays the white privilege enjoyed by those about whom he writes. Indeed, this is surely a core point of the book, and it is consistent with one of Vance's few explicit mentions of race and his only mention of white privilege, which comes in the book's preface:

> There is an ethnic component lurking in the background of my story. In our race-conscious society, our vocabulary often extends no further than the color of someone's skin—"black people," "Asians," "white privilege." Sometimes these broad categories are useful, but to understand my story, you have to delve into the details. I may be white, but I do not identify with the WASPs of the Northeast. Instead, I identify with the millions of working-class white Americans of Scots-Irish descent who have no college degree. To

their color.[37] Resentment toward those receiving public benefits is as likely to be directed at whites as at any other racial group—especially in overwhelmingly white communities like Middletown, Ohio, where the 2000 population was measured as 87 percent white.[38]

Indeed, when struggling whites who are working observe firsthand those who are not working—as opposed to merely imagining them based on a stereotype like the racialized welfare queen—the resentment is more likely directed at the offending "mooch" in front of one's face than at the distant one. Indeed, this firsthand observation appears to be what annoyed Vance and what animates his conservative position on public benefits. Recall what Vance observed as a high school student bagging groceries in Middletown: food stamp recipients making bad food choices ("a lot of canned and frozen food") compared to their more affluent—and in Vance's self-described "amateur sociologist" assessment—hardworking counterparts, whose carts were "piled high with fresh produce" (all quotations from 138). One must wonder if Vance is aware that canned and frozen food is far less expensive than fresh produce and can be stored longer; it is also more easily and quickly prepared by working parents and the children they must often leave home alone.

Except for his frequent use of "white" to modify "working class" (about fifty times throughout the book), Vance writes as if race is not relevant to his analysis. He also downplays race in discussing why "his people"—hillbillies—tend not to like Barack Obama. Vance writes,

Many of my new friends blame racism for this perception of the president. But the president feels like an alien to many Middletonians for reasons that have nothing to do with skin color. Recall that not a single one of my high school classmates attended an Ivy League school. Barack Obama attended two of them and excelled at both. He is brilliant, wealthy, and speaks like a constitutional law professor—which, of course, he is. Nothing about him bears any resemblance to the people I admired growing up: His accent—clean, perfect, neutral—is foreign; his credentials are so impressive that they're frightening; he made his life in Chicago, a dense metropolis; and he conducts himself with a confidence that comes from knowing that the modern American meritocracy was built for him. Of course, Obama overcame adversity in his own right—adversity familiar to many of us—but that was long before any of us knew him.

President Obama came on the scene right as so many people in my community began to believe that the modern American meritocracy was not built for *them*. (191)

In this passage, Vance seeks to diminish the significance of President Obama's Blackness in the white working-class response to him. Vance presents that response as stemming as much or more from class differences as from racial ones, and I agree with Vance on this matter—up to a point. In the case of Obama—who both is Black and projects an upper-class polish—working-class white resentment is not all about race, as evinced by the many working-class whites who voted for Obama in 2008 and 2012.[39] Bill Clinton could turn on his working-class boy from Arkansas, and George W. Bush could feign "common man" ways if not roots, thus appealing to rural and working-class whites because they were white and because of classed affectation. This was not an option available to Obama, whose Black skin made it difficult—if not impossible—to play the everyman card like his predecessors did, in spite of Obama's working-class upbringing.

But Vance notes that his "new friends"—presumably those he met at Yale Law School and since in the elite milieu where he now abides—are quick to assume the racism of working-class whites. This not only is consistent with postelection 2016 thinking about the white working class, but has also long been a presumption about them. Indeed, white elites project racism onto the white working class.[40]

Vance's point is nevertheless an important one: many working-class whites resent the professional/managerial class—arguably an inferiority complex manifest as anger.[41] This helps explain why many dislike Obama. Animus toward him is not solely (or, for some, perhaps even primarily) about racism,[42] just as animus toward Hillary Clinton is not solely about sexism. Recall the fondness of many working-class white voters in 2008 for another female candidate, Sarah Palin.[43] Class matters—a point often lost in the left's understanding of politics in twenty-first-century America.

Even though Vance does not express them as such, two of his messages about race might be summarized thusly: white people don't equally enjoy the fruits of "white skin" or whiteness more generally, and not every bad thing that happens to a Black person is entirely racially motivated. I agree with these points, and they find some support in recent scholarship.[44] Camille Gear Rich, for example, has admonished, "When scholars talk about white privilege in the abstract, without discussing the host of competing identity variables that complicate white privilege, they risk increasing the salience of whiteness for less race-identified whites in a context that gives whites an incentive to cling to a white identity."[45] Fischer and Mattson observe that the socioeconomic status into which one is born is a better predictor than a child's race of that child's future. But the critical race community and progressive elites generally have not been receptive to scholars like those who would add nuance to America's racial politics by calling attention to the role of class more specifically, to the potency of socioeconomic disadvantage as it afflicts whites.[46] Neither race alone nor class alone (nor gender or sexuality, for that matter) explains everything.

TWO WHITE WORKING CLASSES

Vance engages another concept that explains a great deal about what is happening among those whom outsiders see as a monolithic white working class. Specifically, he draws a line between two white working classes. On the one side of the line are the socially flawed and uncouth but essentially virtuous folks like his grandparents. On the other are Vance's mother and, by his account, many of Vance's generation who have succumbed to various social ills, including familial instability, laziness, and drug abuse. Vance depicts the latter as hapless at best, exemplars of sloth and dysfunction at worst.

Of the two white working classes, Vance writes:

Not all of the white working class struggles. I knew even as a child that there were two separate sets of mores and social pressures. My grandparents embodied one type: old-fashioned, quietly faithful, self-reliant, hardworking. My mother and, increasingly, the entire neighborhood embodied another: consumerist, isolated, angry, distrustful.[47]

There were (and remain) many who lived by my grandparents' code. Sometimes you saw it in the subtlest ways: the old neighbor who diligently tended her garden even as her neighbors let their homes rot from the inside out; the young woman who grew up with my mom, who returned to the neighborhood every day to help her mother navigate old age. I say this not to romanticize my grandparents' way of life—which, as I've observed, was rife with problems—but to note that many in our community may have struggled but did so successfully. There are many intact families, many dinners shared in peaceful homes, many children studying hard and believing they'll claim their own American Dream. Many of my friends have built successful lives and happy families in Middletown or nearby. They are not the problem, and if you believe the statistics, the children of these intact homes have plenty of reason for optimism.

I always straddled those two worlds. (148–49)

Although this is a point on which Vance does not reference any academic literature, various scholars have observed and analyzed the dichotomy he articulates between these two subclasses within the white working class.[48] Indeed, this distinction is another point on which Vance and I agree, though I view the group whom he maligns and distances himself from with greater empathy and compassion.[49] Whether expressed as the divide between those who work and those who don't,[50] the "settled" versus the "hard-living,"[51] the worthy poor versus the unworthy poor,[52] or rednecks (or hillbillies) versus white trash,[53] the dichotomy is nothing new. Joe Bageant even mocked the distinction, quipping, "poor is poor, whether you have to work for poverty or not."[54]

Of course, Vance loves and is deeply loyal to and appreciative of his Mamaw and Papaw, as well as to his relatives who maintain stable family lives and who are, presumably, gainfully employed. But Vance doesn't tell us much about the work or economic circumstances of that extended family (besides his grandparents), other than to say that one of them has a "beautiful house" (239) and several great uncles worked in construction, one with his own business, in Indiana (14, 29). What Vance repeatedly touts regarding several of his and his parents' generations are their happy, intact families, what great parents they are. In short, if these extended family members and other "worthy" folks among Vance's networks are still working class by any definition (that is, they may have migrated upward into the middle class), they are the "settled" variety. Vance himself would be among this group if he retained any claim to the working or even middle class, had he not hit the jackpot of admission to Yale Law School and been catapulted into wealth by virtue of the publishing sensation that is *Hillbilly Elegy*.

Academic literature shows that the "settled" harshly judge the "hard-living" and also that they find it very important to differentiate themselves from such ne'er-do-wells, lest they be mistaken for hoi polloi themselves. While racial difference might serve to draw this line in integrated communities, among whites, subtle nonracial markers—sometimes economic, but also cultural— take on enormous significance. It is not surprising, then, that Vance is so harshly judgmental of those among whom he was raised, those who—like his mother and some of his Middletown neighbors and peers—lead disorderly, precarious lives. After all, as Bourdieu points out, "Social identity lies in difference, and difference is asserted against that which is closest, which represents the greatest threat."[55]

Vance's description of two white working classes resonates with me as both accurate and socially and politically significant. But I strongly disagree with his prescription for what ails the "hard living." I am not opposed to hard work, intact families, or participation in faith communities. In fact I gladly and gratefully partake in all three. I do not, however, see these as the miraculous tonic that Vance does. We increasingly understand that phenomena such as the opioid and meth epidemics hit rural and working-class communities first and hardest because these communities' economies had already been devastated.[56] We are beginning to see the "deaths of despair" phenomenon (high rates of suicide and overdose deaths) to be a predictable result of the downward mobility that has resulted from globalization and the neoliberal turn.[57] Intact families won't get us out of this mess any more than Narcan will.[58] People need economic opportunity.

Vance's response to the devastation he saw in his hometown and the region is thus to be expected, not least because he has safely eluded its clutches. As one who works hard, is "settled," is worthy, and yet still claims the hillbilly mantle, he wishes to clearly distinguish himself from those who represent the other side of each of the dichotomies: lazy, hard-living, unworthy, "white trash." Yes, his Yale Law degree and elite employment should now do this differentiating for him, and presumably they do, for the most part.[59] Perhaps Vance documents what he does in *Hillbilly Elegy* not because he needs to do the differentiating so critical to low-status whites. Instead, perhaps he has written it to meet his own emotional needs, to distance himself from his childhood, because he is looking for peace of mind on several fronts. Maybe he wrote it to launch a political career or just to make some money.

Whatever Vance's motivation for writing his memoir and grappling with this divide within the white working class, it is important to bear in mind that the significance of this admittedly broad and fuzzy line between two groups of low-status whites can hardly be overstated. Yet it is a distinction so little known or understood by elites who look at all of Middletown, the Rust Belt, or—in the aftermath of the 2016 election—Trumplandia, and paint the whole lot with the broad brush of unworthy whites, even "white trash." Vance's stance and that of the vast majority of his readers is consistent with the responses Matt Wray, a longtime scholar of low-status whites, tells us have always been associated with "white trash": "moral outrage, disgust, anger, contempt, and fear."[60] Indeed, Vance's assumption that the failure of poor whites is essentially their own damned fault is another way in which *Hillbilly Elegy* serves to confirm the stories we tell ourselves, stories that implicate race as much as they do class—because whites "have race," too.[61] Such narratives affirm our desire to believe in a just world,[62] one where people get what they deserve, where they reap what they sow.

SUSPENDING OUR CRITICAL FACULTIES

As noted at the outset, Vance's message is a conservative one, as evinced most notably in his harsh judgment of the low-education, low-income whites among whom he grew up. Vance places the responsibility for poor and working-class whites' failures—including their downward mobility—squarely at their own feet. A secondary culprit, though, is the government, for fostering what he views as a "culture" of laziness and dependency. Vance acknowledges the tough knocks people like his grandparents took in relation to globalization, but he generally downplays—even in relation to his beloved Mamaw's food insecurity in her old age—the structural factors that led to the decline of the Rust Belt and the diminution of worker wages and protections. In short, *Hillbilly Elegy*—in the parlance of twenty-first-century chattering classes—blames the victims. The problem is that many readers don't see the ways in which the white working class are victims. Many view them only as culprits.[63]

Given Vance's message, it is easy to see why Vance has become the right's latest poster child for its gospel of personal responsibility. If Vance can rise from family dysfunction in and around down-and-out Appalachia, the American Dream must still be accessible to all—at least to those with adequate grit and determination. Indeed, Vance's essential message is the same as that Kevin Williamson purveyed in much harsher terms in the March 2016 issue of *National Review:*

> The white middle class ... failed themselves.
>
> If you spend time in hardscrabble, white upstate New York, or eastern Kentucky, or my own native West Texas, and you take an honest look at the welfare dependency, the drug and alcohol addiction, the family anarchy— which is to say, the whelping of human children with all the respect and wisdom of a stray dog—you will come to an awful realization.
>
> ———
>
> *Nothing happened to them.* There wasn't some awful disaster. There wasn't a war or a famine or a plague or a foreign occupation. Even the economic changes of the past few decades do very little to explain the dysfunction and negligence—and the incomprehensible malice—of poor white America.
>
> ———
>
> The truth about these dysfunctional, downscale communities is that they deserve to die. Economically, they are negative assets. Morally, they are indefensible. Forget all your cheap theatrical Bruce Springsteen crap. Forget your sanctimony about struggling Rust Belt factory towns and your conspiracy theories about the wily Orientals stealing our jobs.... The white American underclass is in thrall to a vicious, selfish culture whose main products are misery and used heroin needles.[64]

What Williamson states with unmitigated vitriol and disdain, Vance states in a folksy, aw-shucks way that one reviewer referred to as "tough love,"[65] another as a "bracing tonic."[66] In short, Vance makes Williamson's core message more palatable, in part because of the overall tone of *Hillbilly Elegy* and in part because he is writing about his own people, including some about whom he still cares.

Not only conservatives but also progressives have touted *Hillbilly Elegy*. The *New York Times* review, for example, called the book a "compassionate, discerning sociological analysis of the white underclass."[67] What the reviewer fails to note is that Vance's compassion is limited to certain members of his family and does not extend to many whom he left behind in the Rust Belt, not even to his mother.

Consistent with the book's reviewers, the majority of my own highly educated acquaintances have praised *Hillbilly Elegy*. Friends and colleagues have marveled at the book, though I have been less certain whether they were gobsmacked by Vance's tumultuous, even traumatic childhood or by his awed response to the hallowed halls of Yale Law School where he learned, for example, the utility of a butter knife and that "networking power is like the air we breathe" (215). *Hillbilly Elegy* introduced many readers to an exotic world they had only imagined, if that.

To be clear, I am not mocking Vance's "hillbilly" ignorance of these matters. I was simply later than he was to catching on to the importance of networking because I did not attend an elite law school and took a different path into the world of elites. As for table manners, I'm still working on those.

As a related matter, Vance's depiction of himself as a rube is somewhat undermined by his account of how he chose Yale Law School and how he presented himself in his admissions application. Clearly, Vance understood the import of an elite legal education; by his own account he was willing to go two hundred thousand into debt to get one (198). The same could not be said of many would-be class migrants.[68] Of his application to elite law schools, Vance suggests he used his working-class Appalachian narrative to catch admissions officers' attention (204). I am not criticizing him for doing so, and I credit Yale Law School for seeing how he represented diversity.[69] However, the fact he knew to write about his family story in his application suggests he was more savvy than he often depicts himself. As for his bragging about the ease of his first semester (200) and the suggestion that he basically hopped off the treadmill that would have led him to a Supreme Court clerkship, I assume they evince his insecurity.

On all of these matters, readers seem to have suspended their critical faculties, but where they seem most acutely to have done so regards those working-class and impoverished whites Vance left behind in Middletown, throughout the Rust Best, and, in fact, across America. Perhaps because progressives are reading their first contemporary tale of white working-class woe (*The Grapes of Wrath* is ancient history after all), they seem especially disinclined to approach it critically. Rather, they appear stunned into deference to Vance's supposed expertise, doled out on the basis of his firsthand observation, offered essentially as anecdote. It is a methodology that the Brookings Institution—citing *Hillbilly Elegy* in a policy paper—referred to as "n=1," meaning the sample size is "1," a single individual, Vance himself.[70] Of course, Vance does not hold his book out as scholarship, but his mere flirtation with scholarly literature and policy and the ways the book has often been received as authoritative do complicate what we are to make of this hybrid text.

Daniel Patrick Moynihan's "culture of poverty" theory—articulated regarding inner-city Blacks—fell from favor decades ago.[71] Yet academics and other elites appear to embrace Vance's rehabilitation of the concept vis-à-vis poor whites. Certainly I have heard few reject it, but then I also did not hear elites criticize Kevin Williamson's *National Review* essay. In the sections that follow, I outline how that very racial difference—liberal elites' different attitudes toward poor whites versus poor Blacks—looms large in their response to *Hillbilly Elegy*.

IGNORANCE OF THE WHITE WORKING CLASS

Vance could say little to surprise me—given that I come from hillbilly stock myself—about what he calls hillbilly culture. My childhood saw plenty of gun-toting, blue-streak cursing, violence, and other sundry dysfunctions. Vance's is just another story from my 'hood, if you will. For me, then, reader reactions to *Hillbilly Elegy* have been far more interesting than the content of the book itself.

In the rarefied world I now inhabit, it seems very few knew anything of the "hillbilly" world before they read the book. Indeed, my colleagues and friends seemed hardly aware that his world exists beyond some Rust Belt abstraction or reality TV caricature, although it has become increasingly familiar (albeit at a safe distance) thanks to the media's "Trump country" tourism following the 2016 election. In my coastal ivory tower, however, Middletown, Ohio, and Breathitt County, Kentucky, remain essentially another planet, their denizens inexplicable aliens. In fact, while Vance's familial circumstances were no doubt traumatizing, his socioeconomic disadvantage was relatively mild in the greater scheme of things. His mother worked as a nurse. He was never homeless. His grandparents maintained two homes after their separation. But elites are generally ignorant of acute socioeconomic disadvantage and therefore not well situated to gauge how dire Vance's childhood was.

Had the narrating classes who have made Vance the toast of the town even a passing familiarity with the milieu from whence he comes and about which he writes, they would not have been so taken with Vance's tale—and they surely would not have been taken in by his policy prescriptions. Were America not so polarized, so geographically segregated along class lines as well as race lines,[72] *Hillbilly Elegy* would have revealed remarkably little to upper-crust readers. As it happens, though, Vance's story has taken elites by storm, in part because it has taken them by surprise.

To be clear, elites are generally also unfamiliar with the lives of poor nonwhites. Nevertheless, white elites are more aware of at least the existence of these communities because poverty and dysfunction are widely depicted as Black and Brown.[73] Such communities are centerpieces of left-leaning policy and law reform agendas, and progressives are highly aware of racial discrimination and racial disadvantage. But poor whites have been rendered largely invisible, absent from the national consciousness.[74] Indeed, "forgotten," "hidden," and "invisible" are adjectives used frequently in the wake of the 2016 election to describe rural and/or white working-class constituencies.[75] Hidden from and invisible to whom, we might ask?

We in academia and similarly elite settings may know people inching up the social hierarchy, people who attended nonelite colleges, who now perhaps even have graduate degrees or are trying to position their children for the Ivy League. But how many in the chattering classes know firsthand anyone like J. D. Vance—someone who grew up hardscrabble, perhaps traumatized by an addicted parent—who has made a massive class migration in a single generation?[76] Further, when people like Vance and I claw our way into privileged social spaces, the pressure to class pass is enormous, meaning others won't always identify us as class migrants.[77] Alternatively, when we are so identified, the collective embarrassment and stigma around class squelches any explicit recognition or dialogue about it.[78]

In short, elites (white elites, anyway) are at least as insular regarding class as they are regarding race. With respect to race, however, progressives articulate a desire to understand racial difference and racial disadvantage, as well as to ameliorate the latter. Not so with respect to low-income, low-education aspiring class migrants who are white.[79] Regarding this population, the liberal presumption that these folks are unenlightened at best, racist at worst, prompts us to keep them at arm's length.[80]

My "ignorance" thesis is supported by the fact that the few progressive reviewers whose musings about *Hillbilly Elegy* are neutralish or outright critical fall into one of two categories: they grew up in the region from whence Vance came and/or they are white class migrants themselves.[81] Indeed, the first time I found myself among a critical mass of *Hillbilly Elegy* detractors was at the 2017 Annual Meeting of the Rural Sociological Society, a gathering of folks who know a thing or two about rural poverty, structural disadvantage, and spatial inequality. Similarly, Appalachian studies listservs and conferences have met the book with hostility. These groups are not buying what Vance is selling; they literally know better.

CONTEMPT FOR THE WHITE WORKING CLASS

Progressives' widespread ignorance of the lived experiences of white working-class America, somewhat paradoxically, leads to my second argument: white elites are contemptuous of low-education, low-income whites. The left has offered no groundswell of offense at Vance's condemnation of his white Appalachian, Rust Belt, and broader American compatriots because of their disdain for this demographic sector, a response that is facilitated by their ignorance. A few have offered a feeble, piecemeal rebuttal at best.[82]

Progressives would undoubtedly protest the attribution of laziness and "bad choices" to Black and Brown people as reasons for their failures. Liberal elites would express the need for greater cultural understanding of the context in which people of color live, work, and make choices. Progressives ridicule Black conservatives such as Justice Clarence Thomas and Ben Carson for not seeing themselves as outliers who are the exceptions that prove the rule of structural racism and the persistence of racial animus. Yet left-leaning elites offer no such protestations regarding Vance's presentation of himself as the product of his own industry, nor any renunciation of his attendant disdain for those who have not pulled off such a Houdini-like escape from the stickiness of the working class.

In the same vein, progressives take structural disadvantage very seriously when it afflicts racial minorities and thus manifests as structural or institutional racism.[83] But they fail to see similar patterns—or when they do see them, they downplay them—when the victims are white.[84] This attitude is reflected in an expression often heard in the academy, "you're white, you'll be alright," or that which is suggested by the sarcastic quip "white people's problems." As I have written elsewhere, "Poverty is not endemic to whiteness and, indeed, is anathema to it. Whites are (supposed to be) invulnerable, autonomous, independent and self-reliant. Because the world loves and embraces whites, it not only expects but also facilitates their success. Whites who are poor thus have only themselves to blame. . . . Their shortcomings are thus rendered all the more glaring juxtaposed against the advantage of white skin."[85] As Matt Wray has observed, these people have white skin but they are not quite white. They do not enjoy the benefits—at least not all of the benefits—of whiteness.

The depths of despair phenomenon has been widely associated with low-income, low-education whites.[86] The brother of one such victim focused on whiteness as a factor: "There is an expectation for [white people] to keep it together. People think, 'Hey, you are white. You are privileged. So why do you have so many problems? Maybe you are the problem.' . . . There isn't a lot of space for them to be vulnerable."[87] This is the flip side of our conflation of our poverty problem with our racism problem—the presumption that Blacks are poor and poor people are Black.[88] That conflation has given us an excuse for being ignorant of white poverty, but it is surely not the only reason that we continue to overlook the phenomenon of white economic distress. A key reason we look past white poverty is because it defiles whiteness, causing us to flinch and avert our gaze.[89] Recall Packer's deconstruction of the phrase "white working class," quoted above, which in twenty-first-century America has been increasingly conflated with "white trash," with "alienation from the 'founding virtues' of civic life."[90]

This is where Vance's policy-infused memoir comes in. Vance does what most of us—consciously or not—wish to do: he distances himself from white losers. In Vance's case, that requires a distinct rejection of his own mother.

To further illustrate my point, consider for a moment an alternative scenario in which Vance was an African American man writing about low-income, low-education African Americans who have not shared in his success. Or if Vance were Latina writing about the low-income, low-education slice of the Latinx community from whence she came. In those alternative scenarios, progressives would have met Vance's highly judgmental message with widespread denunciation and criticism. Such a scenario would be tantamount to Barack Obama, in his memoir *Dreams from My Father*, condemning those he worked among as a community organizer in Chicago, even while basking in his own success as the obvious fruits of his own labor. Or imagine Justice Sonia Sotomayor, in her best-selling memoir *My Beloved World*, taking complete credit for her class migration from the Bronx's Puerto Rican American community to a seat on the US Supreme Court, all while saying the Latinx youth and young adults left behind simply lacked the grit and discipline to achieve similarly lofty goals.

Progressives might have read such alternative books, but only to be better equipped to condemn them. They would not have let these accounts persist undisputed, as somehow authoritative on the character of low-income African Americans or Latino/as. Left-leaning folks would have disputed the implication that the life trajectories of these minority populations are all down to personal responsibility and might well have called out Obama and Sotomayor not only as outliers, but also as race traitors.[91] Not so with Vance and *Hillbilly Elegy*. Instead, liberal elites can feel a bit of an affinity for J. D. Vance, even "like" him, because he has "cleaned up well," because he aspires to be elite, too, because his Yale Law degree has conferred that status on him. But we have always been suspicious of the white working class, uncouth and presumptively racist as they are.[92] *Hillbilly Elegy* confirms aspects of this long-standing narrative, and so we fall for it, hook, line, and sinker.

THE MYTH OF MERITOCRACY

An alternative explanation—or perhaps more accurately, a complementary one—for progressives' embrace of *Hillbilly Elegy* is that liberal elites are not so much clueless about the white working class and/or disdainful of them as they are politically motivated to deny their struggles. Progressive elites may be complicit in not disputing Vance's tough-love policy prescription for an implicitly unworthy white underclass because to do so would call into question their own merit. In short, to recognize Vance as the exception to the rule of stagnation or downward mobility for socioeconomically disadvantaged whites would reveal "meritocracy" to be the myth that it, in fact, is.[93] Needless to say, elites do not want to go there. As long as the American Dream is alive and well—as Vance's story arguably establishes it to be—elites can (somewhat ironically) also see themselves as products of that dream, that meritocracy, even if they are in fact trust fund babies, born with proverbial silver spoons in their mouths. Never mind that the American Dream has become a pipe dream for the vast majority of working-class whites, just as it is for the vast majority of working-class people of color.

This narrative is not undermined by what we know about structural racism, nor about racism's other forms. Progressives see and acknowledge that racial and ethnic minorities are not playing on a level playing field with whites. The left is well aware that the "meritocracy" does not work for people of color, to whom different rules and another reality apply.

Yet progressives resist the potency of class disadvantage for those with white skin. Most academics refuse to see how structural disadvantage, as well as contempt-driven discrimination, can thwart the life prospects and upward mobility of low-status whites.[94] Just as Vance presents himself as enjoying the fruits of his sheer native ability, hard work, discipline, and grit (oh, and don't forget the dash of good luck), so successful whites wish to see ourselves. In short, even the liberal response to *Hillbilly Elegy*—and not only the conservative one— is confirmation bias at work.

CONCLUSION

One very poignant vignette in *Hillbilly Elegy* comes in the book's conclusion. Vance holds up fifteen-year-old Brian, whom Vance is mentoring, as an illustration for what our country—and "hillbillies"—are getting and doing wrong. Vance writes of taking Brian to a fast-food restaurant and noticing "little quirks that few others would,"[95] such as the fact that Brian didn't want to share his milkshake and that the young man "finished his food quickly and then looked nervously from person to person. I could tell that he wanted to ask a question, so I wrapped my arm around his shoulder and asked if he needed anything. 'Y-Yeah,' he started, refusing to make eye contact. And then, almost in a whisper: 'I wonder if I could get a few more french fries?' He was hungry. In 2014, in the richest country on earth, he wanted a little extra to eat but felt uncomfortable asking. Lord help us" (253). Vance's outrage is palpable, and justifiably so. I share that outrage, though I am skeptical that so few would have seen the boy's "quirks," such as not wanting to share his food. I have often wondered what people who fail to support food programs (e.g., SNAP/food stamps, free and reduced-price school lunches) think they are accomplishing by keeping kids hungry. I tend to conclude that this stance is explained by a desire to visit the sins of the parents (perceived or real) on their children. Never mind that hungry kids don't perform well in school, are more likely to have disciplinary problems, and—as a result—further aggravate parental stress. Never mind that when kids go hungry, their potential is thwarted, and their future—as well as that of our nation—is put at risk. Childhood hunger is a pipeline to adult dysfunction.

Yet Vance is apparently among those who see no role for food programs that could alleviate Brian's hunger. His solution to hungry kids like Brian is for their parents to get and stay married and go to church. His solution is for Brian's parents not to be white trash. But marriage and church don't feed the kids, regardless of the kids' skin color. Why, then, is the left not outraged at Vance's policy prescription for a hungry white teenager in Appalachian Kentucky? Progressives would be apoplectic if Vance were saying this about a hungry Black teenager in Detroit.

In a similar vein, Vance holds up the French as more successful than US parents because children in that country are less likely than US children to be exposed to numerous parental partners (228). At the same time, Vance completely overlooks the more comprehensive French welfare state, one where subsidies and stipends prevent children from being hungry or homeless. These are the very fundamentals of social welfare policy, yet most readers of *Hillbilly Elegy* seem not to have noticed Vance's sleight of hand, his decision to focus on family structure to the complete neglect of the safety net.

Where is the indignation, the progressive groundswell of outrage by middle- and upper-class whites in response to *Hillbilly Elegy*? The book has elicited no mainstream protestation of support or defense of poor or working-class whites. What we are left with, then, is an apparent endorsement of Vance's condemnation of those who—unlike him, now comfortably ensconced among "the haves"—are unable to escape the place or livelihood that once guaranteed them a decent working-class living, one that allowed them to aspire to middle-class standards and stability, but which now leaves them essentially among the working poor.

This acceptance of Vance's message by elite whites across the political spectrum is bad news for people of color as well as for poor whites because it is one more way in which affluent whites prevent cross-racial coalition building among the socioeconomically disadvantaged.[96] Indeed, it reminds me of what Dr. Martin Luther King Jr. observed about white elites during Reconstruction, about the genesis of the Jim Crow era: that elite whites used Jim Crow to segregate the races, to thwart coalition building, to prevent poor whites from seeing what they had in common with Blacks.[97]

Elite whites are still driving wedges between poor whites and Blacks, though I would like to think progressive elites are doing so unwittingly. But vilifying poor whites while expressing concern for the interests of poor Blacks only drives deeper that wedge between two constituencies who desperately need to be in coalition with each other. The acceptance of *Hillbilly Elegy*'s politics—a politics inflected with race as much as with class—is yet more evidence of that unfortunate phenomenon.

NOTES

Thanks to Ann M. Eisenberg, Christopher Chavis, Jasmine Harris, Emily Prifogle, and Amanda Kool for comments on earlier drafts and to Anujan Jeevaprakash for research assistance. Liliana Moore managed the manuscript capably, patiently, and with good cheer.

1. J. D. Vance, *Hillbilly Elegy: A Memoir of a Family and Culture in Crisis* (New York: HarperCollins, 2016).

2. Joe Bageant, *Deer Hunting with Jesus: Dispatches from America's Class War* (New York: Crown, 2007); John Hartigan, Jr., "Unpopular Culture: The Case of 'White Trash,'" *Cultural Studies* 11, no. 2 (May 1997): 316; Nancy Isenberg, *White Trash: The 400-Year Untold History of Class in America* (New York: Penguin, 2016); Matt Wray, *Not Quite White: White Trash and the Boundaries of Whiteness* (Durham, NC: Duke University Press, 2006).

3. Molly Ball, "Hillbilly Elegy Writer Won't Seek Office," *Atlantic*, September 14, 2017, https://www.theatlantic.com/politics/archive/2017/09/hillbilly-elegy-writer-wont-seek-office/539949/; James Hohmann, "The Daily 202: Why the Author of 'Hillbilly Elegy' Is Moving Home to Ohio," *Washington Post*, December 26, 2016, https://www.washingtonpost.com/news/powerpost/paloma/daily-202/2016/12/21/daily-202-why-the-author-of-hillbilly-elegy-is-moving-home-to-ohio/5859da6ee9b69b36fcfeaf48/?u tm_term=.1ae48f2230a0.

4. Elanor Krause and Richard Reeves, "Rural Dreams: Upward Mobility in America's Countryside" (Brookings Institution, September 5, 2017), https://www.brookings.edu/research/rural-dreams-upward-mobility-in-americas-countryside/.

5. Sarah Jones, "J. D. Vance, the False Prophet of Blue America," *New Republic*, November 17, 2016, https://newrepublic.com/article/138717/jd-vance-false-prophet-blue-america.

6. Karen Heller, "'Hillbilly Elegy' Made J. D. Vance the Voice of the Rust Belt. But Does

He Want that Job?," *Washington Post*, February 6, 2017, https://www.washingtonpost
.com/lifestyle/style/hillbilly-elegy-made-jd-vance-the-voice-of-the-rust-belt-but-does-he-
want-that-job/2017/02/06/fa6cd63c-e882-11e6-80c2-30e57e57e05d_story.html?utm_
term=.d848b73b94ab.

7. Frank Rich, "No Sympathy for the Hillbilly," *New York Magazine*, March 19, 2017,
    http://nymag.com/daily/intelligencer/2017/03/frank-rich-no-sympathy-for-the-
    hillbilly.html.

8. Mark Ferenchik, "J. D. Vance Draws Crowds, and Questions about Political Future,"
    Columbus Dispatch, July 31, 2017, http://www.dispatch.com/news/20170731/jd-
    vance-draws-crowds-and-questions-about-political-future.

9. Amanda Erickson, "A Hillbilly's Plea to the White Working Class," *Washington Post*,
    August 4, 2016, https://www.washingtonpost.com/opinions/a-hillbillys-plea-to-the-
    white-working-class/2016/08/04/5c1a7a56-51ca-11e6-b7de-dfe509430c39_story
    .html?utm_term=.c60ef2dbf4d9; Jennifer Senior, "Review: In 'Hillbilly Elegy,' a Tough
    Love Analysis of the Poor Who Back Trump," *New York Times*, August 10, 2016,
    https://nyti.ms/2jAuPgc.

10. William R. Easterly, "Stereotypes Are Poisoning American Politics," *Bloomberg
    News*, December 16, 2016, https://www.bloomberg.com/view/articles/2016-12-16/
    stereotypes-are-poisoning-american-politics; "Why Donald Trump Speaks to So Many
    Americans," *Economist*, August 11, 2016, http://www.economist.com/news/books-and-
    arts/21704774-why-donald-trump-speaks-so-many-americans-promises-promises?fsrc=
    scn%2Ftw%2Fte%2Fpe%2Fed%2Fpromisespromises.

11. James Hohmann, "The Daily 202: Want to Know Why Trump's Winning Ohio?
    Drink a Beer with 'The Deplorables' in Boehner's Old District," *Washington Post*,
    October 4, 2016, https://www.washingtonpost.com/news/powerpost/paloma/
    daily-202/2016/10/04/daily-202-want-to-know-why-trump-s-winning-ohio-drink-a-
    beer-with-the-deplorables-in-boehner-s-old-district/57f288a6e9b69b0592430082/?pos
    tshare=1241475588947475&tid=ss_tw.

12. Rich, "No Sympathy for the Hillbilly."

13. Lisa R. Pruitt, "Acting White? Or Acting Affluent? A Book Review of Carbado &
    Gulati's *Acting White? Rethinking Race in Post-racial America*," *Journal of Gender, Race
    & Justice* 18 (2015): 159; Jill Fraley, "Invisible Histories & the Failure of the Protected
    Classes," *Harvard Journal on Racial & Ethnic Justice* 29 (2013): 95.

14. J. D. Vance and William Julius Wilson, "Race, Class, and Culture: A Conversation
    with William Julius Wilson and J. D. Vance," Interview by Camille Busette (Brookings
    Institution, September 5, 2017). Wilson told Vance that he was an outlier—that
    they were both outliers given where they are now in relation to their childhood
    circumstances.

15. Jonathan Davis and Bhash Mazumder, "The Decline in Intergenerational Mobility after
    1980" (Federal Reserve Bank of Chicago, 2017).

16. Anne Case and Angus Deaton, "Mortality and Morbidity in the 21st Century"
    (Brookings Papers on Economic Activity, 2017).

17. bell hooks, *Where We Stand: Class Matters* (New York: Routledge, 2000); Trina
    Jones, "Race, Economic Class, and Employment Opportunity," *Journal of Law and*

Contemporary Problems 72 (2009): 52; Lisa Pruitt, "Welfare Queens and White Trash," *Southern California Interdisciplinary Law Journal* 25 (2016): 289.

18. Sam Harnett, "What We Talk about When We Talk about the 'White Working Class,'" *KQED*, November 7, 2017, https://ww2.kqed.org/news/2017/11/07/what-we-talk-about-when-we-talk-about-the-white-working-class/.

19. Isenberg, *White Trash*; Lisa Pruitt, "Welfare Queens and White Trash," 289; Wray, *Not Quite White.*

20. Nancy Leong, "Identity Entrepreneurs," *California Law Review* 104 (2016): 1333.

21. Barbara J. Flagg, "Fashioning a Title VII Remedy for Transparently White Subjective Decisionmaking," *Yale Law Journal* 104, no. 8 (1994): 2009, 2035. Transparency in this context means the "tendency for whiteness to vanish from whites' self-perception."

22. Barbara Ellen Smith, "De-gradations of Whiteness: Appalachia and the Complexities of Race," *Journal of Appalachian Studies* 10 (2004): 38.

23. Ibid.

24. Devon W. Carbado and Mitu Gulati, *Acting White? Rethinking Race in "Post-racial" America* (New York: Oxford University Press, 2013); Cheryl I. Harris, "Whiteness as Property," *Harvard Law Review* 106, no. 8 (1993): 1707–91; Peggy McIntosh, "White Privilege: Unpacking the Invisible Knapsack," *Peace and Freedom Magazine*, July and August 1989, 10–12; Camille Gear Rich, "Marginal Whiteness," *California Law Review* 98 (2010): 1497; Vance and Wilson, "Race, Class, and Culture." In a September 2017 conversation on "race, class, and culture" sponsored by the Brookings Institution, Vance made the point that working-class whites resent being told they are the beneficiaries of white privilege. The transcript from that exchange includes the following: "When I talk to folks back home, very conservative people . . . what I find no openness about is when somebody who they don't know, and who they think judges them, points at them and says you need to apologize for your white privilege."

25. Ruth Frankenberg defines whiteness as the cumulative way that race shapes the lives of white people. See Frankenberg, *White Women, Race Matters: The Social Construction of Whiteness* (Minneapolis: University of Minnesota Press, 1993), 1.

26. Vance suggests the Scots-Irish are culturally distinct, focusing on their ethnicity rather than their skin color, similar to Jim Webb, *Born Fighting: How the Scots-Irish Shaped America* (New York: Broadway Books, 2004). As Ignatiev has observed in considering "the Irish," a loss of focus on ethnicity, e.g., the Irish, the Scots-Irish, Italian-Americans, leads to a merging of these distinct ethnic groups into a collective "whiteness," which serves only to oppress nonwhites. Noel Ignatiev, *How the Irish Became White* (New York: Routledge, 1995). See also Karen Brodkin, *How Jews Became White Folks and What That Says about Race in America* (New Brunswick, NJ: Rutgers University Press, 1999).

27. Wray, *Not Quite White*, 139.

28. I say "oddly" here because many progressives seem to revel in the "self-flagellation" implicit in white privilege. See Cedric Johnson, "An Open Letter to Ta-Nehisi Coates and the Liberals Who Love Him," *Jacobin Magazine*, February 2, 2016, https://www.jacobinmag.com/2016/02/ta-nehisi-coates-case-for-reparations-bernie-sanders-racism/.

29. Carbado and Gulati, *Acting White?*; McIntosh, "White Privilege."

30. Pruitt, "Acting White?," 159.

31. Harnett, "What We Talk About"; Jones, "Race, Economic Class, and Employment Opportunity"; Cheryl Harris, "Keynote: Cheryl I. Harris" (September 2014, YouTube video, 1:16:27, posted December 2016), https://www.youtube.com/watch?v=cRV14I7e0R0.

32. Elizabeth A. Fay and Michelle M. Tokarczyk, *Working-Class Women in the Academy: Laborers in the Knowledge Factory* (Boston: University of Massachusetts Press, 1993); Chris Offutt, "In The Hollow," *Harper's Magazine*, November 2016, https://harpers.org/archive/2016/11/in-the-hollow-2/; Lisa R. Pruitt, "The Geography of the Class Culture Wars," *Seattle University Law Review* 34 (2011): 767; Joan C. Williams, *Reshaping the Work-Family Debate: Why Men and Class Matter* (Cambridge, MA: Harvard University Press, 2010).

33. Michelle M. Tokarczyk, "Promises to Keep: Working Class Students and Higher Education," in *What's Class Got to Do with It? American Society in the Twenty-First Century*, ed. Michael Zweig (Ithaca, NY: Cornell University Press, 2004), 166.

34. Charles M. Blow, "She Who Must Not Be Named," *New York Times*, December 4, 2010, https://nyti.ms/2J0bkqW.

35. George Packer, "Hillary Clinton and the Populist Revolt," *New Yorker*, October 31, 2016, http://www.newyorker.com/magazine/2016/10/31/hillary-clinton-and-the-populist-revolt. Joan Williams and Charles Murray have also documented this shift in thinking about the working class. Murray, *Coming Apart: The State of White America, 1960–2010* (New York: Crown Forum, 2012); Williams, *Reshaping the Work-Family Debate*. The *Wall Street Journal* similarly expressed this white working-class decline by comparison to the "inner city" in a 2017 feature, but it framed the comparison as rural vs. urban rather than explicitly Black vs. white. Janet Adamy and Paul Overberg, "Rural America Is the New 'Inner City'," *Wall Street Journal*, May 26, 2017, https://www.wsj.com/articles/rural-america-is-the-new-inner-city-1495817008.

36. Ian Haney-Lopez, *Dog Whistle Politics: How Coded Racial Appeals Have Reinvented Racism and Wrecked the Middle Class* (New York: Oxford University Press, 2015).

37. Alec MacGillis, "Who Turned My Blue State Red?," *New York Times*, November 20, 2015, https://nyti.ms/2k4RPRt; Terrence McCoy, "How Disability Benefits Divided This Rural Community between Those Who Work and Those Who Don't," *Washington Post*, July 21, 2017, http://www.washingtonpost.com/sf/local/2017/07/21/how-disability-benefits-divided-this-rural-community-between-those-who-work-and-those-who-dont/?utm_term=.99b92e4e68cf; Pruitt, "Geography of the Class Culture Wars," 767; Jennifer Sherman, *Those Who Work, Those Who Don't: Poverty, Morality, and Family in Rural America* (Minneapolis: University of Minnesota Press, 2009).

38. "QuickFacts: Middletown City, Ohio; United States. Census 2000" (US Census Bureau), http://censusviewer.com/city/OH/Middletown.

39. Sean McElwee, Jesse H. Rhodes, Brian F. Schaffner, and Bernard L. Fraga, "The Missing Obama Millions," *New York Times*, March 10, 2018, https://nyti.ms/2Gdurxm (reporting that 9 percent of those who voted for Obama in 2012 voted for Trump in 2016).

40. Martha Mahoney, "Segregation, Whiteness and Transformation," *University of Pennsylvania Law Review* 143 (1995): 1667.

41. Richard Sennett and Jonathan Cobb, *The Hidden Injuries of Class* (New York: Norton, 1972).

42. Pruitt, "Acting White?"

43. Pruitt, "Geography of the Class Culture Wars."

44. Pruitt, "Acting White?"; Pruitt, "Who's Afraid of White Class Migrants? On Denial, Discrediting and Disdain (and Toward a Richer Conception of Diversity)," *Columbia Journal of Gender and Law* 31 (2015): 196; Pruitt, "Welfare Queens and White Trash," 289.

45. Rich, "Marginal Whiteness," 1565.

46. Claude Fischer and Greggor Mattson, "Is America Fragmenting?," *Annual Review of Sociology* 35 (2009): 442. To be clear, while Fischer and Mattson's data point speaks to upward mobility, it does not take into account the types of discrimination and abuse experienced by virtue of skin color.

47. Vance's focus on consumerism, isolation, anger, and distrust is consistent with the observations of Joe Bageant, who a decade earlier used similar adjectives to describe liberals' view of working-class whites: "angry, warmongering bigots." Bageant, *Deer Hunting with Jesus*, 13. But Bageant's overall view of working-class whites is far more compassionate than Vance's, and Bageant offers a sympathetic perspective on working-class consumerism, an issue Vance returns to with a vengeance in his book's conclusion. There he sharply criticizes poor families for spending on their children at Christmas, suggesting they should instead buy their children books as gifts, as his wife's family did. See Bageant, *Deer Hunting with Jesus*.

48. Williams, *Reshaping the Work-Family Debate*; Sherman, *Those Who Work, Those Who Don't*.

49. Pruitt, "Geography of the Class Culture Wars."

50. Sherman, *Those Who Work, Those Who Don't*.

51. Williams, *Reshaping the Work-Family Debate*.

52. Timothy Egan, "Good Poor, Bad Poor," *New York Times*, December 19, 2013, https://nyti.ms/2mfqOzX; Noah D. Zatz, "Poverty Unmodified? Critical Reflections on the Deserving/Undeserving Distinction," *University of California Los Angeles Law Review* 59 (2012): 550.

53. Bageant, *Deer Hunting with Jesus*.

54. Ibid., 9.

55. Pierre Bourdieu, *Distinction: A Social Critique of the Judgment of Taste*, trans. Richard Nice (Abingdon, UK: Routledge, 1984), 479.

56. Shannon M. Monnat, "Deaths of Despair and Support for Trump in the 2016 Presidential Election" (Pennsylvania State University Department of Agricultural Economics, Sociology, and Education Research Brief, December 4, 2016).

57. Case and Deaton, "Mortality and Morbidity in the 21st Century"; Joel Achenbach and Dan Keating, "A New Divide in American Death," *Washington Post*, April 10, 2016, http://www.washingtonpost.com/sf/national/2016/04/10/a-new-divide-in-american-death/?utm_term=.79882723584d.

58. Monnat, "Deaths of Despair."

59. Class migration is, in fact, rife with complications, as Vance's story suggests. Rarely is it easy or seamless. I would be curious to know the extent to which Vance is truly an insider now,

among elites, simply because of his Yale law degree, or whether his familial pedigree means he will in some ways remain a persistent outsider.

60. Wray, *Not Quite White*, 8.

61. Flagg, "Fashioning a Title VII Remedy," 2037; Pruitt, "Acting White?," 159; Pruitt, "Welfare Queens and White Trash," 289.

62. Melvin Lerner, *The Belief in a Just World: A Fundamental Delusion* (New York: Springer, 1980).

63. Mahoney, "Segregation, Whiteness and Transformation"; Lisa R. Pruitt, "The False Choice between Race and Class and Other Affirmative Action Myths," *Buffalo Law Review* 63 (2015): 988.

64. Kevin D. Williamson, "The Father-Führer," *National Review*, March 28, 2016, https://www.nationalreview.com/nrd/articles/432569/father-f-hrer. Although Williamson refers to the "white middle class," the milieu he describes seems more consistent with what Vance and others call the white working class.

65. Senior, "Review."

66. "Why Donald Trump Speaks."

67. Senior, "Review."

68. Pruitt, "Who's Afraid of White Class Migrants?"

69. Ibid.

70. Krause and Reeves, "Rural Dreams."

71. Patricia Cohen, "Culture of Poverty Makes a Comeback," *New York Times*, October 17, 2010, https://nyti.ms/2kqyPx9; Daniel Patrick Moynihan, "The Negro Family: The Case for National Action" (Washington, DC: Office of Policy Planning and Research, US Department of Labor, 1965).

72. Bill Bishop, *The Big Sort: Why the Clustering of Like-Minded America Is Tearing Us Apart* (New York: Houghton Mifflin, 2008); Sheryll Cashin, *Place, Not Race: A New Vision of Opportunity in America* (Boston: Beacon, 2014); Murray, *Coming Apart*; Robert D. Putnam, *Our Kids: The American Dream in Crisis* (New York: Simon & Shuster, 2015).

73. hooks, *Where We Stand*; Jones, "Race, Economic Class, and Employment Opportunity"; Pruitt, "Welfare Queens and White Trash," 289.

74. hooks, *Where We Stand*; Pruitt, "Welfare Queens and White Trash," 289; Pruitt, "Acting White?," 159.

75. Lisa R. Pruitt, "The Women Feminism Forgot: Rural and White Working Class Women in the Era of Trump," *Toledo Law Review* (forthcoming).

76. Pruitt, "Who's Afraid of White Class Migrants?," 196.

77. Lisa R. Pruitt, "How You Gonna' Keep Her Down on the Farm . . . ," *University of Missouri Kansas City Law Review* 78 (2010): 1085; Pruitt, "Acting White?," 159; Pruitt, "Who's Afraid of White Class Migrants?," 196.

78. Pruitt, "Who's Afraid of White Class Migrants?," 196.

79. Pruitt, "False Choice," 981; Pruitt, "Who's Afraid of White Class Migrants?," 196.

80. Pruitt, "Who's Afraid of White Class Migrants?," 196.

81. Jones, "J. D. Vance"; Jedediah Purdy, "Red-State Blues," *New Republic*, September 14, 2016, https://newrepublic.com/article/136328/red-state-blues; Betsy Rader, "I Was Born in Poverty in Appalachia. 'Hillbilly Elegy' Doesn't Speak for Me," *Washington Post*,

September 1, 2017, https://www.washingtonpost.com/opinions/i-grew-up-in-poverty-in-appalachia-jd-vances-hillbilly-elegy-doesnt-speak-for-me/2017/08/30/734abb38-891d-11e7-961d-2f373b3977ee_story.html?utm_term=.38e16bda3f65&wpisrc=nl_popns&wpmm=1.

82. Jones, "J. D. Vance"; Purdy, "Red-State Blues"; Rader, "I Was Born in Poverty in Appalachia."

83. Cheryl I. Harris, "Whiteness as Property," *Harvard Law Review* 106, no. 8 (1993): 1707–15; Johnson, "Open Letter."

84. Cf. Priscilla A. Ocen, "Birthing Injustice: Pregnancy as a Status Offense," *George Washington Law Review* 85 (2017): 1163. Ocen's commentary in this piece defies this general rule.

85. Pruitt, "Welfare Queens and White Trash," 303.

86. Case and Deaton, "Mortality and Morbidity in the 21st Century."

87. Kimberly Kindy and Dan Keating, "Opioids and Anti-anxiety Medication Are Killing White American Women," *Washington Post*, August 31, 2016, http://www.washingtonpost.com/sf/national/2016/08/31/opiods-and-anti-anxiety-medication-are-killing-white-american-women/?utm_term=.6ce399e647da.

88. hooks, *Where We Stand*; Jones, "Race, Economic Class, and Employment Opportunity"; Pruitt, "Welfare Queens and White Trash," 289.

89. Pruitt, "Welfare Queens and White Trash," 289; Wray, *Not Quite White*.

90. Nicholas Confessore, "Tramps Like Them," *New York Times*, February 12, 2012, https://nyti.ms/2kzWgb0; Murray, *Coming Apart*.

91. Noel Ignatiev and John Garvey, *Race Traitor* (New York: Routledge, 1996).

92. Mahoney, "Segregation, Whiteness and Transformation," 1667.

93. Lani Guinier, *The Tyranny of the Meritocracy: Democratizing Higher Education in America* (Boston: Beacon, 2015); Annette Lareau, *Unequal Childhoods: Class, Race, and Family Life* (Berkeley: University of California Press, 2011); David A. Leonhardt, "Welcome College Diversity Push," *New York Times*, December 7, 2017, https://nyti.ms/2AYsXa9; Eli Wald, "Success, Merit and Capital in America," *Marquette Law Review* 101 (2017): 2.

94. Pruitt, "Acting White?," 159.

95. I find this self-congratulatory assertion bizarre. Certainly the vast majority of people who are parents would pick up on what Vance thinks he is extraordinary in seeing.

96. James Gray Pope, "Why Is There No Socialism in the United States? Law and the Racial Divide in the American Working Class," *Texas Law Review* 94 (2016): 1555.

97. Martin Luther King, Jr., "How Long, Not Long" (speech, Selma to Montgomery March, Selma, March 25, 1965).

PRISONS ARE NOT INNOVATION

TEXT AND PHOTOGRAPH BY LOU MURREY

CHATTANOOGA, TENNESSEE: Young folks from Appalachia in solidarity with communities at the Southern Movement Assembly fighting for prison abolition. This is not the Appalachian apathy and isolation readers of *Hillbilly Elegy* might expect; this is young people working with people across geographic boundaries to fight a $444 million federal prison in eastern Kentucky because we know that our communities deserve better and we know that a just future for Appalachia doesn't look like supporting the prison-industrial complex.

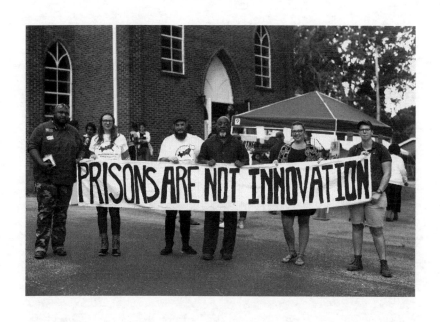

DOWN AND OUT IN MIDDLETOWN AND JACKSON: DRUGS, DEPENDENCY, AND DECLINE IN J. D. VANCE'S CAPITALIST REALISM

TRAVIS LINNEMANN AND CORINA MEDLEY

It is curious how people take it for granted that they have a right to preach at you and pray over you as soon as your income falls below a certain level.

—George Orwell, *Down and Out in Paris and London*

IN DECEMBER 2016, not long after J. D. Vance's *Hillbilly Elegy: A Memoir of a Family and Culture in Crisis* had climbed atop the *New York Times* best-seller list,[1] garnering rave reviews from pundits and the public alike, Eric Eyre of the *Charleston Gazette-Mail* published a multipart series detailing how three pharmaceutical companies had helped fuel the highest drug overdose rates in the nation's history.[2] Eyre found that in just six years, McKesson, Cardinal Health, and AmerisourceBergen had dumped nearly nine million pain pills on the tiny hamlet of Kermit, West Virginia, population 392. All told, nearly 780 million hydrocodone and oxycodone pills—some 400 pills for every man, woman, and child in the state—found their way to Kermit and the other small towns that dot the southern West Virginia coalfields.[3] Although a system was in place to intervene in cases of "doctor shopping" and "suspicious orders," state and federal agencies had ultimately done little to halt the flood of pills that, over the same period, had taken more than seventeen hundred lives from the sparsely populated corner of West Virginia.[4] While Eyre was eventually honored with a 2017 Pulitzer Prize for investigative journalism, his account of greed, neglect, and death has yet to register in the ways that has *Hillbilly Elegy*. From back-flap endorsements by high-profile conservatives to the *New York Times* and network news, Vance's memoir has been lauded for giving voice to the discounted denizens of the southern Appalachians and postindustrial Rust Belt. Reviewing the book in the *New York Times*, for instance, Jennifer Senior gushed that Vance offered "a compassionate, discerning sociological analysis of the white underclass that has helped drive the politics of rebellion, particularly the ascent of Donald J. Trump."[5] Others, however, found very little sociology in *Hillbilly Elegy*. Writing in the *New Republic*, Sarah Jones rebuked the book as little more than "a list of myths about welfare queens repackaged as a primer on the white working class" and derided Vance for his lazy conclusion that "hillbillies themselves are to blame for their troubles."[6] Although they take up the same conceptual terrain and moment in history—postindustrial West Virginia, Ohio, and Kentucky—Vance and Eyre begin and thus end at radically different ontological positions. Whereas Eyre's work is a muckraking account of the political and economic collusion leading to the "opioid crisis," Vance's self-referential account of a "family and culture in crisis" holds that nearly all hardships, including those with drugs and alcohol, whether ending in acquiescence or triumph, are simply matters of individual choice, character, and will. Mapping a Lamarckian culture of poverty onto the conditions of poor white "hillbillies" in the Ohio and Kentucky Appalachians he called home, Vance's story is one of determination and chance, utterly devoid of honest engagement with questions of history and political economy, outside of a clichéd understanding of his "Scots-Irish" heritage as irrevocably violent and tribal. Nevertheless, as we write in the fall of 2017, *Hillbilly Elegy* has sat near the top of the *New York Times* best-seller list for more than sixty weeks, while the corporate malfeasance at the center of the Appalachian opioid crisis uncovered by Eyre remains a mostly disregarded strapline, Pulitzer be damned. In order to grapple with the politics of the unfolding opioid crisis, in this chapter we read *Hillbilly Elegy* as diagnostic of what Mark Fisher called *capitalist realism*.[7] Here Vance's is not simply a story of determination and triumph, but rather a moralizing tale that reaffirms the view of the poor as a morally deficient, self-defeating lot best kept cordoned off from conventional society, while simultaneously upholding the overriding belief that there is simply no alternative to the present social order.

MORALLY INDEFENSIBLE, SPATIALLY EXCLUDED

Before moving forward, it is important to distinguish the broader current of respectability politics that underpins Vance's narrative from analyses of the opioid crisis taken up in other contexts. For instance, as Julie Netherland and Helena Hansen have rightly shown, in the northeastern United States in particular, public debates surrounding the opioid issue have advanced a public health approach favoring care and treatment over policing and punishment.[8] For Netherland and Hansen and others, when compared with the bygone "crack era," this "gentler war on drugs" as the *New York Times* described it, is compelling evidence of a powerful double standard breaking along racial lines, ushering poor black and brown drug users into prison while diverting privileged middle- and upper-class whites into medical care.[9] Recently speaking on the issue, civil rights advocate Michelle Alexander suggested, "White people now feel a kinship to drug users and abusers that they did not feel when the faces of addiction were black and brown."[10] While such a double standard is an obvious and undeniable facet of the long history of the US drug war, in the context of the Rust Belt factory towns and southern Appalachian coalfields upon which Vance situates his argument, the binary between care on the one hand and punishment on the other is less clear. Indeed, as Josh Keller and Adam Pearce report, the highest incarceration rates in the United States are found not in one of New York's five boroughs, but in a placid corner of southern Indiana.[11] The sentences handed down for drugs, particularly opioids, in Dearborn County, bordered by the Ohio River, a stone's throw from Ohio and Kentucky, are routinely the maximum allowed by state sentencing guidelines. Following the practices of other sparsely populated, politically conservative jurisdictions, the punitive tactics of local prosecutors grounded in notions of "personal responsibility" emerged as a preemptive attack on the "heroin epidemic," despite an attendant increase in violent crime.

In a longer view, Brett Story and Judah Schept have shown how, in eastern Kentucky, the political economies of extractive industries have aligned, over time, to fashion a carceral landscape underwritten not by the real or imagined threat of crime or even an ideological commitment to law and order, but by the immutable forces of racial capitalism, private property, and wage labor.[12] Here, as Ronald Eller famously documented, massive swaths of land and mineral and natural resource rights were bought on the cheap, yielding untold wealth for absentee deed holders while locals were left in poverty and the land in disarray.[13] With the rise of strip mining and mountain top removal, the combination of abundant yet poisoned land and dire economic conditions has made Appalachia prime prison-building territory, both in terms of available real estate and as an economic program.[14] In other words, the century-long "big steal," as some call it, has birthed an attendant political economy of punishment that has neither the intention nor the ability to deviate from established prison building, policing, and punishment practices. It is no surprise to us that in the rural South, the drug war, as a system for the management of idle and largely disposable populations, has retained its most punitive dimensions. So while Vance might decry his family and friends for skating on the government dole and others might suggest that the opioid crisis has softened police and prosecutors, it is our firm contention that in southern Appalachia, and other disregarded parts of the rural United States, the drug war has grown neither kinder nor gentler.

It could be that Vance's story, considering its popularity, simply came along, or rather reappeared, at the right time. While he might not speak for the white working class, the release of his book did time perfectly with the final days of the 2016 presidential election and the unlikely rise of Donald Trump. Again, as Jones put it, in the run-up to the Trump era, the national media that were "fixated on the spectacle of white trash Appalachia" went looking for an interpreter and anointed Vance their "representative in-exile."[15] It was, however, from solidly within the right itself that the overstated and now largely disproven link between the ambiguous "white working class" and Trump's seemingly impossible victory emerged first, and perhaps most forcefully.[16] Writing in the *National Review* just ahead of the release of *Hillbilly Elegy*,

Kevin Williamson scolded the "morally indefensible" inhabitants of Rust Belt factory towns for heartening Trump's divisive politics:

> It is immoral because it perpetuates a lie: that the white working class that finds itself attracted to Trump has been victimized by outside forces ... but nobody did this to them. They failed themselves.
>
> If you spend time in hardscrabble, white upstate New York, or eastern Kentucky, or my own native West Texas, and you take an honest look at the welfare dependency, the drug and alcohol addiction, the family anarchy—which is to say, the whelping of human children with all the respect and wisdom of a stray dog—you will come to an awful realization. . . .
>
> The truth about these dysfunctional, downscale communities is that they deserve to die. Economically, they are negative assets. Morally, they are indefensible. . . . The white American underclass is in thrall to a vicious, selfish culture whose main products are misery and used heroin needles. Donald Trump's speeches make them feel good. So does OxyContin. What they need isn't analgesics, literal or political. They need real opportunity, which means that they need real change, which means that they need U-Haul.[17]

Echoing the elitism of the Republican establishment and the dead arguments of Charles Murray,[18] Williamson's attack on the "vicious, selfish, culture" of the "white American underclass" is, like Vance's, not far removed from the Reagan era campaign against inner-city "welfare queens." Carrying forward the tradition of H. H. Goddard, Oscar Lewis, Daniel Patrick Moynihan, and Murray, Williamson points to the tangle of "welfare dependency, drug and alcohol addiction" and "family anarchy" as evidence of the radical alterity of the rural poor and engages in a powerful racializing practice, driving a rhetorical wedge between bourgeois whiteness and its degraded variants.[19] Of course, in *Hillbilly Elegy*, of the many social ills with which Vance and his fellows tangle, drugs and alcohol are not only a consistent presence, but somehow positioned as the chief cause or catalyst of spoiled families and futures. Introducing himself in a TED talk on "America's forgotten working class," Vance establishes this particular vision of personal and community difficulty:

I came from a southern Ohio steel town, and it's a town that's really struggling in a lot of ways, ways that are indicative of the broader struggles of America's working class. Heroin has moved in, killing a lot of people, people I know. Family violence, domestic violence, and divorce have torn apart families. And there's a very unique sense of pessimism that's moved in. Think about rising mortality rates in these communities and recognize that for a lot of these folks, the problems that they're seeing are actually causing rising death rates in their own communities, so there's a very real sense of struggle.[20]

Though he hints at it here and in his book, Vance never really articulates an understanding of family and community difficulty beyond the ahistoricism of drugs, violence, and despair simply "moving in." This sort of achronological causality is built upon or quickly lapses into a powerful sort of victim blaming, whereby the poor and poor communities are deemed wholly responsible for their predicament.

Indeed, as the late 1980s "crack panic" reminds, drug-driven decline is a convenient and popular explanation for difficulties experienced by communities of all kinds, even those outside the familiar confines of the city and its ghetto.[21] For instance, a few years before Vance, journalist Nick Reding had his own *New York Times* best seller, *Methland: The Death and Life of an American Small Town*, describing how methamphetamine and moral vacuity festered at the rotting core of the rural Midwest "heartland." Though somewhat more attuned to structural conditions that made job loss, out-migration, and capital departures unavoidable obstacles for the small Iowa farm towns he visited, Reding, too, emphasized drug-driven individual failings as a catalyst of community decline.[22] What tends to link books of this type, while they prove incredibly popular, is that their titular subjects almost never actually exist empirically. That is to say, both *Methland* and *Hillbilly Elegy* are artifacts of conservative textual poiesis that draws upon and gives life to certain political geographies and subjectivities.

This is not to say that these creations are fabrications, utterly without material consequence. As historian Anthony Harkins has shown, the "hillbilly" has long been a powerful rhetorical tool privileging urban and industrial understandings of social order through the denigration of rural ways of life as backward and antimodern. Of course, the most long-standing and consistent attack on the hillbillies, "rednecks," and "poor white trash" thought to inhabit the rural United States has been oriented around work ethic or, rather, lack thereof. Harkins documents that as early as the 1700s, wealthy landholders and religious and political leaders characterized the largely isolated, small-scale subsistence farmers of the Appalachians as "unhealthy" and "slovenly" outsiders, who eschewed the "natural order" of "hard work and purposefulness" due to their undeniably deficient character.[23] The ancient and widespread contempt for those who flout the strictures of social expectations and live outside the conventional labor market has its roots in Europe and the transition from feudalism to early agrarian capitalism and mercantilism. As William Chambliss and others (see, for instance, Linebaugh) have shown, mass deaths during the Black Plague necessitated the coerced mobilization of idle and freely mobile subjects who had, to that point, managed to live outside the system of landlordism.[24] The enclosure of common lands that provided the poor a means of subsistence and the development of vagrancy statutes enforced by local authorities were powerful methods taken to force the poor to join the ranks of the new economic and social order and work for a wage. As political theorist Mark Neocleous has argued, the anxieties generated by unruly outlaw subjects are thus foundational to the development of the system of wage labor and the adjoining police power engineered to enforce it. Born in response to the threats posed by "masterless men," police helped introduce and enforce a system to "transform the idle, derelict poor, into rational calculating individuals in pursuit of clearly defined economic goals."[25] We might count books like *Hillbilly Elegy* and *Methland*, with an implicit focus on drug-driven moral failings of the idle and jobless poor, as part of this discursive and ideological lineage, helping to imagine and locate the landscapes upon which the contemporary "masterless" are thought to flourish, or at least call home.[26] Drawing upon this ideological line, Vance and his ilk subtly advance an exclusionary vision where, in the words of Williamson, generations of "welfare dependency, drug and alcohol addiction, and family anarchy" are partitioned from the more polite and upstanding members of American society.[27]

In some ways then, exclusionary narratives of drug-driven decline offer a textual counterpart to the popular "ruins" movement in photography, which often takes up Appalachia as its subject. As J. P. Leary suggests, aided by audiences' faulty assumptions of photographic truth, images of rural squalor and rotting cities tend to aestheticize, dramatize, and romanticize poverty without confronting its origins or offering an alternative account of resilience and resistance.[28] Like their "ruin porn" counterparts, both Vance and Reding invoke the grim imagery of death and decay to bolster their rhetorical mode of decline. *Elegy* is of course a gesture meant to honor the departed, in this case Vance's prayer for the regressive culture of the white working class, while Reding similarly points to the death of a particular set of cultural traditions presumably unique to the *American small town*.

Like the flawed assumption of photographic truth that underpins "ruin porn," Vance's rhetorical requiem is aided by an assumption of realism. How, the logic goes, could critics, particularly coastal elites, doubt the accounts of Vance's own life? However dubious Vance's autobiographical realism may be, sitting just below its surface is another, more insidious form of realism that fills out the memoir's distinct ideological form. This is a political and economic sort of realism—dubbed by the late Mark Fisher *capitalist realism*—which exhorts Vance's readers "to get real" and to recognize that the sort of survival of the fittest individualism that characterizes neoliberal capitalism is simply the "way things are."[29] As literary critics Alison Shonkwiler and Leigh Claire La Berge note, realism, including the variety employed by Vance, "has long been considered the aesthetic mode most intimate to capitalism."[30] Yet, capitalist realism is not simply an aesthetic or mode of representation, but an ideological formation that, in Fisher's words, "occupies the horizons of the thinkable" and eclipses, for many, even the ability to imagine how things might be different (8).[31] Returning to his TED talk, we find traces of this sort of ideological closure in Vance's description of his home: "So for starters, there was a very real sense of hopelessness in the community that I grew up in. There was a sense that kids had that their choices didn't matter. No matter what happened, no matter how hard they worked, no matter how hard they tried to get ahead, nothing good would happen."[32] The sense of hopelessness that Vance describes mirrors perfectly the conditions of Fisher's capitalist realism. Not only do Vance's townsfolk possess a particularly grim outlook on their own economic chances, they have lost the ability or will to even speculate about a different future. Here, tales of good jobs and prosperous communities recede into a nostalgia-clogged collective memory and vanish from the ambitions of the young. As we will demonstrate, the notion that the present system offers no hope for the future other than bootstrap determination is precisely the perverse individualistic ethos that perhaps accounts for *Hillbilly Elegy*'s wide appeal. By identifying and tracing Vance's capitalist realist ontology to its ancient origins, we situate *Hillbilly Elegy* within an ideological lineage that polices race, class, and even geographic lines through fearful and cynical appeals to abandon the "white working class" to circumstances supposedly of their own making.

DOWN AND OUT IN MIDDLETOWN AND JACKSON

Paying close attention to what Vance says and, importantly, what he doesn't say about the world of poor white hillbillies, we read *Hillbilly Elegy* symptomatically to outline a few themes consistent with Fisher's capitalist realism. At its most superficial level, *Hillbilly Elegy* emerges from and reaffirms the long-standing mythos of American meritocracy. Not unlike the recent case of Reginald Dwayne Betts, who at the age of sixteen was sentenced to prison for a carjacking and, like Vance, also made good by graduating from Yale Law School, today's "rags to riches" or "jail to Yale" stories offer hopeful lessons on the promises of the American Dream.[33] The importance of the Algerian myth, though primordial, cannot be understated, as it lies at the heart of the present social order. The only way to make it in a world resigned to "how things are" is to follow the rules and work extremely hard. Yet Vance goes beyond simply recuperating a long-standing capitalist ideology of recognition or redemption through material success in the conventional labor market. He asks his readers to "feel" the circumstances of his life and the lives of his fellow hillbillies. As he puts it early on in *Hillbilly Elegy*, his primary aim was not to convince his readers of the well-documented problems of the postindustrial Rust Belt, but to "tell a true story" about what it "*feels* like when you were born with it hanging around your neck" (8, emphasis added). As such, Vance's memoir can be understood in terms of what Fisher described as "affective management"

(74), a particular cultural form or template that offers a reaffirmation of what we already think and, more importantly, feel about a particular subject.[34] Vance writes,

> I want people to know *what it feels like* to nearly give up on yourself and why you might do it. I want people to understand what happens in the lives of the poor and the psychological impact that spiritual and material poverty has on their children. I want people to understand the American Dream as my family and I encountered it. I want people to understand how upward mobility *feels*. And I want people to understand something I learned only recently: that for those of us lucky enough to live the American Dream, the demons of the life we left behind continue to chase us. (2, emphasis added)

Taking Vance at his word, we can say that he aims at a sort of affective interpellation, asking his audience to adopt his politics and take his side. To accomplish this, Vance conveys an overwhelming sense of resignation, tinged with pessimism, cynicism, and pity. He writes, "Our neighbors had a kind of desperate sadness in their lives. You'd see it in how the mother would grin but never really smile, or in the jokes that the teenage girl told about her mother 'smacking the shit out of her.' I knew what awkward humor like this was meant to conceal because I'd used it in the past. Grin and bear it, says the adage. If anyone appreciated this, Mamaw did" (142). The idea that the only recourse for most of the people he describes is to "grin and bear it" is again an underlying mantra of capitalist realism: *there is no alternative, this is as good as it gets*. For Vance, it is no surprise that "working-class whites" are a pessimistic lot; what he aims to get at and thus remedy is the cause of this despair. He explains,

> It is unsurprising, then, that we're a pessimistic bunch. What is more surprising is that, as surveys have found, working-class whites are the most pessimistic group in America. More pessimistic than Latino immigrants, many of whom suffer unthinkable poverty. More pessimistic than black Americans, whose material prospects continue to lag behind those of whites. While reality permits some degree of cynicism, the fact that

hillbillies like me are more down about the future than many other groups—some of whom are clearly more destitute than we are—suggests something else is going on. (4)

The resignation to having little agency or control over one's life approximates the fatalism long associated with Appalachian people and also what Fisher dubbed *reflexive impotence*, "akin to the deflationary perspective of a depressive who believes that any positive state, any hope, is a dangerous illusion" (5). As Vance describes in his book, "There is a lack of agency here—a feeling that you have little control over your life and a willingness to blame everyone but yourself. This is distinct from the larger economic landscape of modern America" (8).[35] As opposed to Fisher, however, who sees reflexive impotence as the direct byproduct of political economy, Vance sees the fatalistic outlook of his tribe simply as an issue of culture, an error in collective thinking and therefore something to be solved by a good old-fashioned change in attitude. Relaying one of the many lessons of his grandparents, he recalls, "Mamaw and Papaw believed that hard work mattered more. They knew that life was a struggle, and though the odds were a bit longer for people like them, that fact didn't excuse failure. 'Never be like those fucking losers who think the deck is stacked against them,' my grandma often told me. 'You can do anything you want to'" (36). Not unlike his friend and mentor Charles Murray, who has long attacked the "white underclass" for its failings, Vance invariably traces a person's individual experiences and life chances back to an ambiguous yet totalizing culture that seemingly determines laziness and defeatist thinking. In other words, as he puts it elsewhere, "hillbilly values spread with hillbilly people" (21).[36]

This sort of cultural fatalism, of course, determines Vance's understanding of substance abuse difficulties—no doubt conditioned by his mother's struggles—as somehow equal parts disease and individual choice. On the one hand, Vance pathologizes drug and alcohol difficulties as an inheritable trait, while on the other he reaffirms his faith in human agency. As he describes,

When Mom came home a few months later, she brought a new vocabulary along with her. . . . Drug addiction was a disease, and just as I wouldn't judge a cancer patient for a tumor, so I shouldn't judge a narcotics addict for her behavior. At thirteen, I found this patently absurd, and Mom and I often argued over whether her newfound wisdom was scientific truth or an excuse for people whose decisions destroyed a family. Oddly enough, it's probably both: Research does reveal a genetic disposition to substance abuse, but those who believe their addiction is a disease show less of an inclination to resist it. Mom was telling herself the truth, but the truth was not setting her free. (116)

So while Vance is seemingly willing to entertain that his mother's lifelong battle with drugs and alcohol—a battle that greatly conditioned his worldview—might be an inheritable condition, or even linked to the "stress of paying bills" and the pain of her father's death, he ultimately has little sympathy for her and others like her for their apparent inability to make good decisions and to stop making excuses (115).

It is precisely the capitalist realist ontology, one that shields the system from critique by framing social problems as problems of only the individual, that negates possibilities for politicization and collective action. As Fisher argues, by privatizing problems such as these and "treating them as if they were caused only by chemical imbalances in the individual's neurology and/or by their family background—any question of social system causation is ruled out" (21). As such, individualistic accounts of both failure and triumph found within the pages of *Hillbilly Elegy* perform the trick of hiding the inequalities built into the present order in plain sight.

This is not to say that Vance sees no utility in collective action; the question is how such a collectivity might be realized. Indeed, for Vance, drug users provide powerful support for an approach to social relations that favors privatization, bureaucratization, and a libertarian state that involves itself little in the lives of its subjects. We can see clear residue of this sort of thinking in Vance's recollection of the "good old days" of beneficent corporations and stable wage labor. He recalls, "As Mamaw used to say, 'Armco built this fucking town.' She wasn't lying: Many of the city's best parks and facilities were bought with Armco dollars. Armco's people sat on the boards of many of the important local organizations, and it helped to fund the schools. And

TRAVIS LINNEMANN AND CORINA MEDLEY

it employed thousands of Middletonians who, like my grandfather, earned a good wage despite a lack of formal education" (53). For Vance and his kind, the social is stitched together by private corporations, churches, and families (and as his later life shows, the military, one of the only forms of institutional welfare acceptable under neoliberalism). Stepping in to pick up the slack when Armco raised his grandmother's insurance premiums, Vance prided himself for being the rugged individualist "protector" rather than questioning a corporation and a system that would ignore the needs of its most vulnerable, writing, "Paying for her health insurance made me feel, for the first time in my life, like I was the protector. It gave me a sense of satisfaction that I'd never imagined—and how could I?" (167).

Of course, Vance's ahistorical "take care of your own" ethos has its roots in the political backlash against Johnsonian welfarism, to say nothing of Nixon's race-baiting Southern Strategy. Vance adds, "As far back as the 1970s, the white working class began to turn to Richard Nixon because of a perception that, as one man put it, government was 'payin'' people who are on welfare today doin' nothin'! They're laughin' at our society! And we're all hardworkin' people and we're getting' laughed at for workin' every day!'" (140). The lesson here, in place for more than a century and directly in line with the present neoliberal order, is that the free market, in terms of both unrestrained corporate power and the spirit of the indomitable capitalist subject, is the core of a healthy society. This is the ideological closure characterized by capitalist realism. As Fisher describes, "An ideological position can never be really successful until it is naturalized, and it cannot be naturalized while it is still thought of as a value rather than a fact. Accordingly, neoliberalism has sought to eliminate the very category of value in the ethical sense. Over the past thirty years, capitalist realism has successfully installed a 'business ontology' in which it is *simply obvious* that everything in society, including healthcare and education, should be run as a business" (16–17). Thus for Vance, a capitalist realist par excellence, only flawed workers—those who have failed to succeed or lost faith in the "dream"—take handouts or look to game the system. Likewise, strip mining, mountain top removal, outsourcing, downsizing, and "corporate welfare" cannot ever be understood in terms of corporate malfeasance, let alone class war. Rather, they are simply sound business decisions. Indeed, for Vance none of these things can account for the condition of his brethren, for after all, his is a book that offers a final requiem for the hillbilly's *culture*. He writes,

> Nobel-winning economists worry about the decline of the industrial Midwest and the hollowing out of the economic core of working whites. What they mean is that manufacturing jobs have gone overseas and middle-class jobs are harder to come by for people without college degrees. Fair enough—I worry about those things, too. But this book is about something else: what goes on in the lives of real people when the industrial economy goes south. It's about reacting to bad circumstances in the worst way possible. *It's about a culture that increasingly encourages social decay instead of counteracting it.* (7, emphasis added)

A BRUTAL STATE OF AFFAIRS

As we have briefly described, Vance's laissez-faire capitalist realism underpins and overlaps with a long-standing ideology that holds that the poor are a population to be loathed, feared, and controlled. As historian Nancy Isenberg recently detailed in her exhaustive account of the historical development of the ancient term "white trash," the fixation with controlling and punishing poor whites lays bare the contradictions between the mythical ethos of the American Dream and the immutable reality of life in a profoundly unequal society.[37] Unsurprisingly, the survival of the fittest ethos that structures *Hillbilly Elegy* has emerged in local and national policy discussions of the "opioid crisis." Locally, a member of Middletown's city council, Dan Picard, made national news when he proposed a perverse "three-strikes" solution to the costs of providing emergency medical care to overdose victims. Picard suggested that the Municipal Court require a first-time patient to complete community service work equal to the costs of emergency medical services (EMS), roughly eleven hundred dollars. Picard suggested that on a second overdose the cost be doubled, and on a third, the city should withhold EMS services, effectively imposing a de facto death sentence.[38] Defending his controversial proposal, Picard doubled down on the harsh "message" of capitalist realism: *you are on your own.* "I want to send a message to the world that you don't want to come to Middletown to overdose because someone might not come with Narcan and save your life. We need to put a fear about overdosing in Middletown."[39]

Of course, the driving concern here is not the welfare of drug users or even public safety, but the city's bottom line. And though it does not seem that they spoke in concert, around the same time a local police official voiced similar suggestions. Richard Jones, sheriff of Butler County, in which Middletown sits, vowed that the personnel under his supervision would never carry Narcan (Naloxone), the relatively inexpensive and highly effective treatment for opioid overdoses. Responding to criticisms of the ruthlessness of his decree, the sheriff quipped that it was not he who rendered a death sentence, but individual users who make the decision "when they stick that needle in their arm."[40] The ruthless neglect that would allow people to die of an easily treatable condition requires an understanding of the problem that places blame squarely at the feet of the dead. Of course, this sort of cold indifference and resignation lies at the capitalist realist core of *Hillbilly Elegy* and twins with the "brutal state of affairs" identified by Alain Badiou in his reflections on the nature of evil. He writes, "We live in a contradiction: a brutal state of affairs, profoundly inegalitarian—where all existence is evaluated in terms of money alone—is presented to us as ideal. To justify their conservatism, the partisans of the established order cannot really call it ideal or wonderful. So instead, they have decided to say that all the rest is horrible. Sure, they say, we may not live in a condition of perfect Goodness. But we're lucky that we don't live in a condition of evil."[41]

Unsurprisingly, the Trump administration's response to the opioid problem also powerfully articulates the cynical resignation to "business as usual" that characterizes capitalist realism. In an October 2017 speech, Trump declared the opioid crisis a national public health emergency, in order to, among other things, authorize federal emergency funds. Calling the problem the "worst drug crisis in American . . . and even world history," Trump offered little beyond platitudes and the impotent politics of "just say no." Unsurprisingly, he took the opportunity to wheel out his now-patented brand of race baiting, blaming the "crisis" on "dangerous criminal cartels" somehow "allowed to infiltrate and spread throughout the nation," and invoked the fabricated nexus of immigration/drugs/crime in order to tout his southern border wall.[42]

Lost in his administration's facile response is that the "crisis" permits some to profit greatly from the suffering of others. For instance, while Trump insists his approach to the crisis will be a "beautiful thing to see," his enacted "tax reform" changes will make it much more difficult for the needy to access treatment programs through Medicaid. What's more, as Daniel Denvir recently reported, aided by increased demand, price hikes, and other production maneuvers, increased aggregate sales of Naloxone—from roughly 20 million in 2011 to nearly 280 million in 2016—marked a boon for some of the same companies that have profited from the sale of opioids.[43] Yet perhaps the most stunning bit of hypocrisy illustrated by the Trump administration's approach to the opioid crisis was his attempt to appoint Pennsylvania Congressman Tom Marino as his "drug czar" (director of the Office of National Drug Control Policy). As the *Washington Post* and NPR revealed, legislation sponsored by Marino, under the guise of "ensuring patient access," profoundly limited the DEA's ability to investigate "doctor shopping and suspicious orders" and greatly increased pharmaceutical diversion to his home state and other states hit hardest by addiction and overdose deaths.[44] From invoking failed Reagan-era politics of "just say no" to allowing the pharmaceutical industry and its adjuncts to drive national policy, when it comes to "the worst drug crisis in American . . . and even world history," it is quite clear to us that the fox is guarding the henhouse.

And so it seems, for now, it is business as usual for the postindustrial Rust Belt and southern Appalachia, as the crisis of the moment has opened up new avenues for the enrichment of some on the misery of others. Over yonder sits a new mode of extraction, a complex if you will, organized around the opioid problem, with the police and prison at its center. If we are to discover a better, more humane solution to the conditions that make the opioid problem a reality, we will not do so in self-referential accounts such as Vance's that stubbornly invest in a nostalgic if not illusory past and refuse to admit that a different future is possible.

NOTES

1. J. D. Vance, *Hillbilly Elegy: A Memoir of a Family and Culture in Crisis* (New York: HarperCollins, 2016).
2. Eric Eyre, "Drug Firms Poured 780M Painkillers into WV amid Rise of Overdoses," *Charleston (WV) Gazette-Mail*, December 17, 2016, http://www.wvgazettemail.com/news-health/20161217/drug-firms-poured-780m-painkillers-into-wv-amid-rise-of-overdoses. According to the government's own estimates, in 2016 drug overdoses took the lives of more than fifty thousand Americans, outpacing the number of accidental deaths resulting from automobile accidents and gun violence. https://www.cdc.gov/nchs/nvss/deaths.htm.
3. Eyre, "Drug Firms Poured 780M Painkillers into WV."
4. Eric Eyre, "'Suspicious' Drug Order Rules Never Enforced by State," *Charleston (WV) Gazette-Mail*, December 27, 2017, https://www.wvgazettemail.com/news/health/suspicious-drug-order-rules-never-enforced-by-state/article_3c9f1983-9044-5e97-87ff-df5ed5e55418.html.
5. Jennifer Senior, "Review: In 'Hillbilly Elegy,' a Tough Love Analysis of the Poor Who Back Trump," *New York Times*, August 10, 2016, https://nyti.ms/2jAuPgc.
6. Sarah Jones, "J. D. Vance, the False Prophet of Blue America," *New Republic*, November 17, 2016, https://newrepublic.com/article/138717/jd-vance-false-prophet-blue-america.
7. Mark Fisher, *Capitalist Realism: Is There No Alternative?* (Alresford: John Hunt, 2009).
8. Julie Netherland and Helena B. Hansen, "The War on Drugs That Wasn't: Wasted Whiteness, 'Dirty Doctors,' and Race in Media Coverage of Prescription Opioid Misuse," *Culture, Medicine, and Psychiatry* 40, no. 4 (2016): 664–86.
9. Katherine McLean, "From 'Junkies' to 'Soccer Moms': Newspaper Representations of Overdose, 1988–2014," *Critical Criminology* 25, no. 3 (2017): 411–32; Katharine Q Seelye, "In Heroin Crisis, White Families Seek Gentler War on Drugs," *New York Times*, October 30, 2015, https://nyti.ms/2k2aZr8.
10. Kirsten West Savali, "Michelle Alexander on the War on Drugs: The Color of Drug Users Got Whiter, the Nation Got Nicer," *Root*, October 17, 2017, https://www.theroot.com/michelle-alexander-delivers-fiery-keynote-at-dpa-s-2017-1819453125.
11. Josh Keller and Adam Pearce, "This Small Indiana County Sends More People to Prison Than San Francisco and Durham, NC, Combined. Why?," *New York Times*, September 2, 2016, https://nyti.ms/2jQTP20.
12. Brett Story and Judah Schept, "Against Punishment: Centering Work, Wages and Uneven Development in Mapping the Carceral State," *Social Justice: A Journal of Crime, Conflict and World Order* (forthcoming).
13. Ronald D. Eller, *Miners, Millhands, and Mountaineers: Industrialization of the Appalachian South, 1880–1930* (Knoxville: University of Tennessee Press, 1982).
14. Judah Schept, "Sunk Capital, Sinking Prisons, Stinking Landfills: Landscape, Ideology and the Carceral State in Central Appalachia," in *The Routledge Handbook of Visual Criminology*, ed. Michelle Brown and Eamonn Carrabine (New York: Routledge, 2017), 497–513.
15. Jones, "J. D. Vance."

16. Mike Davis, "The Great God Trump and the White Working Class," *Catalyst: A Journal of Theory & Practice* 1, no. 1 (2017): 151–72.

17. Kevin Williamson, "The Father-Führer," *National Review*, March 28, 2016.

18. Charles Murray, *Coming Apart: The State of White America, 1960–2010* (New York: Crown Forum, 2012). Murray has for years warned of the sins of the "white underclass," most recently in *Coming Apart*.

19. Emelie K. Peine and Kai A. Schafft, "Moonshine, Mountaineers, and Modernity: Distilling Cultural History in the Southern Appalachian Mountains," *Journal of Appalachian Studies* 18, nos. 1/2 (Spring/Fall 2012): 93–112. As Peine and Schafft have shown, drugs and alcohol have for centuries been used as such a wedge to reaffirm the understanding of the entire Appalachian region as backward, antimodern, and ultimately unsalvageable.

20. J. D. Vance, "America's Forgotten Working Class" (TED: Ideas Worth Spreading, September 2016), https://www.ted.com/talks/j_d_vance_america_s_forgotten_working_class.

21. Paul Draus and Juliette Roddy, "Ghosts, Devils, and the Undead City: Detroit and the Narrative of Monstrosity," *Space and Culture* 19, no. 1 (2016): 67–79.

22. Nick Reding, *Methland: The Death and Life of an American Small Town* (New York: Bloomsbury, 2010).

23. Anthony Harkins, *Hillbilly: A Culture History of an American Icon* (New York: Oxford University Press, 2003).

24. William J. Chambliss, "A Sociological Analysis of the Law of Vagrancy," *Social Problems* 12, no. 1 (1964): 67–77; Peter Linebaugh, *Stop, Thief!: The Commons, Enclosures, and Resistance* (Oakland: PM Press, 2014).

25. Mark Neocleous, *The Fabrication of Social Order: A Critical Theory of Police Power* (New York: Pluto Press, 2000). In conceptual terms, these independent individuals appeared as "dissolute condition of masterless men, without subject to Lawes, and a coercive Power to tye their hands." As "masterless men" free from the traditional authorities that existed under feudalism, their social, economic, and political condition appeared to undermine the social order and they were considered disorderly. It is in this context that the police project has its roots (ibid., 3).

26. Travis Linnemann, *Meth Wars: Police, Media, Power* (New York: NYU Press, 2016).

27. Williamson, "Father-Führer." Here it is useful to recall Michel Foucault's discussion of the plague in *Discipline and Punish*, wherein the leper colony and the plague city formed as dialectical modes of discipline, the former a zone of banishment and the latter a space where subjects were to produce normality by perpetually examining themselves and others for signs of impurity. Michel Foucault, *Discipline and Punish: The Birth of the Prison* (New York: Vintage, 2012), 197–98.

28. J. P. Leary, "Detroitism," *Guernica*, January 15, 2011, https://www.guernicamag.com/leary_1_15_11/.

29. Fisher, *Capitalist Realism*.

30. Alison Shonkwiler and Leigh Claire La Berge, eds., *Reading Capitalist Realism* (Iowa City: University of Iowa Press, 2014).

31. Yet even those who endorse the validity of the contentious notion of Appalachian

fatalism argue that its origins lie in material conditions—poverty and isolation—rather than immutable cultural traditions.

32. Vance, "America's Forgotten Working Class."

33. Bari Weiss, "Admit This Ex-Con to the Connecticut Bar," *New York Times*, August 9, 2017, https://www.nytimes.com/2017/08/09/opinion/admit-this-ex-con-to-the-connecticut-bar.html.

34. Fisher, *Capitalist Realism*.

35. Sandra Lee Barney, *Authorized to Heal: Gender, Class, and the Transformation of Medicine in Appalachia, 1880–1930* (Chapel Hill: University of North Carolina Press, 2003).

36. Charles Murray, "The Coming White Underclass," *Wall Street Journal*, October 29, 1993, A-14, http://www.aei.org/publication/the-coming-white-underclass/.

37. Nancy Isenberg, *White Trash: The 400-Year Untold History of Class in America* (New York: Penguin, 2016). By no small coincidence, the roots of this ideology perhaps run deepest in the region Vance has called home. As historian Keri Leigh Merritt has recently shown, in the Antebellum South, wealthy slaveholders mobilized the criminal law, particularly vagrancy statutes and alcohol ordinances, in order to keep poor whites from mixing with and inciting black slaves in hopes of maintaining the slave economy and preserving the broader bourgeois order. See Keri Leight Merritt, *Masterless Men: Poor Whites and Slavery in the Antebellum South* (Cambridge: Cambridge University Press, 2017).

38. Maia Szalavitz, "Ohio Lawmaker Suggests Letting People Die If They've Overdosed Twice Before," *Tonic*, June 27, 2017, https://tonic.vice.com/en_us/article/zmejd9/ohio-lawmaker-dan-picard-three-strikes-let-people-die-if-theyve-overdosed-twice-before.

39. Ed Richter, "Middletown Councilman Has 'No Regrets' about Overdose Comments," *Journal-News*, June 29, 2017, https://www.journal-news.com/news/middletown-councilman-has-regrets-about-overdose-comments/iRyfMw7KvWABWfUUw8qV6H/.

40. Cleve R. Wootson Jr., "Why This Ohio Sheriff Refuses to Let His Deputies Carry Narcan to Reverse Overdoses," *Washington Post,* July 8, 2017, https://www.washingtonpost.com/news/to-your-health/wp/2017/07/08/an-ohio-countys-deputies-could-reverse-heroin-overdoses-the-sheriff-wont-letthem/?noredirect=on&utm_term=.ca78dc23f83e.

41. Christoph Cox and Molly Whalen, "On Evil: An Interview with Alain Badiou," *Cabinet Magazine Online* 5 (2001): 2.

42. "Remarks by President Trump on Combatting Drug Demand and the Opioid Crisis" (White House, October 26, 2017), https://www.whitehouse.gov/briefings-statements/remarks-president-trump-combatting-drug-demand-opioid-crisis/.

43. Daniel Denvir, "These Pharmaceutical Companies Are Making a Killing Off the Opioid Crisis," *Nation*, December 20, 2017, https://www.thenation.com/article/these-pharmaceutical-companies-are-making-a-killing-off-the-opioid-crisis/.

44. Bill Chappell, "Tom Marino, Trump's Pick as Drug Czar, Withdraws after Damaging Opioid Report" (National Public Radio, October 17, 2017), https://www.npr.org/sections/thetwo-way/2017/10/17/558276546/tom-marino-trumps-pick-as-drug-czar-withdraws-after-damaging-opioid-report.

RESPONDING

KEEP YOUR "ELEGY": THE APPALACHIA I KNOW IS VERY MUCH ALIVE

IVY BRASHEAR

DELLA COMBS BRASHEAR had had enough.

She backed her Cadillac long-ways across the one-lane road in front of her house, lit the Virginia Slim in her mouth, pulled her .38 pistol from her purse, and waited, stone-faced and determined, for the next coal truck to come along.

The trucks had been running day and night up and down the head of the Left Fork of Maces Creek in front of her house every day for weeks. They were coating every bit of furniture in and outside her home with a thick layer of gray coal dust. Her kitchen counter; the rocking chair she sat in while watching *The Price Is Right* in the morning and *Wheel of Fortune* in the evening; the porch swing; the hanging ferns that encircled the porch. Nothing could escape the intrusive, insidious dust kicked up from the road by the trucks as they barreled back and forth to the strip mine on the overlooking mountain. The dust swirled in thick, gray clouds around the house, seeping in under the front door and closed windows. It buried everything. No matter Della's efforts to keep the tides at bay, coal-dust tsunamis were inescapable.

There's only so many times a woman bound to the code of Clorox, Pledge, and Windex can clean up after someone else's mess before the time comes to act.

She wasn't afraid of jail. "They'll give me three hot meals a day and a place to sleep," she proclaimed to my Dad when he tried to persuade her to remove her one-woman barricade. And she wasn't really making a political stand against an oppressive, thieving industry. She was more interested in defending her home from unwanted, unclean intrusions.

She didn't make the trucks stop forever; but, they did turn around and go home that infamous day when she couldn't take it any longer. A small victory for a woman who fought for nearly everything she had.

Fierce is a good word for Della Combs. Fiercely loyal to her children and grandchildren. She once threated a coach at the local high school so he would give her son a letterman jacket. Fierce advocate for doing unto others as you would have them do unto you. Legend has it she kept most of the hungry children in Christopher, Kentucky, fed their entire childhoods. Fierce mountain woman who had big dreams of city life, playing piano and singing in Chicago or New York City, but who instead married a man her mother picked for her before she graduated high school. She stayed with him until the end of her life because of a fierce sense of duty.

To me, though, she was Granny Della. A fierce storyteller who had the most enormous zest for life and love, with the heart to match. Her laugh seemed to always echo off the walls and reverberate off the hills that held the holler. Music was her one true love, second only to the fierce, expansive love she had for her family. Made-up songs about everyday life rolled over her lips as easily as the fog rolls into the valleys. She would often catch a word someone spoke to her, and trail off into a song containing the word.

"The sun sure is shining bright today," someone would say. She'd answer in melody: "In the pines / in the pines / where the sun never shines. . . ."

She always wore pink lipstick and white powder, and clip-on earrings. She had arthritis in her toes from a youth spent in high heels with matching dresses. She was a beautiful woman. Once, she took her two firstborn to have their portraits made in Hazard, and the photographer was so struck by her beauty, he insisted on taking her portrait too. She's wearing pearls in the photo. She was always put-together like that. She maintained a standing hair appointment every Friday at Dascum's Beauty Shop in Vicco. She always had short hair, which she preferred, even for her only daughter, my Mom, who preferred the opposite of almost everything her parents wanted.

Granny Della got her driver's license and earned her GED when she was in her forties. She kept a newspaper clipping in a drawer that was a picture of her and her fellow GED recipients that year. She lived a life of confinement in some ways, always meeting others' expectations, and sidelining her own dreams in the process. Her middle age was about reclaiming her independence—creating a life outside her husband and her children. She was, and remains, one of the fiercest, strongest women I've ever known.

I grew up her neighbor. We lived just up the hill from her, and I knew her door was always open to me. I could run down the hill, and into her house without warning any day, and she would welcome me in, offering me food and conversation. I was often in her kitchen as she put up peaches in Ziploc bags for winter, or watered her beloved hanging ferns that encased her porch. She played piano every Sunday at Lone Pine Baptist Church—the family church founded by my great-grandfather, less than a mile from my home. When she told me I had "piano fingers," I felt so special, like she had chosen me to carry on her music. Sometimes, Mom and I would visit in the evenings, and watch *Wheel of Fortune* with her. In the summer, her porch would be full of family who lived within a mile radius. Great aunts and uncles, cousins, neighbors. Life updates and family stories would be swapped late into the gloaming hours of the evening.

Granny Della was gregarious and outspoken, once telling a man to "get a life and get a job," and another time telling Lone Pine's preacher he was wrong about God not giving people talent they didn't have to learn. Everyone knew where they stood with her, and where she stood on certain issues. Mostly, everyone knew you didn't cross her, or disrespect her. They revered her, and praised her, and followed her lead. She was one fierce mountain woman, and it showed.

But, I would never, ever—in my wildest dreams or imaginings—disrespect her in any format because of her fierceness by calling her a lunatic, as J. D. Vance so often refers to his Mamaw in his memoir, *Hillbilly Elegy*.

The way he describes this woman, whom he claims to revere and credits as the reason he made it out of his low-income life in suburban Ohio and into Yale Law School, is shameful. It displays a willingness to sell out his family members by tapping into a long history of distorted, false, and intentionally made stereotypical images of central Appalachia that have been imposed on the region by outside media makers for nearly three hundred years, ever since the first white land prospectors were sent into the region by George Washington himself.

Vance's willingness to tap into that long history of misleading images of the place and people who live there proves his end game: monetary gain and national notoriety to bolster a potential political run for office—supported, of course, by his carefully created and curated self-image as the so-called "expert" on the white working class of Appalachia, a place in which he has never lived. His only connection to its realities were visits with grandparents who traveled home for short periods for a few summers when Vance was a child.

However, what's more insidious about his rise to fame on a book largely made up of descriptions of Appalachian stereotypes he attempts to pass off as universal truths is the fact that people will read his book, and assume all Appalachian people, if they are smart, are trying to actively run away from their culture; they will understand it to be less than and the people they came from to be crazy lunatics. This, to me, is one of the more personal attacks that Vance hurls at Appalachian people in his 261-page simultaneous fetishization and admonishment of my culture.

Elegy has no class, no heart, and no warmth. It's a poorly written appropriation of Appalachian stereotypes about violent, ignorant, and slovenly hillbillies who refuse to help themselves despite having every opportunity to do so.

Vance makes broad generalizations about class and wealth, insinuating that everyone living in the region lives in poverty, or among some mythical ruins of working-class life. He clings to that fictionalized past of working-class nostalgia, and assumes that all our problems come from white men being out of work. He paints the region white, completely erasing the economic and cultural contributions and existence of Appalachian people of color. And perhaps most glaring of all, he blames the people of Appalachia for the economic and social problems they now face, which, in actuality, they had very little hand in creating.

The systemic challenges Appalachia faces, such as poverty, drug addiction, economic collapse, and poor public health, have been caused almost entirely by the capitalist greed of extraction companies. From salt to timber to coal to gas, absentee companies have stripped Appalachia of every resource from which they could make a buck, and left very little wealth behind. Just like my Granny Della having to Clorox the coal-dust grime from her porch furniture, Appalachian people have been left to clean up the various economic, social, public health, and environmental messes extraction companies have dumped upon us, leaving very few internal or external resources from which to build.

Big media have highlighted and exploited these systemic challenges and problems in recent years, and used them to identify Appalachia as the scapegoat for all of America's social and economic ills. If we can just solve the problem of Appalachia, they posit, we can save America. Naturally, since big media seemingly always choose the path of least resistance, J. D. Vance has become their "Appalachian Darling," appearing on news shows and on panels of so-called middle America experts. *Hillbilly Elegy* also benefited from a great deal of coincidence in the American social change calendar, published at precisely the right moment to become a part of the national zeitgeist about the largely exaggerated and much misunderstood role of the "white working class" in the election of Trump.

As a result, thousands and hundreds of years of lived Appalachian experience, and almost fifty years of dedicated Appalachian scholarship, have been stepped over by the national media in favor of the misleading, oversimplified, and stereotypical narrative about Appalachia that fits their preconceived notions of the region: a self-named death poem about a place that most people have long since already buried in their hearts and minds.

Much has been missed in the hype about *Hillbilly Elegy*; most importantly that it presents Appalachians as a forgotten people who aren't worthy of anything but derision and pity, and who cannot be helped because we refuse to help ourselves. Vance writes—and many who've read his book believe—that our very DNA betrays and condemns us to a life of strife, regardless of what monumental efforts at change we might make.

The book also assumes there is some special sect of the working class that is especially dedicated to straight, white men. This narrative line of thinking and acting is now largely understood as a dog whistle for white supremacist ideology. In fact, when white supremacist neo-Nazi groups descended on

Pikeville, Kentucky, in April 2017, the flyers and messaging they disseminated on social media co-opted the very bootstraps language Vance uses repeatedly in *Elegy*. It also can't be ignored that Vance was outed in 2017 as having met with Steve Bannon, former aide to Donald Trump, executive chairman of Breitbart News, and well-known race baiter.

His narrative of the region also badly distorts its true demographic diversity. It ignores any person who is brown, black, queer, or progressive and, by default, assumes these groups of people simply do not exist in the region, and even if they do, aren't worth talking about or investing in. Rife with fragile masculinity, *Elegy* forgets that most men in the region are no longer coal miners, or factory workers, and that they haven't been for some time, and that their understanding of masculinity is no longer tied to old ideas about what it means to be a man.

Vance also actively diminishes, glosses over, and ignores the reality of the critical role that Appalachian women play, and have played, in the economy and in shaping the region's culture and understanding of itself. Appalachia, in fact, is a very matriarchal culture. We revere our grandmothers and mothers. We follow their lead as they enter the workforce because their husbands have been laid off. For generations, they have grown and harvested our food and fed our bellies three times a day with snacks in between. They have stood on picket lines when men were banned from doing so. They have chained themselves to bulldozers and refused to leave their homes. They prop up our economy in a way that is largely ignored and made invisible and unimportant in false narratives like Vance's. In reality, the work and contributions of women, people of color, and queer folks across the region are vital to its past, present, and future survival.

In short, *Hillbilly Elegy* presents an Appalachia in which my experiences and those of my family, and those of many of the people I know and love in the region, do not exist. It erases my story: a young, queer Appalachian with roots ten generations deep in eastern Kentucky, whose ancestors settled the head of the Left Fork of Maces Creek five generations ago, in the 1830s. I hold within me the fierce loyalty and determination of my Granny Della, the unconditional compassion of my Granny Hazel, the individuality of my parents, and the mountain heart and soul—the pride and dignity—of all my ancestors combined.

I come from a culture and a family of dignity and grace and laughter and joy—none of which exists in J. D. Vance's fictitious Appalachia. I spent my childhood running in the hills with my cousins and older brother. Family gatherings for birthdays and holidays and Sundays were our reality.

We were surrounded by our ancestors from whom we heard stories of their youth and what it was like to grow up as the children of subsistence farmers. We learned about the intense difficulty of that life—farming all day, until dark, waking up the next day, and doing it all over again. But, we also learned of the intense dignity of that life. What it meant to till the earth on which my family still lives at the head of the Left Fork of Maces Creek, and how it felt to have everything they ever needed to live and thrive at their fingertips, grown or raised or made with their own hands. How they took care of each other, no matter their socioeconomic status or their political leanings or the hardships one family might have faced more severely than another. We learned lessons of self-reliance and community building from them.

My parents co-owned a gas station in Jeff throughout my childhood, and I spent many evenings and weekends making the store my playground. I built forts out of cases of pop, and played Legos in the office just behind the counter. Students from neighboring Dilce Combs Memorial High School snuck away to Jeff Mart between classes and on their lunch breaks for hots dogs and pop. Some of them even worked for my parents. There were regulars who came into Jeff Mart every day just to be somewhere in between work and home. They were coal miners, construction workers, county officials, teachers. All walks of Appalachian life.

I grew up at Viper Elementary with my classmates, whose parents also worked in a broad mix of jobs. I'm sure some of their dads were coal miners, though I only remember kids of nurses and teacher's aides, and mechanics. We played basketball together, and were on the academic team together. We tried to learn instruments together so we could be in the band. That didn't work out so well for me, but I did enjoy playing Pokémon with the other Gameboy nerds in my class. Just like I enjoyed playing "Donkey Kong" and "Zelda" on Super Nintendo with my brother and cousin after school every day. We played until we made it to the end and beat the whole game. Video games were a favorite past time when I wasn't reading *The Diary of Anne Frank* or writing my own stories for fun.

In high school, I played soccer. I went to prom. I hung out with my friends on the weekends. We went to the movies and watched the latest releases. We went to the high school hangout spots: Perry County Park and the local Applebee's. We made our grades, we passed our classes, we graduated, and many of us went on to college or some other form of postsecondary education. Most of the people I knew in high school are now happily employed as nurses and lab techs, or teachers, or pharmacists or lawyers. Most of them are married with young children. Many of them still live in their home region of Appalachia, because contrary to what Vance would have his readers believe, most of us are not actively trying to leave our home because of cultural deficiencies we can overcome or escape only by getting as far away as possible. Instead, most of us are trying to stay and raise our families in the place we know and love.

I certainly do not discount the difficult childhood that Vance lived through and his own lived experience that he describes in detail in his book. However, I do take great issue with the ways in which his narrative of the region erases and erodes any Appalachian experience outside his own non-Appalachian experience by reinforcing repeatedly that Appalachian "hillbilly" culture is somehow deficient and morally decrepit, and that it is something to be overcome and escaped from without looking back.

Misrepresentation of Appalachia matters for several reasons. It obscures and intentionally eclipses the pride and dignity of being Appalachian—pride and dignity I personally and many other Appalachian people feel deep within ourselves. Pride and dignity that I was told stories about by my elders, that my high school friends expound upon on Facebook, that my aunt Delilah Sue once told me to never forget and never lose. *Hillbilly Elegy* instead tells us—like so many false narratives before it have—that we should be ashamed of who we are, where we come from, and the people in our blood. It says to us that we aren't worthy or deserving of anything more than being the butt of a joke. Such messages hit us hard in our guts, because the truth is way more complicated and way more real, and nobody likes tales to be carried about them.

Hillbilly Elegy not only demeans Appalachians, it presents a hackneyed, stereotypical view of the region to everyone who doesn't live there and who have no connections to it. It plays right into the ways in which people outside of the region have already been conditioned to see us. It gives them permission to not care about investing in our future because, according to Vance's book, Appalachian people don't deserve saving, and they wouldn't appreciate it anyway, and the best hope for the region and its people is to write them all off as an inevitable and unavoidable loss—a lost people consumed by the fault of their DNA that the rest of America just couldn't save, despite their best efforts.

Appalachians have been fighting back against that narrative for decades. Although he likely thinks his views and opinions about the region are revolutionary, J. D. Vance adds nothing new to the conversation about Appalachia. In fact, he only recycles and updates old narratives we Appalachians have heard a million times before: we are a deficient people not worthy of anything more than what we've already been given, not sophisticated enough to bring into the mainstream, and not important enough to be used as anything more than pawns by coal company owners, mass media makers, and would-be Ohio politicians.

Perhaps the thing that bothers me most about Vance's narrative is his unabashed misrepresentation of my home region without so much as a backward glance to make sure he didn't run over anyone on his road toward national prominence.

Hillbilly Elegy actively and intentionally ignores and excludes the real life, lived experiences of all but a minority of Appalachian people. It ignores my fierce Granny Della and my Granny Hazel, who smelled of starch and taught me how to feed the chickens and always had breakfast waiting for me when I had to stay with her on a sick day. It certainly doesn't tell the stories of my Grandpa Earl, who liberated concentration camps, who referred to me exclusively by my middle name, Jude, and who always had a Werther's candy ready for me. My Poppy Harold's story is left out. He was too young to enlist during World War II, so he signed up as a Victory Farm Volunteer, and worked for a time on a dairy farm in northern Maine during the war. Both he and my Pa Earl were water boys for the WPA, carrying water to workers building roads near their homeplaces for twenty-five cents a day. Poppy Harold was a construction worker with an eighth-grade education who's built dozens of homes and buildings in Perry County. To this day, he lists FDR as his favorite president.

The multifaceted lives of my Mom and Dad are also left out. They hung Modigliani and Van Gogh and Paolo Soleri prints on the walls of our home. They played NPR every Sunday morning while Dad fried bacon and made scrambled eggs for us before we went to Sunday school at Lone Pine. They fought the dam at Red River Gorge, the racists in Hazard, the strip-mining companies for which Dad used to work. Mom worked on an Appalachian oral history project in the early 1970s through Alice Lloyd College. She was editor of the long-since-defunct *Mountain Review Magazine*, which was a publication of Appalshop, the media, arts, and cultural center in Whitesburg that blossomed out of a War on Poverty program. Until he started working at Trus Joist, a wood-product manufacturing factory just outside of Hazard, Dad was home to cook supper for us every day. To this day, the sound of a range hood going and water boiling on the stove brings me incredible comfort.

Late in life, they both went back to school and got their degrees. Mom got her teaching degree and recently retired after a decades-long career. Dad became a respiratory therapist after Trus Joist left town when their tax breaks dried up. He's still working at the local hospital.

These men and women lived, and still do live, complex lives in the mountains, and harbor complex thoughts. They raised families and helped build communities in the mountains. They carried, and still do carry, deep knowledge of land and place in their heads. But you won't hear their stories in narratives such as *Hillbilly Elegy*. Instead, Vance relies on easier, lazier stories based heavily on stereotypes rather than taking a more nuanced approach to complicate and expand the narrative of a diverse place full of diverse people.

Hillbilly Elegy's danger is that it continues the long tradition of presenting Appalachia as a monolithic region and a group of people characterized only by laziness and violence and dislike of anyone or anything different. For those of us who are trying to shift the narrative of our place toward one that is more honest and complex as a means of rebuilding our communities and our economy, Vance's book is akin to mining coal in the modern era with a pickax. It is increasingly difficult to reclaim and reshape the story of Appalachia when we constantly have to fight back against misleading and harmful portrayals of the region that are rabidly consumed and mass marketed to people not from this place who are unwilling to seek a deeper understanding of people and place.

This is the cycle of media exploitation of Appalachia, and J. D. Vance knows it well. He has used it to produce a *New York Times* best seller and a career commenting on Appalachia's challenges that never delves deeper than the surface level. He sees what he wants to see, and what he must see in order to fulfill the decades-long narrative of the lazy, ignorant hillbilly. Perpetuating this narrow view is increasingly detrimental to Appalachia's economic revival that has picked up considerable steam in the past ten years.

There is no way we can rebuild a brighter future in the region—one that is non-extractive and regenerative, and that considers the lives, opinions, and wealth generation of all our neighbors as valuable—if we don't complicate our narrative by making it more diverse and more real. And if we must consistently pause our work to fight back against lazy and ignorant stories disseminated like propaganda about our universal laziness and ignorance, we will have very little time left to tell more honest stories about the region.

And the truth is, we are an incredibly diverse people in ethnicity, race, class, beliefs, and thoughts, just like any other place in America. We are the descendants of native peoples, slaves, subsistence farmers, coal miners, homemakers, school teachers, sharecroppers, business owners, Eastern Europeans, and Africans. A rapidly increasing number of us have come from Mexico or South America. We are gay, straight, and everything in between. We are Democrats and Republicans, and more than anything, most of us don't vote at all because of apathy and disenfranchisement. Some of us are coal miners, but more of us work in health care. Some of us live in abject poverty, a few of us live in extreme wealth, and most of us live in the middle, trying desperately month to month to make it all work. In these ways, we are very similar to any other rural place in America right now, just trying to figure out our place in a twenty-first-century world that has, for the most part, left us to fend for ourselves.

Whether J. D. Vance or anybody else in big media's orbit wants to admit it, those of us who are from or who currently live in the region are *all* Appalachians, and we all have a story to tell about the place we love—the place where our bones are from, the place Vance could only dream of ever truly knowing.

My Granny Della had had enough that day she stopped the coal trucks with her .38 pistol. Although she didn't end up in jail, and never faced any punitive action for taking her stand, she took matters into her own hands because, as the descendent of generations of people who had to do for themselves just to survive, she inherently knew that's the way of Appalachian people. Perhaps, rather than the false narratives about our DNA being encoded with laziness and poverty, the true makeup of our genes is intense self-reliance. We've always had everything taken from us, and we've always had other people telling us—and everyone else—who we are. So, we've had to make do with what we already had for decades.

As a result, we've become experts at cleaning up other people's messes. We've cleaned up the messes and environmental disasters left by extraction companies, and the artificial messes corporations tried to make between and among races. And we've worked to clean up the mess big media have made us into. And long after we clean up what J. D. Vance has done, we'll go on living in this place, making stories here and telling them to anyone who will listen. Maybe someday our complex stories will overpower the simpler, false narratives about our place. Until then, we'll be waiting to clean up any new messes, while simultaneously building our brighter future despite the narratives telling us we can't do it, and that we aren't worth it. We simply know better, and more than anything, we've had enough of those lies.

HE SAID/SHE SAID

CRYSTAL GOOD

HE doesn't speak for me.
HE doesn't know me.
HE is Scots-Irish.
HE is not Affrilachian. Mamaw said he can't even spell it.
HE likes to talk about himself. Too much about himself.
Mamaw said that's normal in the Rustbelt. We aren't sure where
    HE is from.
HE is a memoir.
HE is a best seller.
HE went to Yale Law y'all.
HE is fight or flight first class.
HE takes out white trash in Black Lives Matter bags.
HE is not a Redneck. Mamaw is a Redneck. Mamaw always with her red
    bandana on.
HE didn't vote for the welfare of Miss Appalachia Welfare Queen.
HE has class mobility.
HE parks his car at the White House.
HE doesn't have any bumper stickers. Mamaw said that's a lie
HE has one: TRUMP
HE does not drive a Subaru.
HE has a vanity plate: Make America Great Again.

HE is punctual, right and on the times.

HE goes to the movies with Opie.

HE was a gift. Mamaw said I bet git to the library if I want to read that crap.
    She won't let

HE come in the house.

HE was already checked out.

HE came in the mail. My rich uncle sent,

HE is a lawyer.

HE loves his Mamaw. I love my Mamaw too.

SHE is mountain wise. She just tricked me to read,

HE—Hillbilly Elegy.

THE HILLBILLY MIRACLE AND THE FALL

MICHAEL E. MALONEY

IN THIS ESSAY, I present an overview of the migration of people from the Cumberland Mountains of Kentucky and Tennessee to southwestern Ohio and northern Kentucky, describe the variety of communities we established, provide a narrative of my own family's experience, and contrast that with J. D. Vance's family story in *Hillbilly Elegy*. I use the framework of the Miracle and the Fall to explain some of the differences between Vance's family narrative and mine. By the Miracle, I mean the enormous success story that Appalachian migration was for most of its participants. By the Fall, I mean the economic collapse some of our families, individuals, and communities experienced in the wake of automation, deindustrialization, and globalization. This collapse affected some but not all Appalachian communities in southwestern Ohio and northern Kentucky. The application of this framework for this essay is that my family story is about the Miracle. Vance's story is about the Fall. Both narratives describe part of the reality.

THE MIRACLE

The story of the Cumberland mountain people of eastern Kentucky and eastern Tennessee is intimately bound up with the communities in northern Kentucky and southwestern Ohio where so many of us migrated during the twentieth century. Although our migration peaked in the period between 1940 and 1970, Appalachian enclaves in such places as northern Kentucky, Cincinnati, Dayton, Norwood, and Middletown began at least as early as the 1920s. Men came to work in such factories as Newport Steel, Stearns and Foster in Lockland, Armco in Middletown, Frigidaire in Dayton, General Motors in Norwood, and Champion Paper in Hamilton. Appalachian men, through much of the twentieth century, built the cars and appliances, made the paper, built the houses, cut the trees, and drove the trucks that helped make America and those cities what they are today. The women entered the workforce too. They worked in factories such as Avon, Kenner Toy, and Nutone. They worked as waitresses, maids, and cleaning ladies. Those who managed to get through college became a large workforce component of such fields as teaching, nursing, and secretarial work. About 10 percent of these men and women became business owners and professionals.[1] The vast majority, though, remained blue-collar workers, some in union jobs with good benefits, others in the secondary labor force where work was hard, wages low, and benefits (health, retirement, etc.) inferior. About 20 percent at some time had to resort to welfare and other kinds of transfer payments. Heavy drinking was common among younger men, but most matured and became solid family providers. Until recently, other substance abuse was not a big problem. Most men and many women were able to retire with pensions and health benefits. In fact, as late as 1990, family composition in working-class Appalachian neighborhoods was similar to that in white affluent areas except in the poorest areas such as Cincinnati's Lower Price Hill. This means that most children had two parents as well as some extended family support.

When I think of Appalachian communities in southwestern Ohio and northern Kentucky, four images come to mind. The first is miles and miles of modest homes in the cities and scattered suburbs owned by first-, second-, and third-generation Appalachians. Second, I think of assimilated Appalachians living in bigger suburban homes or in gentrified sections of the cities. Third, I think of low-income enclaves such as Cincinnati's Lower Price Hill and South Fairmount, where most people are renters. Finally, I think of families living on small farms or in mobile homes along the side of the rural highways extending out from Cincinnati, Dayton, and Indianapolis. A comprehensive understanding of the world of former Appalachian migrants needs to include all such places, not just abandoned factory towns like Middletown and Portsmouth, and also the different classes in most communities. Jackson,

Kentucky, J. D. Vance's parents' home town, for example, has a prosperous suburb where many professionals and merchants live.

During the period of the great migration of the mid-twentieth century, some urban Appalachian neighborhoods gained notoriety as rough and rowdy "ports of entry" for the migrants. The most famous perhaps were Cincinnati's Over-the-Rhine, Dayton's Fifth and Wayne, and Chicago's Uptown. There were similar migrant enclaves in many Midwestern and Mid-Atlantic cities and places like Cabbagetown in Atlanta. The inner areas of smaller cities like Hamilton and Middletown in Ohio and Newport in Kentucky were less known but of equal importance as entry points.

Nonetheless, the so-called ports of entry were never home to the majority of Appalachian migrants. From the earliest days of the great migration, Appalachians followed their kinship and friendship networks to affordable housing and jobs throughout the tristate region. Typical among the outlying communities that attracted people from eastern Kentucky is the town of South Lebanon in Warren County, Ohio. South Lebanon was a tiny village in the 1940s. The main source of employment was a mushroom packing factory, but the men and women who moved there from Breathitt and other eastern Kentucky counties could carpool to jobs in Dayton and Cincinnati's northeastern suburbs. Kash D. Amburgy, a radio evangelist, merchant, and housing developer from Owsley County, Kentucky, built five hundred homes by 1960. Today, the South Lebanon area is a booming part of the Cincinnati-Dayton urban sprawl. There is still a blue-collar core, but many of the new homes cost $225,000 to $1 million. This shows that blue-collar enclaves do not inevitably decline. Several largely Appalachian communities in southwestern Ohio have flourished as Cincinnati and Dayton's suburbs expand.

Many of the first-generation migrants to South Lebanon had only an eighth grade education or less, but nonetheless newcomers often stayed with relatives until they, through friends or relatives, got on at one of the factories. Their children typically finished high school, and some were able to get factory jobs; some got postsecondary training or a college degree and went into fields such as sales and service. This shows that Appalachians still retain a certain resiliency, since from the 1960s on the region's manufacturing base with its union-scale jobs and benefits has shrunk rapidly.

The experiences of my generation (people born in the 1930s and 1940s) have been documented by the late James Brown of the University of Kentucky, as well as by his associates and students.[2] These scholars interviewed families in Beech Creek in Clay County, Kentucky, and followed them to South Lebanon, Ohio, and other migrant destinations. What they found was not massive social network breakdown and disorder as could have been expected and was often alleged but functional systems of mutual support within the migrant streams and the "stem-and-branch" families created by migration. Indeed, the migration was so successful that they concluded that for so many people with such little formal education to have migrated in such a short period of time without causing great social upheaval was one of the miracles of twentieth-century American history.[3] However, if one focuses exclusively on the poverty, family breakup, crime, and school failure in the ports-of-entry neighborhoods, one would call them "slums." Herbert Gans in *The Urban Villagers* presented an alternative designation for such places as Boston's Italian immigrant North End—an urban village. He defined this as a place where newcomer ethnic groups rebuild their social structure before moving on to better neighborhoods. This process certainly describes what happened to many of the urban Appalachian families I have worked with in my fifty years of community work in Cincinnati. There were many families, of course, who became casualties as deindustrialization, automation, and globalization replaced the system in which a worker could spend a lifetime with one company and even pass a job along to a child or relative.

THE FALL

The processes of deindustrialization and globalization have certainly taken a great toll. So has gentrification. Most of the urban Appalachian port-of-entry neighborhoods no longer exist. The Appalachians who lived there have been replaced by some combination of urban renewal, gentrification, or ethnic succession. Some of the "second stage" neighborhoods like Cincinnati's South Fairmount and East Price Hill, which are a bit higher in socioeconomic status and have more single-family housing than the original urban villages, still have Appalachians but also have become more ethnically diverse. These neighborhoods were also hit hard by the 2008 recession as families who had taken out risky real estate loans often found themselves evicted after bank foreclosures.

The 2008 recession (in many places, really a depression) seemed to be a turning point for many urban Appalachians and other working-class Americans, a time when the new reality of the postindustrial world set in. Good jobs with a living wage and good benefits were often no longer available. As a result, men and women often had to work two jobs to make ends meet, and many of the jobs people had to take were strenuous and led to injuries and chronic pain. This set the stage for the substance abuse epidemic that has destroyed so many of our families.

It is important to recognize that the "hard living" lifestyle that J. D. Vance's family exemplifies is not new.[4] This way of life with its violence, family discord and breakup, neglect of children, and substance abuse (usually in the form of smoking and drinking) has always been there for a minority of urban Appalachians. It is not fair or accurate, however, to depict this lifestyle as typical of all of Appalachian culture. Instead, we should recognize that this culture includes the positive as well as negative adaptive practices that people employ to cope with their social and economic circumstances. The positive practices include a large informal economy and mutual support.[5]

James Brown and his colleagues in their research in Clay County and South Lebanon in the 1960s described these adaptive practices among rural and urban Appalachians as functional and positive. Rhoda Halperin found the same in her studies of rural Appalachian Kentucky in the 1980s and her ethnographic work in Cincinnati's East End in the 1990s.[6] Brian Alexander, the author of *Glass House*, a study of what happened when a corporate raider shut down a factory in Lancaster, Ohio, found that "it wasn't people's culture that caused the opioid epidemic in Lancaster and Portsmouth . . . it was corporate greed."[7]

Millions of American working-class families have experienced a fall. They have either lost faith in the American Dream or lost the discipline it takes to realize it. Many have also lived in segregated enclaves where strong role models were absent. When did the Fall occur? In Jackson and the Three Forks area of Kentucky where the Vances and Maloneys originated, it happened slowly over time as jobs in oil, timber, mining, and agriculture declined. In Middletown, it happened as Armco (now AK Steel) cut back production in the 1980s, just as Vance was growing up in the Garfield neighborhood. My sister, Nina, and her family were living there then too, and I visited often. I could see the gradual change in the quality of life in the neighborhood. My own nieces and nephews and grandnieces and grandnephews seemed to have adapted to the changing economy, but home ownership and independence seemed to be harder to come by for many of their neighbors.

Another window into the consequences of these changed economics comes from my conversation with Mike Miller, a staff person from the Kentucky River Area Development District (KRADD) who has lived in Jackson much of his life. He says Jackson is in some ways a better place now than when he was growing up there. Lee's Junior College, now Kentucky Community and Technical College, offers four-year degrees through Morehead State and some master's degree programs. There is a hospital now and two high schools. But some of the changes Miller describes are for the worse. The population has declined 30 to 40 percent. "The working people have left," he reports. "The number of poor people is not up but the percentage is because of the population drop. Families used to have six kids. Now they have one or two. There is family breakup and drug abuse. Very few Breathitt County families have no one who is not an addict. Part of it is economics. Some people became disabled through work. My mother had an ironing lady. She developed arthritis and could no longer iron. The doctor put her on pain medications. Her social security was three hundred a month, not enough to cover rent, food, and utilities. She found she could take half of the medications, sell the rest and double her income. When I was a kid, better off people used drugs. Now everybody can afford them." He continued:

Fifteen years ago, Breathitt County had fifteen to nineteen thousand people. The next census may show eleven thousand. The only age group that is growing is the fifty-five to sixty-four group. The workers go to Alabama to work in the mines, to Lexington, to Georgetown, Kentucky [Toyota plant]. The people who worked on the railroad had to leave to keep a job. If you exclude retirement income there are still 50 percent [of the people left] who are on government assistance. In the eight KRADD counties, four to six thousand miners have lost their jobs and each mining job lost takes out two to three related jobs. The drug abuse is related to poverty. This has compounded in the last seven to eight years. If the truth were known, and it isn't, there is a death from overdose every two weeks in Jackson. That is twenty-six deaths a year in a town of twenty-three hundred.

I had expected Miller to tell me things in Jackson were not as bad as Vance describes. I was heartbroken by the conversation. I told Miller so and he said, "I am too."[8]

These changes marked the Fall of Jackson and Breathitt County. Times had always been tough. Hard living was always the lifestyle of some families. But it had now become more the norm than the exception. And it isn't true just for Jackson. In *Glass House*, Brian Alexander describes the Fall of the edge-of-Appalachia town of Lancaster, Ohio, when corporate greed caused the shutdown of the glass factory. Sam Quinones described the same Fall of Portsmouth, Ohio, in his book *Dreamland: The True Tale of America's Opiate Epidemic* and how the negative impact of deindustrialization and globalization was followed by the opioid epidemic.

The core of Middletown and Hamilton in Butler County, Ohio, also experienced the Fall. So did Dayton's East Side neighborhood and some of Cincinnati's neighborhoods, East and Lower Price Hill and Riverside-Sedamsville most notably.[9] At the same time, as these cities experienced relative decay, a whole new city of West Chester flourished in Butler County, just up I-75 from Cincinnati. Immediately to the east, Warren County seems to thrive as well with very low poverty and unemployment rates and growing suburbs. Thousands of upwardly mobile urban Appalachians live in these prosperous new exurbs. South Lebanon's core of modest homes built by Kash Amburgy and other Appalachian migrants is now surrounded by suburbs with new expensive homes. It is my intention here not to explain the stark difference in the fate of these communities but to note that the majority of urban Appalachians do not live in neighborhoods where poverty and social network collapse is the norm.

MY FAMILY'S STORY

My personal and family narrative is in some ways the same as and in some ways different from that of J. D. Vance. Like the Vances, the Maloneys came to the Three Forks area of eastern Kentucky (where the three forks of the Kentucky River meet) in about 1805. They founded the village of Maloney in Lee County, but I was born in Breathitt County a few miles upriver from Maloney. I mostly grew up in Lee County, but Jackson, home base of Vance's family, has also been part of my world since early childhood.

The Maloneys lived in the Three Forks area from 1805 to 1917. They then moved to Middletown, then to the West Virginia coalfields. In 1936 a group of Maloneys came back to Breathitt County from the West Virginia coalfields. My grandparents, parents, and Uncle Marvin's family bought fifty acres of land and built three log cabins in Spencer Bend. I was born there in 1940. Although the feuds that gave "Bloody Breathitt" its name had ended by 1916, the county still had more than its share of violence during my childhood. My grandfather killed a man who tried to rob his sawmill. My father killed one man in a West Virginia coal mine for making a disrespectful remark, another for drawing a gun on him, and another who had murdered my uncle Dewey in Middletown, Ohio, where Dad had worked at the Rolling Mill (Armco Steel, where J. D.'s grandfather later worked). My dad served six months in Moundsville Prison for one of his killings but was released after he proved the other man drew his gun first. He was not prosecuted for the other two. My paternal grandmother once threatened to geld a man with her corn knife when she thought he was making a pass at her. This is quite similar to J. D.'s account of his grandmother who nearly shot two men for attempting to steal the family cow (15). As it was for Vance, telling stories of these and neighbors' incidents of violence was a family pastime. Some of the victims, it was determined, "needed kilt" (deserved to be killed); others were simply caught up in an Appalachian version of a Greek tragedy. My uncle Dewey, for instance, was killed because of his involvement in a love triangle. My father was killed when I was two years old because he took back money that had been stolen from him.

My mother's response to Dad's violent death was to move her children ten miles away so that her sons would not perpetuate a feud with the Sheltons and Johnsons she thought responsible for the murder. As a result, my four sisters finished high school as boarding students at local missionary "settlement" schools and were sent outside Appalachia to colleges run by other Christian institutions. None of them got a four-year degree, but all were taught the social skills that young ladies needed to know. Only one of my four brothers got to go to high school, and he dropped out in his junior year, got married, and joined the Air Force.

The vehicle for my family's migration to southern Ohio was my second oldest sister Jeanne. At the end of World War II, she married a returning soldier from War Creek, Kentucky, a community near my birthplace in Spencer Bend. They settled in South Lebanon in Warren County, north of Cincinnati and near Middletown. Jeanne and her husband Frank bought a house that became the family's beachhead for migration and adjustment to life in Ohio. Each of Jeanne's younger siblings migrated, one at a time, and stayed with Jeanne and Frank until they got jobs and found housing of their own. Jeanne and Frank's house became a social gathering space for our extended family. Jeanne and Frank served as mother and father to the urban branch of this Appalachian stem-and-branch extended family. When one of my brothers got his girlfriend pregnant, Jeanne said, "Now Joe [not his real name], you know you have to marry that girl," which he did. The extended family thus enforced the moral code just as it provided access to jobs, emergency loans, medical care, help with child care, car maintenance, advice, and much of what would someday be provided by social service agencies. As each of my siblings got married and established their own households, they still, to one degree or another, lived within this support system.

The extended family operated like a village. My brother-in-law, Bennie Frazier, worked at Armco and ran a body shop on the side. He served as a mechanic for several other Maloney households. My sister-in-law, Verneda, attended to my sister, Jeanne, when she was suffering from cancer. Several of the women and some of the men had fantastic cooking skills. Family gatherings were usually not planned but seemed to happen spontaneously, and there always seemed to be a pot of beans, cornbread, fried potatoes, and some kind of meat. Or you might just get a bologna sandwich or a dish of fried green tomatoes. In any case, one never went hungry at these gatherings. The social and even economic support of these family networks was invaluable.

Schwarzweller, Brown, and Mangalam described these systems in *Mountain Families in Transition*, and Rhoda Halperin later documented them in *The Livelihood of Kin: Making Ends Meet the Kentucky Way* and in her study of Cincinnati's East End neighborhood.[10] My family's narrative matches both those of Schwarzweller et al. and Halperin on the one hand and that of *Hard Living on Clay Street* on the other. When my family first moved to South Lebanon, some of the men were involved in a certain amount of whoring, weekend drinking, and barroom fights. The Appalachian working-class moral code admonished young men to sow their wild oats while they were young. I was gay and not attracted to this lifestyle but remember enduring a certain amount of social pressure to do the same. For my generation, the pattern was for men to marry, settle down, and become decent family men. Some women also fell into a wild "honky tonk" (hanging out at bars) lifestyle but, like the men, eventually most settled down and raised a family. For my family and most of my generation of migrants, therefore, hard living was either nonexistent or a life cycle phenomenon associated with the teen years through the midtwenties. Men and women who did not "settle down" were pariahs in their communities.

For Vance's family, trips "down home" to Jackson seem to have been the source of a sense of identity and rootedness. Often these return trips were tied to short-term economic hardship, as they were for my family. During the 1940s and 1950s, when my older siblings were trying to get established in South Lebanon, Middletown, and Waynesville, layoffs were common in Ohio factories. During these hard times, my siblings would show up at our place on the hilltop in Lee County. Then when the men got "called back" or found another job, they would return to Ohio. This is one of the ways the extended family helped provide stability. I think these visits for Vance's family and mine were a way of staying rooted in the kinship and friendship systems and in the values of hard work, solidarity, and respectability.

INVOLVEMENT IN COMMUNITY LIFE

My generation of migrants also became embedded in Ohio communities. They established their own churches, bars, and restaurants. In this world you could spend your entire week with minimal contact with people who were not from eastern Kentucky or Tennessee. If you were lucky enough to work in a union shop, though, you would meet people from other cultures in the union hall as well as on the assembly line. These other workers often wore rings that marked them as protestant members of a Masonic order or Catholic members of the Knights of Columbus. Though they had started as outsiders in their factories, Appalachian men eventually became the leaders of many of the labor unions in southwestern Ohio and northern Kentucky. In the 1960s the factories began to hire African Americans, and this added more diversity to life in the factories.

First- and second-generation Appalachians also became active in other community structures. In South Lebanon in the 1960s, the elementary school principal was from Breathitt County and hired my sister Jeanne as school secretary. She bought a typewriter and a Gregg manual and taught herself to type. Along with the principal, she became a mentor and role model to hundreds of migrant children. Likewise, when I visited the city of Moraine, a Dayton suburb, in the 1990s, I discovered that the mayor and most of the city council members were first-generation Appalachian. These men and women were working class, and none had more than a high school education, but with the help of a professional city manager they were doing a good job of governing the city. At the time Moraine provided fifty thousand jobs to Dayton-area residents. In Warren County, first- and second-generation members of my family also became active in the government of South Lebanon, leading the community action and senior services agencies. The Waynesville Maloneys (three generations) are still active in the Democratic Party, and one grandnephew became a communications staff person for Congressman and Governor Ted Strickland.

During the 1970s a factory in Lebanon (Warren County) shut down and moved south in order to hire cheaper labor. My brothers Charles and Victor organized the workers and the community to buy the factory and continue production of stove parts. Charles did the organizing, Victor the "preaching" (marketing) to gain community support. These two self-educated men were among the mentors who helped shape my politics, my life, and my career. Their children include a world leader in the Church of God in Cleveland (Tennessee), one of Lebanon's most prominent citizens, the founder of a million-dollar tech company, and the head librarian at the University of Cincinnati in Blue Ash.

Just as my sister Jeanne's family helped hold our kinship network together, they also contributed to the life of South Lebanon as a community. Jeanne's oldest child, Frances, married Larry Sargeant, the son of one of the first Kentucky families to migrate to South Lebanon. Larry for many years directed the combined community action and senior services agencies. He worked effectively with Warren County officials to develop social services and senior housing. Frances became a health worker, as did their two daughters. Although one daughter had a temporary substance abuse issue related to chronic illness, both married into other Breathitt County families and raised their children well. Larry and Frances bought a section of South Lebanon called Amburgy Hill, and sold some of the timber on it to pay for street construction. They named the streets for family members and developed homes for their daughters. When Larry retired, he opened a gun store in South Lebanon. Continuing a tradition of community service by her mother Jeanne, Ann Gross Herald became a member of the town planning commission. Jeanne's son, Frank Edward, found a steady public service job, and his daughter, Brooke, became chair of the Department of Nursing at Miami University Regionals.

By 2000, there were over 150 descendants of my parents living in southwestern Ohio and perhaps 30 living in Georgia, North Carolina, Florida, California, and Texas. The Texas branch includes a union organizer, a well-known Appalachian filmmaker, and an artist. The members of the third generation, like their parents, are social activists. Our family reunions are usually held in Warren County. Usually, at least six of the nine branches of my parents' descendants are represented at reunions and other family gatherings such as funerals and weddings. Divorce has become acceptable. One sibling and I and several of the 36 second-generation Maloneys did have breakups, but each remarried and the two-parent family is still the norm. We have three LGBT and one interracial household. An informal survey of the 180-member clan shows that only four are chronic alcoholics, one of whom became a certified alcoholism counselor, two with substance abuse issues both recovering, two with mental health and substance abuse issues, and two deaths due to substance abuse. Only one of the 180 has been unable to maintain a functional family life. Only one of the women remained a single parent after divorce. This is not a shabby record for a family that grew out of a dirt-poor coal mining and subsistence agriculture background.

COMPARISON TO VANCE

Vance's narrative also acknowledges the role of the extended family as a support system helping enforce the proper moral code. His grandfather served him as a math tutor when J. D. was discouraged with school and a potential dropout. His grandmother was always there to provide shelter and protection when conditions with his drug-addicted mother were dangerous or otherwise intolerable (148). He also acknowledges the role of uncles, aunts, and his sister as emotional support and role models. His narrative also acknowledges the existence of the "stem-and-branch" family when he talks about his family's visits back home in Jackson.

For many migrant families, church life is an extension of the kinship network in collaboration with other families. For these folks, church is a source of emotional support and mutual support in times of crisis. Church is an "inside" institution entirely controlled by the families served. In Vance's narrative, however, the church does not come across as being helpful to him or his family. I have no issues with this part of his story, as I outgrew fundamentalist Protestantism when the preacher could no longer answer my questions. I embraced Catholicism and studied for the priesthood but eventually outgrew that as well and embraced existential philosophy.

For most of my siblings, religious faith had nothing to do with religious conversion or church membership. Our faith was passed on through home-based knowledge of the King James Bible. There was a pattern among the Appalachian men I grew up with of using a religious conversion as a way of breaking the hold of habitual drinking and other behavior they regarded as sinful. This was sometimes followed by a period of church attendance. Otherwise, our relationship with God was direct and not mediated by the church. We had carried the Protestant revolt to its extremes. We believed in heaven and hell, aspired to uphold biblical teachings, and lived by the Golden Rule. Religious fervor and efforts to convert others were regarded with suspicion. The family was not only the primary social unit; it was virtually the only social unit, and it mediated all others including the church. If an Appalachian family did not like what was going on in church, it could try to intervene, withdraw, or even start a rival congregation.

My brother, Victor, wanted to be a preacher, but he was too much a free thinker to really fit in with church culture. Nonetheless, I do believe that the church was important to him and his wife, Verneda. They attended regularly at times and church was a source of friendship and emotional support for them. Their son, Mitchell, became a successful church builder (renewing small congregations) in the Church of God, Cleveland Assemblies. He became pastor of the mother church in Cleveland, Tennessee, and built a new $11 million church for that congregation. He is now an international official in his communion. When his younger brother, Philip, was in danger of becoming involved with a criminal set in South Lebanon, Victor sent him to stay with Mitchell in Detroit. Philip was converted and became a very successful evangelist. While Mitchell was a straight arrow, Philip was closer to Elmer Gantry, not in moral character but in style. He was flamboyant, sometimes standing on the pews as he held his audience transfixed by his eloquence. Sadly, Philip had some health issues, became addicted to his medications, lost his home and family, and became something of a recluse thereafter.

To his credit, Vance acknowledges the existence of such families as mine when he describes two types of urban Appalachian families. There are those like his grandparents whom he describes as old-fashioned, quietly faithful, self-reliant, hardworking (148, 239). He also says "there are many intact families" and affirms that "many of my friends have built successful lives and happy families in Middletown or nearby" (149). The other type of family, though, he claims as his world. It is a world in which people don't work hard, don't maintain their homes, and don't provide for their children or even protect them. Why is this narrative so different from that which applies to my own family?

Part of the answer, I think, lies in the fact that our family experiences were different. We both lived in female-headed families, but our mothers were vastly different. I was sometimes hungry or barefoot in the summer, and often wore clothes from the missionaries' "hoolie barrel," but they were washed clean on a washboard and I always knew I was loved and felt safe at home. In contrast,

J. D.'s mother was an addict and often neglected his needs. There were episodes of violence. Fortunately, he also had loving grandparents who provided some of the security and push every child needs to succeed.

Vance chose to focus more on the families that are failing and on parents who are not advancing themselves or helping their children to advance. My mother never expected to escape poverty, but she gave her children the expectation that they would. In the same way, most of my siblings worked in factories but pushed their children to finish high school and either go to college or pick up a trade.

The fate of migrants from Breathitt and other eastern Kentucky and Tennessee counties thus presents a very complex picture. *Hillbilly Elegy* does not, as a memoir, encompass all this complexity. It does, however, shed light on the "hard living" that often follows mass migration and the hardships involved in adjusting to life in a new place and the Fall that so many communities have experienced over the past several decades. Vance, like Harry Caudill before him, expresses disappointment in his people. Caudill talked about "fertile and amoral females" and people who had become dependent on the dole.[11] Vance says, "We spend our way to the poorhouse" (146). He refers to a "welfare queen" and writes, "Our homes are a chaotic mess" (146). He says the only stable families his relatives created were those in which someone married outside "our own little culture." Most of my associates who grew up in working-class Appalachian families identify with most of Vance's personal and family narrative. We and our families have experienced violence, economic struggles, and emotional deprivation as well as the joys and comforts of life in extended families. Those of us who are upwardly mobile also have suffered the strains and tensions of living in two worlds and making choices between leaving a familiar world and staying. Vance describes these strains very well.

In his own way, Vance does extoll the virtues of the stem-and-branch Appalachian family. I believe he recognizes the ways in which his family's ties to down-home relatives were a source of strength to them, a connection to roots and a sense of who they were as people. The Blanton uncles and Mamma Blanton and Aunt Bonnie were prominent figures to J. D. (171–72). His grandparents were a source of emotional and physical protection. After his grandmother died, he lived happily with Aunt Wee's family for a while.

He says of his grandparents that he was "supported by two living hillbillies, and part of a family that for all its quirks, loved me unconditionally" (113).

Although he is clearly disappointed at the number of dysfunctional families in his old neighborhood, he does not put all the blame on hillbilly culture. He acknowledges the role of structural economic factors, such as the collapse of the factory system, which had once provided good jobs to our people. He admits the need for better public policy (206). He even acknowledges that something is wrong with America's opportunity system, writing in reference to the findings of a recent study by Raj Chetty that the authors found that "a lot of European countries seemed better than America at the American Dream" and that "more important, they discovered that opportunity was not spread evenly over the whole country. . . . It was in the South, the rust belt, and Appalachia where poor kids really struggled" (241–42). This, in turn, affects people's expectations. Vance cites the Pew Economic Mobility Project, which determined that 42 percent of working-class whites report that their children's lives will be more economically successful than those of their parents, whereas over half of blacks, Latinos, and college-educated whites believe their children will be better off. "Even more surprising," the study concludes, "42 percent of working class whites—by far the highest in the survey—report that their lives are less successful than those of their parents" (144–45). Here Vance makes it clear that the problems of his people's culture are rooted in economic realities and the failure of public policy. He clearly separates himself from those conservatives who encourage poor whites to blame the government for their problems (194). I wish he had said that some also encourage them to blame other minorities and women, but Vance neither acknowledges the reality of Appalachian diversity nor deals with racism in his book. Nonetheless, I agree with his conclusion that blaming others rather than asserting one's own control reinforces behaviors that block upward mobility. People's expectations do affect their behavior.

For the first time since the publication, in succession, of Michael Harrington's *The Other America*, Jack Weller's *Yesterday's People*, and Harry Caudill's *Night Comes to the Cumberlands* in the early 1960s, Appalachian poverty is in the national limelight. J. D. Vance may not be the spokesperson we Appalachians wanted, but he is, for the moment, the spokesperson we have. As the reader can see by the tone of this essay, I believe the Appalachian movement needs to claim this hillbilly, embrace him, and support his ability to call for better public policy to address the personal and social network breakdown that automation, deindustrialization, and globalization have wreaked on our people. We need to challenge Vance's use of "culture of poverty" language and his alleged leaning toward genetic explanations of poverty.[12] We also need to elaborate on and mobilize around Vance's critique of an American social service system that Appalachians often find to be more of a problem than a help. The fact that a self-described "hillbilly" has gained this kind national platform has the potential to either promote another round of Appalachian "victim blaming" by the media and the political and intellectual classes or help challenge us to work harder at the kind of cultural revitalization and political movement needed to help create the kind of opportunity systems working-class Americans of all races and ethnicities so badly need. I certainly hope it is the latter.

NOTES

1. "Greater Cincinnati Survey" (Institute for Policy Research, University of Cincinnati, 1990).
2. Harry Schwarzweller, James Brown, and Walter Mangalam, *Mountain Families in Transition* (University Park: Pennsylvania State University Press, 1971).
3. Ibid.
4. Joseph T. Howell, *Hard Living on Clay Street: Portraits of Blue Collar Families* (Garden City, NY: Anchor Books, 1973).
5. See Rhoda Halperin, *The Livelihood of Kin: Making Ends Meet the Kentucky Way* (Austin: University of Texas Press, 1990).
6. Ibid.; Rhoda Halperin, *Practicing Community: Class Culture and Power in an Urban Neighborhood* (Austin: University of Texas Press, 1998).
7. Brian Alexander, interview by the author, October 28, 2017.
8. Mike Miller, interview by the author, November 3, 2017.
9. Michael E. Maloney and Christopher Auffrey, *The Social Areas of Cincinnati: An Analysis of Social Needs*, 5th ed. (University of Cincinnati, 2013), 159ff.
10. Halperin, *Practicing Community*.
11. Harry Caudill, *Night Comes to the Cumberlands: A Biography of a Depressed Area* (New York: Atlantic Monthly Press, 1963), 286.
12. See Elizabeth Catte's *What You Are Getting Wrong about Appalachia* (Cleveland: Belt, 2018), 65ff.

ELEGIES

DANA WILDSMITH

When Jim Wayne Miller saw the mountain ways
his grandpa had lived were starting to disappear,
he wrote them down to save what he loved. Briers,
he named the men of his granddaddy's day
because they were sharp and tough and stuck tight
to family. A few decades passed,
along came another Jim, born in the gap
between that reverenced past and what might
have been if the Briers had stuck around
instead of dying or fleeing to mill towns
where anger and drugs drove hope underground
and kids like J. D. ended up passed around
like colds. So J. D. wrote to save what he grieved:
a heartless home place his heart can't leave.

IN DEFENSE OF J. D. VANCE

KELLI HANSEL HAYWOOD

THE RECENTLY RENEWED media jest of the coalfields has come on the coattails of another phenomenon spearheaded by champions who wait to critique every commentary or representation of Appalachia. Appalachian academics, nonprofit employees, journalists, and activists have expressed adamant disdain for J. D. Vance and his *New York Times* best-selling memoir *Hillbilly Elegy: A Memoir of a Family and Culture in Crisis*. If you Google the book and "criticism," you'll find enough to keep you reading for a few days. The most complete and well written of these criticisms comes from Bob Hutton, a senior lecturer of history and American studies at the University of Tennessee in the urban Appalachian city of Knoxville. Hutton's "Hillbilly Elitism: The American Hillbilly Isn't Suffering from Deficient Culture. He's Just Poor," published in *Jacobin* in October 2016 (and presented in revised form in this volume), convincingly accuses Vance of writing to play into the need of white elites to have a scapegoat for the problems of working-class America, based on the assumption that capitalism creates the opportunity for upward mobility if one is rightly motivated to pull oneself up by one's own bootstraps. Hutton writes, "But of course, the book is not aimed at that underclass (few books are), but rather a middle- and upper-class readership more than happy to learn that white American poverty has nothing to do with them or with any structural problems in American economy and society and everything to do with poor folks' inherent vices."[1]

So who has the right to tell the story of coalfields Appalachia? So many of us are tired of Appalachia being portrayed as all white, ignorant, addicted, unhealthy, and self-sabotaging. Yet, while it is true that our communities are not homogenous, and we have a wide variety of beliefs about who we are and how to go about fixing things here, there is truth to stereotype whether or not we like to admit it. In most coalfields counties, 80 to 90 percent of the community identifies as white. Most of us are considered working class or unemployed, and few have a college education.[2] Check the numbers. When adjusted for population, four of the top five states for drug overdose deaths in 2016 were Appalachian states.[3] The number of babies in the United States needing hospitalization for being born addicted has nearly doubled in the last four years, and the greatest increase has been in a region of states that includes Kentucky.[4] Kentucky also ranked seventh highest in 2017 in the most obese states category.[5] And on and on. While there are individual variants within these overall statistics, it cannot be ignored that there is a narrative here being overlooked. In the unwillingness of our own champions to publicly admit that these truths matter, we are missing the opportunity to create a real community-led movement with the potential to effectively address the deeply rooted trauma we have experienced at the hands of corporate colonialism and indentured servitude.

The onslaught of these various critiques demonstrates an aversion to acknowledge and rightfully address these statistically concrete facts about our own communities. The fact that J. D. Vance has become a media celebrity for both liberals and conservatives partly on the basis of his claiming the status of a bona fide Scots-Irish hillbilly is not pleasing to many living and working in the thick of the Appalachian coalfields. Those who take strong offense to the book feel Vance is telling the wrong story of Appalachia, or not an Appalachian story at all. They are among those who feel ownership in the voice of Appalachia and of the perception of its white working class consumed by the outside world.

Taking a deeper look into the reaction to Vance's memoir gives us insight into the collective psyche of those of us who identify our work as Appalachian-centric. In her essay that she read at the 2017 Appalachian Studies Association conference in Blacksburg, Virginia, criticizing J. D. Vance and his memoir (as part of the panel responding to *Hillbilly Elegy* that helped prompt this volume and that is revised in this book), Ivy Brashear said, "The fact that people will read his book and assume that all Appalachian people are trying to actively run away from their culture, and that if they are smart, they will understand it to be less than and the people they came from to be crazy lunatics is, to me, one of the more personal attacks that Vance hurls at Appalachian people in his 261-page simultaneous fetishization and admonishment of my culture."[6] Yet, Vance writes in many places in his book that hillbilly culture has served him as much as it has hindered him. Can this not be said for any culture, and is it not a good thing to examine this truth? Here's one passage in particular from *Hillbilly Elegy* that illustrates his perspective:

> Mamaw would kill anyone who tried to keep me from her. This worked for us because Mamaw was a lunatic and our entire family feared her.
>
> Not everyone can rely on the saving graces of a crazy hillbilly. Child services are, for many kids, the last pieces of the safety net; if they fall through, precious little remains to catch them.
>
> Part of the problem is how the state laws define the family. (243)

Clearly, Vance uses plain language here about his reality with a clear sense of pride in what it did for him and his success.

The question of who or what is Appalachian plays a chiding role in many of the arguments discounting Vance's book as anything but representative of the Appalachian experience and culture. University of Kentucky sociologist Dwight Billings, for instance, says of Vance, "He has only visited family members in eastern Kentucky, or attended funerals there. His inventory of pathological traits—violence, fatalism, learned helplessness, poverty as a 'family tradition'—reads like a catalog of stereotypes that Appalachian scholars have worked so long to dispel. Vance's Appalachia is refracted through the distorted lens of his own dysfunctional family experience."[7]

While we can say that Billings is right, for Vance's book does at times read like a catalog of stereotypes, there are statistics that show that these stereotypes are grounded in some degree of reality. Furthermore, whatever the dysfunction in his family, Vance and his kin are undeniably Appalachian.

He is from Middletown, Ohio, by birth, which is situated in a county that borders Clermont County, Ohio, which, according to the Appalachian Regional Commission, is part of Appalachia. Frank X. Walker of Danville, Kentucky, in Boyle County (outside ARC designated counties), has coined the term Affrilachian to identify himself as African American and Appalachian. However, if we use the same map to define Vance as not Appalachian, then neither is Walker. Appalachia is proud of Walker, as we should be. He is a tremendous poet and social advocate. Walker claims us. So does Vance. Yet, it seems a great many would like to dictate who, given equivalent geographical credentials, can claim us and part of our story and who cannot, as Walker has been accepted as having an Appalachian experience, but Vance has not.

J. D. Vance is the product of colliding worlds, just as my community's Trump voters are. He holds, first and foremost, the idea that the American Dream is obtainable for any American citizen and that the traditional American family is still described as father, mother, and children. Yet his story is also readily identifiable as "hillbilly." Vance's mother was raised by Appalachian parents who visited their childhood home in Breathitt County as often as possible, as many displaced Appalachians did and do. Vance himself spent a great deal of time in Jackson with his great grandmother and his grandmother's siblings. Vance's writing or his perspective cannot therefore be discounted by saying his narrative is "non-Appalachian."

If you read the canon of much popular Appalachian literature, you will find an often-romanticized version of life not unlike that of the southern "Moonlight and Magnolias" literary genre. The reality on the ground is much barer bones and earthier. Vance raises some hard questions, especially for those of us in the coalfields of Appalachia who are facing the biggest upheaval our economy has seen in a very long time with no tangible plans for how to fix it. All we have is the "silver buckshot" as those in the region working in community development and "just" economic transition like to call the effort of throwing out many ideas to see which ones stick.

Vance's book is a memoir. It is not his responsibility to write the experience of his critics, or mine, or yours. He has used his family's experience to give a human story to a class and region in crisis. Vance uses his story to explain how parts of our culture that served us well under past conditions are no longer doing so. It is not a surprise that he would question how he, of all people, could end up where he is today and to ask himself, if he has been able to advance financially, why can't others? It is a question that he doesn't claim anywhere in the book to have an answer for. The closest he comes is when he writes, referring to himself and a young (presumably) Appalachian boy he consoled, "We do need to create a space for the J. D.s and Brians of the world to have a chance. I don't know what the answer is, precisely, but I know it starts when we stop blaming Obama or Bush, or faceless companies and ask ourselves what we can do to make things better" (256). There is absolutely something to be said for attempting to determine the origins of these problems, and in doing so, to discover possible solutions for today. We can also get so caught up in getting the backstory right that we forget the people themselves, a great many of whom have no context for their problems aside from their family story. Placing the blame for our problems in the right spot does nothing to get us past where we are now. What will change if the right people are blamed for the region's despair?

Vance does not make any secret of being a conservative thinker, though he is far less doctrinaire than those who adhere to Tea Party politics or fundamental evangelical values based in religious duty. This conservatism makes him a target for those who want to discredit his ideas, and even his "right" to make any definitive comments on Appalachia. Those who see Appalachia's difficulties as complex and varied reject Vance's simplistic conclusion: "These problems weren't created by governments or corporations or anyone else. We created them, and only we can fix them" (256). By "we," he means the people of Appalachia, but also the Rust Belt and other white working-class Americans. I too believe his explanation is too simple, but I think his larger point is sometimes missed. Vance also writes, "Public policy can help, but there is no government that can fix these problems for us" (255). This statement, coming earlier in Vance's conclusion, provides the basis for the meaning of his latter statement. Like any one-dimensional piece of writing, lines taken out of context can seem heinously immoral. It is up to Appalachians to fix these problems, but first we must admit the problems Vance's family story highlights are real and not uncommon among Appalachians living today. If these problems are left unaddressed, they will hold back, if not altogether squash, any real progress toward diversifying the economy and attracting people to the region to spend money.

Sure, Vance does a poor job of describing Appalachia's actual diversity. He also relies on studies done by people with questionable theories of poverty, gender, and race (like Charles Murray, an American Enterprise Institute scholar and graduate of Harvard and MIT, whom the Southern Poverty Law Center has labeled a white nationalist) to explain certain social trends. Yet Vance also mentions being influenced by William Julius Wilson, an African American Harvard sociologist who is considered progressive and whose book Vance read at age sixteen (144). Most importantly, he brings to light the issues of addiction, generational poverty, and learned behaviors of how to work government systems for relief. Vance adds to those realities accounts of the inability to find work, and the human costs of low educational attainment and interpersonal violence. Then he dares to mention that, despite a myriad of grants, policy reform, and welfare relief thrown at these problems, we are experiencing the same issues we tried to address in the 1960s. What is true about many of these efforts, regardless of how well-intentioned they may have been, is that we cannot pinpoint that this or that project worked and will have a lasting effect after government changes, the grant expires, or individual community organizers come and go. These existing programs are a drop in the bucket, just a beginning, and many do not directly address over the long term any of the problems Vance raises. Vance has come under serious criticism for presenting current eastern Kentucky in a vacuum, with no mention of land usage, coal wars, or an extraction economy, just what he sees when he goes back home. What would a poll of eastern Kentuckians look like, if they were asked about the major issues their region faces today? Even if totally cognizant of the area's history that brought the region to its current state—and most of our families do have a strong tradition of preserving orally their specific family experience—what would that "knowing" do to tangibly address what is going on in front of them every day? Analyzing the wrongdoings and placing a time stamp on when this or that problem began is useful only to academics or those wanting to debate the history of the region in the context of its current dilemma. We know how we got here pretty well. Now what? The region needs help now.

Hillbilly Elegy is subtitled and highlights "a culture in crisis," and Vance is right here too. There *are* aspects of our way of life that allow these problems to continue. The most troubling of these cultural drawbacks is the way we handle problems that cause us to seem weak, embarrassed, or, by some standards, immoral. We pretend they do not exist, at least in public. By airing our dirty laundry, Vance has triggered the response of people scrambling to show that these problems do not define us. Yet, to those in the thick of these realities, they often do.

To negate Vance's personal experience and his claim to his own identity is to say his story does not matter and does not have a place equal to or among our own. It also says that his right to his interpretation of the social environment that allowed his experience to occur is invalid. Consider, for instance, "The Trillbilly Worker's Party," a new podcast created by some of the region's thinkers. Their first episode was called "J. D. Vance Is a Snitch." One of the hosts suggested that she wants to buy Vance's mother a drink for her woes.[8] Yes, the podcast is in jest, but it shows that we don't allow some things to be spoken in mixed company. In publicly mentioning the problems we as a culture are trying to hide, Vance requires us to answer for them. In today's Appalachian studies activism, community development, social justice, progressive, nonprofit world, that laying bare is far from the popular thing to do, but it is nonetheless necessary.

One of the most troubling aspects about all the energy folks have spent criticizing J. D. Vance is that other books written by Appalachians that take on problems like addiction in a humanizing, beautiful way, especially Carrie Mullins's *Night Garden*, have gone somewhat overlooked on the national stage.[9] Why can't we spend time highlighting examples that might educate a national audience about the day-to-day realities of these issues? Why can't our writers and journalists with an outlet in the national arena engage in a more productive conversation? In the words of Jon Falter, a Whitesburg resident who has been five years drug free, "This problem is not going anywhere." This is the truth of addiction. It is true of the depression and fatalistic attitudes. It is true of the violence that widespread drug addiction enables. It is also true about the generational poverty that can result in a "chicken or egg" argument about its relationship to social dysfunctions. With 61 percent of Kentuckians believing their children will be worse off financially than they are and one in three reporting that a friend or family member has a problem with addiction to prescription pain medications, we must recognize that it will take far more than what is currently happening on the ground before we see any meaningful change in the severe issues plaguing our homeland.[10] Vance is not wrong or reinforcing false stereotypes by bringing up this situation as he experienced it, whether or not you agree with his simplistic analysis. I commend him for it. Now, what are we going to do about it? We must first claim the problem and the part of it that is cultural, and then better explain the part that is a direct result of corporate money gone awry and failures in public policy.

Jared Yates Sexton, another white Appalachian man of working-class origin, recently wrote of *Hillbilly Elegy*, "The thesis at the heart of *Hillbilly Elegy* is that anybody who isn't able to escape the working-class is essentially at fault. Sure, there's a culture of fatalism and 'learned helplessness,' but the onus falls on the individual."[11] Vance intentionally wrote his memoir to be readable by someone who has zero background in Appalachian history, to be quickly consumed. It was written to be a springboard for deeper conversations, as Vance has clearly illustrated through his numerous interviews with both conservative and progressive media outlets. It is not an academic text. It is Vance's experience and Vance's conclusions drawn by the shape of his experiences and written to encourage action before it is too late. As Sexton highlights, Vance writes, "Whenever people ask me what I'd most like to change about the white working class, I say, 'the feeling that our choices don't matter.'"[12] How effective do we think we can be at addressing our problems from within? It seems not much since we are consistently waiting on funding from somewhere, waiting on a nearly obsolete industry to revive, waiting on the powers that be to notice and take pity, waiting on another day. Sometimes our choices do not seem to matter, especially when we are wondering where our next meal will come from.

It is time to stop debating whether Vance is right or wrong—Appalachian or not. It is pointless and distracting from what we should be doing. We should be getting into the parts of the community that national reporters seem to find with exploitative ease and get the real story, claim it, and understand it. This is the necessary conversation we must have, so that we can then take action to redeem that story. Let's stop hiding from the issues and criticizing this man for a book that is mostly memoir, only a small part commentary, and even a smaller part political polemic.

Vance has given voice to things that I and others I know have experienced firsthand. I value his story and the questions it raises. I hope that eventually the debate about the man's character will be put to rest and we will instead start taking a deeper look at the realities of life this work lays bare. I had the opportunity to exchange emails with Vance after I read his book. He wrote to me, "I love my people, and I really hope that comes through in my book. But for all the beauty, there are families like mine and yours, and we've got to recognize the good in those families and the bad if we ever hope to help them."[13]

NOTES

1. Bob Hutton, "Hillbilly Elitism," *Jacobin*, October 1, 2016, https://www.jacobinmag .com/2016/10/hillbilly-elegy-review-jd-vance-national-review-white-working-class-appalachia/.

2. Kelvin Pollard and Linda A. Jacobsen, *The Appalachian Region in 2010: A Census Data Overview Chartbook* (Population Reference Bureau, prepared for the Appalachian Regional Commission, September 2011), http://www.prb.org/pdf12/appalachia-census-chartbook-2011.pdf.

3. Centers for Disease Control and Prevention, "Drug Overdose Death Data," https:// www.cdc.gov/drugoverdose/data/statedeaths.html.

4. Hannah Rappleye, Rich McHugh, and Ronan Farrow, "Born Addicted: The Number of Opioid-Addicted Babies Is Soaring," *NBC News*, October 9, 2017, https://www .nbcnews.com/storyline/americas-heroin-epidemic/born-addicted-number-opioid-addicted-babies-soaring-n806346.

5. "The State of Obesity in Kentucky," https://stateofobesity.org/states/ky/.

6. Ivy Brashear, "Why Media Must Stop Misrepresenting Appalachia," *Huffington Post*, April 10, 2017, https://www.huffingtonpost.com/entry/i-am-appalachian-too-a-response-to-hillbilly-elegy_us_58ebe93ae4b081da6ad006be.

7. Dwight Billings, "Review of Hillbilly Elegy" (Occasional Links & Commentary on Economics, Culture, and Society, August 10, 2016), https://anticap.wordpress .com/2016/08/10/hillbilly-elegy/.

8. Trillbilly Workers Party, "Episode 1: J. D. Vance Is a Snitch," https://www.mixcloud .com/trillbillyworkersparty/jd-vance-a-snitch/.

9. Carrie Mullins, *Night Garden* (Lexington, KY: Old Cove Press, 2016), http://oldcove .com/projects/night-garden-by-carrie-mullins/.

10. Foundation for a Healthy Kentucky, "Health Issues Polls for 2012," http://healthy-ky .org/res/images/resources/KHIP6-American-Dream.pdf and http://healthy-ky.org/ res/images/resources/KHIP5-Rx-Drug-Misuse.pdf.

11. Jared Yates Sexton, "Hillbilly Sellout: The Politics of J. D. Vance's 'Hillbilly Elegy' Are Already Being Used to Gut the Working Poor," *Salon*, March 11, 2017, http://salon .com/2017/03/11/hillbilly-sellout-the-politics-of-j-d-vances-hillbilly-elegy-are-already-being-used-to-gut-the-working-poor.
12. Ibid.
13. Email exchange, August 29, 2016.

IT'S CRAZY AROUND HERE, I DON'T KNOW WHAT TO DO ABOUT IT, AND I'M JUST A KID

ALLEN JOHNSON

THE GRIM REALITY is that most children raised in dysfunctional families become dysfunctional adults.

My head nodded a stoic "yes" at the presenter's introductory remark. I was attending a workshop in the mid-1970s to add continuing education units to maintain my West Virginia social worker license. At the time, I worked with an Appalachian Regional Commission (ARC) pilot project to provide intervention services for children at risk for abuse or neglect. Some of my clientele outwardly appeared like happy functional families. I knew better. These families lived chaotic lives. My dossier of known or suspected maladaptive family traits included alcohol dependency, domestic violence, truancy, poor hygiene, improper nutrition, and emotional abuse. Poverty was a common thread. The children had innate potential for happiness and success in life. I liked my kids, and on a certain level, I liked their adult figures, too. Yet family dysfunctions seemed so entrenched, and social services to address the need so inadequate, that I often felt I proverbially was "banging my head against a brick wall."

My workshop presenter then stated his theme that breathed hope for my future work: "About 15 percent of children raised in dysfunctional families beat stacked odds to become successful, happy, community-contributing adults. We call these people 'transcenders' in that they have overcome limiting and negative childhood experiences. They have transcended from a negative life experience to a positive outcome. This session will discuss factors that influence potential positive outcomes for children in dysfunctional homes."[1] As I read J. D. Vance's *Hillbilly Elegy: A Memoir of a Family and Culture in Crisis*, my mind continually raced back to the challenged families I had directly worked with over twelve years. I also reflected on my involvement with all socioeconomic strata across my home, Pocahontas County in rural West Virginia, for over forty-five years. Vance's family during his growing-up years was unique, as are all families, yet I felt as I read that I knew his folk, that Vance's Mamaw, Papaw, sister, mother, and neighbors were not at all strangers to me. I thought, too, of people I know who are overcoming the obstacles stacked against them and are now on a good trajectory toward happiness and life fulfillment. My own childhood background had been within the stability of a functional family and community. What could I learn from *Hillbilly Elegy* that might help me better understand and contribute to my own rural Appalachian community?

A person rescued from drowning will later wonder, "How did I get into my predicament? Could I have prevented it? Who rescued me? What do I owe?" In the same way, Vance has written a memoir to analyze his life. He ranges far as he examines his family upbringing, his Appalachian heritage, his cultural milieu, his own psychological responses, his eventual breaks in life, and his sense of obligation to give value back to the hillbilly people he identifies himself with. To many readers, his best-selling and award-winning book is an eye-opener into the hidden lives of struggling Appalachian families. To some critics, though, the book touches a raw nerve by ripping open an underbelly of Appalachian hillbilly stereotyping and presenting it to readers unfamiliar with the complexity and breadth of Appalachia. To me, what is most significant is that J. D. Vance overcame adverse childhood experiences (ACE) to become successful in life and profession, and to be sought after as a commentator on the challenges of Appalachia, the working class, politics, and American society. Every one of us is raised within the matrix of family, community, and culture. How accurately then does Vance's story of being "a cultural emigrant from one group to the other" (252) interpret the struggling resilience and resource capacity of working class, Appalachian-background people as they intersect with the dominant, foreign-to-them American culture? Is Vance's own story of transcending structural limitations a template for the struggling Appalachian context? My essay explores these questions.

THERAPEUTIC REMEMBERING AND TELLING

> This is the story of my life, and that is why I wrote this book. I want people to know what it feels like to nearly give up on your life and why you might do it. I want people to understand what happens in the lives of the poor and the psychological impact that spiritual and material poverty has on their children. I want people to understand the American Dream as my family and I encountered it. I want people to understand how upward mobility really feels. And I want people to understand something I learned only recently: that for those of us lucky enough to live the American Dream, the demons of the life we left behind continue to chase us. (2)

As J. D. Vance explains in the first pages of *Hillbilly Elegy*, to help readers to understand his story, he had to first figure it out for himself: "There is an ethnic component lurking in the background of my story." For Vance, that ethnic component is the culture and lifestyle of his multigenerational Appalachian family that he characterizes throughout his volume and early on: "Americans call them hillbillies, rednecks, and white trash. I call them neighbors, friends, and family" (2–3).

Did J. D. Vance write his memoir as a step toward his own healing and growth from childhood trauma? Donna F. LaMar, an experienced clinical psychologist who has worked extensively with adults successfully transcending ACE, points out important stages that clients must process in order to transcend ACE. Painful suppressed emotional feelings must be uncovered and expressed: "Revisiting is the re-experiencing, remembering, and re-feeling of the past to gain an adult perspective and understanding of what happened to us as children. Revisiting is handling all the feelings as well as the problems and conflicts (issues) left from the experiences of childhood."[2] Sidney Jourard, who pioneered a self-disclosure therapeutic model that emphasizes reciprocity of openness and disclosure between therapist and client, stresses the same thing. One of Jourard's steps to transcending is "an openness to sharing experiences with oneself and with others fully and freely, with little defensiveness."[3] Certainly *Hillbilly Elegy* seems to do just this.

LaMar underscores the essentialness of lancing and healing childhood trauma wounds. "As with any infected wound, the less airing, the more painful the wound and the more energy needed to contain it. If one is to cleanse and heal shame and secrets, they must be expressed or aired." She insists, therefore, that family secrets should be vented. "Secrets are often generations old and have been passed down through the years to each new generation. With the understanding comes a choice of continuing the secrets or stopping the generational dysfunction surrounding them."[4] Those who buck up the courage to honestly confront and expose their shames and secrets, she emphasizes, experience an exhilarating feeling of freedom and a burst of energy.[5]

Jeannette Walls, who wrote the best-selling and critically acclaimed *Glass Castle,* her memoir of growing up in her own dysfunctional family, had a similar experience when she came to terms with her difficult past. She spent her teen years with her three siblings and parents in Welch, West Virginia. Their home was a ramshackle hut, their clothes little more than rags, their food often picked out of school garbage cans. Her father rarely worked and drank excessively, while her spaced-out mother left the children to fend for themselves. The local community scorned them. As soon as she could, Walls escaped to New York City to carve out a successful career as a news columnist.[6]

In an interview with Gary Thompson of *PhillyNews* about the movie based upon *Glass Castle,* Walls reflected upon her childhood. "Poverty isn't just about being hungry or cold," she said. "The killer thing is, you think you are less than other people. You think there is something wrong with you, that's the most devastating thing. So I just carried that around with me. I felt that if people knew, they would hate me." Walls quietly kept her secret for two decades. Writing her memoir became an emotional experience. "I had tried to distance myself from it and pretend that it hadn't affected me, that it wasn't part of me. The first time I reread what I'd written, I was kind of shocked. It was cathartic."[7]

Healing from ACE involves expressing gratitude for one's new life. Walls and Vance each express gratitude for "the good luck" to be a survivor now empowered and willing to help others transcend. In this light, writing *Hillbilly Elegy* and giving subsequent public lectures and media interviews have served as self-therapy for J. D. Vance. Vance hopes to inspire and challenge those who have suffered ACE to honestly examine and express their own background traumas. Furthermore, he hopes his memoir will evoke deeper understanding and reciprocity from the wider spectrum of society including those insulated by their privilege from the lives of the "teeming masses" and that he can serve as a kind of bridge between these national power-broker "Yale-types" and everyday Americans in Appalachia and beyond.[8]

There is broad medical evidence of the long-term harm caused by ACE, and it is now popular parlance in social science research and practice. ACE categories include physical abuse; sexual abuse; emotional abuse; physical neglect; emotional neglect; intimate partner violence; mother treated violently; substance misuse within the household; household mental illness; parental separation or divorce; and incarceration of a household member.[9] Frequency and severity of abuse, and age and resiliency of the child also influence the degree of traumatic impact. Beginning in 1998, researchers at the Centers for Disease Control and Prevention launched an ongoing public health study of ACE.[10] The results of this and other studies point to strong links between childhood trauma and higher adult rates of depression, violent behavior, chronic disease, substance abuse, criminal incarceration, and other undesirable outcomes.

ACE theory includes a biochemical component that correlates to stress. Gabor Matte, for instance, has worked with addicted populations in Vancouver and studied the impact of high family stress on children. He writes,

> Happy, attuned emotional interactions with parents stimulate a release of natural opioids in an infant's brain. This endorphin surge promotes the attachment relationship and the further development of the child's opioid and dopamine circuitry. On the other hand, stress reduces the numbers of both opiate and dopamine receptors. Healthy growth of these crucial systems—responsible for such essential drives as love, connection, pain relief, pleasure, incentive, and motivation—depends, therefore, on the

quality of the attachment relationship. When circumstances do not allow the infant and young child to experience consistently secure interactions or, worse, expose him to many painfully stressing ones, maldevelopment often results.[11]

In her volume *Transcending Turmoil*, LaMar writes, "Transcenders are individuals who grow up in difficult, painful, destructive families and emerge with a meaningful, productive way of life. These individuals, as children, somehow maintain a sense of self strong enough to withstand the onslaught of abuse and neglect from their families."[12] She continues, "Children in dysfunctional families do not get the nurturing or the protection they need to grow and develop into healthy, productive adults." Typically, such children take on their parents' dysfunctional character traits and family relationship patterns, which they as adults then pass on to their own offspring.[13] J. D. Vance underscores this intergenerational impact throughout *Hillbilly Elegy*, noting his own family's ancestral patterns as well as at-large Appalachian cultural traits.

As a youngster, Vance experienced frequent violent family fights, a drug-addicted mother, and, most disturbing to him, his "mom's revolving door of father figures" (15, 228). And yet his own life trajectory has been very different. Why are some children "resilient," that is, able to maintain an inner core that survives childhood trauma and rebirths into healthy, stable adulthood? Vance answers that his coarse, ACE-scarred grandmother saved him: "Reams of social science attest to the positive effect of a loving and stable home. I could cite a dozen studies suggesting that Mamaw's home offered me not just a short-term haven but also hope for a better life. Entire volumes are devoted to the phenomenon of 'resilient children'—kids who prosper despite an unstable home because they have the social support of a loving adult" (149).

Why is, say, Jeannette Walls successful, happy, and highly functional? Her family was deeply impoverished, her parents were highly unstable, and her neighborhood and classmates mocked her. However, a high school English teacher, Jeanette Bivens, invited Walls to be the first seventh-grader ever to join the staff of the school newspaper, *The Maroon Wave*. Bivens gave Walls a critical spark that kindled into a harnessed fire once she left home.[14]

Resilient children begin their transcendence through emotional separation from their dysfunctional setting. This can be from a singular crisis or from a series of compounding traumatic episodes. This key turning-point decision becomes an emotional divorce from their families. According to LaMar's research and experience, the average age of this turning-point decision is ten to thirteen years.[15]

This was the case for Jeannette Walls's sister. In her book, Walls vividly describes how her older sister Lori and she secretly saved earnings to escape from their home misery in Welch. Shortly before Lori's high school graduation and her planned bolt to New York, their dad discovered the hidden trove, stole it, and squandered it on a three-day drunken spree.

> "I'll never get out of here," Lori kept saying. "I'll never get out of here."
> "You will," I said. "I swear it." I believed she would. Because I knew that if Lori never got out of Welch, neither would I."[16]

Lori did escape to New York City and got a toehold with a place to live and a job. Jeannette began counting the days to her graduation so she could join her sister. Then she hatched the idea of moving in with her sister at the close of her junior year. Even though her guidance counselor, Ms. Katona, ridiculed the idea and warned her that she would miss her senior year, Jeannette had her eureka moment walking home, reflecting on what Ms. Katona had urged. She decided that her advice was not compelling. "I had almost a hundred dollars saved, enough to get me started in New York. I could leave Welch in under five months.... I got so excited that I started running... I ran faster and faster."[17]

Likewise, Vance's turning-point decision came in his high school sophomore year when his mother demanded he give her a jar of his urine for her random sample to the nursing licensure board. Mom knew hers was dirty from prescription drugs. J. D. exploded upon his mother, venting years of bottled up hurt, disappointment, fear, and hopelessness. His mother broke down in tears, but Mamaw, also present, talked him into giving his mom the sample. "I know this isn't right, honey. But she's your mother and she's my daughter. And maybe, if we help her this time, she'll finally learn her lesson" (131). "Though I followed Mamaw's lead," Vance writes, "something inside me broke that morning." Later that day, when Mamaw told J. D. she wanted him to live with her permanently, he accepted (132). This turning point made all the difference to J. D., who thrived under Mamaw's consistent care, perceptive discipline, and loving encouragement through the rest of his high school years.

Vance effusively credits his hillbilly Mamaw for saving him from a bleak future, and giving him enough confidence and self-control to venture out from his imprisoning emotional and cultural cage. She is a powerful example of what LaMar calls a "significant other":

Significant others are the *most important* factors in surviving. Most transcenders actively seek relationships that involve them with a more nurturing, protective world. These important relationships offer love, acceptance, support, kindness, and a feeling of being special. Significant others also provide role models, examples of alternative lifestyles, and hope for the future by demonstrating another way to live. The nurturing and protection that come from relationships are remembered vividly for years. Even what seem to be the smallest of gifts from others are priceless gifts to the transcender.[18]

Dwight Diller, an accomplished traditional Appalachian banjoist, also recalled his own "significant other." As a child, he bumped around from relative to relative as he took flight from his emotionally abusive mother. "My dad had left when I was young. But an uncle and aunt ran a beer joint. I'd stay with them a lot. I'd sit at the bar with the men and they'd accept me being there. Wouldn't talk down to me. I absorbed their stories. They'd take me hunting, fishing. I internalized my rhythm from the juke box, hearing Johnny Cash, Little Richard, Jerry Lee Lewis."[19]

As Vance and Diller attest, transcending from a dysfunctional family can be daunting. The emerging transcender may be embarrassed by a lack of normal relational social skills. When J. D. began dating his future wife Usha, for instance, he often dealt with conflict in the hotheaded way he had absorbed from his family and he feared he would not be able to escape negative family patterns. This is a common response of ACE survivors, for as LaMar has written, "There is a totally confusing, feeling 'crazy' time that occurs when new and old patterns of operating are functioning at the same time. . . . They [the survivors] especially need to know that they are doing well and are going to make it."[20] Fortunately as Vance writes, Usha gave him just this type of consistent reassurance (246). In doing so, he followed the path of other transcenders who experience relief and joy as they consistently develop positive social relationships, gain academic and workplace success, and further their emotional distancing from their dysfunctional families. "As the memory and all its feelings are revisited," LaMar writes, "transcenders gain thoughts and insight into their behavior as well as their emotional patterns . . . gain a deeper knowing and understanding of themselves . . . [and] glean each experience for every bit of learning about themselves and their world."[21]

As life under Mamaw had its calming, healing effect, J. D. began to question his family, community, and culture. At age sixteen he was identifying with books he read on social policy and was beginning to connect the dots. He learned that many mountain folk had fled Appalachian poverty by moving to northern industrial jobs, only to be stranded when factories closed. Government programs too often exacerbated dependency and family breakdown rather than opening pathways for them to rebound. Still, he wondered, even if structural problems contributed to the dysfunction of families, why did so many of his neighbors make bad choices? National politics, marketplace adjustments, and government programs were all factors, but so too was human agency. The puzzle was complex and multifaceted. "It would be years," he writes, "before I learned that no single book, or expert, or field could fully explain the problem of hillbillies in modern America. Our elegy is a sociological one, yes, but also about psychology and community and culture and faith" (144–45).

TROUBLES IN APPALACHIA

Having spilled the guts of his family's secrets and shame in *Hillbilly Elegy*, Vance sallies forth to analyze people like his kin and their culture. Partly as a result, Vance's widely read, best-selling book has elicited controversy and raised many potential questions: Since in the minds of mainstream Americans Appalachians already carry heavily caricaturized stereotyping as ignorant, immoral, and unhygienic, is the popularity of *Hillbilly Elegy* due to its voyeuristic appeal? Does the book paint with negative broad brushstrokes all Appalachian people? Does Vance blame the victim rather than the victimizers who have exploited labor, the environment, and politics? Has he cherry-picked examples from his own life that he projects into a faulty social theory? Does he pejoratively use the word "hillbilly"? Is Vance pseudo-modest while trumpeting his accomplishments culminating in a Yale Law School diploma? And has he, in unrealistic and exaggerated terms, too narrowly defined the American Dream as constituting only a prestigious degree, an elite circle of friends, and sumptuous wealth?

Is Vance's memoir analogous to that of a troubled and abused region and the pathway he dreams for its transcendence? Vance is right when he says that some regions in the United States are struggling economically and socially—in particular, Appalachia and the Rust Belt. Quality-of-life statistics for Appalachia are unquestionably disheartening. In almost all categories of social stability and health including levels of poverty, environmental degradation, years of education, business conditions, job participation, physical and emotional health, rates of drug abuse and opioid addiction, access to quality Internet, access to basic services, levels of smoking, rates of obesity, levels of social mobility, percentage of population loss, and overall happiness, the region ranks near the bottom in numerous studies and polls.

In the Gallup-Healthways "Well-Being Index" (published annually since 2008), West Virginia has been fiftieth in state rankings and Kentucky typically forty-ninth every year. Furthermore, West Virginia ranked last during the consecutive years 2009–13 in the subcategories of life evaluation, emotional health, and physical health. That is, West Virginians across the socioeconomic spectrum reported themselves to be the most hopeless, unhappy, and sick people in the nation. During that time frame, Gallup-Healthways also measured data for all 435 US congressional districts. These numbers revealed that West Virginia's Third District, in the southern tier of the state, and Kentucky's Fifth District, in the eastern part of the state, hovered at rock bottom of those indices. Neighboring districts were only a tick higher. These districts encompass deep Appalachian culture and a coal mono-economy, and have suffered massive waves of population out-migration.[22] *Forbes,* a global media company focusing on business, investment, technology, entrepreneurship, leadership, and lifestyle, recently ranked West Virginia last for business.[23] CNBC also produced a low ranking, summarizing grimly, "In an economic death spiral, West Virginia is America's worst state for business in 2017. . . . West Virginia workers are the least educated in the nation. Fewer than 12 percent of residents over the age of 25 have a bachelor's degree, according to the U.S. Census Bureau."[24]

The steep population loss is one of the most troubling facts facing much of Appalachia. Historical coal-producing areas have been depopulating for decades, personified in J. D. Vance's grandparents' relocation from eastern Kentucky to the southern Ohio manufacturing town of Middletown. West Virginia reached its peak population in 1950, according to US census figures, and has been on a downward trend ever since, losing 8 percent of its people while the nation's population has more than doubled. Traditional coal mining communities in eastern Kentucky, southern West Virginia, and southwestern Virginia are hemorrhaging residents at a rate of up to 2 percent per year.[25] Moreover, the majority of rural Appalachian counties are aging and have an older median age.[26] Meanwhile, younger, talented, career-oriented people desiring upward mobility are emigrating from Appalachia in pursuit of modern broadband, vibrant social opportunities, cultural diversity, and a clean natural environment.

Statistical analyses therefore clearly substantiate Vance's conclusion that, taken as a whole, Appalachians in their home and diasporic regions are in difficult straits. When people are in such a dark tunnel with no end in sight, despair brings on social behaviors that are puzzling to outsiders. Why, for instance, did Donald Trump win not only all fifty-five West Virginia counties in the Republican primary, but 70 percent of the state's tally in the national election? Likewise, why did Bernie Sanders win all fifty-five of these same counties in the Democratic Party primary? Most bizarrely, why did Keith Judd, a convict in a Texas prison, win over 40 percent of the 2012 Democratic Party primary votes in the state and carry ten counties against incumbent President Obama? Do these results not reflect that Appalachia's underemployed, sick, and despairing voter population has lost faith in the conventional mainstream political system and is willing to hazard blowing it all up for a fresh start? What's to lose when your current path is heading off a cliff?

Nor is West Virginia or even Appalachia unique in this way of thinking. *Strangers in Their Own Land: Anger and Mourning on the American Right* is a brilliant analysis of working-class white communities in conservative rural southern Louisiana, where levels of poverty, health, education, and environmental degradation are analogous to those in broad swaths in Appalachia. The author, sociologist Arlie Russell Hochschild, traveled out of her liberal Berkeley bubble to interview hundreds of Louisiana locals. She imagines a play, "The Deep Story," that explicates the resentment and despair of many white working-class males. This is my synopsis of this "Deep Story" written in Hochschild's style:

> Imagine yourself as a white male standing in a long line leading up a hill that will crest over into the American Dream. Your grandparents once stood in that line, as did your parents. Through hard work, pluck and scrap, and playing by the rules, they moved forward to a better life. You, too, are standing in that line working hard, living a moral life, and playing by the rules. But alas, your line is not moving. It has been standing still. Even worse, the line you've been standing in for so long is now moving backward!
>
> And then you discover, much to your dismay, people cutting line in front of you and moving forward. Black people because of affirmative action. Immigrants and refugees because they will work for lower pay. Women who used to stay at home and raise the kids. Even people who are not even trying to work yet are getting a living with food stamps and housing vouchers and free health care. And now, over there, it looks like President Obama is helping these people cut in front of you. Maybe Obama was a line cutter himself.
>
> You might say to yourself, I've tried to not to blame others, yet I keep hearing catcalls calling me a racist bigot, ignorant redneck, white trash, and blaming me for my not moving forward.
>
> Meanwhile I'm underemployed and cannot afford a nice home and car like my parents and grandparents did. I so much want my wife and our kids to have comfort, security, nice things and vacations. I'm failing my family, and this shatters my dignity. I'm getting tired and angry

standing in this line that's going backward for me. Sometimes I feel like giving up.[27]

J. D. Vance understands this "Deep Story" well. In July 2016, he was interviewed about Appalachian people's enthusiasm for Trump. Following are excerpts:

> What many don't understand is how truly desperate these places are, and we're not talking about small enclaves or a few towns—we're talking about multiple states where a significant chunk of the white working class struggles to get by.
>
> ———
>
> The two political parties have offered essentially nothing to these people for a few decades. From the Left, they get some smug condescension, an exasperation that the white working class votes against their economic interests because of social issues. . . . Maybe they get a few handouts, but many don't want handouts to begin with. . . . From the Right, they've gotten the basic Republican policy platform of tax cuts, free trade, deregulation, and paeans to the noble businessman and economic growth.
>
> ———
>
> Trump's candidacy is music to their ears. He criticizes the factories shipping jobs overseas. His apocalyptic tone matches their lived experiences on the ground. He seems to love to annoy the elites, which is something a lot of people wish they could do but can't because they lack a platform.[28]

Although Vance makes clear in numerous interviews and lectures that he is not a Trump supporter, he understands the popularity that brought the man to the presidency. Trump is not condescending to working-class people. Trump says he understands their pain, and promises they will be in the forefront of making America great again. Trump's blustery, offensive, and exaggerated speech is how working-class people talk among themselves about politics.

When much of the white working class feel they have been hopelessly left behind by decades of impotent government policies, voting for a promised political paradigm change is energizing.

ABUSE OF LAND AND PEOPLE

Vance astutely recognizes the pain and despair many Appalachians feel. Yet *Hillbilly Elegy* gives short shrift to external forces that have forged much of the culture in Appalachia. For instance, noting the family breakdown, drugs, and bad choices, Vance writes, "These problems were not created by governments or corporations or anyone else. We created them and only we can fix them" (255–56). Vance dismisses how continued systemic manipulation and exploitation of the Appalachian region and its people have significantly contributed to the social pathologies that he critiques. The plundering of Appalachian resources has bequeathed a wreckage of impoverished land and people. Just as Vance had to realize he was in an abusive family and dysfunctional setting in order to transcend it, so he should recognize and analyze the abusive economic and political powers Appalachians need to transcend.

Decades of large-scale timber and coal extraction have bent Appalachian culture into structural pathologies. To list just some examples: (1) the early era of dangerous working conditions engendered a "live for the day" mindset that has been passed down through generations, stifling long-term planning for education, personal health care, and savings; (2) company towns controlled workers, creating an ethos of dependency that continues through a coal mono-economy; (3) regional politics (and politicians) is so beholden to these extractive industries that it often disengages from economic diversification; (4) constant grinding degradation of land and people induces apathy; (5) workers in rural areas often have to accept jobs with long commutes or stay-overs, which negatively affects family life; (6) high wages ($50,000 annually) in coal mining for workers with only a high school degree disincentivized furthering education, leading to a lower overall educational ethos in a coal-mining community, and if and when laid off, miners have been and continue to be reluctant to retrain or accept lower paying work; and (7) the opioid addiction plague began when Purdue Pharma targeted southwestern Virginia for high OxyContin sales because of its high coal-miner-related Medicaid and disability rates.[29]

Furthermore, Appalachian children of the diaspora have been subjected to degrading prejudice. The late Larry Gibson was known worldwide for his courageous fight against mountaintop removal. He inspired many to join him against the odious mining practice that ruined his boyhood home, Kayford Mountain, and many other locations. During the coal layoffs in the 1950s, Gibson's family moved from West Virginia to Cleveland seeking work. He recalls his first day in school as an eleven-year-old enrolling in fifth grade, wearing his best new clothes, a pair of bib overalls and brougham work boots:

> I was in class just a few minutes when the principal came. "Come with me, young man," he said, taking my hand. "We're going to put you back to the third grade, because your standard of education is not up to ours." That got me mad. I knew they were taking two years of my life. They didn't give me a chance, test me or anything. Then when I got in the third-grade room, the teacher had me get in front and said to the class, "Okay, you kids, I want you to go home and bring this boy some clothes tomorrow because he doesn't have any." I had my best clothes on. That day they took away my dignity, my pride, all the respect I may have had for myself. So I did what they put me to. I gave up. Fought in school every day.[30]

Much can be made about outsiders stereotyping hillbillies. The more insidious stereotyping, however, can often come from inside the community. Children in dysfunctional families have enough of an uphill battle without being further and unjustifiably stigmatized. My wife indirectly experienced this sort of insider class prejudice when we relocated to a rural West Virginia community in 1973. She had been hired as the first-grade teacher at Valley Head and came home from her first day of school orientation with steam pouring from her ears. The principal had given her a list of her students. "See, you are new here, so I need to tell you about the students you will have." He did not know the students, but living in a small community, he did know their families. "You'll enjoy these youngsters, Mrs. Johnson," he said, naming off several students whose parents were solid community members. "They'll learn, and they'll behave. But let me tell you about some of these other kids. Their parents are no good, and that's how these kids will turn out. Don't feel badly that they won't learn. Just try to make them behave." That year my wife poured herself out for her students. At the end of the school year nine months later, every student was at or above grade level.

VISITING THE PAIN AND ENVISIONING THE HEALING FOR APPALACHIA

So how can we respond to this seemingly insurmountable set of problems, and how can insights from Vance's book help do so? As a path forward, let me extrapolate transcender theory into an admittedly hypothetical, semi-analogous social construct for significant sectors in Appalachia. In doing so, I am cognizant that we in Appalachia are diverse and multifaceted, that a majority of us Appalachian people are functional, successful, fulfilled persons, and that most of our neighborhoods are solid, friendly, and supportive places to live and rear a family. Yet just as transcenders have had to honestly face up to their dysfunctional upbringings, build the courage to step out of those malignant situations, and give voice to their past, so those of us who love our Appalachia must squarely recognize those factors that are holding back too many of our neighbors from vibrant, promising, and fulfilling lives, and gird up our will to forge the means to transcend.

Let me briefly look at factors that can contribute to thriving individual and community life: jobs and economics, family, education, and community and spiritual support. Each is conditioned on the presence or absence of core virtues including work, thrift, respect for others, kindness, generosity, forgiveness, mercy, and love that is genuine, self-sacrificing, and tough.

"Jobs! Jobs, more and better jobs," pounds the unceasing drumbeat of every elected or wannabe politician. Good-paying jobs will be the panacea for Appalachia. But are there enough capable workers for the jobs of the new economy? In Appalachia, as in much of America, there is a sharp divide: those who work incredibly hard, responsibly, skillfully, and those who don't. Besides working alongside fellow employees in various jobs, I've had administrative oversight over hundreds of employees, have hired many and fired a few. I could write volumes on the virtues, coveted by companies across the nation, of the majority of hardworking Appalachians such as Vance's Papaw, who he writes in the 1950s was one of thousands of fellow Appalachians actively recruited by Armco for their hard work capability (27–28). But I also share Vance's lament about communities with too many indolent young men who, to use a local expression, find ways to "get by" on relatives, girlfriends and spouses, government and charity programs, and the underground economy. Vance writes about his experience, for example, as a seventeen-year-old working at a grocery store. Living with his Mamaw, he recalls, money was tight. Resentment swirled up in Vance as he saw federal and state income taxes deducted from his small paycheck while people on welfare had cell phones, bought steaks, and gamed the food stamp system through the soda pop black market. Vance infers this was the time he began questioning the social aid policies of the Democratic Party (138–40).

For West Virginia, statistics and anecdotes from local employers bear this out. In 2015, West Virginia held the dubious distinction of being the only state in the nation that had fewer than half its adults holding down a job. Analysts looked for causes. Mining jobs had fallen off; the state also had a higher-than-average median age, high rates of obesity and diabetes, the nation's highest rate of disability (over 20 percent), and the worst labor force participation rate (which measures those who are employed or are "ready, willing, and able to work"). Those who are healthy, educated, and married fare well in employment; there just aren't enough of them to spur robust economic development. West Virginia's 11 percent rate of adults holding a bachelor's degree is the nation's lowest.[31] A local employer running several businesses tells me he has plenty of unfilled jobs: "I have twenty employees. I could use ten more. Can't find them. All the good workers already have jobs. There's plenty of jobs around to be had, but not people willing to work or who are dependable. Drugs are worse than ever, just awful. So many can't pass a drug test. Others, they're just plain lazy." Unable to acquire sufficient laborers, he is selling one of his promising businesses and abandoning his plan to purchase another.[32] An employer in the health field tells me more of the same. "I used to place help-wanted ads and get twenty applicants," he reports. "Now weeks go by without an applicant. It's that way everywhere. It's harder to find working-class people. Everyone is told to go to college. Those that don't, half cannot pass a drug screen or background check. I'd hire a busload of Mexicans in a heartbeat because they'd work."[33]

A person's work ethic and skill set are formed through the influences of his or her family, social group, and community pillars such as school and church. Positive reinforcement for capable work is essential, whether it is affirmation from a parent, teacher, peers, or coach, or later, from the incentive of fair monetary compensation. The poor score for Appalachia in the Gallup-Healthways Life Evaluation points to hopelessness and despair as a likely contributing factor for why too many people give up trying to obtain and maintain gainful employment.

Economic stability must be rooted in strong communities, school, family life, and churches. Just as a stool needs sturdy legs to stand, children have improved prospects when the "legs" of family, school, community, and moral virtue are sturdy and mutually supportive partners. If any of these legs is weak, as is the case with children living with dysfunctional families, then the other legs must step up with added strength.

Although Vance had a chaotic growing up, he had the strengthening benefit of a family supportive of education. His mother was salutatorian of her high school class, and while raising her children she earned an associate's degree in nursing at a community college. She enthusiastically helped him with school projects, regularly took him to the local library, and encouraged him to read. Vance writes, "Mom cared about enterprises of the mind. Nothing brought her greater joy than when I finished a book and asked for another" (60, 65). His grandfather helped him practice math weekly (59–60). His limited-educated Mamaw reached deep into her sparse financial resources to buy her grandson a $180 graphing calculator for a high school honors math class, and scolded him into excelling in it (137–38). His Mamaw also demanded that he get a job to learn the value of a hard-earned dollar. Vance writes that his community experience as a cashier at a local grocery educated him "into an amateur sociologist" as he observed the traits of his customers (138–39). These experiences plausibly laid the groundwork in developing his political, economic, and social theories.

Teachers and administrators in our schools try but cannot fully compensate for dysfunctional households. State standards push schools for academic achievement, yet some of their students cannot learn until their deep emotional needs are addressed. Such children must have rays of hope each school day that bring them an intrinsic sense of satisfaction and success, like Jeannette Walls thriving on the staff of her school newspaper. Our students need to be knowledgeable and proud of their heritage, culture, and environment. Community members can teach traditional Appalachian music, history, ancestral background, and the local nature. Some of our local male school custodians, for instance, take on a few boys to help them, becoming de facto mentors and role models. When Dwight Diller substituted as a middle school music teacher, he taught students traditional Appalachian music. "A lot of the mountain kids were in the slow classes," he recalls, "but they sang the words much better than the elite kids."[34] Hands-on vocational skills can begin in elementary school to benefit not only the children from working-class families but those whose future might be in white-collar employment. An "it takes a village to raise a child" mentality is especially needed if ACE children are to transcend. The village must embrace these children so they can have hope and emulate positive, engaged role models. ACE children especially need to watch how adult leaders cope with conflict, stress, failure, and success. Involved role models can inculcate virtues such as honesty, kindness, generosity, forgiveness, humility, confidence, dependability, respect for others, mercy, and tough love. They can demonstrate helpful life skills such as how to tie a necktie, how to look someone in the eye and give a handshake, how to bake a cake, how to follow proper table manners at a sit-down meal, and how to stick with a difficult task to its completion. For several years, I worked in behavior management services with children and their families. Our most successful intervention involved role modeling through our trained staff, including summer-employed college students, with behaviorally challenged children in one-to-one settings and in group settings. Much of the time they just hung out together.[35]

Another example of successful role modeling is the Mountaineer Challenge Academy near Kingwood, West Virginia, a boot-camp-style program run by the West Virginia National Guard and funded by the US Department of Defense. The program accepts on a voluntary basis sixteen- to eighteen-year-olds who are at risk educationally for a twenty-two-week stint. A day begins with a five o'clock wakeup for an hour of physical training, then barracks maintenance, followed by breakfast, academic study, and classes in life coping, goal planning, and job skills. During my time in social services, I assisted two troubled young men to apply. Both of my clients completed their GED, one of them after starting out from a third-grade proficiency level. Their families were ecstatic with pride at their sons' accomplishments and the dignity, confidence, and social manners they now exhibited.[36]

I have seen the benefits of such interventions many times. During my eleven years as director of our county library system, we encouraged music teachers to use our facilities at no charge to teach young people traditional Appalachian banjo, fiddle, and guitar.[37] Our library developed an extensive collection of books and videos on Appalachia and West Virginia, along with local histories and family genealogies. I often smiled when I'd see at our Internet-connected computer tables the socioeconomic spectrum of our citizenry. After school, latchkey children use the gym run by our local Parks and Recreation organization.

High Rocks Academy is another example. Started in 1996 by middle school librarian and gifted education teacher Susan Burt, it is a local nonprofit that operates two-week summer camps for girls beginning high school along with weekly sessions for academic enrichment. During camp each girl gets to take care of a riding horse, help with camp chores, and experience drama, journaling, and overall confidence building. Burt observed a worrying trend that girls in her community began middle school with positive energy and sunny dispositions, excited about their future, but soon began to downslide, failing to live up to their early potential. As a result, doors to their futures began closing and their choices became few. She designed High Rocks as a way to step in to provide girls with self-confidence, social relationship skills, and academic capability as a strong head start in life.[38] High Rocks as well as an Upward Bound program give teens, often from families with no college experience, maturity, confidence, and experience with academic rigor they will need for success in competitive colleges.

Religious institutions are the most visible expression of shared virtues in America, and J. D. Vance is cognizant of the transformative power of faith. As he writes in *Hillbilly Elegy*, during the brief times he lived with his biological father's family, he experienced a happy, functional, loving family life in large part because his dad's church provided tangible social, emotional, and financial support for struggling people in the congregation. Vance states:

I think it's important to point out that Christianity, in the quirky way I've experienced it, was really important to me, too. For my dad, the way he tells it is that he was a hard partier, he drank a lot, and didn't have a lot of direction. His Christian faith gave him focus, forced him to think hard about his personal choices, and gave him a community of people who demanded, even if only implicitly, that he act a certain way. I think we all understate the importance of moral pressure, but it helped my dad, and it has certainly helped me![39]

Although Appalachians predominantly express Christian belief, the majority of them do not participate in a church congregation. Nevertheless, church engagement has long played a crucial supportive role in the region, even though it has long been mischaracterized. As Deborah Vansau McCauley's exhaustive research reveals, "American Protestantism in particular has historically and consistently interpreted the worship practices, belief systems, and church traditions of the mountain people as the religion of a sublime subculture of poverty and the product of powerlessness and alienation"; she has seen the people of the region as "waiting for the salvific actions of the home missionaries to *help* mountain people and their region partake of *Christian civilization*." Yet, in reality, "these worship communities and the ongoing and very strong influences of mountain religious culture beyond the doors of the mountain church house are arguably the most important and most prominent stabilizing force in the sociocultural life of the region."[40]

In other words, McCauley asserts that mainstream churches are patronizing and condescending to what Vance might describe as hillbilly churches. His Mamaw's Christian faith stood at the center of her life. She sent much of her spare income to her Jackson, Kentucky, home church, and her confidence in God kept her hope alive in times of despair. Would a county seat "First Church" welcome into the fold the menthol-smoking, uneducated, peel-the-paint-cussing, hillbilly Mamaw? Would someone like Mamaw be willing to change her lifestyle in order to accommodate congregation gatekeepers? Congregation memberships seem as sharply drawn along lines of class, culture, and race as they are in theology and practice.

Tragically, many of these mountain churches are dying off, and the emotional catharsis, confidence, and hope provided by vibrant mountain church life is waning in many rural communities. This results in a loss of role modeling, compassionate service, and moral virtues for the larger community. Are there churches that are willing to make needed adaptations to help struggling families and children to transcend? Or will eleven o'clock Sunday morning continue to be the most class-segregated hour in America?

It is important to remember, in this context, that Jesus was a hillbilly. He grew up in Nazareth, a small town in Galilee of a few hundred closely related persons. The Bible records a derisive comment from Nathanael when he is invited to see Jesus. "Can anything good come out of Nazareth?" he sniffs.[41] As are "hillbillies" today, Galileans were harshly stigmatized by urbanites as backward, crude, and irreligious, and as a people who spoke with a peculiar accent. Obery Hendricks writes, "Galileans had a distinctively accented pronunciation of Hebrew that caused them to slur their words in what was thought to be a 'country' way. This accent sometimes resulted in mispronunciations that made Galileans objects of ridicule."[42]

Numerous studies positively correlate religious practice to desirable social characteristics such as lower rates of illegitimacy, divorce, suicide, and poverty, and higher levels of self-esteem and marital satisfaction. Church congregations have the God-given mandate to warmly and humbly invite to their welcoming table those who are struggling. In so doing, such congregations exert great effort and self-sacrifice while risking community misunderstanding, and rejection and ingratitude from those to whom they reach out.

While outside help is desirable and needed, Vance emphasizes that individual responsibility and agency are essential for positive outcomes in children and, cumulatively, in society. More than anything else, children need stable, competent parental figures. Writing from his own life experience and backed by a plethora of studies, Vance offers a succinct synopsis of the root of much social malaise. "I think that any social policy program would recognize what my old high school's teachers see every day: that the real problem for so many of these kids is what happens (or doesn't happen) at home" (244). Nationally what is happening at home is a seismic negative shift in marriage, cohabitation, and divorce that is impacting children and massively contributing to income inequality. This shift is exacerbated within less educated populations, including those in Appalachia. Less educated women are five times more likely to be cohabitating, and such relationships on average last only about two years. Fewer than half of the children in cohabiting households are living with both biological parents, compared to 90 percent of those living in married couples' households. Fathers with less education are also significantly less likely to live with their children, which negatively impacts their children's outcomes.[43] One news story reports that "researchers estimate that between one-fifth and two-fifths of the growth in family income inequality is due to a difference in marriage patterns between Americans of higher and lower socioeconomic status, determined by educational achievement. And projections show that the gap in marriage will continue to widen over time."[44]

In contrast, stable educated families invest more quality time in their children. They are more likely to read to their children, which studies show is the single most important activity in predicting future success in school. According to Read Aloud, "Some children will hear thirty million fewer words than their peers before age four. Studies have shown the number of words a child knows when entering kindergarten is predictive of future learning success."[45] Role-modeling fathers who read with their children and help them with their schoolwork overcome the too-prevalent attitude that associates "accomplishments in school with femininity," which Vance notes was commonplace among his male high school classmates (245).[46] There are available resources and opportunities for parents wanting assistance even in rural communities to gain at little to no cost, including GED tutoring, computer skills, library access, and parenting help. Most communities have volunteers with hands and hearts willing and capable to help struggling families. That too many choose not to avail themselves of these uplifting opportunities is the elegy.

ARE WE LISTENING?

I began this essay with a quest: to define the significance of *Hillbilly Elegy*, a mission that began during the 2017 Appalachian Studies Conference when

I heard an esteemed panel critically deprecate the book. I was puzzled, since I had read the book more positively. I had read Vance's approach as one that drew from his life's experience growing up in a dysfunctional family within an ailing Appalachian diasporic cultural and community setting that seemed to predestine him to a bleak future. Fortunately, timely interventions jumpstarted Vance's transcendence to a promising future. His tumultuous childhood was diametrically different than my own, yet we both have Appalachian experience and knowledge of real problems in our region and its people. Over the years I have come to know a modest number of people who have grown up in highly dysfunctional families yet have "beaten the odds stacked against them" to become successful, happy, altruistic adults. Their analysis of life and society is a perspective that deserves an objective hearing, especially if it can be used to improve the likelihood that environmentally distressed children can transcend into positive adult outcomes.

I was at the same conference for a panel discussing a recent publication by the Catholic Committee of Appalachia, *The Telling Takes Us Home: Taking Our Place in The Stories That Shape Us*. It is a "People's Pastoral" that seeks to give voice to the marginalized, poor, and discarded people of Appalachia. It states in part: "And so before daring to offer any call to action, we have simply asked people in Appalachia, and in particular, those who are struggling, a simple, but very profound question: 'What is it like to be you? And further, what is it like to be you in this place?' We know that there are voices we have not heard closely enough in the past. Some people within our communities have stories that we are only now beginning to hear."[47]

Hillbilly Elegy is J. D. Vance's story of growing up in a chaotic family. He examines his family strengths and pathologies, offers an interpretation through his Appalachian diaspora context and culture, and tries to analyze how he ended up happy and successful despite the fact that life's cards were stacked against him. As *Telling Takes Us Home* makes clear, the voiceless poor are seldom heard unless someone with agency can give them a platform to speak to ears that will listen, hearts that care, and hands that can empower. Although Vance is no longer voiceless and poor, he speaks out of the confusing, hopeless time he had growing up. Vance speaks to his own hillbilly people and for his own hillbilly people so that the nation will understand and care.

The Telling Takes Us Home asks, "Can we really hear the cry of the poor, and take our place among the excluded, if befriending the poor and marginalized is uncomfortable, and we don't always like what we hear when we listen to their struggles and ideas?"[48] I titled this essay "It's Crazy Around Here, I Don't Know What to Do about It, and I'm Just a Kid." J. D. Vance is no longer a kid, his life is no longer crazy, and he writes his memoir to help people recognize how they too can do something about it.

NOTES

1. Because the workshop was forty years ago, my words in quotes are my reenactment of the thrust of the speaker's theme.
2. Donna F. LaMar, *Transcending Turmoil: Survivors of Dysfunctional Families* (New York: Plenum, 1992), 106.
3. Sidney M. Jourard, *Disclosing Man to Himself* (New York: Van Nostrand, 1968), 233, quoted in LaMar, *Transcending Turmoil*, 101.
4. LaMar, *Transcending Turmoil*, 201. Donna F. LaMar, telephone interview by the author, October 27, 2017. LaMar reaffirmed the value of disclosing one's traumatic childhood to the healing process. "One 'must' face up to and 'express' one's painful experiences!"
5. LaMar, *Transcending Turmoil*, 202.
6. Jeannette Walls, *Glass Castle* (New York: Scribner, 2005).
7. "'Glass Castle's' Jeannette Walls: I Get Why Trump Won, Why Don't Others?," *Philadelphia Inquirer Daily News*, August 10, 2017, http://www.philly.com/ philly/entertainment/movies/glass-castle-jeannette-walls-donald-trump-woody-harrelson-20170810.html.
8. Words in quotation marks are mine, not Vance's. In a lengthy interview with Rod Dreher, Vance is quoted as stating, "I'm a big believer in the power to change social norms. To take an obvious recent example, I see the decline of smoking as not just an economic or regulatory matter, but something our culture really flipped on. So there's value in all of us—whether we have a relatively large platform or if our platform is just the people who live with us—trying to be a little kinder to the kids who want to make a better future for themselves. That's a big part of the reason I wrote the book: it's meant not just for elites, but for people from my own clan, in the hopes that they'll better appreciate the ways they can help (or hurt) their own kin." See Rod Dreher, "Trump: Tribune of Poor White People," *American Conservative*, July 22, 2016, http://www .theamericanconservative.com/dreher/trump-us-politics-poor-whites/.
9. Substance Abuse and Mental Health Administration, "Adverse Childhood Experiences," September 5, 2017, https://www.samhsa.gov/capt/practicing-effective-prevention/prevention-behavioral-health/adverse-childhood-experiences.
10. V. J. Felitti, R. F. Anda, D. Nordenberg, D. F. Williamson, A. M. Spitz, V. Edwards, M. P. Koss, and J. S. Marks, "Relationship of Childhood Abuse and Household Dysfunction to Many of the Leading Causes of Death in Adults: The Adverse

Childhood Experiences (ACE) Study," *American Journal of Preventive Medicine* 14 (1998): 245–58.

11. Gabor Matte, *In the Realm of Hungry Ghosts* (Berkeley, CA: North Atlantic Books, 2008/2010), 197–98.

12. LaMar, *Transcending Turmoil*, 3.

13. Ibid., 21.

14. Walls, *Glass Castle*, 203.

15. LaMar, *Transcending Turmoil*, 42–43.

16. Walls, *Glass Castle*, 229.

17. Ibid., 236.

18. LaMar, *Transcending Turmoil*, 72.

19. Allen Johnson, "The Rhythm of Dwight Diller," *Goldenseal*, Winter 2014, 16. The quotation is a summary from notes taken during interviews with Diller.

20. LaMar, *Transcending Turmoil*, 126.

21. Ibid., 172.

22. Gallup-Healthways, http://www.well-beingindex.com/. See also https://www.eight-rivers.org/Pocahontas/Quality-of-Life_Studies.html.

23. "Forbes Best States for Business, 2016 Ranking," *Forbes*, https://www.forbes.com/places/wv/.

24. Scott Cohn, "America's Top States For Business," *CNBC*, July 11, 2017, https://www.cnbc.com/2017/07/11/west-virginia-americas-worst-state-for-business-in-2017.html.

25. "Human Health Impacts," *Appalachian Voices*, http://appvoices.org/end-mountaintop-removal/health-impacts/. This web page correlates strip mining with human health impacts as well as population loss.

26. Kelvin Pollard and Linda A. Jacobsen, "The Appalachian Region: A Data Overview from the 2008–2012 American Community Survey Chartbook" (Appalachian Regional Commission, 2014), https://www.arc.gov/assets/research_reports/DataOverviewfrom2008-2012ACS.pdf.

27. Arlie Russell Hochschild, *Strangers in Their Own Land: Anger and Mourning on the American Right* (New York: New Press, 2016), 135–51. The wording in these paragraphs is mine, synthesized from Hochschild's key points and in her style.

28. Quoted in Dreher, "Trump."

29. Barry Meier, *Pain Killer* (New York: St. Martin's, 2003.)

30. Larry Gibson, interviewed by Michael and Carrie Kline, ca. 2010, KK-CT-025-057 side A, Michael and Carrie Nobel Kline Collection, Berea College Special Collections and Archives, Berea, KY. Gibson grew up in an abusive, often impoverished home. He was a school dropout. He worked as a custodian at a General Motors factory until disabled, then returned to his boyhood Kayford Mountain and became incensed at the surface mine destruction. He received skillful support to become an activist and charismatic leader, even speaking to standing ovations at Yale, Stanford, and other influential forums. Gibson was a classic transcender. He died in 2012.

31. David Gutman, "Age, Poor Health, Low Education Keep Half of W.Va. Jobless," *Charleston (WV) Gazette-Mail*, January 18, 2015, https://www.wvgazettemail.com/business/age-poor-health-low-education-keep-half-of-w-va/article_f9b87625-de63-5062-99a9-9aef4663be8e.html.

32. Kenneth Varner, telephone interview by the author, November 5, 2017.
33. Jud Worth, telephone interview by the author, November 7, 2017.
34. Based on conversations over the years with my friend, Dwight Diller.
35. Timberline Health Group, Marlinton, WV, late 1990s. The office is now closed.
36. Mountaineer Challenge Academy, http://wvchallenge.org.
37. Pocahontas County Free Libraries, Marlinton, WV, http://www.pocahontaslibrary.org/index-1.html.
38. High Rocks, https://highrocks.org/.
39. Dreher, "Trump."
40. Deborah Vansau McCauley, *Appalachian Mountain Religion: A History* (University of Illinois Press, 1995), 7–8.
41. John 1:46.
42. Obery M. Hendricks, Jr., *The Politics of Jesus* (New York: Doubleday, 2006), 70. Dr. Hendricks is a biblical scholar at New York Theological Seminary and an Ordained Elder in the African Methodist Episcopal Church.
43. Shelly Lundberg, Robert A. Pollak, and Jenna Stearns, "Family Inequality: Diverging Patterns in Marriage, Cohabitation, and Childbearing" (US National Library of Medicine, National Institutes of Health, 2016), https://www.ncbi.nlm.nih.gov/pmc/articles/PMC4861075/.
44. Lindsey Cook, "For Richer, Not Poorer: Marriage and the Growing Class Divide," *U.S. News & World Report*, October 26, 2015, https://www.usnews.com/news/blogs/data-mine/2015/10/26/marriage-and-the-growing-class-divide.
45. Read Aloud West Virginia, https://readaloudwestvirginia.org/.
46. Each year, our county newspaper publishes a group photo of high school honor graduates. I notice that typically about two-thirds are female.
47. *The Telling Takes Us Home: Taking Our Place in the Stories That Shape Us* (A People's Pastoral from the Catholic Committee of Appalachia) (Spencer, WV, 2016).
48. Ibid., 7.

"FALLING IN LOVE," BALSAM BALD, THE BLUE RIDGE PARKWAY, 1982

TEXT AND PHOTOGRAPH BY DANIELLE DULKEN

MY PARENTS took refuge in the mountains of western North Carolina from the systems of "meritocracy" that J. D. Vance's book champions. My mother was raised by working-class immigrants. My father was raised by well-to-do socialites. The deep green forests of the now receding eastern hemlock lured them toward an imagined life in which the demands of labor and status were secondary to a relationship with the natural world. As they journeyed up the Saluda grade along I-26, their Land Cruiser became a chrysalis cradling them through a transformation. They sloughed off material expectations and adopted communities and landscapes in the Mountain South, which in turn nurtured their romance, and soon, their family.

My father, a carpenter, made a life for himself in Horse Shoe, North Carolina. My mother took odd jobs to support him. In 1985, while hiking in Pisgah Forest, my mother's water broke. I was born the next morning. Sometime during the next thirty years, my parents divorced and my father relocated further into the mountains. There, he built himself a house out of hemlock.

Holding this page from my mother's scrapbook, I see how person and place can become intimately entangled. "A geography of the heart" is how bell hooks describes her relationship to her home in Appalachia. When I look at these photographs of my parents I understand what she means.

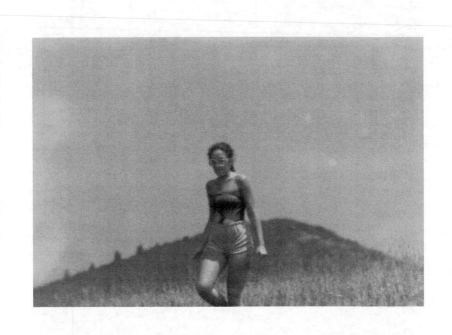

BLACK HILLBILLIES HAVE NO TIME FOR ELEGIES

WILLIAM H. TURNER

I IMAGINE that around the same time in the spring of 2013 that J. D. Vance and his bicoastal brain trust were polishing up the galley proofs of *Hillbilly Elegy: A Memoir of a Family and Culture in Crisis*, Ron Eller and I were huddled in Boone, North Carolina, with Karida Brown at the annual conference of the Appalachian Studies Association (ASA).

Ron, now retired from his thirty-five-year distinguished professorship in the History Department at the University of Kentucky (including a decade-long stint as Director of its Appalachian Center), was then still basking, always modestly and humbly, in the glow of his award-winning 2013-published tome, *Uneven Ground: Appalachia since 1945*.[1] He and I were gathering close with Karida—then a graduate student in the Sociology Department at Brown—to buff up our plans for a panel I had arranged titled "Demography of Blacks in Appalachia: 1980–2012," which I had proposed months earlier to Karida, whom I have known since the hour of her birth.[2] I invited Ms. Brown to join the panel to discuss the major themes of her dissertation on blacks' out-migration from eastern Kentucky. When I sent Ron the synopsis of her work and asked him to join me in introducing this brilliant young scholar to our ASA colleagues, he averred, "Wow! Karida's research substantiates those positive traits about Appalachian families and culture that we've been conveying now for eighty years between us!"

When the session ended, Ron and I stood to the side and watched with a degree of smug delight as at least three dozen of the attendees peppered her with questions and a tangible excited level of warmth, and asked her to flash back through her PowerPoint slides. The three of us left twenty-five minutes later only because the conference staff politely insisted they had to make room for the next session. Karida exited the room, her belongings chested, yet still smiling radiantly and spiritedly engaged with people who now seemed like her "followers." Her stories about blacks in and from Appalachia had exposed a shimmering light. Not a requiem in her entire presentation!

"Yes, really," I heard Karida—a Temple University graduate who holds a master's degree from the University of Pennsylvania, say again and again, "my father and mother were born and raised in Lynch, Kentucky, in Harlan County. There were twenty-three [!] children between the two families, and my grandfathers were coal miners, both for at least forty years, having migrated to Harlan County in the late 1920s from Central Alabama." She told the story of her parents—Richard and Arnita—who, like 99 percent of their contemporaries, left the Lynch Colored School in the mid-1960s and migrated to their Promised Land.[3]

In investigating what happened to the dozens of black families or individuals who migrated between 1950 and 2000 from a coal camp in Harlan, Letcher, or Perry counties in eastern Kentucky, Karida found that for most, their migratory endpoint—their Promised Land—was not New York City, where her parents settled, but more likely Ohio—Cincinnati, Cleveland, Columbus, Dayton, or Middletown—not insignificantly, the same place J. D. Vance's mother and grandparents settled. Same migratory route. Very similar chronicle, timeline, and collective Appalachian working-class memoir, but with a twist—that of the Appalachian black working class.

Before the weekend of the 2013 ASA conference was over, I introduced Karida to my old colleague and friend Bill Ferris, the event's keynote speaker. A folklorist from Mississippi specializing in African American music, Ferris is the Joel R. Williamson Eminent Professor of History at the University of North Carolina at Chapel Hill and Senior Associate Director of the Center for the Study of the American South. After the conference, Karida invited Bill Ferris onto her dissertation committee as outsider reader, and he invited her into his network at the Center for the Study of the American South.

Within a year, the Eastern Kentucky African American Migration Project (EKAAMP) was born. In the words of its website, it is a "public humanities project designed to document and archive the unique cultural history of a diaspora of African Americans who partook in an intergenerational migration into and out of the Appalachian region of eastern Kentucky throughout the 20th century. The Appalachian region often escapes the collective consciousness of Americana. Even when representations of Appalachia do enter the cultural-historical discourse in academia or in the media, African Americans are rarely inscribed into the social heritage of this region."[4] Karida's project is intended to reinscribe African Americans into this regional experience. Karida went on to receive her PhD in sociology from Brown University in 2016, earning the 2017 American Sociological Association's Best Dissertation Award. Her dissertation, "Before They Were Diamonds," "traces the formation of an African American mining community in Eastern Kentucky, and its transformation into a diasporic community when the mines closed and the Civil Rights Movement created mobility opportunities."[5]

JET AND *EBONY* MAGAZINES: CHANNEL FOR BLACK APPALACHIANS' VALUES

I was born around the time—1946—that blacks in the coalfields of eastern Kentucky moved toward a half century of labor, at the bottom of the working class.[6] With the mechanization of the industry, they began to migrate, en masse, to spaces later called the Rust Belt, cities like Detroit and Cleveland, where people of color populate America's hyperghettos. My grandparents' and parents' generations, by and large, had migrated from Central Alabama to the coal counties of eastern Kentucky between 1900 and 1940. My mother was born in Harlan County (Benham) in 1924.

They were no different than J. D. Vance's people, except, of course, for the lingering effects of what C. Vann Woodward called "The Peculiar Institution," and the intergenerationally transferred status associated with second-class citizenship. While Vance never addressed why his family and the culture that influenced their values failed—what precipitated the crisis—black people from

Appalachian coal camps and elsewhere knew the answer. They had lived, since slavery, in a failed system. I never, if ever, heard anybody early on in my life use the word "capitalism," but it was clear to me that the system under which we lived did not permit the even and equal flow of economic resources and opportunities. I experienced—as did my peers—a system in our coal camp that allowed a privileged few, the "boss" class, to have resources that we were denied. That same racialized system waited for us when we migrated; and we knew how it worked. We were taught to accept the fact that the system would not change the rules that privileged the majority of white people and discriminated against the majority of people who looked like us. We were taught to change the system by dreaming that we could do better if we acted and behaved as though we could improve our situation by staying together as families and working twice as hard as whites to get half as much from that system.[7]

I read *Hillbilly Elegy* with more than three decades of study and intervention work in black communities in eastern Kentucky, southwestern Virginia, and southern West Virginia and with Karida's work in mind. In the summer of 2016, as Karida was completing her dissertation, I visited a number of childhood friends in the network of what we called the Eastern Kentucky Social Club. In that group there is a strong emphasis on the "can-do" spirit that is best exemplified in the life mission of John Johnson, the founder of Johnson Publications, the issuer of *Jet* and *Ebony* magazines. Born into poverty and privation in Arkansas City, Arkansas, Johnson, like my grandparents' generation, migrated to Chicago, where he created for himself a place in the pantheon of the American rags-to-riches experience. Over the years, Johnson received numerous awards and accolades for his contributions to society and was awarded the Presidential Medal of Freedom by President Clinton in 1996. At the time, Clinton credited Johnson with giving "African Americans a voice and a face, in his words, 'a new sense of somebody-ness, of who they were and what they could do.'"[8] Blacks leaving the colored schools of eastern Kentucky with the migratory stream that carried Vance's grandparents to Ohio went with this same "make something of yourself" attitude and an attachment to the belief that one could and must "succeed, against all odds."[9] Black people throughout Appalachia's warren of coal camps were imbued with the message of resilience contained in the Black National Anthem, "Lift Every Voice and Sing," which resonated regularly in (segregated) school and church settings, going back to when it was published in 1905. Some appropriate lyrics:

> Sing a song full of the faith that the dark past has taught us,
> Sing a song full of the hope that the present has brought us;
> Facing the rising sun of our new day begun,
> Let us march on till victory is won.[10]

BEEN TO THE MOUNTAINTOP: A SAMPLER OF SUCCESS ALONG LOONEY CREEK IN HARLAN COUNTY, KENTUCKY

It has been my privilege in ethnographic work and community service—and in my personal life—to come to know personally or peripherally just about every respectable, high-achieving African American to come out of the Appalachian coalfields, those who adhered to the values of both Booker T. Washington and W. E. B. Du Bois.[11] Likewise, I can say the same about the most reprehensible ruffians—like the ones in Vance's family—from the same region. In my work, inspired by Johnson, I have chosen to concentrate on the former group—like the ones I visited in the summer of 2016.

I started from my newly adopted home in Houston with a stop in the elegant home of Dr. Frieda Outlaw, my high school classmate, who now lives in suburban Nashville. The chief administrator of a state health agency, Frieda took her bachelor's from Berea College, her master's in psychology from Boston College, and a doctorate in psychology from Catholic University. Frieda and I were born two weeks apart in the Hospital of Notre Dame in Lynch, Kentucky, in the summer of 1946. During our visit, we phoned and chatted with her sister Rita, also a Berea grad who later earned a master's degree in mathematics from Michigan. Rita recently retired after a long distinguished career with IBM. I told Rita—who almost won the big prize on *Jeopardy* a few years back—how all the homefolks in Harlan County were still amazed with her Harvard-grad daughter, Skylar, who earned a perfect score on the SAT and now works for the National Security Agency. During our conversation, I told them how Frieda's friend and fellow Berea grad Jim Branscombe had brought

Hillbilly Elegy to my attention. "Don't you get tired of reading that crap about mountain people?"[12] Freida asked, deadpan. Not a question.[13]

During my visit, Freida's husband, Lou, who holds a doctorate in philosophy from Boston College and is a tenured professor of philosophy and African American studies at Vanderbilt, took me for a spin in his airplane, a Diamond DA40 with Garmin 1000 avionics. Lou hails from Starkville (Oktibbeha County), Mississippi—an Appalachian Regional Commission–designated Appalachian county. Up, up, and away from slavery to freedom.

From the Outlaws, I took a flight to Washington, D.C., where I visited with Bernard Bickerstaff, seventy-four, longtime head coach and front-office executive in the National Basketball Association. Bernie, a native of Benham, near Lynch, became the youngest head coach in NCAA Division I history, when, at twenty-four, he starting calling the shots at San Diego State University. He had worked in a coal mine outside Cumberland briefly after high school (1960), just before going to Cleveland, Ohio, to live with relatives. Bernie earned a scholarship to play basketball for Rio Grande College in Ohio. After college, over a four-decades-long career at the highest level in his profession, Bernie has been the head coach for the NBA's Seattle SuperSonics, Denver Nuggets, Washington Bullets/Wizards, Charlotte Bobcats, and Los Angeles Lakers. At the time of this writing, Bernie is a front office executive with the Cleveland Cavaliers; his son, John Blair, is the head coach for the Memphis Grizzlies.

Driving not far from Bernie and Eugenia's well-heeled neighborhood near Embassy Row in the nation's capital, I next arrived in the Southeast region of the city to visit with other childhood neighbors, the Freeman brothers—James, Jr., "Junebug" (now seventy-four), and my classmate, Willie, better known at home as "Tank"—both Army veterans and retired D.C. policemen. We talked again of how their father was one of those who left Lynch in the "middle of the night" to avoid the bill collectors from the company store. After being laid off at the US Steel–owned mine in Lynch in 1958, he migrated to New York City. We laughed about the government-issued bologna and cheese they survived on at that time; later when the two brothers left the military service, they purchased a home in Washington for their parents and younger siblings.

In nearby Maryland, I visited with my first cousin's Lynch Colored School classmate and best friend, Betty Freeman, the half sister of the Freeman brothers. Betty, eighty-two, is a retired coordinator of high school counselors for the Aurora, Colorado, school system. She graduated from Tennessee State University and lived for forty-seven years in Denver, but moved to Oxen Hill, Maryland, three years ago, to be near her brothers and grown children—who were committed to "take care of Mama." Delecia Eller, her oldest, is completing a doctorate this year, while her youngest daughter, LaDoncia, is an administrator for a federal cyber security agency. Betty says, emphatically, "I expect the same high achievement from my six grandchildren."

Betty's fellow 1958 Tennessee State graduate was yet another Lynch Colored School graduate named Willis "Bunny" Thomas, now deceased. Bunny was an All-American basketball player who was on the starting team for more than a decade with the world-famous Harlem Globetrotters. How well I remember—I was fourteen at the time—when dozens of black kids gathered at the bottom of the street from my home, in front of the pool room and juke joint—when Bunny came home in a brand spanking new white 1960 drop-top convertible Thunderbird. He was *somebody*, the personification of the black role models covered every week and month in *Jet* and *Ebony* magazines. In Harlan County in 1960, we were, to be sure, isolated from the rest of the world, but we had homefolks who came back regularly whose lives were marked by unusually high achievements and accomplishments, living legends who let us young ones know that we too could "be somebody." Fact is, every one of the eleven Thomas children—their dad an Alabama-born and -raised Methodist preacher and US Steel–employed coal miner—graduated from college. Another person in the generation of Vance's grandparents, General Pearson (his given first name), left Lynch Colored School in 1950 to study and graduated from the Howard University School of Medicine in the nation's capital. Son of Harlan County black coal miner. Graduate of Lynch Colored School. 1950. Medical school graduate. Think about it!

After four weeks on the road, I arrived back in Houston where my childhood friend, Reverend Dr. Franklin Callaway, also from Benham, ferried me from the airport to his ginormous home in the Woodlands section of America's most diverse city. A retired Air Force veteran and IBM executive, Frank holds a bachelor's degree from Texas Christian University and a doctorate in systematic theology from Louisville Presbyterian Seminary. We connected in a three-way call to his brother-in-law Kevin, a VP at Verizon in Atlanta, and his brother Tony, holder of the MBA and owner of an in-home health care business in Raleigh. He asked about Tony's daughter, Tiffany, who graduated from Wake Forest University with a chemistry degree and from Harvard Medical School. Tiffany, a certified cardiologist, did her residency at Duke School of Medicine. Her grandfather, Harris Callaway, whom I knew all my life, was a Harlan County coal miner and father of fifteen.

Tony's wife, Patricia, focused her University of Kentucky–awarded doctoral dissertation, "'Don't You Fall': Resilient and Academically Successful African Americans' Literacy and Family Involvement Practices," on Benham High School, from where Frankie and Tony and their thirteen siblings graduated. The Callaway family of Benham personified the highest expression of the attitudinal and cultural values that influenced the local blacks who became high achievers. There was an extraordinary and disproportionate number of such high achievers.

In our conversations about "whatever happened to so-and-so from Benham," we brought up the name Jeffrey McDonald, one of Frank's classmates. Jeff, who lives in Saint Louis, holds an undergraduate degree from Kentucky State University and an MBA from Boston College. He retired two years ago after a successful thirty-eight-year career as an accountant and comptroller at various companies including Monsanto, DuPont Chemical, and Ralston Purina. Jeff's younger sister, Bettye McDonald Powell, is vice mayor of Trotwood, Ohio, but a stone's throw from Vance's home ground of Middletown.

After our call with Kevin and Tony, we then teleconferenced with my brothers—Tony, Karl, and Jeff—who live in Cincinnati, New Orleans, and Indianapolis, respectively. Tony, who has owned his CPA firm for almost four decades, graduated from Western Kentucky University after spending a year at Notre Dame. Karl is married to Cicely, a Vassar grad and Vanderbilt University–trained pediatrician. Their sons, Lawliss and Justin, were raised in New Orleans and earned their bachelor's and master's degrees at Morehouse College and the University of Kentucky and at Stanford University and Columbia University, respectively. Justin is an executive at Google and lives in Palo Alto, California. Karl holds a bachelor's degree in philosophy from Fisk University and a master's in diplomacy and international economics from Kentucky and co-owns a thriving seafood import-export company with his Chinese American business partner. We all joked about how our youngest brother Jeff, sixty, has sold each of us Mercedes-Benzes over the years, "exporting" them to our various homes from Indianapolis where for the past three decades he has been among the top Mercedes salespersons in the Chicago-area market. He has also sold Mercedes to his Lynch high school classmates, Kenny Austin, an anesthesiologist in Fort Wayne, Indiana, and Dwayne Baskin, a Kentucky grad and now an executive with a major electrical wiring firm in Indianapolis.

After these calls we remembered Paul Gaffney, the Tennessee Wesleyan College graduate who, like Bunny Thomas, played for the Globetrotters, for fifteen years, under the handle "Showtime." Because we were talking about friends from home with stellar resumes in professional athletics, Paul reminded us of Larry Kirksey, from Harlan, who had just retired from a long coaching career in the NFL. Among others, Larry coached the 49ers' premier wide receiver Jerry Rice. We chatted as though we'd been together the week before, although most of us had not seen each other in several years.

I finally arrived home, having nearly finished reading and taking notes in the margins of my by then dog-eared copy of *Hillbilly Elegy*. I was greeted by my daughter Kisha, a Spelman College and Temple University graduate and college history professor and fashion designer and entrepreneur. My sons are also both college grads. William, the older, is a Morehouse, Kentucky, and Clemson grad and now an associate in one of Houston's largest architectural firms—Kirksey and Associates. Our youngest son, Hodari, is a master machinist for a company that supplies parts to a Houston-based oil and gas conglomerate. Hundreds of books and artworks specific to Appalachia adorn the bookshelves and walls in my home. Unlike Vance's family, neither we nor any of this sampling of blacks with Appalachian roots have lost our way back to the future that our upbringing provided.

IF BLACK HILLBILLIES CAN MAKE IT IN AMERICA, THEN WHAT'S VANCE'S FAMILY'S EXCUSE?

Why these stories about blacks with roots in the eastern Kentucky coalfields? What do these bits and pieces about the lives of just a few of my lifelong friends and family—and our kith, kin, and kind—have to do with the way J. D. Vance remembers his family and his people?

If indeed Vance's grandparents represent the white underclass in America, then my grandparents and parents and those of the folks I met and talked with (as well as several dozen others I did not) during the month I read his book represent the black underclass. All of us were born and raised in the coal camps of Harlan County, Kentucky—at the base of Black Mountain, Kentucky's highest peak. We could be found in Harlan City (in the "colored section" known as "Georgetown"). There are many similar stories of other Black Appalachians such as the Olinger family from Perry County, in Hazard, but a stone's throw from Vance's Jackson. The oldest son, Glenn, was an academic scholarship recipient—but also a stellar athlete—at Kentucky's famed Centre College and recently retired from his work as a science teacher and football coach from the Fayette County School System. His brother David studied at Berea College and UK law, while both of the girls in this high-achieving Black Appalachian family graduated from Transylvania University in Lexington. My brother Jeff is married to their sister, Millie Olinger, regional marketing manager for a major pharmaceutical company based in Indianapolis. Their daughter Whitney graduated in the spring of 2018 from Hampton University in Virginia. Two of Whitney's cousins, my brother Tony's daughters—Camille and Brittany—also graduated from Hampton and work in professional capacities.

The press gives Vance profuse recognition and high praise for his family stories even as he holds them responsible for their misfortunes. One generous reviewer noted that his people "did not step off the Mayflower and become part of America's ascendant class." To that, I quote Malcolm X: "We didn't land on Plymouth Rock, Plymouth Rock landed on us." The fact is that blacks like my people were the initial underclass in America. Vance believes that "learned helplessness" and a pervasive fatalism have invaded what he calls hillbilly culture and proceeds to argues that because too many hillbillies have endured hard times and adversity for too long, too many of them feel that there is nothing they can do to change their lot.[14] It is easy to focus on the pessimism and estrangement of Appalachia's underclasses, white and black, or for that matter, of any working-class people anywhere in America. But unlike Vance,

I opt instead to focus on the socioeconomic realities that explain poverty as a structural, systemic issue. In a capitalist economy, the choices of government policy makers and the corporations that lobby politicians play a large role in both creating and maintaining poverty.

New York Times reviewer Jennifer Senior also wrote of Vance, "His ancestors and kin were sharecroppers, coal miners, machinists, millworkers— all low paying, body-wearying occupations that over the years have vanished or offered diminished security." Slavery was, figuratively speaking, a boon for the white underclass, for had the free labor of people of African descent not been exploited for nearly four hundred years, Vance's working-class whites would have a label much more pejorative than "hillbilly." At that level of analysis, *Hillbilly Elegy* might have been subtitled *Thank God for Black People*.

Just like Vance's people, Black eastern Kentucky migrants poured into locations like Middletown, Ohio, shortly after World War II. As the case studies abridged above show, they lived out their lives, coping and adapting— some thriving—like many of their white counterparts from the region. I am repulsed by the word "hillbilly" in the title of the book, next to the contextually pejorative usage "elegy." Another marketing ploy, I thought, another "Appalachians as Other," this era's Appalachian attention grabber. Requiem. Dirge. Funeral song. Another bizarre and offensive portrayal of Appalachians. Vance trotted out a worst-case scenario of a family that came to represent not only the whole region, but also any working-class whites who supported Donald Trump for president of the United States. I thought, at least in this case, "Good that we black Appalachians have always been invisible," not part of this latest account of "strange and peculiar people."

Growing up, we knew well about the negativity of being colored, Negro, black, African American, or whatever the *nom de jour* at any given point in the historical experience of people of African descent. We were taught at colored schools in the mountains about W. E. B. Du Bois's double consciousness. Being Appalachian on top of the hardships produced by our racial identity and class status was triple trouble. It added another layer to these misrepresentations, an old offensive stereotype that Vance revived in *Hillbilly Elegy*.

BETWEEN HARRY CAUDILL AND MALCOLM X

In 1966 I exchanged Christmas gifts with Dr. John Bell Stephenson, one of the founders in 1977 of the Appalachian Studies Association and the president of Berea College at the time of his death in 1994. Stephenson gave me a copy of Harry Caudill's *Night Comes to the Cumberlands* (1963), and I gave him *The Autobiography of Malcolm X* (1965). During the intervening half century, my concentration on blacks in Appalachia has consistently oscillated around race and class and the ways all Appalachians have been broadly defined, usually without differentiation, as "economically peripheral upland Southern whites."[15]

I thought I had seen and read every stereotype drawn from the century-long use of the label "hillbilly" until I read J. D. Vance's discourse. Considering it in comparison to the depth of analysis and understanding of Malcolm X on urban blacks or Caudill on white highlanders would be like the FBI treating white extremist groups like the KKK and Neo-Nazis the same as they treated what they called black "radical organizations" such as the Southern Christian Leadership Conference, founded by Dr. Martin Luther King Jr. Imagine what you get when you compare Minister Louis Farrakhan's Nation of Islam to Alicia Garza and the Black Lives Matter Movement.[16] There simply are no comparisons. There is one standard of analysis that explains the treatment of the black working class and another for poor whites.

If history offers any lesson, it is that there are extreme, isolated, and individualized examples of values and behavior and outcomes within any marginalized groups. This is not to say that Vance's hillbillies are phantoms, but they are not representative of all poor whites. Similarly, if he had referenced the lives of even one single poor black family in his narrative, their woes or triumphs would not be taken to represent the entirety of Black Appalachian migrants. The fact that he did not mention the experience of blacks in Middletown—those who migrated from the same region as his family— shows that he sees racial discrimination as both understandable and even to be expected, when it comes to blacks. But when the same financial inequality and attendant insecurity applies to whites, even those making the wrong choices, the narrative becomes incomprehensible and should be seen as an unendurable, existential threat of the first order. Vance says, essentially, "this just should not happen to white people in America."

Most people I know, such as the ones I talked to during my travels in 2016, are not trying actively to run away from their culture and their families are not in crisis. I would be the first to acknowledge that there are also some pure lunatics, and some outrageous, crazy, foolish, and harebrained black people—just like members of Vance's family—who migrated from the eastern Kentucky coalfields. Like Vance, I too know—in my own extended family and among families in my network—individuals and families who may be worthy of derision and pity, people who cannot be helped because they refuse to help themselves to America's opportunities. But I also recognize the impact of systemic, racist, capitalist oppression and the impact of economic transformations on their lives—forces they could not control even if they could control themselves and behave according to the prescription for success.

Historically, a far higher percentage of African Americans than whites have been and remain working class. In Appalachian settings like the ones from which my family and Vance's grandparents migrated, African American coal miners were at the very bottom of the working hierarchy: they were the last hired, the least likely to be promoted, largely excluded from unions, and the first displaced by the mechanization of the mines. During my father's years working in an eastern Kentucky coal mine, between 1933 and 1980, my people, much more than Vance's, experienced the inequality and disparities that came with life in a coal camp.

In the 1950s, African Americans shouldered the worst of the advent of labor-saving mechanization of the coal mines, and they went off to Ohio (places such as Cincinnati, Cleveland, Dayton, Middletown, and Columbus) or to Chicago, Milwaukee, Louisville, Lexington, Flint, Pontiac, Detroit, and beyond, where many have stayed. In Michigan and Ohio, black migrants from Appalachia once again faced racism and were confined to the positions that proved to be most susceptible to mechanization. When cities like Detroit began to show signs of desertion—as imported cars drove the American-based auto industry to the Pacific Rim and Mexico—blacks were the first casualties of the economic crash.

It is clear that most blacks who left coal camps after they lost their jobs and migrated to areas similar to where Vance's grandparents did kept their hopes alive and pursued the American Dream. Karida Brown's work, for instance, shows that black working-class people from the eastern Kentucky coalfields were able to adapt to negative shocks and keep going; they code-switched with the rhythms of a long history of hard times, discrimination, challenges, and sacrifices.

In reviewing this essay, Ron Eller commented on its main point: racism and structured, institutionalized inequality and disparities, and why some working-class blacks exhibit higher levels of optimism about the future than poor whites—why the blacks are less likely to exhibit desperation, depression, and suicide, a fact recognized long before Vance set to paper the crisis of his people:

> I have long wondered why some poor whites fail to have higher expectations for themselves and their children and become fatalistic about their condition while some blacks with a deep history of persecution and the absence of privilege can be driven to succeed? Is it in fact a product of racism itself that white privilege appears to grant some status to poor whites, and when they fail to succeed (because of class and the capitalist system) they accept their condition and develop a failed identity (blame themselves) while finding others to blame for keeping them down? Thus does systemic racism also prevent poor whites from recognizing their own political and economic injustices? And for mainstream whites, the failure of poor whites from Appalachia to succeed must be a product of their own individual decisions and culture (thus their hillbilly culture in Vance's terms) since, as whites, they ought to be able to achieve the American Dream but choose otherwise. The "racialization" of Appalachia as white (our contemporary ancestors) not only sustains a larger apartheid system in America but sustains an unequal form of capitalism within the society as well.[17]

My generation of black coal camp natives never had an expectation to inherit anything, but we were inculcated by our elders with high expectations, optimism, and big dreams that were passed down. They passed their values—"I can get ahead"—on to the next generation, and I have done the same to my own adult children, born outside Appalachia, now Vance's age in their thirties and forties.

Vance ignored African American working-class people; and by excluding them, he missed a critical point of reference because their experiences could have given his family a warning as to what was coming and how to survive it. As Dr. Martin Luther King Jr. famously said, as though he too had been raised in Harlan County, "I have been to the mountaintop, and looked over; I may not get there with you, but we will get to the Promised Land."

Hillbillies like the ones Vance remembers—and eulogizes—can and will reach the Promised Land. That is, only if hillbillies, and those who seek to understand us, don't take too seriously these craftily though deceitfully written premature autopsies of Appalachian people like the one composed by J. D. Vance.

NOTES

1.   Ron Eller, *Uneven Ground: Appalachia since 1945* (Lexington: University Press of Kentucky, 2013).
2.   http://appalachianstudies.org/annualconference/2013/.
3.   Thomas Wagner and Phillip J. Obermiller, *African-American Miners and Migrants: The Eastern Kentucky Social Club* (Champaign: University of Illinois Press, 2004).
4.   Eastern Kentucky African American Migration Project, http://ekaamp.web.unc.edu/.
5.   https://www.brown.edu/academics/sociology/karida-brown.
6.   William H. Turner and Edward J. Cabbell, *Blacks in Appalachia* (Lexington: University Press of Kentucky, 1985).
7.   John Hope Franklin, *Mirror to America* (New York: Farrar, Straus and Giroux, 2007).
8.   Myrna Oliver, "Obituaries: John H. Johnson, 87; Innovative Publisher Built an Empire from Ebony, Jet Magazines," *Los Angeles Times*, August 9, 2005, http://articles.latimes .com/2005/aug/09/local/me-johnson9.
9.   John H. Johnson, with Lerone Bennett, Jr., *Succeeding against the Odds: The Autobiography of John H. Johnson* (New York: Amistad Books, 1993).
10. James Weldon Johnson and J. Rosamond Johnson, "Lift Every Voice and Sing," https:// www.youtube.com/watch?v=ya7Bn7kPkLo.
11. W. E. B. Du Bois, *The Souls of Black Folk* (Chicago: A.C. McClurg, 1903), and Booker T. Washington, *Up from Slavery: An Autobiography* (New York: Doubleday, 1901).
12. William H. Turner, "Another Take on Hillbilly Elegy," *Daily Yonder*, August 16, 2016, http://www.dailyyonder.com/review-another-take-on-hillbilly-elegy/2016/08/16/14807/.

13. William H. Turner, "The Canaries in Appalachian Coal Mines Were Black," in "The Future of Appalachia," *Now and Then: The Appalachian Magazine* 32, no. 2 (2017).

14. Jennifer Senior, "Review: In 'Hillbilly Elegy' a Tough Love Analysis of the Poor Who Back Donald Trump," *New York Times*, August 11, 2016, https://nyti.ms/2jAuPgc.

15. Sherry Kaye, "Recasting the White Stereotype of Southern Appalachia: Contribution to Culture and Community by Black Appalachian Women" (MA thesis, East Tennessee State University, 2016).

16. Ta-Nehisi Coates, *We Were Eight Years in Power: An American Tragedy* (New York: One World, 2017).

17. Ron Eller, email to the author, January 25, 2018.

PART II

Beyond
Hillbilly Elegy

NOTHING FAMILIAR

JESSE GRAVES

The world held us like a cup,
or a deep bowl the stew of our lives
could be poured into.
We lived in a valley, in foothills
of ancient mountains. The trees
waited for each generation to be born,
to keep them company as they watched
over us from high above.
I heard stories about grandmothers,
grandfathers, great, great-great, and beyond,
farther back than we had pictures
or letters or deeds with illegible names.
Each step I took across the upper ridges
fell deep inside a broad old footprint.
What to call it, a link in a chain,
leaf on a tree, step on an ascending ladder?
Nothing familiar contains it—more like dirt
pressing together in a shared piece of ground,
swelling with rain water, feeding roots
and the busy mouths of insects,
giving life to what it can never watch grow.

HISTORY

JESSE GRAVES

Every hour changes something forever.
Or changes something for another hour.
Watch the clouds at the far end of sky,
how slowly they move toward you,
how the blue above seems inviolable.
Watch for an hour and the mottled
streak of gray-threaded horizon
reaches over like a lid across a box.
The box you are in feels like history,
permanent change and no warning,
myths of cycles and repetition.
The loop you are in is imaginary;
it's a new world every hour.
No history here.
Mountains for eternity, a few scattered
tribes, hunting and gathering,
supplanted by farmers, also hunting,
gathering, and going hungry most days,
then a railroad, a teachers' college,
highways and chain restaurants.
When it all disappears, deer and coyotes
will stake out new feeding grounds,
trout will flourish in cold, swift streams,
mountains for eternity, clouds ever passing.

TETHER AND PLOW

JESSE GRAVES

Wherever we went, we carried a chain
across our shoulders, and tied to the end
of the chain was a ploughshare that dug
deep ruts out of the roads we travelled.
Each link of the chain bound us
to a home we didn't want, an accent
no one else could understand,
some few dollars we didn't have.
Whoever passed us on the road
bestowed their judgment,
made us feel the weight of their eyes
as they shifted quickly away from ours.
The plow's long tether cut into
our flesh, bruised us into the bone,
and it bound us together, made us
love one another, more than we loved
ourselves. We carried the weight,
and the weight was our reward.

ON AND ON: APPALACHIAN ACCENT AND ACADEMIC POWER

MEREDITH McCARROLL

"LET'S GO around the room and say where we're from." It was my first day in a class called "Experiencing Appalachia" during my first year of college.

"Raleigh," someone said.

"Just outside of Charlotte," said another.

"High Point."

The professor continually nodded as the circle made its way to me.

"Haywood County," I said.

Her eyebrows raised in respect.

My home was only about a hundred winding miles from the classroom in which I was sitting, but "Haywood County" suddenly became more than a place to me. It was a marker of identity.

On day one of class, I learned that the region's boundaries have been constantly contested. I was told that migratory patterns explain some of the dialects of the mountains. And I came to understand that I was Appalachian.

I knew that I was a mountain girl. My family had been in Haywood County for generations and one branch of my family tree started or stopped— depending on your perspective—when the Cherokee were marched through. But I had to take a class called "Experiencing Appalachia" to even know that I was Appalachian.

To "experience" the region, we studied the *Foxfire* magazines like those that lined the bookshelves in my childhood living room. We practiced churning butter. We read about quilting. Some of this resonated with me because it was familiar. My Granny painstakingly taught me to quilt one summer, which mostly meant that I spent time watching her pull out all of my sloppy handwork. My Granny and Pa, who lived next door, grew and canned tomatoes and green beans. I knew the differences between half-runners and blue lakes, and know of no sound more satisfying than the *pop* of lids sealing on the kitchen counter in the late afternoon. But there were plenty of Appalachian traditions that I did not know. And there was nothing markedly Appalachian that we did because we *had* to. It is true that I had eaten groundhog on a camping trip and could name most of the local peaks by sight, but it is also true that I bought incense and spirulina at a health food store in Asheville. I ate more tempeh than I did fatback, and I loved Ani DiFranco and Doc Watson equally.

After graduation, I moved to Boston and became, for the first time, an outsider. Like so many before me, it took leaving home to understand it. I suddenly saw details in contrast and became proud of my heritage. I grew tomatoes on the fire escape because it connected me to my Granny, whose tomatoes were a month ahead and a foot taller. As distance helped me understand what it meant to be from the mountains, I began to deeply miss them. I felt like Ivy Rowe in Lee Smith's *Fair and Tender Ladies* when she says that she's like her daddy and needs a mountain to "set her eyes against."

Yet while I was proud of my home, I was also learning that powerful stereotypes about Appalachia had arrived in places like Boston well before me and had influenced the way that even the most considerate people thought about me. The banjo lick from *Deliverance* backed many introductory conversations when I said where I was from. Instead of calling people out for their ignorance, I distanced myself from Haywood County. I laughed along. I waited longer and longer before saying where I was from. I blended in. During this time I applied to graduate school. During visits to prestigious universities in Boston I actively tried to talk right, to be correct, to hide my accent. One lingering linguistic marker caused me the most panic when I slipped. Long after I attached Gs to my gerunds and bleached out the local color from my language, I stumbled over the word "on." My mom told me to put my *coat on*—and those words rhymed. She told me to call her when I was *on the road*. And those words rhymed. To my Appalachian tongue, "own" and "on" were pronounced exactly the same way. But not for the rest of the world, I learned. This reminder that I was not from around here meant, to me, that I might not belong in a Boston graduate school.

I learned to always use adverbs. I took my groceries from a buggy and put them in a cart. I (nearly) stopped calling my hat a toboggan. I forced my vowels into shape. It worked. I got into graduate school. I got a PhD. I learned to pass. But I lost my voice. With Granny's chiding in my ear—"You're talking uppity now that you live in Baaaaahston"—I developed a new way of speaking. And it wasn't until a decade later that my own repressed voice echoed back to me in West Virginia.

Writer and activist Silas House spoke at a conference addressing the theme of "New Appalachia," urging his audience to bring civil rights issues for LGBTQ people into our classrooms, our scholarship, and our conversations in order to make Appalachia a safer place. New Appalachia, for House, was tied to Old Appalachian activism. As soon as he began speaking, I began to understand the new in light of the old. Combined with a quiet, intricate thoughtfulness, his manner of speaking awakened in me memories that I had long put to rest. In one moment, his voice cracked as he was overcome with emotion remembering the violence enacted upon queer youth in Appalachia. Throats tightened across the room. He paused and then said quietly, "And it will go on and on and on . . ." until we—teachers and writers and students in this room—commit to change. To an outsider, it might have sounded like he was saying "own and own and own." But when I heard Silas House repeat this word in this context, I felt the ground shift beneath me. Because while he talked about justice, I heard the timbre of my Pa. As he read his own poetry, I heard the cadence of my Aunt Betsy. As he addressed his audience, I heard my mom talking. I heard established scholars speak in accents and it did not change the content of what they were saying. It did not change the power of their intellect. Then I stood up to deliver my paper about the politics of representation in Appalachian film. My Gs were intact. My vowels stood up straight. My "on" was not my "own." And I felt a powerful loss—of my own voice, my own accent.

Television shows, movies, and cartoons rely lazily on the assumption that viewers will signify a southern accent with a lack of intelligence. It is still acceptable in popular discourse to mock "rednecks" and "hillbillies." "Reality" shows exoticize Appalachia as a safer space to show how the other half live, without much interrogation of authenticity. People say to lighten up. It's just a movie. It's just a TV show. It doesn't matter. But it does. It mattered to me as I left home, thinking that the only way to be a legitimate scholar was to attend college in New England and change my voice. I had learned to talk right, but I had gotten it all wrong.

I can't change the fact that my Granny's great-granny was raised as a white girl after her own biological parents had to leave her on the Trail of Tears. Passing for white, she had no choice but to assimilate to her surroundings to fit in. I'm unable to trace my way back to that culture that was taken from her and connect to a past that was not allowed to happen. But I can claim the past that I have known. Now that I have learned to articulate issues about representation and gender politics, I want to do so in my own voice—to let my vowels relax into the shape that they wanted to take all along. I want to honor the voices that were the soundtrack to my upbringing and respond to the calls of Uncle Joe, Granny, Aunt Lena, Aunt Betsy, Pa, and Mom. I want to draw thick that perforated line to my past. I want to claim the voices belonging to my people.

———

Granny mostly made clean patterned quilts with a recognizable order. But her mother-in-law made crazy quilts, piecing together scraps and favorites, remnants and set-asides. Combined, polka dots, solids, and gingham formed something alluring beyond any pattern. I loved these crazy quilts, and as I struggled my way through my first stitching, I thought that perhaps the style would be easier than the log cabin quilt I had settled upon. Knowing this wasn't the case, Granny took one of Ma's quilts down and with few words taught me how to judge it. Flipping it over, she revealed the even, measured hand stitching that held the mismatched pieces together. In it I saw how a thing is made whole, how the intricate gathering together of the unlikely can make sense. I am reminded of it now when I consider the seemingly disparate layers of my own voice and identity—multigenerational Appalachian, first-generation college graduate, economically privileged, queer, feminist, antiracist, mother, writer, teacher. I am reminded of that quilt when I look around and see the multiple ways to be Appalachian and to speak Appalachian. Perhaps with some attention, the voices of the past will not be lost, but can find a way to go on and on and on.

OLIVIA'S NINTH BIRTHDAY PARTY

TEXT AND PHOTOGRAPH BY REBECCA KIGER

THIS IS A PHOTO I made of my daughter on her ninth birthday. She has always been a water baby, so it was no surprise when she requested a pool party. All of the children in her class were invited. They swam, ate cake, ran, and played ball in the field at Grand Vue Park in Moundsville, Marshall County, West Virginia. As the cobbler's kid has no shoes, my daughter often lacks photos of her life. I find occupying the same space as a mother and a photographer to be difficult. In one I'm an active participant and in the other I'm an observer. However, this is a moment I am glad to have captured, not only for our family, but for purposes beyond. This photograph ended up being the cover image for the Looking at Appalachia project for almost a year, and it ran on the Lens blog of the *New York Times*. Its surreal elements delighted so many folks. I think this image not only gives a sense of place about where my daughter is growing up, but challenges stereotypes about who we are as Appalachians. She is strong, active, and loving life.

KENTUCKY, COMING AND GOING

KIRSTIN L. SQUINT

For my grandmothers

LEAVING HOME

In the early 1950s, a woman jumps from a bridge into the Ohio River. She is saved by a man who rows a boat from shore when he sees her jump. She is disappointed when she wakes up on the Kentucky side of the river, with weeds in her hair, because she is still alive.

The Cincinnati newspaper that reported the story described the woman simply as "a mother of two." It mentions nothing of her husband who came home whiskey drunk the night before and tried to beat her with a baseball bat. The scene wasn't new. What was new was her fourteen-year-old son stepping in to stop him. That's why she took a taxi cab to the bridge.

This is a story I have tried to write many times. It is not my story, but it is my family's story. My mother's people always said she was crazy, because why else would a woman try to leave her children like that? Everybody already knew she drank in bars and never set foot in a church. My father's family never said anything about it. Especially my father. He was that fourteen-year-old boy.

The story that I had always heard—that Mamaw Hazel was crazy—stayed with me until I was in my mid-twenties and asked her about it. She had lived in Florida during my childhood, and it was only when she moved back to Cincinnati with her second husband (to die "at home" as she put it) that I got to know her. She is the one who told me about the river weeds in her hair and my first papaw's abuse. After our talk, I went to the Cincinnati Public Library and read what had been written about her in the newspaper.

My father had a horrible fear of heights, especially crossing the bridge that connected Newport to Cincinnati, the one we walked across to go to Reds baseball games when I was a kid. He kept his eyes focused straight ahead and never let me stop to look at the water. Of course, I didn't know about my mamaw's attempted suicide then. Later I realized that even though it wasn't the same bridge, it was close enough.

I didn't know Mamaw Hazel when I was a child because she lived far away, and my dad never talked to her. The grandmother I knew, Grace, refused to let me called her "grandma" because she didn't want anyone to think she was like Ma Kettle, and she sure didn't want me or anyone else in her family listening to bluegrass music because she felt embarrassed when she heard those "twangin' banjos." I am sure that she never read or watched *Deliverance*, which as Anna Creadick points out is the source of much Appalachian banjo shame,[1] but perhaps she was impacted by social osmosis, or perhaps her distaste for bluegrass music was older than that cultural touchstone. As an adult, I understood that she had been hurt by the stereotypes of Appalachia, those that must have plagued her when she and my granddad moved up to Newport, so he could work at the steel mill. She was a fourteen-year-old girl in Berea when they married. He was the friend of her older brother, twenty-one when they married, a former one-room schoolhouse teacher and builder of what he called "those hand-shakin' roads" they built back in the mountains of Wolfe County (since you shake hands with yourself coming around a switchback). Along with her warm hugs, biscuits, and homemade candies, I remember my grandmother's devotion to the Pentecostalism of my mother's side of the family. As a five-year-old, I sat in a small church in Newport in the pew next to my grandmother, listening to my uncle preach. When it was time to sing, I would stand beside Grandmother and listen to her belt out "That Old Rugged Cross," tears streaming down her cheeks, her hand high in the air. Sometimes she or other parishioners would get so taken with the spirit that they would head down the aisle of the church so the preacher could lay his hands on them while they spoke in the holy tongue. To me that church was a mystery, one that sometimes revealed itself in the gospel songs that brought goose bumps to my skin, in the fervent pitches of preacher's sermons, and in the warm, thick, comforting arm of my grandmother, who would hold me close to her.

This was the grandmother I knew, not Mamaw Hazel. Like her fellow church members, Grandmother Grace believed that women should only wear dresses and keep their hair long and forgo makeup and nail polish. You didn't want to look like a jezebel in the eyes of God, you obeyed your husband, and you sure didn't up and leave your children. My most clear image of her is from my five-year-old perspective, when my family moved in with her and Granddad for a couple of years. She was a petite woman with long, thick, silver hair that she often let me brush and braid but that was usually piled in intricate curls, poufed, and pinned all over. She wore long polyester dresses, stockings to her knees, and thick-soled shoes that laced up. Looking back, I realize that her appearance certainly suggested a particular Appalachian cultural group, but I believe her faith blinded her to this. It was the popular culture stereotypes of mountain people that Grandmother Grace disavowed.

In the years after Mamaw Hazel tried to commit suicide, she divorced my first papaw, remarried a man who was making a good living as a bookie in the "sin city" that was Newport in the 1950s, and watched her oldest son (my father) get married at sixteen to my mom, who was pregnant with my brother. My parents both quit school, and when my father decided that working in a chicken slaughterhouse was the worst possible fate, he signed up for four years in the Air Force. The pay and the benefits were so much better than any of his other options that once his Air Force tour was finished, he signed up for the Army and became a career military man. Sometime during those early years of my parents' marriage, Mamaw left Kentucky. She and her new husband headed down to Florida where they could run a hotel together, close to sunny beaches and a racetrack where he could continue his bookmaking work.

During my childhood, I knew Mamaw Hazel only from 1950s photographs, a tall, slender woman posed next to her two sons, wearing a short-sleeved dress that was cinched tight around her waist and swirled around her knees. Or posed next to one of her two husbands, both tall men, barrel-chested with thick hair combed in a jaunty side part. They looked a lot alike, my papaws, though the first one lost much of his hair as he aged. The picture that I remember most though is a headshot, her alone, chin tipped over one shoulder, cheeks artificially rosy, as is often the case in old photographs. Her nose is thin, her cheekbones well-defined. Her hair is fashionably curled and cropped close to her neck. Her eyes are dusky with a light of laughter or maybe mischief shining just beyond the darkness. Everyone always said she was beautiful, and I thought so too. When she told me about waking up on that riverbank, disgusted to find river weeds in her hair, I wondered what the man who saved her life thought.

RETURNING HOME

I was a surprise child, the "first of the second string," as my dad liked to call me, the one who came four years before he retired from his twenty years in the Army working as a military intelligence officer. I was born in west Texas, and if my dad had had his druthers, that's where we would have stayed, under the big open Texas sky, blue like bluebonnets, blue like my eyes, he said. I was his "little Texan." But my mom was tired of "being dragged all over the world" as she put it, so they headed back to Kentucky. Dad substituted his dream ranch for a seventy-acre farm he was given by his dad in a rural county in northern Kentucky. Unlike my older siblings, I grew up in Kentucky, in a holler next to Grassy Creek, in a house my dad built almost entirely by himself.

When I was nine or ten, my dad starting driving me down to Corbin, in Laurel County, where he had spent his early years. That was where Mamaw and Papaw had come from before their journey up to Newport for a better life. Those road trips with my dad are some of my fondest memories of him. We would belt out songs a cappella, especially his two favorites, "The Battle of New Orleans" and "Dixie." Our conversations covered the geologic history of Kentucky, which we could see in the rocks that had been blasted through to make I-75, the Civil War (prompted by our singing), and his childhood, which seemed like a much happier time than his teenage years, which he never talked about.

In Corbin, we would always stay with my Aunt Nanny (on my first papaw's side), who claimed she had raised my daddy and who had an extensive collection of salt and pepper shakers filling tall china cabinets and table surfaces throughout her kitchen and dining room. I would spend hours examining her shaker collection. Some were ceramic, some were glass, some were metal. My favorites were the realistic-looking ceramic corn cob pipe shakers. When dad drove me around Corbin, he would point out the houses that his grandfather, a carpenter, had built, and he told me about his mamaw, who sold the eggs her chickens laid and made the best corn pone he had ever eaten. We would always stop at Uncle Coy's (on Mamaw Hazel's side), my dad's favorite relative. Uncle Coy lived in a modest brick house that was stuffed full of books and smelled like tuna fish. Uncle Coy is the only member of my family who I knew had gone to college, earning a degree in journalism from the University of Kentucky. While Dad and Uncle Coy reminisced, I thumbed through the books on his coffee table. The one that I found both appealing and repelling and read every time I was there was *101 Uses of a Dead Cat*. I knew the book was supposed to be funny, but it also made me unsure of Uncle Coy, like there were things about him I didn't understand.

My dad's favorite stories were about his daddy taking him fishing on the Laurel River when he was a boy. Dad never did take me fishing down there, but he did take me to Cumberland Falls, a magnificent crashing of water and light, the "Niagara of the South." It was the prettiest place I had ever seen. My dad proudly told me that Cumberland Falls had a world wonder, its "moonbow," a spectrum of color visible under the falls during the full moon. I would try to imagine that moonbow as we made our way through the Daniel Boone National Forest, seeing a different version of my dad—a happier, younger one.

LEAVING AND RETURNING, THIRD GENERATION

Like Mamaw Hazel and my dad, I left Kentucky. I couldn't wait to leave for as many years as I can remember. I wanted adventure, like what the rest of my family had when Dad was stationed in Japan and Hawaii and Washington and Maryland—places I had never seen. I also knew there was a seed of unhappiness in the house I grew up in, that perhaps began when two people married too young or when they realized they had been apart for so long that they never really knew each other.

My quest took me away to college, and I became the first woman in my family to earn a bachelor's degree. After finishing the coursework for my master's degree, I found myself among the mesas and canyons of northwestern New Mexico, teaching English in a high school on the Navajo Nation.

Teaching became my profession, and after years of working in community colleges, I eventually entered Louisiana State University to pursue a doctorate. My journey of being educated and becoming an educator took me to six states and revealed some truths to me.

Being a white teacher on an Indian reservation was my first experience as a demographic minority. Having attended a poor public high school in a predominantly white county in Kentucky and two Midwestern colleges with very little racial diversity, I struggled to understand the concept of my own privilege. How could I, someone who had grown up ashamed of the lack of education and perceived poverty of my own family, be a representative of a history of oppression? I was twenty-three years old, not trained as a teacher (my master's degree was in creative writing), and I was in unfamiliar territory, literally and metaphorically. I resigned from my position before the school year was out, because I was overwhelmed by the many things I could not control, such as whether or not my students had eaten breakfast or would be hitchhiking home from school or their desire to learn the things I was supposed to be teaching them.

As a graduate student studying colonial and postcolonial theory at LSU, I realized that living on the reservation lay bare the bones of US settler colonialism to me. I read French theorist Albert Memmi's *The Colonizer and the Colonized* and learned of the colonizer who goes to the colony, realizes his or her position of privilege, and then chooses to exploit it.[2] Then there is the colonizer who goes to the colony and refuses—refuses to participate in the exploitative system and leaves. I left my job, but of course, within the system of settler colonialism, it is impossible to truly leave. Had I understood that when I was twenty-three, I would have finished out the school year for the sake of the students I left behind, whose names and faces I still remember.

I continued to teach in community colleges once I finished my master's degree and enjoyed the work tremendously because, even though I hadn't attended a community college, like many of my students, I had been a first-generation college student. I understood how challenging it could be to explain the importance of your education to family members who may not understand the choices you are making in your personal life such as studying instead of helping them in some way. I understood how a college education changes you—that you look at the world differently, and as a result, you look at your family and yourself differently.

Being a first-generation college student also helped me relate to my students at the historically black university in Louisiana where I taught for five years while completing my PhD. While there, I often felt compelled to share Erica Abrams Locklear's research on women in Appalachia who gained new literacies only to find themselves alienated from their community for their difference.[3] I explained that higher education had worked in that way for those women and for me, and so many of my students would nod their heads in agreement. They knew how it felt to be the first in the family to head into these deep waters, and that even though their loved ones on shore cheered them, they didn't always know how to help when it was time to navigate the rapids.

I learned a lot about myself from Erica's research on Appalachian women, which she often shared with me during our walks around the LSU lakes. Erica and I became friends early on in our doctoral program partly because she was the only person I met pursuing an academic career who had spent part of her childhood on a tobacco setter like I had. We often talked about our families, hers in North Carolina and mine in Kentucky. She was hoping to get a job back in North Carolina, and I had an idea I wanted to live in Texas because it was where I was born. My dad had died from cancer after my first year at LSU, and I somehow thought that living out his dream of returning to Texas would give his spirit—and mine—some peace. We also talked about what it meant to be women from Appalachia, where we fit in the world, and how much our grandmothers had shaped us.

I never got that job in Texas. Instead, I found myself leaving Louisiana for a tenure-track position in the piedmont of North Carolina. One year into my assistant professorship, I had a son. My husband joked that I brought us to North Carolina so I could raise my baby in a place like my home in Kentucky. This is a joke because academics in the humanities rarely get to choose where they live and welcome pretty much any opportunity that comes their way. And yet, there is some truth in what he says. It pleases me to show my now-five-year-old a tobacco field in its various stages of growth and harvest and tell him about how, alongside my dad, I pulled the tiny plants and carefully placed them in a setter when I was a child. The cedar trees that line the fence of our suburban yard are neat and orderly, unlike the wild cedar hills of my family's farm, but they smell the same and still provide a cool shady spot for panting dogs on a hot summer afternoon. We have seasons for wild honeysuckle and blackberries, and we pick them on long walks. My boy has a mama who makes him hand-rolled biscuits not only because he loves them, but also because she believes that biscuit-making is a form of love.

The piedmont of North Carolina is a little drier and rockier than the rolling hills of north-central Kentucky where I grew up, but it is just a couple of hours on the other side of those same mountains of my family's comings and goings. In fact, it is probable that at least one of my ancestors who first settled in Kentucky passed by the area where I live today when he traveled from Rockingham or Stokes County, North Carolina, through the Cumberland Pass. Pierce Dant Hamblin was a veteran of the American Revolution who had fought under George Washington and survived the winter in Valley Forge before marrying, beginning a family, and making the dangerous trek into a territory newly available to settlers as a result of the Treaty of Tellico with the Cherokee Indians.

I think living on the Navajo Nation, the largest Indian reservation in the country, makes me think about what it means that my family's Kentucky heritage is due entirely to a treaty that dispossessed a tribe of the majority of its land. Because of my time in Navajoland, I am a scholar of American Indian literature, but because of my time in Kentucky, I focus on Southeastern Natives. Being in North Carolina gives me opportunities to teach classes about Cherokee history and literature and to mentor Eastern Band of Cherokee students from time to time. Are such actions a form of reparation? No. But in the Southeast, where the long shadow of Indian Removal obfuscates settler colonialism by rendering Natives invisible, talking and teaching are some kind of beginning.

LEGACIES

My father had a faded one-inch scar that cut diagonally across his right eyebrow. I asked him about this scar many times growing up, and he always said that he had been running across the road as a young boy and was hit by a truck. He bounced off the front of the truck bumper and landed in the grass on the side of the road. I was always in awe of this story. I imagined it like a cartoon, the boy bouncing on his bottom like a rubber ball, landing safely in the grass with a deep cut over his eye, but otherwise free from harm.

From an adult's perspective, this story seems highly implausible. People don't bounce, and a small person being hit by a truck implies only one likely outcome. Once Mamaw Hazel told me about the baseball bat, it occurred to me that there might be other sources for that scar, sources my father would not want to share with me.

I recently read an article in the *Atlantic* about how life expectancy in some Kentucky counties is now the lowest in the nation. Contributing factors include "obesity, physical activity, hypertension, smoking, and diabetes, but . . . poverty, education, and unemployment also play a role."[4] Kentucky also has "one of the highest rates of death from drug overdoses" and is home to the country's "poorest white-majority county." The article notes that opioids, "poor diets, and financial strain," the latter brought about by such factors as the dying tobacco and coal industries, are "major reasons" for this trend in life expectancy reduction. Many members of my family have struggled with type 2 diabetes, poverty, and addiction. Reading this article brought on a vivid flashback of the afternoon of my mother's funeral when some of my siblings and cousins divided my mom's prescription antidepressants and pain medications among themselves. The helplessness, anger, and sorrow I felt about such dysfunction compounding an already devastating period wasn't a new phenomenon. In the days following my father's funeral, I watched one of my siblings nearly hit my mother with a vodka bottle. I'm not sure what "normal" is, but our grief, or at least our methods for coping with it, never felt normal.

I don't imagine that these legacies of addiction and violence began with my papaw's alcoholism, but it is the first set of causes to which I can point. At times, I become lost in the painful memories, and I have to remind myself that there are other legacies.

When I was in my late teens and early twenties, Grandmother Grace lived in a nursing home in Newport, high on a hill with a beautiful view of the Ohio River and Cincinnati skyline. As an older high school student and early college student, I would drive up from the farm to visit with her when I had the chance. She was paralyzed on one side of her body from a stroke, so her mobility was restricted to wherever her wheelchair would take her. During my visits, we would sometimes have dinner together in the cafeteria or walk the halls, greeting her friends, some of whom were lucid and some of whom were not. Her favorite days were when the service dogs came to visit, particularly a bright-eyed golden retriever whose fur she would run her fingers through. My grandfather had died ten years before, and she could no longer do things she had always done, like make buckeyes and chocolate and peanut butter fudge for her grandchildren and great-grandchildren.[5] Because she had never gone to a summer camp or lived in a dormitory, the lack of privacy in her shared room in the hospital-like nursing home was a shock. And yet, in the nursing home, my grandmother had a kind of freedom she had never before known. She talked to men and women from different cultural backgrounds than her own. She was independent to the degree that she could be, with no husband or children to care for. She had a lot of time to think.

One summer day before I started college, we were sitting in my favorite space at the facility: an open-air atrium topped with an ivy-covered pergola that overlooked the river and bridges connecting Kentucky and Ohio. I felt so close to my grandmother then, as a young woman, just starting to make my way in the world, and I had a sudden memory that I wanted to confide.

I said, "Do you remember when I was five, and you saw that my fingernails were painted, and you said, 'What do you think Jesus would say if he came down from Heaven today and saw that paint on your nails?!'"

My grandmother's paper-thin cheeks flushed pink, and she cried, "I said no such thing!"

"But you did, Grandmother."

She pulled a tissue from the cloth bag attached to her wheelchair and wiped her eye with her good hand. "Kirstin," she said. "I don't believe Jesus worries about such things."

Something had changed.

When I returned to Kentucky the following winter after my first semester away at college in Illinois, I visited my grandmother, not thinking anything of my baggy sweatshirt or long hair pulled back in a messy ponytail.

Grandmother introduced me to one of her friends by saying, "She dresses like that because she's a college student."

Though I felt awkward because maybe I had embarrassed her, I clearly heard a note of pride in the final two words.

I often think about the differences between the choices I have had and the choices available to the women who came before me. What choices did my grandmothers have? For my grandmother Grace, who married at fourteen and ventured beyond the Appalachian home she had known, she built a world secure in family and faith. She must have felt judged harshly to decide to shed what cultural affiliations she could, the ones she felt certain would mark her as a hillbilly. For my Mamaw Hazel, who left her birthplace, her family, and eventually Kentucky itself, stigma was her reward; I'm glad she had the sense to choose stigma over physical harm.

Grandmother Grace taught me both the importance of faith and the importance of changing when faced with new circumstances. Mamaw Hazel taught me that leaving is sometimes the only thing you can do—that leaving might actually be an act of love. Of course, her leaving scarred my father, an emotional loss forever etched in him, like the scar across his eyebrow. And her leaving became his leaving. Despite the trauma my father experienced growing up, though, he taught me that going places was always an adventure, a way to meet new people, learn new things, and grow, grow, grow. My mother would have been happier if I had just stayed in Kentucky, and in some ways, her conflicts with my father manifested in me, her baby, who just as soon as she could, headed off to college and Paris and Vancouver and New Mexico and Louisiana and lots of other places, none of which were Kentucky.

My father died in 2004, and my mother died from heart failure a year and a half later. Mamaw Hazel died after we lost Dad and before we lost Mom. Grandmother Grace passed much sooner, the summer after I returned from Paris.

I still visit Kentucky on occasion, but the house my dad built was sold, along with our land, and my chats with my parents now take place in a cemetery. Leaving Kentucky meant a disconnection from my family and home community, but it has also meant opportunities my grandmothers never had, like the chance to earn a PhD or support myself financially or backpack across Europe. Certainly my father's encouragement of me to dream big (he was hoping I would become secretary of state) and to persevere regardless of my circumstances helped me to break free from the gendered expectations of my family.

DISCLAIMER

I do not know if all of these details are accurate. My access to the stories has been blocked by the doors of death and dysfunction. What I think I know has been shaped by the pressure of time into glinting shards of memory that sometimes blind me with their brightness. What I do know is that sometimes you have to find yourself in deep water before you can begin again.

NOTES

1. Anna Creadick, "Banjo Boy: Masculinity, Disability, and Difference in *Deliverance*," *Southern Cultures* 23, no. 1 (Spring 2017): 63–78.
2. Albert Memmi, *The Colonizer and the Colonized* (Boston: Beacon, 1965).
3. Erica Abrams Locklear, *Negotiating a Perilous Empowerment: Appalachian Women's Literacies* (Athens: Ohio University Press, 2011).
4. Olga Khazan, "Kentucky Is Home to the Greatest Declines in Life Expectancy," *Atlantic*, May 8, 2017, www.theatlantic.com/health/archive/2017/05/kentucky/525777/.
5. Her buckeye is a peanut butter and powdered sugar ball coated with just enough chocolate to look like the seed of the buckeye or horse chestnut tree.

RESISTANCE, OR OUR MOST WORTHY HABITS

RICHARD HAGUE

*re: Scott McClanahan's dismissal of "the Appalachian Minstrel Show"
and J. D. Vance's "elegy" for hillbilly culture*

When anywhere, even in Rome,
we did as mountaineers would do.
When told to stay inside the lines,
we organized the strike.
When instructed to take our medicine,
we dug ginseng, ran naked in a blizzard.
When told to straighten up and fly right,
we crouched, veered left,
slid on our asses down the holler.
When told to listen up,
we clawhammered, fast,
and sang them down.
When counseled to lighten up,
we hoarded scrap iron and bullet lead.
When told to get real,
we remembered Jack and Old Fire Dragaman
and dreamed up wilder worlds.

When ordered to chill,
we stoked interior fires.
When threatened with arrest,
we clogged beyond their reach.

At prayer, we profaned.
In profanity, we blessed.
In silence, we exhorted.
In poverty, we grew rich.

When silenced,
we became mountain streams
announcing imminent danger.
When nailed down,
we erupted like exploding stills.

Despite brief collaring and cuffing,
we slip our bonds and occupy lost days—
quoting Bible and Mother Jones,
and become gagging, hair-balling cats on
Matewan bloody pillows, mean dogs
gnawing Blankenship-guilty bones.

NOTES ON A MOUNTAIN MAN

JEREMY B. JONES

THIS IS AN ESSAY about Ernest T. Bass, "a fictional character on the American TV sitcom *The Andy Griffith Show*." This is an essay about Ernest T. Bass informed by Wikipedia. And so this, too, is an essay about us. Or them.

This is an essay about Howard Jerome Morris, a Jewish man born in the Bronx in 1919—the classically trained Shakespearean actor who played Ernest T. Bass and whose entry on Wikipedia links to a page titled "Mountain Man."

"A mountain man is a male trapper and explorer who lives in the wilderness."

When my great-great-great-great-great-great-grandfather moved into the mountains where I was raised, the map labeled the area as only "The Wilderness."

In a private college full of smart, wealthy northeasterners, someone once heard me speak and called me "a mountain man." Immediately, I saw Ernest T.

Howdy do to you and you.

I loved Ernest T. more than any character on *The Andy Griffith Show*.

This is an essay about me. *It's me, it's me, it's Ernest T.* This is an essay about a hundred acres in a community named Fruitland in the Blue Ridge Mountains of North Carolina. Or, if you like, this is an essay about a massive region reaching from Alabama to New York. About how every single one of the people living in that streak of the map is a male trapper. Not thousands of male trappers, but—like the body of Christ—we together form Male Trapper. Some an eye. Some a coonskin cap.

Ernest T. Bass appeared in only 5 out of 249 episodes. He threw rocks and wanted to find love.

I loved Ernest T. more than any character on *The Andy Griffith Show*.

Some museums across the country celebrate an Ernest T. Bass Day in their Natural Science sections, inviting people to bring any rocks they're unable to identify. Ernest T. Bass Day takes place on April 1, Ernest T.'s birthday. Citation needed.

My first ancestor to come here to The Wilderness in 1785 grew rich, in part due to his whiskey still. He died in the woods, either bushwhacked or clumsy, at the age of ninety-five. I was born surrounded by the houses of my uncles and grandparents and great-grandparents and great-great-grandparents in 1981. I spent most of my childhood in the woods. My first CD purchase was Dr. Dre's *The Chronic*.

Howard Morris picked up a menu of Southern accents while stationed at Fort Bragg during World War II. From them, he brought Ernest T. to life. He later sang the "Eep Oop Ork Ah Ah" song as Jet Screamer on *The Jetsons*. In 1989, he voiced the French gangster cat named Monte De Zar on *Chip 'N Dale Rescue Rangers*.

I am not a French gangster cat.

I never once considered myself a mountain man until I left the mountains. I didn't know what a mountain man was. I still don't know what a mountain man is.

"Mountain men were most common in the North American Rocky Mountains from about 1810 through to the 1880s (with a peak population in the early 1840s)."

A mountain man is a Jew from the Bronx.

Citation needed.

Ernest T. first appeared on *The Andy Griffith Show* in the episode "Mountain Wedding." After meeting him, Andy says, "If you ask me, this Ernest T. Bass is a strange and weird character."

I loved Ernest T. more than any character on *The Andy Griffith Show*.

One of the earliest portraits of the mountains by an outsider was Will Wallace Harney's 1873 travelogue: "A Strange Land and a Peculiar People."

In college, one of my classes took a weekend trip to the mountains. On a hike, I left the trail and tiptoed a tree fallen across a creek. I picked my way along the rocks peeking from the water, finding sure footing by instinct—avoiding slick algae and shaky stones—so that I could sit by the water and skip rocks on the other side. Two guys started out behind me. Within a few steps, they'd both slipped into the cold water. "You can't follow him out here," a girl hollered from behind us. "He's a mountain man."

"The mountain man, in the Southern Appalachians," Donald Culross Peattie wrote in 1943, "is not a real mountaineer, as are some of the Swiss living at giddy altitudes; he is a forest man."

When I walked into the woods of our family land as a boy, I became Daniel Boone or Davy Crockett. I roamed, carrying a canteen in a fur pouch, a cap gun, and a coonskin hat—all purchased at *Dollywood*. I hid in caves of rhododendron. I dropped down the steep bank of the creek and threw rocks at unseen enemies. I might kill a bear or I might camouflage my whole being into the land of my ancestors and never go inside again. Or I might give it up and play Nintendo.

"The life of a mountain man was rugged: many did not last more than several years in the wilderness."

The Wilderness my ancestor came upon, at the age of seventy-five, was named Flat Rock. Later, it became a mountain getaway destination for wealthy plantation owners in the South. Today, New Yorkers build big houses and retire here.

Years after playing Ernest T. Bass, Howard Morris directed *Richie Rich*, a Saturday-morning animated series about the son of "the world's richest parents." In 1994, Macaulay Culkin starred in a film based on the character. Though *Richie Rich* was set in Chicago, most of the movie was filmed at the Biltmore Estate, a 135,280-square-foot house built by George Vanderbilt in the late nineteenth century—it sits twenty-five miles from the Wilderness of my people.

"It is a strange gorgeous colossus in a vast void of desolation," Henry James wrote to Edith Wharton of the Biltmore Estate in 1905.

This is an essay about being from a vast void of desolation.

To announce his arrival to Mayberry from the mountains, Ernest T. Bass breaks windows. To court women, Ernest T. Bass breaks windows. To threaten men, Ernest T. Bass breaks windows. To send a letter, Ernest T. Bass breaks windows. He is a connoisseur of window-breaking rocks. Often he brings them from home, toting the rocks down the mountain before he commences to smashing up the town. Town is a place that cannot hold Ernest T. He is a man for wild, uncivilized mountains. In Mayberry, he skips through traffic, yelping and laughing—an escaped monkey in a tattered vest and big boots. He cannot be contained, resisting every social norm pressed upon him, escaping from lockup as if by magic only to appear grinning in his ratty britches on the street again: *You ain't seen the last of Ernest T. Bass.*

Wikipedia lists Ernest T.'s occupation as "troublemaker, hillbilly."

My cousins and I found a glass medicine bottle in the woods. In it, we poured gas from a can in the tractor shed. Then, we rolled pages from an old Farmer's Almanac, like a snake, and stood them in the bottle. We liked to watch *The A-Team*. We took some matches and our Molotov cocktail and headed down the Old Road, past our great-great grandparents' empty house and toward the creek and barn. We stopped beside a good-size mud puddle, set the bottle on a rock in the middle of the water, and lit the paper. Before long, one of us got nervous about the flame from the Farmer's Almanac pages, the way it shot up high from the fumes and nearly touched the plants bending over the road. One of us got nervous about the possibility of an explosion a few feet from our young bodies. One of us said to throw rocks into the puddle, in hopes we'd splash enough muddy water onto the bottle to quench the flame before it reached the gas. One of us didn't understand this plan. He said, "Y'all keep missing. Watch this." He smashed the bottle with a precise toss. Water turned to flame. We stepped back and watched what had just been flat, dark water on a dirt road in Fruitland, NC, transform into the sun. We ran back into the woods.

"Television programs of the 1960s such as *The Real McCoys*, *The Andy Griffith Show*, and especially *The Beverly Hillbillies*, portrayed the 'hillbilly' as backwards but with enough wisdom to outwit more sophisticated city folk."

One of the earliest recorded uses of "hillbilly" comes from a *New York Journal* article in 1900: "a Hill-Billie is a free and untrammeled white citizen of Tennessee, who lives in the hills, has no means to speak of, dresses as he can, talks as he pleases, drinks whiskey when he gets it, and fires off his revolver as the fancy takes him."

I never rightly learned to shoot a gun. While my uncles and grandfather and cousins hunted, I never had much interest. I liked to pass from sight in the woods. I'll admit to breaking a few windows, only once with a rock, but my people didn't touch spirits. They're an abstaining lot, and I didn't have a drink until I was twenty-one on a beach in Costa Rica. I brush my teeth four times a day and own more shoes than most men would admit.

In his first episode, Ernest T. tries to convince Charlene Darling to marry him by boasting of his best attributes: "I can do chin-ups, I'm the best rock thrower in the county, and I'm saving up for a gold tooth."

My junior-year prom date was named Kwang Hee. We went to the strange gorgeous colossus that is the Biltmore Estate in my mint green Ford Probe and danced to R. Kelly.

The word *stereotype* was first used in printmaking in 1798 "to describe a printing plate that duplicated any typography." Once created, the stereotype could be used in place of the original. With a stereotype in hand, who needs the original?

I play the banjo.

One of those Molotov-cocktail-exploding cousins lives a stone's throw from the spot of the burning mud puddle, in a trailer with thirteen guns. Another one of those Molotov-cocktail-exploding cousins is a DJ in Chicago, living in a high-rise condo with his Jewish wife. We are all Male Trapper.

"The 'classic' hillbilly stereotype reached its current characterization during the years of the Great Depression, when many mountaineers left their homes to find work in other areas of the country." During this great migration from the mountains—to places like Detroit and Chicago and Mayberry—the rest of the country cocked its head to the side to catch a load of these mountain men coming into town.

Howdy do to you and you.

In one episode, Ernest T. comes into town, throws a rock through the window of a house, and then goes inside to the party. He intends—as always—to fall in love. Instead, he sticks his hand in the punch bowl and eats the watermelon rinds and runs off giggling. Andy decides to help civilize Ernest T. Andy always decides to help Ernest T., but Ernest T. is resistant. He speaks through his nose, he doesn't understand unnecessary niceties, he throws rocks. "Now, Ernest T., we're just trying to help you fit into society," Andy says.

I imagine mountain men arriving to Cleveland and Detroit in 1930, 1940. They open their mouths and windows break.

In college, I stopped saying *reckon*. I kept an eye on *used to could*. I flattened out those long i's that rounded my mouth. I sent Ernest T. back to the mountains and settled down into my seat. Inside. Windows closed.

I don't chew my cabbage twice and you ain't heard the last of Ernest T. Bass.

In another episode:

Andy: He's made a lot of progress since the last time he was in town.

Barney: Oh, so he shaved the back of his neck; what's so great about that?

"*Stereotype* derives from the Greek words *steros,* meaning 'firm, solid' and *typos,* meaning 'impression.'"

I'm supposed to say that Ernest T. is wise, that he carries more sense than those townsfolk trying to dress him up or educate him or keep him indoors. It's not true. Ernest T. is, as Barney Fife forever names him: *a nut.*

I loved Ernest T. more than any character on *The Andy Griffith Show.*

I could never get comfortable out of the mountains. I lived in other countries, in a big city, at the beach, in the rural Midwest. I felt forever itchy in those landscapes, always looking at the horizon, waiting for some land to rise up that I could run off into. Eventually, I moved back to the Wilderness.

Ernest T. isn't wise, but he is his own man. And he is willing to fight to stay that way, no matter what Town tells him. In the face of their fine dining or jails, he laughs and runs off. Back into the mountains. Ernest T. is in the town, but not of the town.

I live in the Wilderness with city water.

Right or wrong, I'm here to fight. Unless you run away with fright. And if you wonder who I be . . .

Okay, okay, here it is: a stereotype is a window. Flat, clear, firm.

Every morning I drive past my great-great-great-great-great-great-grandfather. I wave to the tall headstone above where he rests on his former Wilderness— alongside a paved road and massive church and a housing development—and head off to teach college. In rooms full of male trappers, I hope what I'm saying when I say *we're making art here* is *we're breaking windows*. I'm saying: Go down the mountain if you must, but for the love of God take a rock.

A rock is you.

It's me. It's me.

(Unless otherwise indicated, all quoted material comes from Wikipedia.)

THESE STORIES SUSTAIN ME:
THE *WYRD*-NESS OF MY APPALACHIA

EDWARD KARSHNER

WHEN I WAS IN HIGH SCHOOL, I started seeing this girl who had just moved in from Dayton. Her family had bought the old tree nursery in Pickaway County that ran right up to the Ross County line. It was the day after Christmas and I was going to meet her extended family for the first time. I went to her house wearing my Christmas finery: a flannel shirt from JCPenney and a nice pair of moc-toed St. John's Bay work boots. She told me I looked like a "Hillbilly" and sent me home to change. That stung. It was the first time I had ever been called a *Hillbilly*, a word I associated with the Clampetts, old Warner Brothers cartoons, and Snuffy Smith. But not me. Not my family. We were "country," from the hills. My Dad preferred "the old ways." My Mom rolled noodles out on the kitchen counter. We listened to mountain music. But, so did everyone else. We weren't unusual. Yet, at that moment, when the word *Hillbilly* crawled out of her mouth and attached itself to me, I felt a truth to it. I felt shame. Even though I was unaware of it, the Hillbilly seemed to know what I was.

In his book *The Rhetoric of Appalachian Identity*, Todd Snyder writes, "The Hillbilly is everything outsiders have been taught to believe about Appalachians, everything they've been told to believe about Appalachians. The Hillbilly is everything Appalachians have been taught to believe about themselves, the rhetoric they both reject and consciously (and subconsciously) uphold."[1] Snyder nails the irony of trying to define Appalachianness: it is too often done by those on the outside. Growing up in the hills and hollers, I didn't see the need to define it—it just was. However, what the Appalachian learns about being a Hillbilly is a caricature created by outsiders and it is this image, presented from the outside where "the Hillbilly [is] told his own life story from the perspective of others."[2]

Books like J. W. Williamson's *Hillbillyland: What the Movies Did to the Mountains and What the Mountains Did to the Movies* and Anthony Harkins's *Hillbilly: A Cultural History of an American Icon* offer a historical perspective on the development of the Hillbilly media construct. Most recently, J. D. Vance's *Hillbilly Elegy* illustrates, maybe unintentionally, the role these media constructions have in the development of a Hillbilly identity. Roger Abrahams writes that identity is built on "the stories one tells oneself or one's community. The sum of these stories constitutes the life history of the individual or the group."[3] The role story plays in the construction of who we are, where we are, should never be underestimated. The question becomes, who has the right to choose the stories we tell ourselves?

In raising two "halfalachian" children Off in northeastern Ohio, I have become painfully aware of the role narratives and counternarratives have in constructing Appalachian identity. We are the stories we tell. For this reason, I feel an important step in reclaiming the vitality of our Appalachian identity is to reconsider our own folk narratives in order to inoculate ourselves against the disruptive and dangerous media narratives that distort Appalachian metaphysics into Hillbilly porn. As I have tried to do with my own children, I want to stress the power of folklore to develop and maintaining heritage and culture by affirming traditional values of family and place.

It is easy to dismiss the obvious versions of Hillbilly porn. As a genre, Hillbilly porn exemplifies Roland Barthes's idea of "mythologies" where, on one end of the spectrum lives the monster as depicted in the granddaddy of Hillbilly porn, *Deliverance.* On the other end dwells the conceptual clown exemplified by the Hillbilly minstrel character Larry the Cable Guy. These characters are obvious. It is in the more subtle, academic, or political narratives where the most redirection of attention is done. Presented as objective truth, with the legitimacy of degrees and academic presses, Appalachians are told what they are or aren't. There is a *cunning*, meant in that old mountain sense, in these stories that pretend to not be stories, where the Appalachian, as rhetorical audience, is transformed from insider to outsider and steered out of the flow of personal history and tradition into the vacuum of Off—a reality that will, very much, remake us in its image.

No story is more cunning than Jack Weller's 1965 *Yesterday's People*. This is the book that defines Appalachians as a gloomy, fatalistic, backward-looking people imprisoned by their own adherence to a life long gone. Weller constructs this reality by blending the most pessimistic qualities of cultural tradition with the helplessness of philosophical fatalism. Weller writes, "While tradition can thwart the planners and molders of industry, education, and society in general, fatalism can so stultify a people that passive resignation becomes the approved norm."[4] This is the moment when reporting, reinforced by mass media narratives, transforms the Appalachian into the Hillbilly— depicted as either a monster lurking in the dark woods of history like the degenerate, cannibal hillbillies in the movie *Wrong Turn*, to be feared, or a pathetic clown, like Jethro Clampett, stubbornly fixated on a primitive existence, to be ridiculed.

Weller deepens his "fact" by making the point that Appalachian fatalism is justified by a belief in theological happenstance. Weller offers a quote, attributed to no one, to make his point. "If that's the way God wants it, I rekon that's the way it'll be," says the reimagined mountaineer. I'm sure, as well, that this is the very lens that directed Vance to depict his Appalachia as being marked by "spiritual and material poverty."[5] In the stories I was taught, however, this kind of metaphysical laziness toward adversity would have been treated like blasphemy.

In my folk narratives, rather than be subjected to them, I become part of the story. Christine Pavesic writes that these folk stories are "an experience rather than a possession."[6] Each story is an interaction with the past, an opportunity to reconsider the moment now—the imagination always directed to what should be done in a future that inevitably comes. Storytelling is more than just the story. It is how the story is woven together and how meaning emerges as an organic outgrowth of awareness, thinking, speaking, and doing. In "Bless Its Heart: The Irony of Appalachian

Literature," Maurice Manning explores the genre of Appalachian literature, explaining that in Appalachia, "a world of art is in front of you . . . [there] is a larger art of being alive in the world." If we take Paul Zolbrod's definition of art as "transforming awareness into an ordered pattern," we discover that Appalachia is not devoid of art but awash in it.[7]

It is this art that gives Appalachians their own, unique cosmovision. Rodger Cunningham defines cosmovision as a "systematic structure of meanings implying an orientation to the cosmos; in short, a folk ideology and at the same time, a specifically, spiritual phenomena."[8] Ricky Dale Mullins puts it simply: "Being an Appalachian is more than being from the area; it's a way of thinking, a mindset."[9] Manning describes this mindset as a choice we make to participate in this wider, allegorical world of art: "All we have to do is go forth and trust that the human imagination, wherever it resides, will call to life the things that matter to us all and present them as a pretty, a toy for thought and a wonder for the soul."[10] That is what people from Off don't get. Vance and Weller's stories re-create our region as a wasteland—a barren place in the final stages of social decay brought about by the inaction of a lazy, ignorant people. But, in my stories, there is no fate, no stagnation. There is only our choice to participate in or ignore creation. Now, good people will make bad choices and bad people will make good choices. My brother is fond of saying, "Admitting you aren't perfect is the first step to getting better." Every choice is made with an eye toward making the self, world, situation better, more complete. Manning's "pretty" emerges from those choices as the stories we tell others about ourselves.

In the gloaming, I sit my kids down on the front porch or at the supper table. The TV, tablets, phones turned off, we consider the day's events (local, personal, and national) in light of the lessons taught to us by the stories of our own people. I tell my children their stories—spinning a yarn in that very real sense of pulling a thread from here and there, twisting each one into a sturdy cord, tethering them firmly to the who of where they are.

Our stories start in the middle with my Great-Grandparents, Amy and Eli Fisher. They were schoolteachers in Putnam County, West Virginia. Great-Grandma had to stop teaching when she married in the early 1920s and when they left Red House for Spud Run, Ross County, Ohio, Great-Grandpa couldn't find work as a teacher. He hired himself out as a farm hand, cutting corn, then cutting lumber and doing day labor. Great-Grandpa Eli didn't accept adversity as God's will. He understood, as the Good Book teaches, that the only creature not declared "good" was the human being. He believed that humans were a work in progress with a duty to complete themselves as "good" by finding those moments to dress and keep creation. Disappointment was not to be met with resignation. It was embraced as opportunity.

My Uncle Wes says that Great-Grandpa started to notice the need for a veterinarian in their holler and the one adjacent. My Great-Grandparents collected and saved textbooks. At night, they would read these to their kids by the stove. Great-Grandpa took an animal husbandry textbook and learned to animal doctor. Uncle Wes said, "Old Eli was sharp enough to see a need and take to it."[11]

Like Vance, Proverbs 24:30–34 equates material poverty with spiritual poverty: "I went by the field of the slothful, and by the vineyard of the man void of understanding; And, lo, it was all grown over with thorns, and nettles had covered the face thereof, and the stone wall thereof was broken down. Then I saw, and considered it well: I looked upon it, and received instruction. Yet a little sleep, a little slumber, a little folding of the hands to sleep: So shall thy poverty come as one that travelleth; and thy want as an armed man."[12] However, unlike Vance, Proverbs also connects, through allegory, experience, thinking, and doing. A field that is never turned over, plowed up to the rich soil underneath will never be green. A brown, weedy, nettled field will never feed its people. The metaphor is clear: poverty, whether spiritual or material, is rooted in not using the imagination—in not seeing the connection between creative thinking and physical act. If the mind doesn't push the body, the body will never challenge the mind. It is the separation between awareness and act that leads to fatalism.

I have to think that my Grandpa Ralph Fisher saw it that way, too. When my Great-Grandparents left Red House, they bought, sight unseen, eighty acres on Spud Run Road. What they found was eighty acres of hills and hollers without a flat piece of land to farm. Eventually, they moved down the road to sharecrop a farm owned by a man who lived in Chillicothe.

Grandpa was drafted in 1941 and spent the war years Off in the Aleutian Islands. When he returned, four years later, he had saved enough money to buy the farm they worked. My Great-Uncle Joe said, "Then we were in our own house. Not someone's property. We all lived there—we couldn't get thrown off." This was also where I was born. Grandpa accepted the war that interrupted his life with an opportunistic pragmatism. He never let the draft rob him of his freedom to act, to plan ahead. As he was free to choose, he chose to free his family. In doing so, he has come, in my family, to represent the very essence of ethical responsibility. Time and time again, as I tell my kids their stories, I am reminded that we, through our choices, make who we are and, in the process, create a paradigm of action for others.

In 1946, Grandpa married my Grandma, Annabelle "Wrought Iron Annie" Fisher. I always thought her nickname had to do with her being tough, strong, and that she could be pressed without breaking. In Appalachia, everyone has a "fierce granny" story. I think it comes from the fact that we all either had or knew a fierce granny. These women loom large in our collective, mountain imagination and have become, depending on who you ask, either a literary trope or a cliché. But, there can be little doubt that so much of our Appalachian identity is tied up in these stories of strong women.

Grandma was widowed at thirty-four and left to raise four children by herself in the early 1960s. Despite the expectations of society and the times, she refused to get remarried, saying, "I didn't want some other man raising my husband's children." She was defiant, but never angry. When we would tell her we couldn't do something or something was too hard, she would answer, "But, you have to." Even after my Uncle Roger, her oldest son, died young at twenty-six, and even though at age forty-four she had buried a husband and a son, she still told us to "get up and do it."

Her big claim to fame was that she was the first woman to run for public office in Ross County, Ohio. After my Grandpa died, Grandma moved to town. My Uncle Roger, being the oldest, noticed in his cynical, teenager way that the politics of town was more of a plutocracy than a democracy. He told my Grandma that only rich people could be in government. She heard fatalism in that "could not" and decided to nip it in the bud. In the mid-1960s, she ran for county auditor and, some twenty years later, was the first woman to run for mayor of Chillicothe.

Of course, she lost both elections. But, what she had earned was her respect. I think she made her point—that there is a difference between power and respect. I want to pass on the knowledge of this difference to my son James and my daughter Alex. Power can manifest itself only when imposed on another. It is an illusion of the most selfish cooperation and is to be confronted and confounded whenever possible. Respect, on the other hand, is something you earn by overcoming the weakest part of yourself, exposed by defeat or humiliation. Respect is yours to share with another person of your choice.

For her, respect was also earned by maintaining your essential nature in the face of an oppressive power seeking to set limits on your ability to make choices. I remember telling her I wanted to drop out of college. She asked "why?" I said, "I just can't do it." She tossed back her head and sang:

> Well, John Henry said to his captain
> Lord, a man ain't nothing but a man,
> but before I let your steam drill beat me down,
> I'll die with a hammer in my hand.

She saw in John Henry a heroic attitude—not suicidal, not resigned to fate. John Henry challenges the steam drill to prove himself superior to the impersonal machine. Like Emmanuel Levinas's hero, John Henry is aware of the "impossibility of annihilating oneself."[13] This heroic vitality is made clear in the last stanza of the song:

> So every Monday morning,
> when the bluebirds begin to sing,
> you can hear those hammers a mile or more,
> you can hear John Henry's Hammer ring.[14]

John Henry's vitality transcends his physical body to live here, in the song, in my Grandma (now passed), in me and in my daughter when we read the picture book or listen to the song. Can little Alex drive steel like a man? Yes, she can. Yes, she will.

I doubt Grandma found this much academic sermonizing in the song. I think her understanding was more in line with Scott Reynolds Nelson, who writes, "It is a song about terrible adversity that somehow produces marvelous things."[15] Appalachian values stress a struggle against adversity, not the passive acceptance of it as the stereotype of fatalism suggests—or demands. What is fatalism, really? It is just the surrender of choice to what "will" happen. I don't deny that this is a worldview. However, one could just as easily choose to see life as being subject to what "could" happen. Rather than fatalism, the "could" gives us not too few but too many anxiety-inducing possibilities. My stories teach me to choose what "should" happen. *Should,* not as certainty, but as possibility. My responsibility becomes to choose the better to bring that possibility to fruition.

This is what is *wyrd* about Appalachian storytelling. The Old English term *wyrd* (Old Norse *urd*) is almost always translated as "fate" and used to characterize the Anglo-Saxons, like the Hillbilly, as gloomy, fatalistic, and pessimistic. However, as Paul Baushatz writes, "if fate's meaning is to be limited to denoting 'that which is spoken' or 'that which has been laid down,' then [fate] translates the context well."[16] Literally translated, *wyrd* does not mean "fate." Rather, *wyrd* is the past tense of "to be," "has become." Rather than determine the future, *wyrd* reveals the past. *Wyrd* manifests itself in the present through stories and art ("laid down by speaking"). In the process, these stories reveal "a realm of experience including all of the accomplished actions of all beings, men, gods, etc."[17] These stories lay bare the possibilities that existed then and may very well exist now—if only we look for them. Understanding how these stories make us is the awareness of the very essence of who we are to become.

Knowing, telling, hearing, and engaging stories of myth, folklore, and family history provides what Wendell Berry calls a "comforting sense of precedent."[18] Our knowledge of the past, through our stories and the complex intertextual networks they form, allows for "the working out of the past into the present (or more accurately, the working in of the present into the past)."[19] *Wyrd,* as "fate," does not limit our agency or doom us to a predestined end. Rather, *wyrd* reveals a structure for what we should do, now. Choosing to act becomes one more story that replenishes the well for the next generation. I think this is the most important lesson: as we take from the well, we also fill it.

The ability to gain and have access to these stories contributes to one's "luck" (Old Norse *hamingja*). Bettina Sommer describes this Norse concept as "a quality inherent in [a person] and [his/her] lineage . . . at once both the cause and expression of the success, wealth, and power of a family."[20] When I teach this concept to my kids, I stress that luck is our inherited *wyrd*—knowledge, in the form of stories, songs, and language that reveal the "root assumptions," of "not the kind of knowledge we possess but the kind of knowledge we are made of."[21] This cosmovision encourages us to reflect on who we are, where we are, and who we should become as we navigate the structures and situations of the environment we are in and the particular moment we are born into. Knowing who we're from depends on the stories we pass down that teach us about our family history and inheritance as a guide to meaningful action.

And there is our spiritual wealth that, while articulating it in his own stories, J. D. Vance can't understand or find. Our wealth is more than material possessions. It is found in our traditions and our stories. These traditions are part of a past we did not make but are subjected to nevertheless. That is what I wish Vance could see—that he, both of us really, have achieved marvelous things. That the obstacles we overcame were not solely part of our Appalachian culture but, more so, imposed on us from the outside. That our accomplishments were not despite our traditions but because of them. The stories of the failures and triumphs of our people became our luck—our strength. The spiritual wealth he overlooks is expressed in the awareness of our ability to use these stories to choose better. My Uncle Wes is fond of telling stories about his abject failures and disappointments. Weller may see these stories as fatalistic resignation. Vance may not find any spiritual wealth in them. But, they miss the point of the story. Uncle Wes ends every story with an admonition, "Don't you dare disrespect me by imitating my bad habits or character flaws."

We all fall short. Even the people in our stories. They cried. They hurt. They drank too much. They died too young. They could be hard when we needed comfort. But, we should never be ashamed of them. Leon Kass characterizes shame as "the painful response to a self-consciously recognized gap between an idealized self-image and the truth about ourselves."[22] The inevitable truth is that no matter how well we choose, we will eventually fail. The power of shame is its ability to pull us from spiritual action to material stagnation. Shame teaches that we win or lose. Our stories, on the other hand, direct us toward who we should be, a goal we strive for constantly, yet consistently fall short of achieving. While shame may rob us of what we feel we could have, it never touches our ability to choose what we should do.

In his introduction to *Hillbilly Elegy*, Vance writes, "I want people to understand something I learned only recently: for those of us lucky enough to live the American Dream, the demons of life we left behind continued to chase us" (2). Now, that's his opinion and he is welcome to it. But, before he lumps me in with his "us," I would like for Vance to study on this: in folklore and mythology, demons, monsters, and dragons all serve to remind the "hero" of the dangers inherent in their metaphysical stagnation. In the *Völsunga Saga*, Sigurd slays his Dragon. But, that is not the whole story. He then sets to eating it. On tasting the Dragon's blood, the story tells us, he could understand the language of the birds. Joseph Campbell glosses it as being able to hear "the song of the universe." The point is, whether positive or negative, we must confront the past if we are to open ourselves to Manning's mystical world where our stories reimagine us as we should be.

It is only in looking back, into tradition, that we know who we are. Silas House articulates what I understand to be the very essence of Appalachian luck: "Wendell Berry says that if you don't know where you're from, you don't know who you are. I think people look at that quote and think he means a physical place . . . but I think he's talking about something much more profound than that. So, I will paraphrase Berry here and put this forth: if you don't know who you're from you don't know who you are."[23] The "Gospel of Thomas" further warns against ignoring one's essential nature: "That which you have will save you if you bring it forth from yourselves. That which you do not have within you will kill you if you do not have it."[24] You can't ignore what and who you are. You can't be what you ain't.

But, a fool will try. On that day after Christmas, when I was eighteen, I went home to change. The work boots were traded out for a pair of Converse high tops and the flannel shirt for an Otterbein College sweatshirt. It was, at that time, an insignificant moment. It was forgotten. It wasn't until the 2015 Appalachian Symposium, held at Berea College, that I began to understand the existential catastrophe that I had participated in. Ending his keynote address, Maurice Manning challenged the audience to "Get more Hillbilly as [you] go." At that moment, I realized I had hidden myself in clothes I had not chosen—setting myself on a long road away from who I should have been. I struggled to be something I wasn't or sought to balance who I knew myself to be with what I thought I needed to be to succeed Off. Manning shamed me that day, making me realize that I had failed at both hiding and passing. I was forced to acknowledge that I was at my best when I was at home with my wife, our kids, my brothers, my parents. I also had to come to terms with the fact that I was unhappy with my professional life because I left the best part of me at home, wearing a flannel shirt and Realtree camo sweat pants and porch sitting in a rocking chair. I was killing myself living what I did not have in me.

I wish J. D. Vance could see his life through the lens of Appalachian storytelling. I want him to understand that living an American Dream not of your choosing is not "lucky," especially if you have to leave behind your own stories and traditions—those best things. Appalachian storytelling teaches us that luck is made when we know and live our traditions; that the *wyrd*-ness of the Appalachian cosmovision is the antidote to material and spiritual poverty. This essential knowledge of how things are strengthens us so that, in the cool of the day, we won't hide in shame when, as Johnny Cash puts it, "the Man comes around." Instead, we can stand boldly in front of the mirror our stories provide and be open to instruction.

NOTES

1. Todd Snyder, *The Rhetoric of Appalachian Identity* (Jefferson, NC: McFarland, 2014), 5.
2. Ibid., 1.
3. Roger D. Abrahams, "Identity," in *Eight Words for the Study of Expressive Culture*, ed. Burt Feintuch (Urbana: University of Illinois Press, 2003), 201.
4. Jack E. Weller, *Yesterday's People: Life in Contemporary Appalachia* (Lexington: University Press of Kentucky, 1965), 37.
5. Ibid., 2.
6. Christine L. Pavesic, *Ray Hicks and the Jack Tales: A Study of Appalachian History, Culture, and Philosophy* (IUniverse, 2005), 8.
7. Maurice Manning, "Bless Its Heart: The Irony of Appalachian Literature," *Appalachian*

Heritage 44, no. 1 (2016): 61–81; Paul Zolbrod, *The Diné Bahané* (Albuquerque: University of New Mexico Press, 1987), 349.

8. Rodger Cunningham, "The Greenside of Life: Appalachian Magic as a Site of Resistance," *Appalachian Heritage*, Spring 2010, 55.

9. Ricky Dale Mullins, Twitter @Rickydale88, August 16, 2017.

10. Manning, "Bless Its Heart," 79.

11. Joseph Fisher, interview by the author, April 28, 2016.

12. *The Bible: King James Version* (New York: HarperCollins, 2008).

13. Emmanuel Levinas, *Time and the Other*, trans. Richard A. Cohen (Pittsburgh: Duquesne University Press, 1990), 73.

14. "John Henry," *AZLyrics*, August 2017, www.azlyrics.com/lyrics/brucespringsteen/johnhenry.html.

15. Scott Reynolds Nelson, *Steel Drivin' Man: John Henry, the Untold Story of an American Legend* (New York: Oxford University Press, 2006), 173.

16. Paul Baushatz, *The Well and the Tree: World and Time in Early Germanic Culture* (Boston: University of Massachusetts Press, 1982), 6.

17. Ibid., 7.

18. Wendell Berry, "Writer and Region," in *What Are People For?* (Berkeley, CA: Counterpoint, 2010), 71.

19. Baushatz, *Well and the Tree*, 11.

20. Bettina Sommer, "The Norse Concept of Luck," *Scandinavian Studies* 79, no. 3 (2007), quoted in Daniel McCoy, *The Viking Spirit* (CreateSpace, 2016), 90.

21. Charles Upton, *Folk Metaphysics* (San Rafael, CA: Sophia Perennis, 2008), 5.

22. Leon Kass, *The Beginning of Wisdom* (Chicago: University of Chicago Press, 2006), 67.

23. David O. Hoffman, Natalie Brandon, and Sylvia Bailey Shurbutt, "Interview with Silas House," http://www.shepherd.edu/ahwirweb/house/pages/essay.html.

24. Ron Cameron, "Gospel of Thomas," in *The Other Gospels: Non-Canonical Gospel Texts* (Cambridge: Lutterworth Press, 2006), 70.

WATCH CHILDREN

TEXT AND PHOTOGRAPH BY LUKE TRAVIS

PITTSBURGH can be overwhelming to someone who spent formative years in small-town Appalachia. The thought of the city alone conjures to small-town citizens ideas of coldhearted hustle and bustle. The hidden beauty of this region, however, is the unknowingly shared values that both small towns and large cities host. The values of family and community mark this entire region. While walking through the Northside of Pittsburgh I feel the same presence of "small-town values" that I did in Port Allegany, Pennsylvania, a small town of just over two thousand, nestled in the Appalachian Mountains. I remember being warned of the harsh environment and lack of values I would encounter when my family moved from the small, rural town to Pittsburgh. However, through my experiences I have learned that these values mark the whole region of Appalachia, and that "small-town values" manifest themselves in different shapes and sizes—they do not belong solely to small towns.

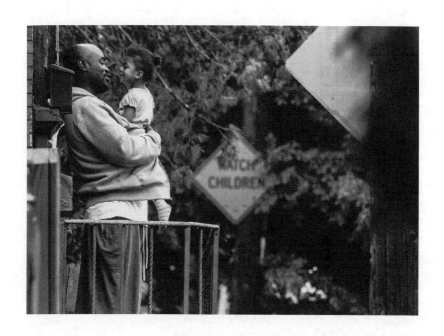

THE MOWER—1933

ROBERT MORGAN

in memory of my father

Far back as I remember I have loved
to cut weeds with a scythe. Some say I took
it after my grandpa and that it runs
deep in our blood. But since I was a boy
I liked to take the blade and trim along
the edges of the field, to make the banks
and even ditches look well groomed, a park.
The odd thing is I like weeds too, the smell
of weeds on hottest days, their steaming scent
through leaves, their wilting in the brightest sun.
I like the way big weeds grow one behind
the other on a slope, and reach into
the light, and crowd each inch of space and air,
with joe-pye weed and hogweed reaching highest.

With scythe on shoulder, whetrock in my hand,
I march off to do battle with the weeds.
I like to take the big stalks down until
the ground is smooth as any Flat Rock lawn.
The question is: where to begin? I stop beside

the hogpen, rest the handle on the ground
and rub the whetstone on the blade. I like
to feel the whet-grains cutting into steel.
I work along the blade and whet it dull
and then brilliant, and turn the scythe to whet
the other side. The blade lights up with my
abrasive strokes. The whetrock on the steel
sounds like an auctioneer, says give me one,
a one, a two. I blow the grime off of
the rock and slip it in my pocket. Oof
and oof the pig says snuffling up against
the pigpen wall. The pig is lively in
the morning cool. But as the day grows hot
it finds a corner spot in shade to nap.

Now it will turn quick as a cat to slam
the pen side, hoping I have come with slop
to pour into its trough. The pig smells sour,
not just the sour of hog manure, but stink
of festering summer mud. It is the sour
of cabbage rot and old dishwater, sour
of juices standing in hoof pools, that spoil,
fermenting. Pen mud, deep and black is greased
with shit and silt and fetid creams, of bone
and marrow jelly. Cobs stink, and stalks of weeds
are pickled in the slime. Each day I throw
fresh weeds into the pen to give the hog
a salad, but they soak into the slime.
The trembling batter of the pen seeps out
through cracks and glitters in the sun. The mud
is thick and deeper than a pillow. Curds
and turds of mud are churned up by the hooves.
Flies hang in glistening veils above the pen.
The air around the grunting swine's a full

rainbow of stinks and fetor, fart and belch
of rotten breath. The dirt below the pen
is where I dig for fishing worms in spring.
The mealy compost there will yield more worms
per shovelful than any place I know,
worms orange, purple, worms with threads like screws,
night crawlers glistening like snakes, and worms
with swollen bands and blister rings, worms flat
at lower ends. I dig a canful there
in minutes, tangled, moistened in the foam
and suds and spit of slime. The muck and musk
below the pen grow best and bigger weeds
than anywhere around. Corn volunteers
from seeds in the manure. And sometimes squash,
or pumpkins sprout there too, grow succulent
from filth. But mostly just plain weeds thrive here,
ragweed and hog, the plantain, ironweed for
the biggest part. But largest of them all,
the pokeweeds, that by August reach out stalks
and leaves with purple veins eight feet or more,
though pokeweed doesn't like the richest ground.
It thrives along the edges of the spill
of hogpen soil, in red clay and leached out dirt
of the old strawberry bed. For starting out
I swing the blade along the path and slice
the canes of Johnson grass that drop like wheat
beneath the scythe. All grass grows jointed stalks
if left to age and go to seed. I sweep
the blade across the ground and cut things off
about two inches high. The stalks and leaves
fall where they grow. This is the way to put
the things on earth in shape, I think. The blade
will hiss as it will swing on bigger weeds.
Weeds grow their stalks like little towers, and have

both tubes and wires inside their spines. Weeds have
a suction in their veins that draws both up
and down and pulls juice from the roots into
the tips. I swing the blade like I would pull
a crooked oar. There is a rhythm I
must find each morning, but it takes a while
to get it right. Some days I never find
the cadence in this dance of labor, or
the perfect pace. Ragweeds have limbs that grow
out from the stalks like shelves, kept stiff by juice
inside the veins, erect and filling out
and stretching in the hottest sun until
the tips wilt just a little and go limp.
The leaves are crisp as dollar bills right off
the press in morning dew; but when they're cut
the leaves turn black and crumble like dried ink.

The big weeds reach out limbs like they resist
my blade. They stand in ranks like soldiers with
their shields of green. Their arms would wave me back,
but I advance one step and swing each time,
and weeds fall back like they are pulled beneath
by undertow. This is a way to make
a fodder of the weeds I think. I swing
but don't think how I'm broke and out of work.
What will I do this fall? There are no jobs
and money seems extinct. It disappeared
and won't come back and nothing seems to work.
Already I can smell my sweat, and scent
of chemicals that rise from weeds. The stubs
that bleed smell like perfumes and spice.
The fumes rise from the leaves like varnish spilled
or powerful solvents that intoxicate
with vapors lifting from the fallen weeds.

There is a blend of scents, of oils, and saps,
of nectar fumes, so strong I feel a little dazed.
The air is lit with herbals fogs and smoke
of incense, choirs of vapors in the air.

Along with smells there are insects that boil
ahead of where my blade will swing. And dust
and bits of thistle, seeds, grasshoppers, fly
wherever weeds are struck and fall. The air
is filled with moths that have been sleeping in
the shade. And white and purple butterflies
are stirred by mowing. Spider webs between
the stalks get torn and spiders jump out of
my way or scurry on the ground as I
advance into their kingdoms with each swing,
big spiders, little, brown or yellow. Some
are black as pearls, and some resemble boats
that run on oars. Leaf mites and hoppers shake
from weeds and boil like dust. Each leaf will hold
a meal of white and yellow lice if you
look close. I sweep the blade close to the ground,
and move ahead in arcs with every step.
I want the field to look like it's been shaved.

My hands are jolted almost out of grasp
I've hit a rock and see the cut the blade
has made among the weed stains on the stone.
This rock I've mowed into before. I grab
the stone and fling it to the pigpen wall,
and hear the pig lunge from one side to slam
into the other wall. I will not be
slowed down, I vow. I won't be stopped from my
ambition to make something grand. Where there
is not a way I'll make a way. Without a plan

there will be nothing meaningful. I'm drunk
with sun and sweat, inspired by heat of labor.
I raise the blade, inspect the edge and find
in blinding sun the metal stained with sap
and bits of leaves and stalks are stuck to steel.
There is a nick along the edge the rock
bit out, a gap within the sharpness. With
a few more nicks like that the blade would be
a total loss. I whet the steel like I
would punish it. The metal's soft and fat
beneath the stone's abrasive touch. Then I
Inspect the edge that's microscopically thin.

My fury makes the sunlight bright and lethal,
and weeds more vivid, leaf and vein stand out.
I glare at every stalk and tendril, stare
at chalky butterflies and clicking crickets.
A quail fires from the weeds like mortar round.
My anger makes the air grow brighter still.
The steams and vapors from the ground rise in
my face. The weeds have molten gold inside
their veins that burns my skin. The weeds stand in
my way like everything I know. I launch
into the stalks again. I mean to quell
the field if possible. The weeds rise up
at me and mock, stampeding in their lush
resistance, rise in ever higher waves
to bury me, defeat me with their floods
of growth, and cover any path or spot
I try to clear. They fling out arms to stop
me once again. And morning glories wrap
on stalks and limbs. Briars rake at everything.
Blackberry canes shoot up like fountains, catch
the fur of fox and rabbit. Chiggers swirl

in bins and wash away in currents with
the flowers and flies. A foam of chlorophyll,
of petals, pollen, honeydew, of bees
caught in the vortex of the blade, in clots
and wads of straw. I swing the blade to slice
the biggest stalks like juicy sapling sprouts.
I mow the catbriars, seedlings of young pines.
I slash through rank on rank of fragrance, queen
of the meadow. Weeds much taller than me.
I swing into the shadows, fight as knight
with sword against the summer's green rebellion,
advancing deeper in the ranks and drawing blood.

Midmorning, I have acres still to do
by dinner time. Below the hogpen those
big weeds are not about to make a truce,
appear to be recalcitrant. I stop
to whet the blade again, then swing sideways
into the fray. I feel as though I swim
in sweat, and sweat flows over me to wash
me from inside, as though I sweat the poison,
the fury out, the sweat baptizing me
within and bleeding out the fester of
the times, resolving all resentments as
I stand on my own land, both cleansed and healed.

CONSOLIDATE AND SALVAGE

CHELSEA JACK

MY MOM, Susan, worked as a quality and production manager for twenty-eight years in Pepsi Bottling Group facilities across west-central Virginia. She started at a plant in the small city of Lynchburg, a place with an uncomplicated love for the Blue Ridge and a complicated attachment to Southern Baptist televangelist Jerry Falwell. Mom worked in Lynchburg from 1986 until 1991 when Pepsi consolidated production in Botetourt County. While pregnant, she even traveled back and forth between *both* plants from 1990 to December 1991. After that initial consolidation, she spent the better part of her career working in the Roanoke Valley.

People take unexpected roads in life and wind up in even more unexpected places. I was born in Virginia Baptist Hospital on Rivermont Avenue in the middle of the night in December 1991. The *place* of my birth was a bit of an irony. Back then, my parents lived on Coffee Road. Coffee runs in the wooded outskirts of the "'03s," which is local slang for the relatively well-to-do (and optically white) households in Lynchburg with an enviable 24503 zip code. Rivermont was an "ironic" place for me to hit the human scene because my parents weren't stereotypical '03 folks, especially Mom who worked full-time in the glamorous men's world of industrial manufacturing in the early nineties.

Roads—and trails and rivers—are important to our story. In 1991, Mom was unable to imagine a comparable salary and benefits elsewhere, and so she decided to stay with Pepsi after the Lynchburg plant stopped producing. She and my dad moved to Bedford County, a few miles from the Blue Ridge Parkway and the Peaks of Otter, so she could commute more easily to the new plant in Botetourt. In her 1987 Nissan Pathfinder, she drove eighty miles every day. Her drive ran along US Route 460 West and ended at the plant on Lee Highway, named after Confederate General Robert E. Lee.

Pepsi moved and we moved. Pepsi consolidated and we consolidated. Despite how successfully workers meet and often exceed corporate production demands, they are almost always subject to consolidation, a practice that seeks to optimize distributional logistics. And so are their families. The Botetourt plant, unlike the one in Lynchburg, was positioned near a major interstate, I-81. In terms of operating costs, it wasn't efficient or competitive for PepsiCo to produce at both facilities. The Botetourt plant offered distributional advantages and could meet Lynchburg's production demands, and so the latter closed.

My mom confronted the possibility of plant closure and insecurity repeatedly throughout her career. In addition to this sense of precarity she shared with all of her coworkers, Mom's career choices had a particular gravity as she was one of few women ascending the ranks to middle management in the manufacturing technology industry during the eighties and nineties—and in the South, no less. She experienced economic mobility, which she never took for granted, and yet she also realized that mobility wasn't painless. As it turns out, the mythic American Dream rarely ever is.

———

I anxiously transferred to a private boarding school in northern Virginia, or what folks down in southern Virginia call "NOVA." For reasons totally obvious to anyone from southern or southwestern Virginia, this was no small cultural betrayal. There's Virginia—and then there's NOVA. This is a social fact.

Whether or not they were good, I had my reasons. I had attended a Catholic school in Lynchburg through my freshman year of high school. As I remember it, my time there had been spent in after-school detention for minor infractions almost always related to dress code violations. My kilt and socks were chronically short, and my shoes were never the right kind of faux leather. The most redeeming experience had been making (what was called) the "Men's Varsity Soccer Team." There was no women's team. Though admittedly, as a teenage girl mystified by older high school boys, this absence was not exactly a hardship.

My decision to apply to boarding school wasn't (exclusively) the result of youthful disdain for an idiosyncratic Catholic education. Honestly, the exact reasons for my decision continue to unfold and make sense a decade after the fact. Looking back, I was a disaffected teen with an active imagination. I may have first gotten the idea to go to boarding school from *A Separate Peace* or *Catcher in the Rye* or *Harry Potter*.

However, *Gilmore Girls* was the point of no return. When I saw Rory Gilmore move from her stereotypically mediocre public high school to Chilton, a fictitious, elite private school, then go directly to Yale University (an exclusive Ivy League school), while effortlessly spellbinding Milo Ventimiglia and Chad Michael Murray (my two favorites among her many suitors), and all the while looking like a wood nymph from a goddamn Lancôme ad—I was literally *SOLD*.

I was a fifteen-year-old with a big imagination chasing after the romance of mobility. When I finally left Bedford County for Alexandria, my experiences of mobility, class, education, and gender weren't nearly as quaint as Rory's fictitious forays into elite worlds.

———

A wise woman once told me that the world is made up of different kinds of unknowns. There are things that one is aware of not knowing. These are called *known unknowns*. For example, I know of econometrics, but haven't the least idea what exactly econometrics is (are?). However, there are things that one is unaware of not knowing. There are things that exist in the world, yet completely escape one's imagination. Those are called *unknown unknowns*.

I encountered this second category, unknown unknowns, when I got to boarding school. There were tricky conversational strategies, gendered dispositions, and signs of good taste that made fitting in socially feel nearly impossible. My new high school had a self-conscious southern aesthetic and ethos, and yet it wasn't a familiar one to me. I was technically from the South, but not the (old or new) *moneyed* South.

Remember when Jack Dawson was invited to dinner with the first-class passengers in *Titanic*? It might seem like a dramatic exaggeration, but I experienced that kind of culture shock during my first few months away at boarding school. I oscillated between feeling mystified by my new surroundings and longing to return to hocking loogies with Rose on the upper deck. Granted, this analogy goes only so far. I came from a middle-class American family. My parents worked really hard to send their kid (having secured financial aid and scholarship money) to this fancy school, and all of my successes have been possible only with their help. I wasn't exactly the mythic American individualist living on a prayer or the fruits of a lucky hand in my last card game.

We were *not* poor. We were also *not* rich. There aren't always readily available ways to talk about the space betwixt and between these two places. When I got to boarding school, I stepped into a baffling world of unknown unknowns wrapped up in learned dispositions toward money, small talk, taste, fitness regimens, body image, art, conservative fashion, and socially acceptable (and unacceptable) ways for millennial women to bond in this place.

One of the most well-attended, unofficial rituals in our dorm was the annual viewing of the Victoria's Secret Fashion Show (of all things). Young women would leave evening study hall early and gather in their respective common rooms to watch. They would gather around glowing dorm televisions, and eager hands would pass bags of chocolate chips and Goldfish crackers and comment on the bodies and outfits of the svelte angels with wings. It felt difficult, if not impossible, to cultivate indifference toward the pressure to be extremely thin. I wasted a lot of time pinching my stomach in front of the bathroom mirror. Looking back on these moments, it felt as if my successful consolidation in this place meant shedding weight, and not just physical pounds. The success of my consolidation hinged on my ability to tread lightly in this new world.

———

In the wake of production consolidation, employees are left in the uncomfortable situation of finishing the job. In 2014, the year I graduated from the University of Virginia, my mom was tasked with "finishing the job" as production at the Botetourt plant closed. "Corporate," as she called the faceless powers that be, had decided to once *again* consolidate production. This time they were moving equipment and employees to an even newer plant at the intersection of I-81 and I-77 in Wytheville, Virginia. When we spoke most recently about Pepsi choosing to stop production at the Botetourt plant, she described what closing a plant meant:

"Let's say you have assets sitting there, which cost hundreds of thousands of dollars. You have to begin moving that equipment to other locations. In my case, I had to coordinate, over two weeks, the disposal of all the ingredients and packaging materials we used, and that had to be done in accordance with the appropriate regulatory agencies. Some things, like lab equipment, had to be sent to Wytheville. Salvage people—there are companies that specialize in this—come into the plant and they bid on equipment. They disassemble it and sell it to other production locations that need it. Our bottle lines could go to a brewery, for example."

I asked if Pepsi makes money off of that salvaging process?

"They can capitalize on it. These assets have value, even if they're just sold for scrap metal."

In the wake of such fragmentation, what forms of salvaging are left to the employees who must return home and pick up their own pieces?

There is death and rebirth in salvage. Salvaged materials represent the end of one chapter and the beginning of another. They tell stories about closures and losses. These materials also travel and begin again, just like the people who worked with these materials.

When Mom's plant closed, there were ingredients and packaging materials that had to be disposed. You can't walk out of a warehouse or production facility and leave these things. That would be like moving out of your apartment with everything left in the fridge. All of those things have to be removed, and the removal process has to follow environmental and legal guidelines determined by the Environmental Protection Agency or Department of Environmental Quality. Mom had spent most of her career at Pepsi doing this kind of quality control work, where she had to ensure that production complied with various health and safety standards.

———

Whenever I lose my footing in life, I return to Joan Didion's essay "On Self-Respect," originally published in 1961. When I come up for air, but am still swallowing water, this essay offers the buoyancy needed to break through to the surface. It came to mind after a recent trip home to Virginia in the summer of 2017.

Didion writes about self-respect as a kind of "separate peace, a private reconciliation," which has nothing to do with the approval of others or reputation. It's a kind of courage that allows a person to leave the expectations of others unmet and to own one's mistakes.

"To assign unanswered letters their proper weight, to free us from the expectations of others, to give us back ourselves—there lies the great, the singular power of self-respect. Without it, one eventually discovers the final turn of the screw: one runs away to find oneself, and finds no one at home."

Without it, one eventually discovers the final turn of the screw: one runs away to find oneself, and finds no one at home.

During my most recent visit home, Dad and I paddled our favorite local section of the James River. It's just a couple miles from Glasgow to Snowden. It's one of our things. We skipped the first rapid after the put-in, which is on the Maury River just before it runs into the James. We always start at this confluence. It's where the two rivers join and become one.

That day I couldn't remember the last time the two of us ran this section of the James. Just like when I was a little kid, we hooted and hollered down Balcony Falls. I'm not sure we even stopped chatting or paddling to consider what line to take. Like riding a bike, some things just stay with you.

Below Little Balcony and Jump Rock, he asked me to snap a picture of his favorite spot on the river. "Flatwater builds character," Dad always says when we hit this section. He's right. It's where folks develop endurance. It's also where the glassy surface affords a clear look at one's self and decisions.

I paddled, peered down at the surface of the water, and reflected on all the ways I had continued to consolidate since I left home for boarding school at fifteen. I had landed somewhat closer to home when I chose to go to the University of Virginia, but after four years in Charlottesville, I consolidated again. That time I went a couple hundred miles up I-81 North in a black Honda Element. I moved with a newly rescued pit bull–boxer mix named Trapper (after Trapper John, MD on *M*A*S*H*). Trapper rode in the passenger seat the whole way, with his head drooped on my guitar case jutting out from the back seat through the center console. I was about to start my first job out of college in a tiny commuter "town" called Garrison on the east bank of the Hudson River about an hour north of New York City.

———

Two days before moving to Garrison, things (seemed to have) ended with my college sweetheart, who had also been my high school sweetheart. I didn't know how to begin or mark a new chapter, so I got a pixie cut. It was a bold miscalculation.

Since I was a kid, I've assessed the promise of a new day based on how my long, wavy brown hair looks right when I wake up. It's an amusing (and vain) eccentricity. This is no secret in my family. It's the butt of many inside jokes. Even when I was in college, Dad would call and greet me by asking whether it had been a "good-hair day." I chopped of all of my hair to shed old energies, to make room for new geographies, to write new autobiographies.

Shockingly, I didn't instantaneously morph into the new Chelsea I'd pictured. I didn't suddenly look like Jennifer Lawrence or Miley Cyrus with a pixie. (*Surprise!* said no one ever.) My best pals would probably say the 'do was fine, but it had all the regrettable wrappings of a well-intended impulse. It's not hard to feel comfortable in your own skin with a flattering makeover, but a spontaneous breakup haircut gone wrong—oh man.

The reality was this: I was looking for a dope haircut to provide confidence that only a *bad* haircut could. Instead of the instant gratification of a quick chop, I needed (but didn't want) to go through the tedious process of "growing out," as folks with Rapunzel goals would say.

In the Hudson River Valley, with mountains that look so similar to the Blue Ridge, I learned another tough lesson that Didion writes about. And I learned it with a bad haircut. "I lost the conviction that lights would always turn green for me." I screwed up at work (a lot). I totaled my car. I had love troubles. I applied unsuccessfully to PhD programs. I navigated health problems that embarrassed me. I saved money and lost it.

———

There's a photo of a pond at sunset in my iPhone. The clouds overhead look like watercolor paints. It's hard to tell up from down.

When Mom texted me this picture, I was working toward my master's at the University of Chicago. I had been looking out across my new backyard, the shoreline of Lake Michigan, when my phone vibrated. Of course, I could see only a sliver of the lake from my apartment window, but it was still a sliver.

I stared at the picture for a minute. It looked like an optical illusion. If you rotated the image clockwise or counterclockwise, the space where earth and water meet took the rough shape of an hourglass. This was my first backyard, an hourglass.

Growing up involves a lot of waiting—what will I become? I suspect that's a question most kids have, but perhaps dreaming takes a particular shape for kids growing up in rural areas. Things are quiet and wide open. Car rides are long and winding. Time feels slow. So much is left to the imagination. My parents taught my brother and me to be attentive to the world's quiet mysteries. Wherever I've gone, this lesson has traveled with me.

"In other words, even on the perfectly ordinary and clearly visible level, creation carries on with an intricacy unfathomable and apparently uncalled for." That's Annie Dillard in *Pilgrim at Tinker Creek*. In 1974, she wrote those words about the creativity of the world surrounding her just outside Roanoke near the Blue Ridge Mountains. That string of mountains is visible in the background of Mom's picture.

Mom texted me the picture of our backyard at sunset shortly after the election of Donald Trump. I found hope in this image. It reminded me that the world around us persists with care, grace, complexity, and beauty, even when humans refuse to do the same.

———

Mom and I are women from different, albeit both precarious, eras in American life: one a baby boomer, the other a millennial. And yet, like the James and Maury rivers, there are confluences where our stories meet. We are skeptical of the myth of the American Dream, or the idea that social and class mobility are always good things. We share an appreciation for strong women, who artfully

notice the world around them. We share gratitude for those things that can be salvaged even in the midst of darkness.

I have traveled with these lessons and, for now, have consolidated in New Haven, Connecticut, where I'm a PhD student focusing on sociocultural anthropology. This is not a story about someone who "got out" of Appalachia. This is not a story about someone who tried to avoid repeating the mistakes of her parents. This is a mother-daughter story of roads and trails taken. It is a story about consolidating so we could travel lightly, and question what it means to uproot.

I'm staying put in New Haven for now, but I've returned to running for exercise in the last year. I've taken to adventuring along the banks of the Mill River in East Rock Park. Even as I've concentrated on grounding myself, I find myself running again. Life in the time of capitalism often means dislocation, whether it's geographic or financial. Kentucky writer Wendell Berry has challenged the idea that the grass is always greener elsewhere, that mobility is always a good thing. He suggests landing, just staying put, and attending to the people and objects of concern wherever that may be. However, after all the consolidating I've done—and all the consolidating Mom's done to get me here—I'm not sure how to heed Berry's call. There's an alluring possibility betwixt and between places. I've been running to this one bridge in New Haven lately. I pause in the middle and breathe. I'm twenty-six, and I am merely in the process of consolidating and salvaging.

I took a picture of that bridge a couple months ago, but have recently been considering what about it caught my eye. My gaze follows the arch of the bridge over the Mill River. From where I stand, angled in a particular way as the photographer, the opposite bank remains out of sight. I fixate instead on the bridge, which connects a vignetted, overshadowed present to an equally ill-defined future.

HOW APPALACHIAN I AM

ROBERT GIPE

THE BUILDING is stone. In one end of it, there is a liquor store. Beyond it, there is a mining camp, with rows of houses built by a coal company for its workers and their families. The liquor store is labeled, in letters painted on glass, Mongiardos. A five-foot man stands behind the counter. His hair lies in waves across the top of his head. The man smiles. There is a camera around his neck. The facing edge of the liquor store's metal shelves carry, in red and black letters, the prices of the bottles of liquor. The facing edge of the shelves are lined with photographs of people taken in the liquor store, or in front of it. There are hundreds of photographs, pictures of coal miners with dust on their faces; pictures of politicians, smiling, with their arm around the man with the wavy hair; pictures of shirtless men with tattoos on their chests; pictures of women in prom dresses; pictures of young men in tuxedoes with their hair parted in the middle. The pictures are printed on paper. They seem, for the most part, to have been shot on film. These rows of pictures on paper tell the story of a drinking people. They are the feathers of a great, drunken bird.

———

The river that runs through Kingsport, Tennessee, generally looks green. A chemical plant sprawls along the river's bank for nearly a mile. The plant sports smokestacks by the dozen, sets of stacks spread across acres. There is endless duct work curving and turning along the walls of the buildings, and between them. There are sheets of gray and green plastic, stories high and embedded with chicken wire, that serve as windows. The buildings are brick. Their smokestacks plume. Belts hiss, gears churn, and machines hum inside them. There is a smell of high school science labs run amok that fills the plant and spreads to the city and countryside around the plant. The smell is vinegary and invasive. One's eyes water at the smell, until one grows used to it.

The plant by the river made the chemicals used to make the film in the camera owned by the wavy-haired man peddling liquor. Thousands of coal miners and their families made it possible for the man with the wavy hair, and others, to make money selling liquor. Thousands of chemical workers made it possible for their picture to be taken. Every trip to Dollywood ever recorded on film, every wedding, every prom, every mug shot, every high school football game, every birthday party recorded in a photograph during the nearly hundred years when all photographs were recorded on film, was more than likely to have been enabled by a chemical made in that plant by the river in Kingsport, Tennessee.

The buildings in the chemical plant are numbered. The building numbered 190 once produced polyethylene and polypropylene pellets. Plastic pellets. Many of those pellets were sold to the company making film. But the machine operators in building 190 also produced plastic pellets for use by other firms. The pellets were shipped around the world, to factories where they were heated and molded into many things, including steering wheels and lawn mower parts, chain saw guards and tampon applicators.

The plastic was mixed in batches upstairs in building 190, in what were called Banbury mixers. Once mixed, the batches dropped into extruders which stretched the plastic into endless strands of brightly colored synthetic linguine. The extruders cooled the plastic pasta in long trays of water, and chopped it into pellets, which dropped into a box capable of holding a thousand pounds, or into larger metal hoppers. Boxes were sealed with metal straps and loaded onto a tractor trailer and taken to distribution, the part of the plant where product was shipped out. Hoppers were taken to the packing area, where they were set on a bagging machine that dispensed the pellets in fifty-pound increments into a double-thick paper bag. An operator set the bag to run through a sealer that glued the bag shut. The operator stacked the bags on a pallet, and the pallet was loaded on a trailer headed for distribution.

In the summers of 1983 and 1984, human beings operated the machines in 190. Human beings loaded the product. Human beings drove the forklifts. During the summers of 1983 and 1984, I was one of those human beings. I drove a forklift, sealed bags, strapped boxes, loaded product onto tractor trailers. Before I went to 190, the only paying work I had ever done was mowing yards. I mowed my family's yard under duress from my father, and the rest of the yards on the street beside our house under duress from my mother. I went to work at the plant to earn more money, under less duress, and so the extruder operators and Banbury operators and shipping operators could take summer vacation.

One of the extruder operators was named Bear. Another was named Moon. They were both stout. They wore their coveralls open in the front. Bear wore safety glasses with clear frames surrounded by perforated plastic. Moon was bald, and had a salt and pepper beard. Bear's beard was red. We were told to take brief but frequent breaks in a glassed-in room called the break shack next to the rods' office. The rods are what we called the bosses. We would sit in the break shack and talk and smoke and rest. One summer, Bear and Moon helped me collect Planters peanut bar wrappers. If I saved fifty of them, I would be able to send off for a free Boomtown Rats album. Bear would fish wrappers out of the trash for me. I was very glad to be able to share my excitement about the Boomtown Rats with Bear and Moon.

One time when they got off second shift, Bear and Moon went frog gigging. They fixed tridents the breadth of a bullfrog's shoulders to eight foot long golf course flagsticks. They walked that night beside creeks and ponds, with miners lights fixed to their belts, shining their lights at the water's edge. When the light hit a bullfrog, his croaking stopped. "There he is," one of them would say, and the flagstick fork would plunge into the frog's back. Bear and Moon made a circle of a wire hanger, bent hooks in either end, and strung the frogs they caught on the wire, gouging it through the frog's bottom jaw. When they returned to their vehicle with a gang of frogs on the wire, they took each frog and halved him at the waist with a big knife, saved the legs, and threw the rest in the weeds. They advised that one soak the legs in salt water before frying them, lest they jump out of the pan, looking for their lost frog.

The extruder operator named Bear is from Lee County, Virginia, which borders Harlan County, Kentucky. Once a young woman took a community college class in Harlan. I was her instructor, and required her to record an oral history. She recorded one with her father, who described for the young woman how his father, the young woman's grandfather, a coal mine operator, had signed a seven-hundred-million-dollar contract to provide coal to the chemical plant in Kingsport. Seven hundred million dollars over thirty years is how the man on the recording put it. Many people in Harlan County mined coal, earned their living, to help that young woman's grandfather honor that contract. Probably, many of them had their picture made during that time. Some probably drank liquor. I cannot say for certain. I do know this: Harlan County was mostly dry during the time of the seven hundred million dollars, and that the man with the wavy hair told me he sold liquor to Harlan County bootleggers during that time, including one, Mag Bailey, who, it is said, put several Harlan County lawyers through law school, and spent very little, if any, time in jail.

One gathers it is easy to die working in a coal mine, particularly an underground coal mine. Roofs fall. Ribs roll. There are explosives and thick cables carrying killing amounts of electricity. There are deadly and volatile gases. Miners need to be on their toes. Miners need to look out for each other. Miners need to know they can trust one another not to lose their heads. So they test one another. They do things like put motor oil in one another's shampoo bottles. There are stories of them strapping young miners together, lip to lip, with electrical tape when they cannot get along, and leave them lying in mine passages until they kiss and make up. There are stories of nailing one another's dinner buckets to the beltline. A miner who cannot tolerate this is not likely to keep his head when death comes knocking. That is the kind of thing most of us would like to know ahead of time, particularly if we knew we would be braving death on a daily basis.

It is not as easy to die on the job in a plastic factory as it is in a coal mine. But there is still danger. Once a man got his hand pulled off in a plastics extruder, and his coworker had to go back and get his wedding ring off a severed finger. And an inattentive operator can destroy tens of thousands of dollars of material in a minute by dropping a raw batch into an extruder, or taking too long a break and letting a hopper overflow onto the factory floor. And so there was hazing in the plastics factory too. For example, a forklift driver had to go outside to get pallets, on which all material was transported, at least once a shift. It was not unheard of for one's fellow operators to fill the plastic bag that lined the thousand-pound boxes with water and drop it on a forklift operator's head from the top of the building when he went out for pallets. The steel cage that covered the top of the forklift would protect the operator from a broken neck, but not the shattering of the bag and the "drowning" of the forklift operator by a hundred gallons of water.

Some of this hazing is meanness for meanness's sake. Some of it is to stave off boredom. But there is also the lesson in the hazing that this is serious, dangerous work, and that a certain capacity for rough treatment is part of being able to stick with the job, part of being a reliable coworker.

Both the plastic factory that I worked in and most of the coal mines I have heard about are predominantly male workspaces. One need not have much imagination to recognize in the hazing a certain macho relish in being "tough enough" to endure the challenges of the job, and a certain amount of defending the space against those who might not immediately fit a relatively narrow definition of who can do the work. Both the mines and the plastic factory, as I have experienced them, are classic creations of industrial capitalism and of the particular strain of patriarchy supporting and supported by industrial capitalism.

———

My mother married when she was nineteen. She was twenty-four when I was born. My mother went back to college when I was old enough to look after my little brother. She went to East Tennessee State University and earned a degree and became a registered nurse. My mother was anxious about her own intelligence and her ability to graduate from college. She finished first in her nursing class. Her father was a vice-president at the chemical plant in Kingsport. Her mother never worked outside the home.

My father married when he was twenty-four. He graduated from the University of Tennessee, which he attended on a basketball scholarship. My father's mother died when he was four. He was raised by his father's sister, and then his father and stepmother. My father attended four different high schools in two states. His father was a storekeeper for the W.T. Grant Company. My father became a supervisor at the chemical plant. He managed the distribution of several warehouses' worth of the raw material that goes into cigarette filters. He died, like many, many people in Kingsport, of cancer.

When my mother graduated high school, her parents sent her to college in northern Ohio, to a school chosen in part because of its distance from my father. When they got together anyway, there was a big wedding, and my parents received a set of silver from her parents as a gift. My mother always told me her mother told her they would get the silver engraved "if the marriage lasted." It did. The silver remains unengraved.

My mother died in 2016. She once ate all the crème out of a pack of Oreos and fed the cookies to the dog while she was talking on the telephone. She once had a doctor wire her jaw shut to help her lose weight. She taught newborns to swim. She took in my cousins when they were in trouble and had nowhere to go, even when she did not agree with what they were doing. She took a job as the patient advocate at the hospital where she was born, and with unflinching diligence brought complaints about the medical care the hospital's patients received to the people who could do something about it. When she retired, the hospital discontinued her position.

When my mother was a child, she and her twin brother were often sent to Erwin, Tennessee, to spend weeks at a time with their paternal grandparents and aunts. Once my mother had the mumps. She said it was the most miserable she had ever been. Her aunt Hazel asked what she could do to make her feel better, and my mother said, "Stand on your head," which my aunt Hazel did. Another time, when my mother was eight, she went out to the coal pile in the back yard of her grandparents' house in Erwin and found her grandfather sprawled across the coal pile dead. There were no other adults around, and so she told a neighbor, who sent her across the street to wait until the situation had been attended to. When my mother told me about it, she was incredulous that she had been sent away. She said, "What did they think I would see that was worse than what I had already seen?"

My mother harbored lawbreakers, spoke for the voiceless, confronted power, did what she thought was right no matter what it cost her, and perhaps most courageously, made her own sense of the world. Once near the end of her life, I was driving her to my brother's house in Wise, Virginia, and a pickup truck drove by with a Confederate flag mounted in its bed. My mother watched the truck sail by, flag flapping in the breeze. She said, "Why would you do that when you know it hurts people's feelings?"

My mother was at once the most fearless and the most nervous person I have ever known. For all the stands she took in her life, she also lived in constant conviction that our doom was nigh. If we did not call her on a semi-hourly basis, we had to be dead. If there was ice on any road anywhere in North America, we needed to stay home (unless we were coming to visit her). In her mind, there was no point to frog gigging, that only trouble could come from it. The same was true of drinking, staying out late, and venturing too far from Kingsport. She rarely traveled without taking her own food, and her favorite part of any vacation was getting home. Worry was the motor of her existence.

My mother loved jokes. She loved stories. She loved playing cards. She loved us all laughing around her table. A primary manifestation of her anxiety was that people in her presence could not possibly have a good time unless she vouchsafed that good time, either by telling a funny story herself or putting impossibly well-buttered food in front of us, or egging on one of us to be entertaining.

When she passed, the funeral took place in the same church where she was baptized and married. There were four hundred people there. My brother and I told all the funny stories on her we could think of. People were laughing and crying, out of their heads. She would have loved it. In the receiving line, we heard a bunch more stories we'd never heard. One woman told me that when she first moved to Kingsport, she went to her first Kingsport party, and when she walked in, there was a woman dancing on a table. Her hostess said, "Don't worry. That's Barbara Gipe. She doesn't drink."

———

My experience in the chemical plant made me want to live deeper in the mountains than Kingsport, and so, much to my mother's chagrin, in 1989, I took a job at Appalshop, a media arts center in Letcher County, Kentucky. In

1997, I took a job at Southeast Kentucky Community & Technical College in Harlan County, Kentucky. As part of my work, I coordinated a community process that resulted in a $150,000 grant from the Rockefeller Foundation to use the arts to respond to the prescription painkiller crisis in Harlan. Our group, which included students at my college, interviewed community members about the prescription opioid OxyContin, the other drugs being misprescribed and abused, and everything else. We took those interviews and, working with playwright Jo Carson, wrote a play called *Higher Ground*.

One of the women we interviewed grew up in a coal camp. Her momma is gone. And her daddy moves to another coal camp, leaving this woman and her brothers, all of them children, to fend for themselves. To make the rent, they run a card game, most of the players coal miners. The woman is asked how she keeps all these grown people playing cards from taking advantage of her. She replies they always keep a fire in the grate, and a poker in the fire, and if any of them came in on her, she would stab them right in the chest with that hot poker.

Another, younger, female interviewee comes from a family with plenty of money. This woman gets hooked on pills, is arrested, and has to go in front of the judge. The day she goes to court there is a room full of the accused there with her. Not all of them have plenty of money. The judge asks the woman, "What are you doing here? You're not supposed to be here. You're from a good family." The woman says, "Everybody in there could hear. And I just wanted to say, 'And they are supposed to be here? It's OK for their lives to be ruined, but not mine?' Drugs don't care who you are. They treat everybody the same."

The stories of these two women ended up in our first play. One of the things we try to explore in the first Higher Ground play is that perhaps we should respond to the drug crisis the way we respond to a flood in our community— collectively, instead of trying to work it out by ourselves. So in the script, we had the card game woman and the good family woman make common cause. But before they could make common cause, we had to find something they had in common. At the time, we had several stories floating around about people who were packrats, and we thought that would be good, because there are people of all classes and backgrounds who are packrats. So we made that the thing these two different unconnected women had in common.

To make the connection between these two characters, we used a story from my experience with my mother. One day I went with her to her safe deposit box. And in there with all her jewelry and money papers, there's an umbrella and a bag of cheese doodles. She left them in there, she said, because one day she came in in a hurry, eating cheese doodles for lunch, and was embarrassed to walk out with them. I was worried that when my mother came to see the play, her feelings would be hurt by that story being in it. I asked her afterward what she thought of the play. She said, "Oh, Robbie, it was wonderful." I asked her what she thought of the safe deposit box story. She said, "See, I told you I wasn't the only one who does that."

By the time we got to the sixth play, even though all the plays had good music and funny stories in them, people wanted something lighter. And so we decided to do a short play that was a funeral like my mom's, where everybody told good, funny stories about the deceased. That play, which is called *Life Is Like a Vapor*, takes a character, Sweet Betty, who we introduced in our fifth play. Her funeral reveals that she has nearly died many times—she falls out of a deer stand when a woodpecker begins pecking her exquisitely camouflaged hand as it holds a tautly drawn bow; she lies about her weight at a zipline, then crashes the zipline and nearly crushes a youth choir; she gets castor bean pulp in her eye, giving herself a nasty twitch; and she nearly drowns, by insisting on a baptism when the water is too high and the current too swift, surviving by stealing food from raccoons washing their meals on a log next to the truck tire in which Betty has become lodged. We knitted these stories, some version of which might have happened to people we know, while sitting in a room at the community college where I work, telling stories, like the ancients, in a circle, where one story leads to another, where tears follow belly laughs, where the competition to entertain is friendly and mutually supportive—the best of spaces, the kingdom of God lit by fluorescents and fueled by corn nuggets from the Dairy Hut.

I wish my mother could have seen *Life Is Like a Vapor*. It is her kind of thing. She did live long enough to see me, encouraged by the reception our plays received, go to the Appalachian Writers Workshop at Hindman Settlement School and then to other writing workshops. She lived to see me publish a novel. She saw me read and get fussed over and written about. All this made her very happy. She wasn't that happy about me going to Mongiardos or really, being around liquor at all. I understand her point. But I am glad to have been there, because Mongiardos is gone, gone like film pictures, gone like my building 190, gone like most of the coal mine work.

Mongiardos wasn't far from Hindman, and one summer we took new friends at the Writers Workshop to see it. That's how we found out it was closed. The building was still there, but the windows were dirty, and the shelves were bare. Those pictures were so beautiful, all those lives caught at moments of greatest joy, darkest despair, and all points in between, and they had all disappeared.

I don't know what happened to those pictures, the feathers of the great drunken bird. Maybe the bird flew away, its feathers intact, rising in wobbly glory above the ridgeline and into the mountain sky, landing somewhere safe, somewhere where there is a person to tell us all the stories of all the people. Maybe. Maybe I will drink less, so I can better remember all the things I have heard and seen, and be better able to tell it, and better able to listen with patience and care to the stories others are telling. Maybe. That would make my mother happy.

———

Well, to sum all this up and get to my topic, which is how Appalachian I am, I would say this: I reckon I'm more Appalachian than some, and less Appalachian than others. I'd say I'm Appalachian enough. I'd say I was raised, by both my mother and my father, to make my own sense of the world. And I was raised to make meaning by telling stories and listening to stories. I was taught that meaning is complex and shifting and difficult to state, and the more stories one adds to one's thinking the harder it gets to make meaning, and that is good, and a good thing to keep in mind when one sees something new—that one won't be able to make any sense of a thing until one hears not one but many stories about it. And I was raised to know that one good thing about stories is that one person might make one meaning out of a story and another person might take a different meaning from it. And I was raised to believe this ability to make our own meaning out of the world is what freedom is, and what joy is, and meaning making is a right we all have. I was raised that we all are obliged to work to make sure everyone has the right and the opportunity to tell their own story and hear everyone else's—the easy story to hear and the difficult, the happy and the sad, the comic and the tragic. And we are all obliged to work to make sure each of us has the right to hear and tell all the stories and each make our own meaning out of them and the world, and if we don't work toward that end, we are cheating our neighbor, and we are cheating ourselves of the joy of living, and should be ashamed of ourselves and should be forced to take long car rides in cars with no radio for all of eternity with people who grew up in places where they didn't learn how to tell stories.

AUNT RITA ALONG THE KING COAL HIGHWAY, MINGO COUNTY, WEST VIRGINIA

TEXT AND PHOTOGRAPH BY ROGER MAY

EVERY SATURDAY, without fail, Aunt Rita cleans the Chattaroy Church of God at the mouth of Chattaroy holler. I went along with her that Saturday and afterward, asked if I could stop and make some portraits of her. She asked if I thought she should change clothes or fix her hair first. I said no, that she was perfect just the way she was. As she walked out along the edge of the valley fill and looked down at the hollers below, something in me knew that this place was in her DNA, too, that she was of and from and because of this place. And she was beautiful. She's never relied on anyone for anything and she's never met a stranger and would welcome anyone who darkened her door. Standing there, she showed me what home looked like right down to the holler and creek. I read no elegy there, only an inscription of love and home.

HOLLER

KEITH S. WILSON

Never mind my skin. I sound:

stoned	to the cops
white	to one side of my family
Californian	to Southerners
Southern	to Californians
Militant	to the creative agency

You might mistake Appalachian for Southern. If you are not Southern. If you are not Appalachian.

An argument for homesteads on the edge: I've touched the Pacific Ocean with my toes. Some of my blood glitters from the bottom of the Other Ocean.

An argument for the middle: family.

Cincinnati, Ohio—1969

Air force brats fold their white socks a certain way. Traces.

When he was a teenager, my dad was bussed from his school to make sure some amount of a Cincinnati school became integrated. It was a better school. He became good at math.

We resist equations, but we cannot just be anything. He never lived in Atlanta, but some of it had to have run off into him. But what about the fields? What about me?

Erlanger, Kentucky—2000

There's a way about the part of Kentucky we ended up.

Northern Kentucky made news recently when James Alex Fields Jr., drove his car into a crowd at Charlottesville. He killed a woman almost exactly my age. James from there as I am from there. Though of course we are a thousand bodies of water apart.

When I was sixteen, I was assigned a group project with a boy in my class I had heard hated black folks. He is dead now, killed while playing with a gun around the time I left Kentucky for Chicago. I remember we seemed exactly alike. We had the same sense of humor. We joked a lot—enough for me to break the ice: is it true? Yes, he said.

That same year, white supremacist fliers were distributed during the night. I heard about it at school. I'd never been hunting, but I'd bought a small hunting knife from a flea market. I kept it in my backpack. Before 9/11, whether or not I was Middle Eastern, Muslim, was less pressing.

In Kentucky, when kids got bored, some of them went hunting.

Every student of color of my high school could fit in one entry of an obituary. Our high school mascot was a Confederate colonel. My school was named Dixie Heights.

I never felt unsafe. I kept the knife in case I ever did.

Northern Kentucky is at the crossroads of the Midwest, the South, and Appalachia. You rarely saw them hung, but any flea market was verdant with the Confederacy.

Where I lived, you could walk a few blocks to the bridge that crossed the Ohio River and walk into Cincinnati. We were the last stop on the Underground Railroad.

Inside the Freedom Center, a museum in Cincinnati dedicated to the Underground Railroad, are two wall-sized quilts by Aminah Brenda Lynn. They are different than traditional Appalachian quilts. None of them is geometric or patterned, or wholly fabric. Their patches are irregular, painted, overlapping. The edges of the quilt don't line up. They are equally complicated, but different. Living in the quilt are the figures of black people.

Biloxi, Mississippi—1983 (1998)

A decade and a half after I was born, I revisit Biloxi. Everything in my parents' neighborhood, my neighborhood, is broken, the swampy green beneath like crabmeat.

You always dreamed of your mother eating gumbo. Your parents said the neighbors made it and everyone shared.

Ordering Indian in Chicago, I choose Bhindi Masala. They warn "Are you sure? It's very spicy." I say, like I dream they say it in Biloxi, I can take it.

Torrance, California—1990

You can find shells in the fields. Fossils of them, anyhow. All of this used to sleep under the sea.

You found an urchin once, in California. It was dark and brittle, like a pinecone gone wrong. You kept it in the yard until it disintegrated. Not into the water, but the ground.

Evolution is a strange thing.

There were hermit crabs in class, which grew out of their shells and moved on to others. There are shells that twirl into themselves smaller and smaller until you cannot see the twirl.

Chicago, IL—2015

Nobody understands meter. Poets say they do.

One of the complications in the complicated science of breaking down the humanity of poetry is the idea of relative stress. The idea goes that the emphasis we put on a syllable, or a word, is never independently strong or weak, but depends upon its neighbors.

Maybe it is impossible to hear "All men hate" as three stressed syllables. You hear power, and stress, first in the word "all"—ALL men hate. Hate as a universal emotion.

Or you hear it strongest in "men"—MEN do the hating.

You hear a word most strongly, and whatever word precedes or follows it cannot be stronger without weakening it, cannot be weaker without strengthening it. Whatever the case, no two can ever be equal.

Florence, Kentucky—2010

About stories: You are a horse, like the ones in the fields not far from where you used to live in Kentucky. Now, because this is a story, a stream runs through you. A stream is like that. How not to see, in the force of a stream, a binary: either the horse will struggle to make it out of the river, or the horse will not move. He will be swept away, silent and still, until watching, all you see is the river.

Relative to the river, there can only be a horse in struggle, or one content to die. Before the river, the horse knew infinity.

When the dominant narrative speaks over you, it would seem that you have drowned. Or, your life would seem to become one of opposition. Blackness knows this. Appalachia, and women, and the impoverished know it.

D. W. Griffith, producer of *Birth of a Nation* (and a Kentuckian), has a statue dedicated to him at Northern Kentucky University, where I studied Appalachian culture for a time. *Birth of a Nation* famously revived the Ku Klux Klan.

I find myself sometimes trying to identify with others. Isn't this human?

Seven thousand smaller streams branch from the Mississippi. A small one might swallow you. A larger one might swallow it.

To ignore the water is deadly. Oppose it.

Revel in it, or be still; speak the river's language. Be swept away.

The Ku Klux Klan was founded in Pulaski, Tennessee. Opposition.

You laid under a homemade patchwork quilt for years, until it wore through, swept away.

You toured in Appalachia as a young poet, and before you read a poem in West Virginia, you ask "Do you have White Castles here?" Someone in the audience heckles "YOU THINK WE DON'T KNOW WHAT WHITE CASTLE IS???" (Who knows where anything starts, to where it extends?)

The head of the English Department is Appalachian. He introduces you to Gurney Norman's *Divine Right's Trip*. He invites you to his home, his garden. Your grades are bad, but he fights for you. In his office, you switch majors, to poetry. You are perhaps one of the only students that gets a personal phone call. You write a poem for his funeral. It is about connection, and fields, and Appalachia. Swept away.

LOVING TO FOOL WITH THINGS

RACHEL WISE

I REMEMBER laughing at the improbability of the call. Sitting in a hotel room after a campus visit in Alabama, I discovered I'd been selected as one of seven visiting scholars at the American Academy of Arts and Sciences in Cambridge, Massachusetts. I hung up the phone, scratched my bare legs itching from the polyester bedspread standard at the Florence Hampton Inn. I spent most of that night staring at the red light on the smoke detector, slipping in and out of consciousness.

My fellowship was with one of the oldest independent policy research centers in the country, an institution affiliated with Harvard University. I felt elated by the keen persistent sense that I was sneaking in, that this was some mistake. Few places are more certain of their cultural, historical, and intellectual centrality than Cambridge. Yet I was going to talk, research, and write about Appalachian literature there.

On September 15, I put on my best pencil skirt and walked a mile in to the Academy from my place on the Medford/Somerville line. There I met the other scholars in my cohort: two men, four women. Of those six, five had some previous connection to Harvard. Their graduate diplomas bore the hefty weight of Harvard, Yale, Brown, University of Pennsylvania, University of Chicago, and Stanford.

I was introduced by the program director like this: "Have you met Rachel? She's an outlander in every way." ("Better than being a flatlander," my father texted in reply.) Had I breached the ramparts? At later dinner parties, the director and my peers would fumble for ways to engage me as if I were an alien species. They were clumsy and revealingly conjured whatever superficial associations they had with Appalachia—

"Do you study bluegrass music at all?" (No. I study literary representations of the region.)

"Is your family musical?" (Groan. I come from a long line of *have never touched an instrument*. Let me tell you about McCowan Church and the hymns of tone-deaf kin.)

"Are you really a coal miner's daughter?" (No, a coal miner's great-granddaughter. Union.)

They would ask why I didn't talk more in our workshops. What do you do when someone means it as a compliment when he says he can't tell from your habitus that you grew up rural poor? How do you laugh off someone who constantly draws attention to how you say words, form the vowels in your mouth?

———

My peers were uncomfortably grappling with everything "Appalachia" might mean. Because in addition to referencing the eastern US mountain chain from which it takes its name, the region also wields immense symbolic heft. In "Writing on the Cusp," Rodger Cunningham characterizes the region's status as a liminal space between North and South.[1] Pervasive stereotypes of Appalachia authorize rhetorical and ideological constructions of the region as culturally deviant. Accounts of moonshining and feuding have, since at least the 1870s, helped popularize the idea of Appalachians as outliers who are either quaint rubes or violent poor white trash, either venerated or disparaged. "Redneck Reality" TV continues to purvey these stereotypes today—look no further than series like *Buckwild, Moonshiners, Appalachian Outlaws,* or *Hillbilly Blood*—and you'll find ample horror films set in the Appalachian mountains—think *Wrong Turn* or *The Descent.* Imagined as deficient in values traditionally associated with the nation's metropoles, including progress, heterogeneity, and education, Appalachia throws into relief the progress that cosmopolitan Americans have made. As Anthony Harkins argues, Appalachians' perceived lack of culture is political; it offloads the nation's sins onto some other constituency elsewhere.[2]

Perhaps nowhere is this phenomenon of intense national projection more apparent than in the 1972 film adaptation of *Deliverance*, which made famous novelist James Dickey's Appalachia. My father was thirteen in Northern Kentucky when it was released, and he remembers his teacher, wide-eyed, telling the class, "That's the way it really is *down there*." Even today, this movie is frequently the defining experience baby boomers have had with the region. *Deliverance* is all about the return of the repressed and the grotesque inseparability of hillbilly bodies and actual trash in the collective consciousness.

Deliverance follows four tourists from Atlanta who seek the thrill of canoeing the fictional Cahulawassee River before it is dammed to generate electricity and water recreation. The first time we see the men outside of their cars is at the Oree, Georgia, gas station. Overwhelmed by the volume of old tires and rusted metal, one of the men, Bobby, smirks, "Look at the junk. Look here. I think this is where everything finishes up. We just may be at the end of the line." The repeated imperative to "look" merges the point of view of the film's imagined audience and its characters. These urban tourists see the Oree gas station's junk and find it remarkable because it makes visible the logical end of a capitalist system based in mass consumption; its junk is horrific because accumulation extends the orthodox cycle of goods—from extraction, production, and consumption to disposal. In effect, nothing ever "finishes up." Capitalism's material excesses mean that trash has to *reside somewhere*. Dickey's Appalachia is an abject space, and *Deliverance* forces armchair tourists to encounter the trash heap along with its characters. This, in turn, means confronting an economic system that trashes both landscapes and people in order to justify their sacrifice to the gods of Progress and Prosperity. The flooding of the valley is an apocalyptic, Genesis-like cleansing of the trashy landscape. In both the novel and film, the urban tourists' survival depends upon their ability to transfer and quarantine the horrors of late capitalism onto the hillbillies they encounter.

I was made to understand this phenomenon anew just as I started an English doctoral program at the University of Texas at Austin. "Travel inside a world apart," begins Diane Sawyer's *20/20* report, "A Hidden America: Children of the Mountains," which aired in 2008. Following the lives of four children in impoverished communities of eastern Kentucky, it drew the show's largest viewership (10.9 million) since 2004 and earned ABC a Peabody Award. "Mountain Dew Mouths" was a phrase on too many lips. People talk frankly and revealingly when they think they are among the like-minded, the kindred. One saucer-eyed graduate student exclaimed to me, "I can't believe people really live like *that*." Another only slightly hyperbolically concluded, "You shouldn't be allowed to vote without a college education." People can become exceedingly gullible where Appalachia is concerned, take every visual portrayal of the region as gospel—whether it's *Justified* (shot mostly in California), *Deliverance*, or, in this case, "Hidden America."

Sawyer and her team worked on the project for two years, traveling fourteen thousand miles in the process. The special documents the dire conditions of Appalachian life and marvels that such abject poverty could exist in a nation of great wealth. Rather than highlight economic systems that perpetuate poverty, "Hidden America" composes an Appalachia filled with people and land in need of outside management. Using subtitles to signal that viewers have truly journeyed into a "world apart," the special ostensibly portrays the region with an ethnographic eye even as it pulls from popular stereotypes about hillbillies. Here Appalachia is a land of nonnormative white bodies and behaviors, poverty, dirt, substance abuse, poor nutrition, bare feet, toothlessness, and ignorance. The ABC special engenders a presumably middle-class audience with a sense of superiority and responsibility to help a population unable to help itself. By pathologizing and quarantining white rural poverty, this documentary and many like it are indebted to the imagery and tone of President Lyndon Johnson's War on Poverty, which continues to contour the way Appalachia is thought of today. Televisual reports have accompanied fifty years of policies aimed at uplifting Appalachia. "Hidden America" is part of a lineage that includes Charles Kuralt's 1964 CBS special "Christmas in Appalachia" and a 1989 CBS *48 Hours* episode "Another America" with Dan Rather. From the televisual archive, the region emerges as an enduring national ward in need of always-external, middle-class intervention.

———

It never occurred to us that we were Appalachian until my father saw it in black and white: "Appalachian immigrant; or child of." It was the early 1990s, and he was applying for work with the city of Cincinnati. People still made jokes about the Norwood hillbillies flocking to work at the General Motors assembly plant:

Q: Do you know why they built the Brent Spence Bridge two levels high?

A: So the southbound hillbillies could drop their shoes to cousins driving in, taking their place on the line.

Ohioans seemed to find it endlessly funny, the idea of hillfolk working monthlong stints so they could send money to the homeplace. They also found it troubling. Heavy migration in the 1950s and 1960s meant that urban dwellers were quick to label white newcomers from anywhere in the rural south as "hillbillies." In February 1958, Albert N. Votcaw lamented about Chicago: "The city's toughest integration problem has nothing to do with Negroes. . . . It involves a small army of white, Protestant Early American migrants from the South—who are usually proud, poor, primitive, and fast with a knife."[3] Appalachia was stereotyped as homogenously rural and white, and its people as regressive and violent hillbillies that had degenerated from decades of isolation. Cincinnati's old government documents and newspapers are similarly rife with anxiety about the mountain scourge.

Like many Appalachian families, ours is a story of migration. With only an eighth-grade education, my grandfather, Julius Wayne Wise, escaped the coalmines of southwestern Virginia and eventually settled in Florence, Kentucky. He was stringing telephone line in the eastern part of the state, but he had a penchant for destroying contracted hotel rooms with his friend. A teetotaler for all ninety-nine years of her life, his mother always said the devil was in the bottle. The telephone company split the friends up, transferring my grandfather to Boone County. There he spotted my grandmother sitting on the porch and took a shine to her. Just eighteen, she conceived, and they married (in that order). This was to her parents' eternal shame.

The third of four children, my father began working construction at eighteen and married at twenty-one. Three years later I arrived with aplomb, "like a football," the doctor said before catching the rest of the Bengals Monday night game. "Another shittin' ass girl," my grandfather remarked as he lay a stuffed Ewok next to me. I was also about twenty inches in length and just as swarthy. "She looks like a sumo wrestler," my uncle snorted, earning daggers from my grandmother.

By 1987, my parents had four mouths to feed. There were lean years of WIC-approved foods and tattered, outgrown hand-me-downs. We'd clean the state highway running by our house on its way to Interstate 71, a troupe carrying black garbage bags full of aluminum cans that earned us sixty cents per pound. We took showers only on Saturday nights, flushed only when necessary because the water in the cistern needed to last. Then my dad found steady work as a city building inspector and, like so many before us, we crossed the river into Ohio, into the solid North. No more garbage bags full or bellies round with Hoppin' John.

My new schoolmates would query if my mother were also my sister. To be "Appalachian" was to be from somewhere else, to be a punch line. When we were made to think about it at all, we did not eagerly adopt the label. Henry James once described Appalachia as a "vast parenthetic," the mountains themselves "brackets applied as it were to the very face of nature." For James the region's peculiar liminality disturbed the very texture of America and the idea of a homogenous "South."[4] This is the lesson I've learned again and again: being from this vast Appalachian parenthetic means always being a little out of place.

———

I escaped that small Ohio town just northwest of Cincinnati. I did not have kids or marry the boy I knew from high school now working across the street at an AutoZone. Instead I got lucky with a combination of Pell grants and scholarships, paying dearly for college in other ways. I spent my undergraduate years at a private liberal arts school where I endeavored to lose my accent and blend in. Through exclusion, course offerings reinforced the idea that Appalachia, rurality, and the working class were categories to be left behind, themselves sites of cultural absence. I learned that the academy, literature, Culture with a capital C, and the middle class were all mutually constitutive.

Losing the Appalachia in me seemed imperative at the time. But I was the student who patched and hemmed her pants with duct tape, went home to pickup beds held together with green clothesline. I could never quite give up the pleasure of stretching out the life of a thing. It still feels like a middle finger. Manipulating material goods in unorthodox ways highlights the nonlinearity of the extraction-production-consumption-disposal cycle. I see in this manipulation a refusal to comply with material norms that seem to justify the logic of class hierarchies. Instead, my family learned to be suspicious of new things. My grandfather believed that the only people who had nice things stole and cheated to get them. Perhaps this is the mentality of a life lived in an extraction zone where wealth and resources never belong to the people or land that produces them. There is satisfaction in subverting a socioeconomic system that requires certain populations to participate at a disadvantage.

I remember the day that I learned about Claude Lévi-Strauss's bricoleur. "So that's what you call my dad." It gave a name to his practices; it gave a name to mine. "Bricolage" provided a bridge between the material conditions of growing up as an Appalachian outside of Appalachia and the experience of inhabiting academia as a class migrant. It legitimized the folk recyclers and tinkerers I'd encountered all my life. When the foreign-sounding word cavorted between my tongue and teeth, I felt powerful. I had a secret. I saw something my peers could not see. It was the first time Appalachia felt like an asset. The figure of the bricoleur helped sanction the tropes of reuse and repurposing I'd seen repeated throughout Appalachian-set texts spanning from Rebecca Harding Davis's *Life in the Iron Mills* (1861) to Holly Farris's *Lockjaw* (2007), from Grace MacGowan Cooke's *The Power and the Glory* (1910) to Harriet Arnow's *The Dollmaker* (1954).

This brief but formative recognition gave me an intensely personal field of doctoral study. Once I decided to make Appalachian literature the focus of my scholarship, I got asked the same question over and over again in various permutations by mostly well-meaning colleagues: "That exists?" "That's a thing?" "What does 'Appalachian literature' mean exactly?" You think there can't possibly be anything triggering about exploring a digital archive in class until your professor laughs, "Why would anyone want to read a novel set in Kentucky?" You come in from delivering a conference paper on an Appalachian poet and tell a fellow graduate student about it. Her response stings like a fresh switch across a bare bottom: "Oh, I didn't know you study incest." It is easy to begin feeling spiteful about incessant "what" and "why" questions. These are questions no one asks the Shakespeare, Emerson, or Faulkner scholar.

If American literary studies and anthologies are any indication, there isn't much to "Appalachian literature." American literary studies that mention Appalachia at all cursorily touch on Mary Murfree's *Atlantic Monthly* publications and, in particular, her 1884 collection *In the Tennessee Mountains.*[5] As the primary representative of Appalachian literature, Murfree is often seen as originating a literary tradition that caricatures the mountaineer.[6] Her short stories appear in Norton's *American Women Regionalists* (1995) and *The Literature of the American South* (1998), while the Norton and Heath American literature anthologies exclude representations of Appalachia altogether. If you want to know how Appalachia typically circulates in an undergraduate American literature classroom—if it circulates at all—look no further than Murfree's mountaineer stories, which were first consumed by the middle-class readers of one of the era's most well-known "quality journals."[7]

This disciplinary marginalization obscures the way that the region has long operated as a powerful and surprisingly versatile signifier in American literary culture. The critical and textual uniformity arising from treatments of Murfree as the region's paradigmatic writer limits the possibility of new critical narratives that undercut reductive characterizations of Appalachia and its cultural output. By taking Murfree as a cursory touch point—feigned due diligence rather than sustained engagement—imagined Appalachia too often emerges as a homogenous folk region synonymous with its things. When it bothers to talk about it at all, American literary criticism showcases an oversimplified and all too familiar Appalachia as the land of spinning wheels, quilts, outlaws, and moonshine stills.

As a graduate student, I longed to read about something familiar—fresh sorghum poured over jowl bacon and biscuits and old refrigerators bungee-d closed, or crazy quilts hung next to shelves full of Dollar Tree figurines. If this Appalachia had no place in American literature's disciplinary conversations, I could not imagine there was a place for me. At its core, what began to animate my work was the necessity of finding a literary and cultural prehistory for an Appalachia that I recognized. This is an Appalachia equally elided by Dickey's *Deliverance* and Murfree's agrarian Tennessee mountaineers, by Discovery's *Moonshiners* and Berea's Log Cabin Craft Gallery. It is an Appalachia that does not reside within popular binaries: poverty-stricken outlaws or artisan folk culture. It is an Appalachia based in radical praxis rather than specific modalities or signifiers. Through the process of recognition, I hoped to imagine ways of inhabiting academia's intellectual and institutional terrain. At its best, my research still feels urgent—both a love letter and one class migrant's struggle with her own out-of-placeness in the academy.

This kind of work is always personal; it is always political.

———

In maintaining the privileges and pleasures of surprise in spite of the static and stereotypical ways graduate work taught me to think (or not think) about Appalachian literature, I began joyfully discovering characters who interact with material conditions around them in ways not wholly expected. I suspect my particular affinity for Grace MacGowan Cooke's infrequently discussed novel *The Power and the Glory* (1910) resides in the way it refuses to fetishize either traditional folk objects or "high-brow" forms of Arnoldian "Culture."[8] Nowhere do we see Bill Brown's sentimental, local object spared the logic of capitalism.[9] Rather, it is a novel that radically shows its mountain characters engaging a wide variety of material objects, reassembled and reused in ways that undercut the class ideologies that sustained industrial capitalism. None of these objects are saved from the "tyranny of use"; the novel provides its contemporary readers no relief from urban scenes.[10]

Cooke drew from her four decades of residency in Chattanooga, Tennessee, when she set *The Power and the Glory* in the Unaka Mountains. With its initial print run of fifteen thousand, Cooke's "story of the humor and heroism of some lives in a Southern mountain town" entered a widespread debate.[11] Propagandists for the cotton-mill campaign commonly argued that the introduction of cotton manufacturing would function as philanthropy that might cure the "Appalachian problem" by offering economic, cultural, and social opportunities to backwoods mountaineers.[12] With the publication of *The Power and the Glory*, Cooke joined fellow skeptics of the positivist industrialization-as-uplift narrative.[13]

Coming of age in an era when culture and refinement increasingly defined national aspiration, and aspiration became synonymous with the desire for a "better" material life, the novel's heroine Johnnie is initially embarrassed by her family's reputation for borrowing rather than buying.[14] She leaves her mountain home to secure work in the textile mills of Cottonville, located in the lower Tennessee Valley. Once there, Johnnie must face brutal labor conditions, poverty, and the hypocrisy of a Progressive-era Uplift Club, and she eventually marries the mill owner, Gray. Johnnie's family, the Passmores, enjoy altered circumstances when her Uncle Pros finally finds his lost mine.

The novel's overriding ethic is one of "fooling"—tinkering with or repurposing objects in ways that resist stereotypically class-based forms of taste. Through their fooling, the Appalachians in Cooke's novel undercut the ability of a normative middle class to define the region and insist on how its people ought to act. "Fooling" also describes using an object to ends for which it was not intended. The Passmore family drinks mountain spring water from a tin tomato can with a string bail attached.[15] This object indicates that the mythical urban/rural boundary is a permeable one. The repurposed tin tomato can and string also establishes the Passmores' mechanical proficiency and competency for improving on what already exists. In "loving to fool" with things, the repurposed mass-produced object comes to signify not only an expansion of mass-marketed convenience foods by 1900 but also creative potential.[16] Uncle Pros engages the materials given him and constructs the makeshift water pail from a disposable container meant for the trash heap. Similarly, he borrows a broken cradle and radiates pleasure at the fact that with a few nails and some twine it will be as good as, if not better than, new.[17] As the Passmore family proves, even when motivated by need, there can be great pleasure in extending the life of an (often inferior) object beyond the sanctions of dominant cultural norms.

Johnnie inherits her uncle's disposition toward "fooling" with things, a sensibility that comes to the fore once she arrives in Cottonville. Although she initially wants to pattern herself after Progressive reformers attempting to uplift Cottonville's female labor force, it is not long before Johnnie actively reroutes her affiliations through a cheap pair of slippers. A fellow boarder, Mavity, lends Johnnie her daughter's slippers for a club dance. Mavity explains that these slippers are the "cheap, ill-cut things" that her daughter Louvania took off and set on the bridge. Able to climb the netting more easily, Louvania then threw herself into the Tennessee River.[18] The reader may well wonder how many workers climbed over netting to end their suffering in the waters below. Not simply a fetishized or sentimental object, the slippers act as vibrant matter that conjures the dead girl.[19] Indeed, Louvania is a present absence at the dance, for the out-of-place slippers make visible her distaste for millwork, as well as the labor it takes to create the capital that supports Progressive uplift clubs. Johnnie embraces the cheap pair of slippers and thus aligns herself with Louvania rather than the uplift women. Society men watch this mill girl and wonder, "What would you say, in her heredity, makes a common girl like that step and look like a queen?"[20] This likening of Johnnie to a queen suggests that she could pass for middle class, but she instead uses the slippers to actively reroute her heredity through working-class subjectivity. In doing so, Johnnie refuses to play the part of a sentimental heroine who is "naturally" middle class.[21]

In encountering the injustices of a capitalist system that inhumanely treats laboring bodies as disposable, Johnnie continually pushes against any readerly expectation that she will conform to the class and gender norms of a typical heroine. She triumphantly reiterates that there is nothing "to be ashamed of in loving to fool with machinery," even if she is a girl.[22] This attitude results in her using scrap materials to create a safety device for the looms, thus improving upon the labor system in which she finds herself. She tells Gray, the mill owner, "I never did get enough of tinkerin' around with machines" when they get "out of order."[23] Her "fooling" involves the transgressive reworking of that which is fundamentally broken. It is bricolage at its finest.

Johnnie's interest in machinery leads to Gray asking her if she would like to pilot his new automobile. When she first drives it, he dismissively fancies her a child with a toy.[24] However, the next time she drives the automobile, Johnnie has to save Gray from an improbable kidnapping plot. Amidst buckshot and bullets, she still has time to feel a sense of power from the very fact that Gray "could not help her. She must know for herself and do the right thing."[25] Johnnie capably drives the novel's prevailing symbol of modernity down the Unaka Mountains. Her gender-bending habit of "loving to fool" is a tendency that just may have taken root in the cradle she first rested in, patched up as it was by Uncle Pros.

I recognized Johnnie. Rural, cash and credit poor spaces can encourage a kind of freedom. In quotidian ways, gender and labor cease to maintain a seamless relationship. There's a picture of great, great Aunt Orlean I kept on my desk throughout graduate school. Her body angled, she's turned her head to grin at the camera. A happy topknot of hair lengthens her face, makes her seem impossibly tall and strong against the backdrop of spindly trees planted in place of the old growth razed by loggers. She's carrying something heavy in a large tin pail. She's wearing men's trousers at a time when women didn't wear trousers. Aunt Orlean handled all her husband's business—all the money and accounts, the buying and selling. Aunt Orlean and Uncle Lon never had kids, and there were more than a few whispers about Aunt Orlean being "quair."

As the oldest child who happened to be born a girl, I helped my mother mow over two acres of grass with an old gas push mower. Red and rusting out, it vibrated my hands raw. I furrowed and hoed, bent for hours in the strawberry patch. I grew tall and strong like Aunt Orlean.

The Power and the Glory also shows Johnnie engaging in scenes that defetishize books that, as symbols of Culture, all too often reinforce class hierarchies. It's a practice I tried to emulate throughout my doctoral work. Johnnie demonstrates that there are ways to fool with even a most sacred cultural object like the literary text. For example, Gray hopes to educate Johnnie out of the working class, but instead of using books to distance herself from her roots, Johnnie uses them as affective mediums that threaten class hierarchies. She spends much of her time "passing her fingers over [a volume of English verses], as one strokes a beloved hand, or turning through each book only to find the penciled words in the margins."[26] Johnnie values Gray's annotations more than the poetry. His gloss is as valuable and relationally significant as the printed content. She experiences the sensation of holding his hand as she touches each leaf of the volume. She values the abilities of the book as an object to be interacted with and circulated. As she looks over Gray's writing, she gathers "the sheets together and press[es] them to her face as though they were . . . the hands of little children."[27] Here the text achieves an affective significance that is intimately tied to use, labor, and production. The repeated mention of "hands" here is telling given the novel's repeated use of "hands" to describe those laboring in the mills. For Johnnie, the book completes a circuit between her, Gray, and the mill hands. In emphasizing touch, Johnnie recalls the mill's morning procession of "tired-faced women with boys and girls walking near them, and, in one or two cases, very small ones clinging to their skirts and hands."[28] In the leaves of the paper, Johnnie brings together Gray and the "hands" needed to produce the materials and capital that make possible the existence of a commodity like the book. By relating to the book as a material—rather than a high cultural—object, Johnnie uses text as a material conduit through which one can reconnect capitalism's cycles of production.

The Power and the Glory portrays books as potentially vibrant mediums of communication. The novel cautions, however, that affective connections must bring to the surface rather than subsume the conditions of the book's production and the subjectivities that condition how the book is circulated, interpreted, and used. Johnnie's reading practices open up new relational, creative, and interpretive possibilities.

———

I never learned to be ashamed of trash. An old washstand sits in my kitchen that was not nice even when it was new. Cheap and mass-produced, it sat nearly sixty years in "Julie's house" at the edge of my family's property on Hazel Mountain—a high spot just over the Dickinson County, Virginia, line. Julie had long been dead, but the furniture remained where she left it, her red house an accretion on the landscape. The washstand came to me with dynamite-crate doors that were scavenged from the coal company's warehouse. The bricoleur who repaired it cared about the details. She fashioned the doors precise and even. When something simpler might have sufficed, she made pulls out of a wooden spool cut in half and secured them with rusted nails and leather washers. A history of coal mining, exploitation, consumption, poverty, and ingenuity coheres in this washstand.

The doors make sense to me. I think of my father stretching out the bridge of his new work boots with canned goods made wider by electrical tape and newspaper. Or watching an old glove wave at me from the windshield of our pickup, a replacement for a busted wiper. This creativity is motivated by generations of need and scarcity, but also by joyful, exuberant play.

When I told my father about this piece, he slightly acknowledged it, instead launching into a lengthy story about a rotary rock polisher. He recounted purchasing a 120-volt alternating-current polisher to tumble a tray full of stones we'd had since the mid-1990s. We had panned for uncut garnets, rubies, and sapphires one summer in North Carolina with my great Uncle Tom. For years they sat in the basement long after we'd forgotten the telltale edges and colors of a spectacular find. My father began the lapidary process, polishing rough stones with a simple, single-drum machine bought for $44.99 at Harbor Freight. Like many cheap, easily procured things, the stone polisher broke— its engine worn out from continuous running. But still it remained in his detached garage where all his projects lived and grew, nestled among the half painted gourds from his garden.

Months later, my father noticed something familiar looking on the side of the road just as he crested the hill on McHenry Avenue. He was there to look at an old carriage house that sits back in the woods about a half-mile from the road. It remains a source of contention—the city wants to tear it down, the neighborhood to restore it. My father pulled into the curb lane, opened the door, and found it was just as he thought: there sat a twelve-volt direct-current pump. Its casing and mounting brackets were broken off during what he assumed had been a fall from a landscaping truck. This motor was the perfect size.

He took it home, cleaned it up, and mounted it in place of the burned out motor. "Craziest thing. It works good," he said to me. "I like fixing old things up, making them work again." The rock tumbler sits humming on the garage floor as I write this, its DC motor hooked up to an old red Husky battery charger. Most would have thrown it away, but I come from a long line of contrarians; we're just plain "ornery," my grandfather would say. And while he might profess otherwise, I knew in the telling of his story that my father understood exactly what I am trying to do here—what I have always wanted to say.

Having exited academia, I now look back on my scholarly work and see how out-of-placeness animates it; I see how it executes the desire to trace out the literary and cultural antecedents of dynamite-crate doors. I utilize familiar scenes of ingenuity and reuse as a provocation for rethinking the stories that American literary critics tell about Appalachia's people, places, and things. In this Appalachia, cars on blocks and sorghum, dollar tree figurines and hand-woven rugs, sit side by side.

Like my father before me, like the Passmores and countless other characters portrayed in scenes of creative reinterpretations, I want to attend to the ways that Appalachia's exclusion from broader disciplinary conversations has left American literary studies bereft. What narratives of American literature—its relationship to regionalism and middle-class readerships—might we overturn by insisting on thoroughly integrating Appalachia into literary histories of industrial and labor fictions? Minority literatures? Of nineteenth- and early twentieth-century local color, which is too often dismissed as a diminutive, palliative predecessor to regional writing? How might persistent attentiveness to literary representations of the region take us far from the familiar critical ruts in which the discipline seems prone to run?[29]

Douglas Reichert Powell's "critical regionalism" and Ann Kingsolver's engagement with what Arif Dirlik calls "critical localism" give literary critics a methodology for preserving the specificity of marginal geographies like Appalachia while analyzing the cultural and political work that literature performs. This potentially allows for a more granular engagement with literary "Appalachia" while still integrating Appalachia into broader American literary studies.[30] Appalachia is filled with distinctive communities, but the significance of this vast mountainous parenthetic for westward expansion, industrialism, Progressive-era reformers, Civil War and reunification, and race and immigration has long occupied the American literary imagination. The region has been integral to the evolution of American literature at least as far back as John Filson's *The Discovery and Settlement and Present State of Kentucke* (1784), Washington Irving's "Rip Van Winkle" (1819), and Robert Montgomery Bird's *Nick of the Woods* (1837). Can we really understand one without the other?

It is thrilling to think of the radical uses to which James's vast, troubling parenthetic might be put. At a time when *Hillbilly Elegy* is used to palatably explain Trump's presidential victory to liberal and conservative readers alike, it has never been more important to tell diverse stories with a keen critical awareness of the subject positions from which we construct those narratives. Literary critics necessarily engage in the political and socioeconomic implications of how we make meaning with the idea of Appalachia.

I want to tell the story of a literary tradition filled with Johnnies who love to fool. This is a literary tradition that radically challenges national progress narratives bound up in classed forms of consumption, aesthetics, and material use. Anthropologist Kathleen Stewart theorizes West Virginia's coal towns as "a space on the other side of the road," a concept influenced by the bricoleur. She argues that space and the lived cultural poetics occurring therein can interrupt the expected and naturalized, thereby functioning as "back talk" to homogenizing nationalist myths.[31] For the story of America can't help but turn in on itself, desiring at times "cut details, sensate memories, remainders and excess excluded from its own abbreviated account."[32] If space and narrative are inextricable, then literary representations of Appalachia are "space[s] in which signs grow luminous." Appalachia's literature is full of cut details and remainders—geographical, cultural, material, formal, and rhetorical—that can be read as gaps in the seamless rhetoric of progress.[33] As characters like Johnnie resist adherence to dominant cultural and material norms, they simultaneously reject Appalachia's construction as a deficient national ward.

As literary critics, our work produces knowledge. We are recyclers who love to fool with things repurposed, reused, and reassembled. These assemblages have the potential to counteract objectifying histories of Appalachian literature. From specific subject positions, critics pursue various investments by imagining the formal and political possibilities that American literary study offers. We reassemble until we are left with an old washstand and its dynamite-crate doors—a critical object grown luminous in its historicity.

NOTES

1. Rodger Cunningham, "Writing on the Cusp: Double Alterity and Minority Discourse in Appalachia," in *The Future of Southern Letters*, ed. Jefferson Humphries and John Lowe (New York: Oxford University Press, 1996), 145–47.
2. Anthony Harkins, *Hillbilly: A Culture History of an American Icon* (New York: Oxford University Press, 2003), 7–10.
3. Albert N. Voctaw, "The Hillbillies Invade Chicago," *Harper's*, February 1958, 64.
4. Henry James, *The American Scene* (New York: Harper, 1907), 381.
5. Murfree is the region's only literary representative in two watershed studies: Richard H. Brodhead's *Cultures of Letters: Scenes of Reading and Writing in Nineteenth-Century America* (Chicago: University of Chicago Press, 1993) and Judith Fetterley and Marjorie Pryse's *Writing Out of Place: Regionalism, Women, and American Literary Culture* (Urbana: University of Illinois Press, 2003). Appalachia is excluded altogether from Stephanie Foote's *Regional Fictions: Culture and Identity in Nineteenth-Century American Literature* (Madison: University of Wisconsin Press, 2001), and Stephanie Palmer mentions Murfree as a virtual footnote in *Together by Accident: American Local Color and the Middle Class* (Lexington: University Press of Kentucky, 2008).
6. Harkins, *Hillbilly*, 30; Allen W. Batteau, *The Invention of Appalachia* (Tucson: University of Arizona Press, 1990), 40; Henry D. Shapiro, *Appalachia on Our Mind: The Southern Mountains and Mountaineers in the American Consciousness, 1870–1920* (Chapel Hill: University of North Carolina Press, 1978), 15; Emily Satterwhite, *Dear Appalachia: Readers, Identity, and Popular Fiction since 1878* (Lexington: University Press of Kentucky, 2011), 27–53. Elizabeth S. D. Engelhardt's *The Tangled Roots of Feminism, Environmentalism, and Appalachian Literature* (Athens: Ohio University Press, 2003) is notable for its considerable exploration of writers predating Murfree, as well as its attempts to broaden the archive by placing Murfree in conversation with lesser-known writers like Effie Waller Smith.
7. Brodhead, *Cultures of Letters*, 80.
8. Cooke published over 135 items in many of the era's national magazines, including *Atlantic Monthly*, *Century Magazine*, *Harper's*, and *Munsey's*. Although little critical work has been done to connect Cooke to local color or regional literature, Engelhardt's chapter "Emma Bell Miles and Grace MacGowan Cooke: Ecological Feminism's Roots, Part 2" helps place Cooke's Progressive Era feminism and environmentalism within the Appalachian region (135–68). Matthew Arnold's 1869 *Culture and Anarchy* (New Haven, CT: Yale University Press, 1994) described culture as "a pursuit of our near total perfection by means of getting to know . . . the best which has been thought and said" (5). See also Lawrence W. Levine's *Highbrow/Lowbrow: The Emergence of Cultural Hierarchy in America* (Cambridge, MA: Harvard University Press, 1988) and John F. Kasson's *Rudeness and Civility: Manners in Nineteenth-Century Urban America* (New York: Hill & Wang, 1990).
9. Bill Brown, *A Sense of Things: The Object Matter of American Literature* (Chicago: University of Chicago Press, 2003), 4. Brown's study is an example of how American literary criticism's focus on turn-of-the-century textual materialism often reifies the assumption that literary regions always function as isolated alternatives to urban-

industrial settings. See also Nancy Glazener's *Reading for Realism: The History of a U.S. Literary Institution, 1850–1910* (Durham, NC: Duke University Press, 1997) and Gillian Brown's *Domestic Individualism: Imagining Self in Nineteenth-Century America* (Berkeley: University of California Press, 1990).

10. Brown, *Sense of Things*, 8.
11. The review "The Power and the Glory" appeared in the November 1910 issue of the *Garden Magazine*, 193.
12. Shapiro, *Appalachia on Our Mind*, 163–70.
13. Bessie and Marie Van Vorst of New York are just one notable example. *The Woman Who Toils* was first published serially in *Everybody's Magazine* in 1902. Employing sentimentality, the Van Vorsts attended to the effects of factory life on the vitality of families and future generations of Americans. Their accounts earned the praise of Theodore Roosevelt and laid the groundwork for a 1907 Bureau of Labor study.
14. Alan Trachtenberg, *The Incorporation of America: Culture and Society in the Gilded Age* (New York: Hill & Wang, 2007), 160.
15. Grace MacGowan Cooke, *The Power and the Glory* (1910; repr., Boston: Northeastern University Press, 2003), 14.
16. Ibid., 122.
17. Ibid., 3.
18. Ibid., 140.
19. Jane Bennett theorizes "vibrant matter" as objects grown luminous and powerful with "vital materiality" that runs through and across both human and nonhuman bodies. *Vibrant Matter: A Political Ecology of Things* (Durham, NC: Duke University Press, 2010), vii.
20. Cooke, *Power and the Glory*, 154.
21. In "Bodily Bonds: The Intersecting Rhetorics of Feminism and Abolition," in *The Culture of Sentiment: Race, Gender and Sentimentality in Nineteenth-Century America*, ed. Shirley Samuels (New York: Oxford University Press, 1992), 92–114, Karen Sánchez-Eppler describes the sentimental convention of reading the body as a sign of identity.
22. Cooke, *Power and the Glory*, 122.
23. Ibid., 82–83.
24. Ibid., 83.
25. Ibid., 345.
26. Ibid., 217.
27. Ibid., 367.
28. Ibid., 34.
29. Studies like Elizabeth Engelhardt's *Tangled Roots* and Chris Green's *Coal: A Poetry Anthology* (Frankfort, KY: Blair Mountain Press, 2006) have paved the way to a more expansive Appalachian literary archive beginning in the mid-nineteenth century, though they have been largely unable to cross the disciplinary divide between Appalachian studies and American literature. Bill Hardwig's *Upon Provincialism: Southern Literature and National Periodical Culture, 1870–1900* (Charlottesville: University of Virginia Press, 2013) accomplishes similar work for the "South" more generally. Though he predictably uses Murfree as his Appalachian literary

representative, he does analyze the national and international concerns of southern local colorists, helping show how scholars might integrate local color into American literary history more generally. Emily Satterwhite's *Dear Appalachia* is expansive and does an admirable job centering Appalachia within broader historicist studies concerned with reception and literary marketplaces. There is ground upon which to build.

30. See Douglas Reichert Powell, *Critical Regionalism: Connecting Politics and Culture in the American Landscape* (Chapel Hill: University of North Carolina Press, 2007) and Ann Kingsolver, "'Placing' Futures and Making Sense of Globalization on the Edge of Appalachia" in *Appalachia in Regional Context: Place Matters* (Lexington: University of Kentucky, 2018), 17–48. Without either essentializing or losing the distinctive qualities of marginal geographies (Johnson City, TN, is his case study), Powell links local concerns to inter/national patterns of history, politics, and culture. A cultural anthropologist, Kingsolver puts place at the center of her historical and ethnographic analyses of how situated individuals affected by transnational policies and industries critique them.

31. Kathleen Stewart, *A Space on the Side of the Road: Cultural Poetics in an "Other" America* (Princeton, NJ: Princeton University Press, 1996), 4–6.

32. Ibid., 5.

33. Ibid., 4.

ANTEBELLUM COOKBOOK

KELLY NORMAN ELLIS

I, Mariah

Parched okra grind up make coffee.
Parched meal or corn make coffee too.

Red corn cobs burned make white ashes.
Sift it and use instead of soda.

Sift meal, add salt and make up with water
Put on collard leaf, cover with another

Collard leaf and put on hot ashes.
Cover with mo hot ashes. The bread will

Be brown, the collard leaf parched up.
Then, roast potatoes and eggs in ashes.

Make persimmon beer. Put old
Field hay in the barrel bottom,

Persimmons, baked corn bread
And water. Let stand bout a week

A fine drink with tea cakes.
Won't make you drunk.

Put black walnuts in ash cakes
Just as good as crackling bread.

Make vinegar out of apples.
Take overripe apples

Ground 'em up an put 'em
In a sack an let drip. Don't

Add no water and when it get
Through drippin, let it sour

And strain and stand for six
Months. Best vinegar ever made.

Keep you' meat an' greens
Well covered with boiling water

And let it all cook some two
Hours. Don't boil fast but just

Let yo pot simmer along slowsome.
A piece of red pepper pod ain't

Going to hurt the seasonin' none,
An use yo gumption when the boiling

Pretty near finished about whether or
Not mo salt are a needcessity.

Clean the chicken nice.
Stuff him with dressing

Grease him all over good
Put a cabbage leaf on the floor

Of the fireplace, put the chicken
On the cabbage leaf

Then cover him good with another
Leaf, and put hot coals over

And around him to roast.
This the best way to cook chicken.*

II. Mistress

When you kill young chickens
Pluck them carefully, truss and
Put them down to a good fire,
Dredge and baste them with lard;
A quarter of an hour to roast;
Froth them up, lay them on dish,
Pour butter and parsley on.
Serve hot.

Gather leaves from fragrant roses
Without bruising, fill a pitcher
With the flowers, and cover
With French brandy, take out the leaves

Fill the pitcher with fresh ones,
And return the brandy; do this
Until strongly impregnated,
Then bottle it;

It is better than distilled rose water for cakes.

Pick greens very clean, and wash.
Look them carefully over again;
Quarter them if they are very large;
Put them into a sauce pan with plenty

Of boiling water; if a skum rises, take
It off, put a large spoonful of salt
In the sauce pan; and boil until
The stalks are tender. See

They are well covered with water all the time
See that no dirt or smoke arises from stirring the fire.
With careful management, they will look beautiful
When dressed.

Sift one quart of meal in a pan
and add a pint of water and teaspoon of salt.
Stir until it is light, and then place
on a new, clean board and place nearly upright
before fire. When brown, cut in squares,
butter nicely, and serve hot.

Take half a pound of the best, roasted,
Ground coffee; boil the same in saucepan
Containing three quarts of water until
The quantity is reduced to one quart;

Strain the latter off, and, when fined of all
Impurities, introduce the liquor into another
Clean saucepan, and let it boil over again, adding
Lisbon sugar to it as will constitute a thick syrup

Like treacle; remove from the fire and when cold
Pur into bottles, corking the same tight down for use.
If milk is at hand, use it *ad libitum.***

WPA Slave Narratives
**The Virginia Housewife* by Mary Randolf

———————

Manumission Menu

cornbread
cracklin'
hot water
hoe
ash cake
okra   corn
tomatoes   squash
chow chow

353

homny biscuits   rice
bream
catfish, buffalo, pan trout
mullet
gut
hen
yard gospel
capon
pluck
butter beans   pinto   white beans
purple hulls
black eyed
shuck
scrapple
pig tails pig ear
oxtails
turkey neck
chitlins
clean
tongue
neckbones
souse
alive
red beans rice
green onions   bell pepper   celery
trinity
roux
red eye

gravy
taters
peanuts beets
watermelon

dig
crawfish
okra stew
shrimp grits
clabber
chess pie, pecan pie, sweet potato
pone   pound cake   raisin pie
sorghum blackberry
cobbler
peach
rubarb apple
cane
cut
hot sauce
ham hock, fatback, gizzard
maw
sweetbreads
squirrel, rabbit, possum
deer
skin
collards, kale, mustards
turnips
pick
buttermilk
chicory
sweet tea
absinthe
julep
bourbon
big house
bukra
boss
swallow

HOW TO MAKE CORNBREAD, OR THOUGHTS ON BEING AN APPALACHIAN FROM PENNSYLVANIA WHO CALLS VIRGINIA HOME BUT NOW LIVES IN GEORGIA

JIM MINICK

STEP 1: HOME.

Home, verb. To find *the* place, as in homing pigeon; not "Let's go home" but "Let's home"; the journey, however long it takes.

Home, noun. The destination; the place where I'm born, again and again, every morning; where I break the fast of darkness with a glass of water drawn from this one well; where I plant and am planted; where I nourish and am nourished; where—despite ticks and bears and isolation—I want to live and die; where—somehow—I come closest to feeling I belong.

If I'm reborn every morning in this one particular spot, then I want to redefine *native*. But can I? Can I claim my chosen home as native ground? Can I be native to this place?

———

For much of the three decades of our marriage, Sarah and I have pursued the idea of homesteading, where we grow what food we can, work at home, if possible, spend little money, and entertain ourselves with books and music-making and walks in the woods. Grand ideals grounded in getting our hands dirty.

But for several years we couldn't answer this one question: What to eat for breakfast? We kept bumping against this problem as we moved toward a simpler diet, away from meat, eggs, dairy and the traditional breakfast foods. And away from my childhood favorites of Sugar Pops, Fruit Loops, and Life. If you don't eat bacon or eggs—though you love the smell and taste of both—and if you don't really want to spend money on expensive granola from the grocery, what do you eat?

Cornbread.

———

The cornbread I ate as a child usually came from a Jiffy Mix box. After teaching all day, Mom would make chili and cornbread for a family of four. I liked it covered with honey.

Sometimes I ate with my grandparents and uncle on the family dairy farm, where in her fluorescent-lit kitchen, Grandma fried bacon in an iron skillet. After the last strip sizzled, she poured cornmeal batter into the grease, and then slid the skillet into the oven. This is one of the traditional and more flavorful ways of eating pone, but unlike Twain, I like to think there are other cornpone opinions.

———

Corn-bread, noun. The soil, sun, wind, and rain transformed into leaf, stalk, and silk, kernel, meal, and bread; *home* made edible; not wheat bread or wafers, but holy good eatin' all the same.

Step 2: Seed, plant, and tend.

Hoe four rows for better pollination. Drop seeds every six inches. Cover and fertilize on top of the row, not in it, otherwise the seeds will rot in the moisture-holding dried poultry fertilizer. Tamp, weed, and mulch. Water as needed. Visit daily.

———

Friends gave me heirloom field corn, two varieties, Southern White Dent and Bloody Butcher. Both have that hardness that can chip a tooth, both have the dent in the end of the kernel when they're fully dry, and both make excellent cornmeal. The Southern White Dent grinds to a pale, almost white yellow; the Bloody Butcher grinds from a dark rich red to a faded denim.

But to grow any corn, you need a patch far from other varieties, so they don't cross-pollinate, and you have to hope that the crows and deer, coons and bear all stay away.

The best way to do that is to stay home.

Cherokee sent their children out to the cornfield to stay all day and chase away crows and other critters. I don't know what they did at night. Maybe a parent relieved the child, or maybe, like us, they just hoped for the best. Which doesn't always work.

I've come home from my day-job to find whole rows of just-sprouted corn plucked from the ground, one small plant at a time. Crows know to wait and watch for the right stage of tender green leaves. They grab the straw-like stem, tug, and pop out the buried treasure—a sprouted seed. Then they eat the kernel and hop six inches to the next, and the next, and the next. One year, I had to replant three times.

———

Confession 1: Sometimes it happens, but usually, I'm not born again every morning. That's the ideal. Thoreau: "To be awake is to be alive. I have never yet met a man who was quite awake. How could I have looked him in the face?" This wakefulness, it seems, even Thoreau sought with little success. But he kept seeking, kept homing.

———

Another year, I was away again, but left Sarah to tend our patch. The sweet corn stood six feet tall, ears filling out, almost ready—that's when they always come. By chance one morning, Sarah stepped out to hang laundry when she saw a black movement, then another. About a hundred yards away, two cubs rolled down the hill below our garden.

"Where's Mama?" Sarah whispered. The cubs chased each other into the meadow before realizing they'd strayed too far. They hustled back through the blueberries, scampered over the potatoes and crashed into the corn. Then

Sarah heard the distinct crack of a corn stalk breaking. Hidden in the middle of the patch, Mama Bear feasted on our corn.

Sarah clapped and yelled. The bear stopped breaking stalks. Then she stepped out of the garden and searched for Sarah who was hidden in the vine-covered deck. One cub even stood on hind feet for a better look. Sarah kept shouting in a deep voice, "THIS IS MY CORN. LEAVE IT ALONE." Finally, the trio climbed the fence and slipped back into the forest.

Sarah waited a while and then inspected. It seems like a bear would eat the whole ear of corn, to chomp and chew green husk, sweet kernels, and hard cob, all of it mashed together in big bites. This bear did not. She stripped back the husk and ate the kernels, nothing else. Just like a person.

———

How would a bear define *home* or *native*? The question is absurd, I know. To most bears, home is where they are. But at a certain age, juveniles are kicked out and forced to roam. So at least once in their lives, bears have to plant themselves again. I wonder if they feel homesickness for where they were born, or nostalgia, even. How do they come to belong to a new place?

———

Home-sick, noun. An illness of displacement (*dis-place*: having no place); a blues too many of us know; simply sick for home.

———

Over sixty-five million human refugees exist in our world. According to the United Nations, at least twenty-four people are displaced from their homes every minute of every day.

Step 3: Harvest, dry, and shell.

Be patient. Listen to the rattle of dried leaves. Get lost in the now-yellow stalks. Then learn the certain yank and twist, downward and out, that pops an ear off. It's a satisfying sound. The leaves, they'll scratch your skin. Pay them no mind. Instead, be ravenous.

———

I hauled ears by wheelbarrow and buckets up to our attic where they dried on the floor for another month. When the end of each kernel had the characteristic dent, I shelled. As a teenager, I helped a cousin shell corn for their cows. I cranked the sheller's worn handle as she fed the ears. Kernels came out in a bucket at our feet while the cobs shot out into a pile. My sheller this time, though, was my thumb, working down the cob, popping small red pills into the mouth of the bucket, a loud rattling slowly muffled as the kernels filled the bucket.

———

I grew up at the edge of a borough of three hundred people in south-central Pennsylvania. My grandparents and uncle lived on the dairy farm a quarter-mile away, a farm that's been in our family four generations. In the fall, I stood on the tongue of the corn wagon, holding onto the tractor fender while Uncle Harry drove out the lane. The tractor and wagon lurched over ruts, the ground close and wonderfully dangerous.

In the field, we waited for Grandpa to make the round in the bigger tractor that pulled the corn picker and the now-full other corn wagon. My job was to unhook and hook wagons, starting with the loaded one. I pulled the pin, dropped it back into the picker, and dropped the tongue onto the ground. Grandpa drove forward, while Uncle Harry maneuvered the empty wagon close enough that I could hook it up without it rolling down the hill. I had to pull that empty wagon into place, steering with the tongue, and then when the holes lined up, I slid the pin in. I signaled to Grandpa and soon more ears banged on the high metal walls of the wagon. I connected the loaded wagon to Uncle Harry's tractor and climbed the wagon's ladder.

As a boy, I liked to help, to scurry between the big pieces of equipment, to yell directions over the din of the picker and engine, but the best part was this return ride. I lay on my back with the hard ears making a rough bed. Tree branches brushed my face because the mound of corn rose ten feet. I plucked leaves, smelled the crushed bruise of cherry. The dry, yellow corn surrounded me in warmth, with the sun pouring down from the blue October sky. To the east, the whole farm spread out—the pond and other fields, the cows and barns, Grandma watching us out the kitchen window. And beyond the homestead lay the town of Newburg with Kittatinny Mountain banking it to the north.

———

The idea—and challenges—of homesteading came for me from Wendell Berry. When I first read his work in my early twenties, our family dairy farm was about to change hands. My grandparents died, and my uncle no longer wanted to farm. But *I* wanted the farm. Yet how? I had little knowledge, no capital, and no real idea of what kind of farming I wanted or could do. Dairy was too demanding with milking twice a day every day, and that's about all I knew. So I chose my love for words over land and landed a "safer" job teaching. Like an old story, the next job took me farther from my old native ground. In my absence, some of that home place sprouted a housing development called Quail Ridge. Most of the farm stayed in the family, but it became instead a rented house and rented land, the pasture overgrazed. The barn filled with cobwebs and rusting equipment. No Minicks farmed any of it anymore.

———

Ahmed at age sixty-seven fled his home in Syria in 2013. When he and his family arrived in Libya, the militia penned them in a barn with other refugees. The soldiers demanded more money, which didn't satisfy them, so they tortured the men and raped the women. Ahmed and his family finally boarded a boat, but the militia demanded even more money. The refugees emptied their pockets, but that wasn't enough. The soldiers began shooting—killing and wounding several and sinking the boat. Somehow Ahmed made it to Malta, but he lost eight members of his family. He felt like he had no reason to live.

The United Nations report says nothing about his past: Where was he born? What kind of work did he do? What was the house like that he had to flee? What happened to it or any gardens, orchards, or seeds?

The report says nothing about these eight family members: Was one Ahmed's wife? How long had they been married? How many children and grandchildren did they have? Were they raped as Ahmed had to watch?

And the report says nothing about his future: Where did he finally settle? What kind of a home and life has he been able to make? Did his new neighbors offer him their equivalent of cornbread?

Step 4: Winnow and grind.

Take two buckets, one empty and the other full of shelled corn. Go outside, preferably on a windy day. Pour the kernels from one bucket to the other, back and forth, while the chaff blows away. If no wind, use a fan.

Freeze for a week to kill weevil eggs. Then store in air-tight, critter-proof containers. Grind as needed.

We use a Vitamix every morning to make a blueberry smoothie. It also comes with a special container and blade powerful enough to grind the hard kernels into fine meal. But only in small batches.

Two warnings about this: a. Wear ear muffs—the Vitamix's engine is loud as a lawnmower running over rocks; b. Sift the meal. Unground bits of kernel chip teeth.

———

When my uncle stopped the corn wagon, I climbed off and then up the conveyer into the crib, which was a huge affair—twenty feet tall, six feet wide, and thirty feet long. My job: push the ears into the corners, make sure the crib filled completely, and avoid getting pummeled by the falling corn. Uncle Harry opened the wagon and soon the corn traveled up to tumble down. A yellow dust fogged over us. At the start, I shoveled, but as the crib filled, the best tool became my body. I threw the ears, then I lay on my back and kicked them into corners. Kernels filled my shoes, my pants, my shirt. The dust lined my nose and stuck to my sweaty skin. When I hit the crib roof with my head, I yelled, several times, for Uncle Harry, who finally heard and stopped the machine. In the sudden silence, I rested on the hard corn to catch my breath.

I don't know the variety of that field corn. And I don't know the source of my grandmother's cornmeal. I doubt they were the same. She had no Vitamix, no grinder. My father remembers going over the mountain to a mill in Amberson Valley. But sometime in the 1950s—long before I was born—that mill closed and the trips stopped, so the cornbread Grandma made for me probably came from grocery-store cornmeal. It might've even been Jiffy-Mix, like my mother's.

We grew sweet corn, enough to feed the whole extended family. Sometimes we roasted it over a pit, that smoky flavor still my favorite.

Our field corn fed the beef cows we ate. And the unpicked scatterings fed pheasants and rabbits that my father and uncles and I scared up from the stubble and shot with our shotguns and ate at Thanksgiving.

But now from a distance of forty years, I understand for the first time that I grew up with an intimate knowledge of field corn that I never directly ate.

———

Confession 2: Today, cornbread fills the majority of my cereal bowl, but I still eat store-bought cereal. I like to mix in Grape-Nuts or something a little sweet for flavor and texture.

———

Our history is full of refugees: the homeless fleeing the Irish Potato Famine, the slaves chained to a future they never chose, the native Americans pushed at gunpoint farther and farther from their homes.

And what about the homeless who line our streets? What kind of refuge have we offered and what cornbread have we broken together?

Ours is a land full of homesick, homesteading, home-torn, home-lusting, home-lost people who somehow—by force or by choice—made a home in this new place. Or they died.

Step 5: Make the cornbread.

1 c cornmeal	1 c buckwheat flour
2 tsp baking powder	1/2 tsp baking soda
1/4 c sugar	Pinch of salt
1 tbs vinegar	1 1/2 c almond milk
1 handful blueberries	

Mix dry ingredients. In separate bowl, mix wet ingredients and then add to dry and stir. Pour into greased pan. Bake at 425 degrees for 30 minutes.

My wife doesn't like this recipe—too dry, "like cardboard," she says. Sometimes we add applesauce. Usually I eat all of each pone by myself.

———

Twain's thesis in "Corn-Pone Opinions" comes from a slave who preaches this: "You tell me whar a man gits his cornpone, en I'll tell you what his 'pinions is." There are no original opinions, Twain contends, only imitation upon imitation. Any original idea, if it could be caught, should be displayed in a museum.

He's right, of course, and still relevant. But forget the figurative. What does this say now—physically—about cornbread? When we don't know where our cornmeal comes from, then it seems we don't know who or what shapes our opinions, or for that matter, our bodies.

———

I've tried other recipes, finally finding ones that taste good without eggs. But we still buy several ingredients. We still depend on others to grow and process and transport and shelve and store and sell the buckwheat and baking soda, vinegar and milk. This will never be a pure, self-sufficient life. That myth died when the weasel beheaded our chickens thirty years ago. So we do the best we can to do as little harm as we can.

———

What is home to a box turtle or a weasel, a monarch butterfly or a basswood or a bass? They all roam, in their way, at least once in their lives. So which place is home—where they start or where they end?

———

Growing up, I had no idea I was an Appalachian or a Yankee. The Yankees I knew were the enemy to my Baltimore Orioles. Those Yankees had all the money to steal pennants and World Series. Those Yankees all lived far away in the biggest city on earth.

As for Appalachian, that was the Trail that ran the flat spine of South Mountain on the other side of the valley. We crossed this trail every time we drove to Gettysburg to visit that other site of known Yankees.

Then I married into a southern middle-class family. Then Sarah and I moved to the mountains of Virginia, the mountains I now call home. Then, finally, I became an Appalachian.

Step 6: Eat.

One summer at the Appalachian Writers Workshop in Hindman, Kentucky, I broke cornbread with Gurney Norman. As the dining room cleared, he went back for seconds, saying in his high, sweet voice, "This cornbread's so good, I want to eat it for dessert, too." He crumbled yellow bits into a cup, added sugar, and poured milk over it all. Between bites, he told me of his childhood with grandparents who taught him the great pleasure of this simple dish.

And that's when I thought, Why not? Why not eat cornbread for breakfast?

But this will probably disgust you, dear reader, just like it disgusts my wife, who makes our daily morning smoothie of blueberries, soymilk, and other ingredients. I don't pour milk over my cornbread, I pour this smoothie. And it is good.

———

What is home to a hummingbird? Is it where she overwinters in Belize or where she nests every year in the beech tree in our Virginia woods? It seems she belongs to both places, so she must have dual citizenship. Or is she simply native to this earth?

———

But to call myself Appalachian is still inaccurate. Just like the word *Virginia*, *Appalachia* encompasses such a huge swath of land that it ignores all of the diversity within the region. So a Virginian from Arlington is the same as one from Jonesville just as an Appalachian from Knoxville is the same as one from War, West Virginia, or Hazelton, Pennsylvania. And ironically, the counties I grew up in are not technically on the Appalachian Regional Commission's map even though they have mountains. So in their specifics, labels become meaningless and even wrong. The cornbread made in these various places reflects how different they each can be.

So if I'm not an Appalachian or a Yankee, who am I? And where am I from?

———

In *The Unsettling of America*, Wendell Berry points out that we've become married to our careers instead of our home places. For twenty-five years, I embraced that challenge and instead of pursuing a terminal degree, which would've been prudent for my career, I pursued a "degree" in blueberries. This choice of paths, of homesteading by creating a blueberry farm, enriched our lives, but not our wallets, so decades later, I finally went back to school for that degree, and as a result, I landed a "good" job—a tenure-track professor position with an ideal teaching load—all of it 350 miles from our Virginia home.

Meaning: I still don't know how to value both career and place in a society that only values the former.

———

Confession 3: I haven't grown any corn in five years because the academic calendar doesn't allow for a long enough season. If we planted it on our Virginia homestead, we'd be in Georgia when the corn came ready to harvest, and though, as a society, we've come to value online teaching and banking and such, we haven't yet—thankfully—figured out online harvesting. So we still grow what we can in this abbreviated season, which is plenty—lettuce and tomatoes, garlic and onions, potatoes, sweet and Irish, blueberries, peaches, kiwis, apples, and pears. But no corn.

The meal for the cornbread I ate this morning was organic, grown in Kansas. Other times, it's local, but not organic.

———

Confession 4: Life is full of compromises.

———

By 2050, according to *National Geographic*, "scientists predict . . . at least 50 million [refugees]" due to climate change. "Some say [this figure] could be as high as 200 million."

Two hundred million Ahmeds.

———

Confession 5: I never thought I'd own two houses—but there it is.

Step 7: Plant Again and Select for Better Seed

For most of my thirty-year career, I've embraced and been embraced by the Appalachian studies community. I love the multidisciplinary, multivoiced approach that helps us understand and celebrate our complex world, and I've made many close and lasting friendships.

But there are still fellow Appalachians who don't know what to do with me, or who shun me because I'm from afar, from Pennsylvania. Forget that I grew up in mountains, that my maternal grandmother had to sell her farm and move to a house trailer, that my small town's main "industry"—besides farming—is the landfill that swallows two hollows and bulges like a giant wart in the middle of the valley, the trucks rolling in from New York and Philly and D.C. even now, forty years after I smelled the first one. In someone else's eyes, it doesn't matter. It's not enough. Those cornpone opinions have crusted and hardened, molded even.

I understand that tired argument in a different way: sometimes those who complain loudest about stereotypes also are quickest to use them. I wish it wasn't so.

And I'm not innocent. I've stereotyped others. I have my own cornpone opinions. And I hold onto this bitter pill of being stereotyped. Let it go, I tell myself. But that's a hard row to hoe in this corn patch called my life.

———

But then I think of Ahmed, and how shallow any stereotype seems. The United Nations report includes a picture of him. He sits on the floor, his back against a doorjamb. He wears a white tank-top t-shirt. His beard is gray turning white, his moustache brown turning gray. He has a long face, receding hairline—and suddenly I see my grandfather in Ahmed's tired eyes, that high, wrinkled forehead, and that one raised eyebrow.

———

When a monarch butterfly migrates, it can travel as far as 2,500 miles from Canada to Mexico. But that journey has become more and more perilous. New weather patterns bring more severe storms, and in both Mexico and North America, we're destroying butterfly habitat through logging, spraying pesticides, and building houses. As a result monarch butterfly populations have plummeted. If butterflies have a concept for war, they're saying we've declared it. When does homeless become refugee become extinct?

———

I once asked Wendell Berry about this word, *native*. He said, "*Native* means born here. But it's possible now to be *born* here but not *made* here. You can live [in one place] and yet be made by imported nutrients and imported influences. If *native* is going to mean anything, you have to say you're born, nourished, and educated to a significant extent in and *by* your place, your local community."

How? By becoming a native *and* a citizen. By learning—when it's possible—to live in one place. By embracing the responsibility that comes with citizenship.

I asked, "Can you become native to a place even if you weren't born there?"

Berry emphatically responded, almost yelling, "We better!"

Step 8: Root and Be Rooted

Home: the particular hills and hollows of a small farm in the New River watershed that I claim; the waters of Big Branch and Cripple Creek and the underground Valley and Ridge aquifer our well taps into 365 feet deep; the Chiswell-Groseclose-Litz soil that grows the corn that feeds us, soil I plan to feed some day with my own body.

Maybe that is the ultimate definition of home—the place where you are buried—the last place you arrive.

Step 9: Plant yourself or die.

Step 10: Plant yourself and die, again and again.

TONGLEN FOR MY MOTHER

LINDA PARSONS

I.
Abed in Quality Care in Lebanon, Tennessee,
my mother has nearly forgotten the rage years,
the jealous years, the secret Darvocet years
a secret to no one, the leaving years of husbands

and daughter, the years of all bitter, no sweet.
A time zone away, I cloak myself in mindful
practice, cloaked for those years' protection,
visiting her in mind and marrow, in what grit

I can muster on my buckwheat zafu. From this
distance, no cold shoulder, no icy tongue to strike.
I practice the ancient tonglen, exchange of self
with other in taking and sending on the breath.

I inhale her poisons of circumstance:
three attic rooms, her grandmother and parents,
four stairstep girls (two slept in the kitchen),
mother humpbacked at the shirt factory,

father drunk and drunk and drunk, sometimes
slipping a little girl under the covers. I take

in the black smoke of suffering as she lies
abed. Take in what fed her rage, her blessed

pills hidden here and yon, her jealous,
her bitter, no sweet. I take storm into
storm, her child's chaos, my child's tightrope,
my tumble again to the sawdust floor.

Her toxins circle, fur stole on my shoulders,
dinner rings on every finger, just as she
would want. I breathe in all the miles
my wheels can bear, the year, at eleven,

I left my mother's people to live with
my father across the state, returning only
a guest. Our separation our cross borne
our time's waste our unanswerable echo

from the Nashville Basin to the Cumberland
Plateau to East Tennessee between us no breath
no blood no redemption no call no response
no mother's hymn to daughter no strike of kin.

II.
On the out breath, I send my father's
Country Squire wagon, the steep grade
west of Rockwood, our Hillbilly Highway
Knoxville to Nashville before the interstate

cut through the Cumberlands. I send
our switchbacks and hairpin curves,
Peggy Ann's Truck Stop, the hopeful shacks
along Route 70 selling quilts pinned

to the clothesline, split-oak and riverbirch
baskets. My own ride hopeful, second
home to first, despite my triggering
presence, reminder of that towheaded girl

slipped from my mother's grasp. My breath
sent in cool white light descends the Plateau
to the Highland Rim, gorge of limestone
and shale, my father braking for the tempest

to come. Breath sent to quell her sorrow
spinning ruined history from the straw
of our drought. I send peace that passeth
understanding, the out breath longer

than the in, unborn seeds to root
and sprout, a river fertile as the Cumberland
rife with hands raised to salvation.
As she lies abed in Quality Care,

I send and send to deaden
the sharp to bleach the stain
to quiet the fight to sweeten
the sour to heal the disheartened

to mend the tear to fly her soon
to the Savior's throne, streets of gold
and pearl where she will take up
her bed she will rise and walk

and shoulder our remainders
in amazement that, like hers, my hair
has struck silver and old and older
we meet in the middle as we never

allowed our former selves as we
could never be in that world back
yonder our back and forth the blind
road we reaped into elegy years

we sent we received in knowing
finally knowing in finding sure
footing our ground at the blooming
the living end of relinquishment

our one shared breath
ordinary in and out
forever and amen
our precious mother load

My response to J. D. Vance's *Hillbilly Elegy* is purely personal and emotional, not grounded in any political or socioeconomic concerns as others have expressed. Like Vance's mother, mine suffers from addiction and mental illness, and like Vance, as a child I escaped to the saner harbor of my maternal grandmother and later my father and stepmother, moving from Nashville to Knoxville to live with them. As I say in the poem, my "Hillbilly Highway" was Route 70 over the Cumberland Plateau, riding to visit my mother and family with such hopes of mending fences, which never quite happened amid her deep sense of my betrayal. Over the years, my writing has inched me toward understanding, peace, and forgiveness. I'm grateful for the opportunity to further explore our trials and errors in this poem, where I illustrate the meditative practice of tonglen for my mother, the taking on of others' suffering and sending peace and compassion on the breath. I practice the same for myself in healing exchange.

OLIVIA AT THE INTERSECTION

TEXT AND PHOTOGRAPH BY MEG WILSON

EVERY FRIDAY NIGHT from July until September the community fills the streets and sidewalks of Old Town Berea for the Levitt Amp music festival. Local activist Ali Blair, who started the festival, says it is "about connection. It's about a community claiming open public space and celebrating what makes it unique and colorful. Art across all mediums, music across all genres, food grown locally and made with love, a diverse intergenerational mix of community members and visitors, a regular reason for Bereans to come together as they are to enjoy what we collectively have to offer—a unique brand of Appalachian culture."

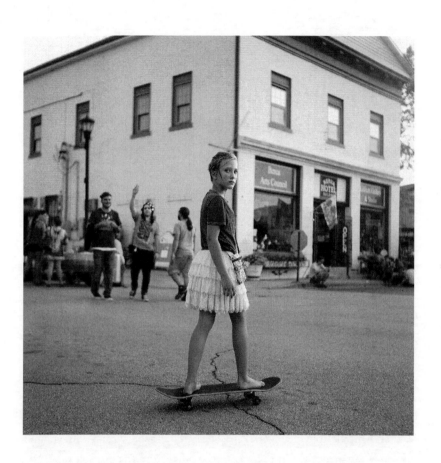

APPALACHIAN APOPHENIA, OR THE PSYCHOGEOGRAPHY OF HOME

JODIE CHILDERS

In this kitchen, the faucet leaks brown drops of water—
Zyprexa, rent to own, buy now, pay later, credit card bills, crumpled
receipts, an empty pack of matches. Pepsi bottle spittoons, ceramic
saucer ashtrays, a free calendar from the bank—it is spring—in this
pantry, or in another pantry just like it, a can of beef ravioli, creamed
corn, unpaid gas bills, ramen noodles in the microwave. In this
kitchen, smoke rings, chain smoke, a shirt hanging on the broken box
fan to dry, plastic pill bottles, powdered milk from Catholic charities,
lithium, Ambien, Klonopin, expired, expired, expired

An emergency call comes in while I'm teaching my Sunday class at a community college in Queens. I have to go back home. The next morning I take an Amtrak from New York Penn Station to Pittsburgh and a Greyhound bus to West Virginia. On the way to the hotel from the bus station, a guy approaches me on the street.

"Look, I know I have a black eye. I got in a bar fight last night. But I'm just a normal guy, I swear. I came down here from Michigan to work for the coal mine. I got an engineering degree. You're not from around here, are you?"

I don't answer.

"This place is crazy," he says.

"Yeah, pretty much."

"You want to hang out? You seem normal."

"Not really."

I don't tell him I'm on my way to the psych ward.

My brother and I are asleep on the foldout bed in the living room. I hear the familiar creak of the rocking chair and the snap of the belt as it hits the floor. I open my eyes.

    Why are you wearing a football helmet, Mom?

    The snap of the belt, the creak of the chair.

    I like my helmet, she says.

The psych ward is not in the same town as Mom's apartment, so I can't stay there. Instead, I book the closest hotel, and I walk a half a mile to the hospital twice a day to visit Mom for our allotted hour and a half. Before this particular break, she had just started taking community college classes, and now her delusions and hallucinations take on the topics and themes of the subjects I teach. She is fixated on her composition course, so we brainstorm her psyche and cluster her paranoid thoughts on scraps of notebook paper while sitting together in the small shared kitchen near the nurse's stand. A man and his son work a puzzle at the next table as we silently free-write.

    She draws a blue circle and writes inside, I want out.

    I know, I write back in an orange circle.

    Home. She writes in block letters.

    I draw a picture of a house.

    Are you going back to New York soon?

    Yes.

    Will I be crucified? She creates a purple circle and writes the
        question inside.

    No, I write inside a blue circle.

    What about Jesus? She draws a cross.

    That doesn't happen in real life.

    Joan of Arc? She challenges me in a red square.

*It is seven in the morning. I am on the floor coloring in stalactites and
stalagmites on the threadbare carpet at Dad's house. My little brother
stands in front of the kerosene heater that has stained the walls with a
layer of grime.*

The phone rings, and I know it's her. I always know.

I need your help.

*Her voice has that odd sound, rapid syllables pushed together,
tachylogia. In crooked bubble letters, I write, Stalactites hang from
the ceiling, Stalagmites rise from the ground*

*I need to finish the poster, the letters pushed together, I need to finish
the poster—*

He's missing, he's gone,

Who?

I saw his face on the milk carton, your brother,

Mom, he's right here,

Who?

My brother,

*your son, my son, stalactites descend, stalagmites ascend,
in the darkness of the cave*

The rules on the Mental Health Unit are strict. All visitors must arrive at
the same time and enter together. We must check any items we bring for the
patients with the staff, no contraband, like the hoodie I brought for Mom one
time. They wouldn't let her keep it because of the string. And once they let us
in, our visits must take place in the public areas. I put my wallet and phone
inside a locker. I never put my stuff in locker six in case Mom sees the key.
Today I choose seven. A better omen.

We sit in stiff plastic chairs in the family waiting room, watching the clock
move, our eyes fixed on the heavy door. Some are regulars. I notice a few
newbies in the mix this time. A man with a beard and a red flannel, a regular,
nods at me. He points out to the newbies that this place is less strict than the
other one, the one down state. His partner disagrees. This is not the first time
I've heard this argument. The newbies defer to the man with the beard. He's
our leader.

It is five minutes past six. "Late again." The man with the beard picks up the phone and calls in. "They said they didn't forget about us. Can you believe that?" He reports back to us.

"Well, they better give us more time then," his partner says.

"This is ridiculous," a newbie chimes in.

Suddenly the doors are opened, "You all thought we forgot about you, didn't you?" says a short haired woman in light blue scrubs.

"Good evening, Sandy," the man with the beard says.

A woman screams from a room.

"Come on in folks," Sandy says.

The staff is beginning to trust me. Today they let me visit Mom in her room. This is a special privilege. I'm a regular.

"It's sad," Mom says. "She had her kids taken away from her." She motions toward the direction of the screaming.

"Just now?" I ask.

"No, not just now. A while back. She's really far gone."

"You should put some of your art up," I say. "The room is too white."

She ignores me. "I don't trust them," she whispers.

"Sandy seems nice," I say.

"She's okay."

"You just have to stay in here long enough to get better."

"But, what if ... you know. ..."

I do know. Symbiosis. I always know. Almost always. "Mom, they're not."

"I don't trust them."

"Just take your medicine, okay?"

"I am. They make me. I don't even know what they're giving me. I just want to see Dr. H. I don't trust the nurses in here."

"They're not putting stuff in your meds."

"They've got everything mixed up. People are getting the wrong meds and everything."

"Mom, stop. I just want you to get out, okay? Just take your meds. How's the food been today?"

"They gave me fruit cocktail. I'm not supposed to have it. It makes my sugar go up."

A few people watch TV. A man sits at a table and plays solitaire.

Hey Cheryl, are those your kids? A lady in a Santa Claus hat and a teddy bear shirt yells across the room to us. Can you bring them over here? I want to meet them.

Maybe later. I have something for you kids. She holds out her hand. Communion, she says.

We both take the bread crumbs from her hands. They smell like cigarettes. We swallow them, washing them down with Kool-Aid from a paper cup.

What happened to your lip? I ask.

This? She touches it and gets blood on her fingers. I jumped off the building. But I was able to fly.

Days pass and the clusters begin to take a more rational tone. We silently try to piece together the story.

Did I bounce any checks before I came in? She writes with a blue marker.

Yes. I respond in green.

Can you call the bank and let them know I'm in here?

I already did.

$$?

Yes. $$$!

Sorry.

I run the house. I am ten. I am eleven. She wakes up from a hundred years of sleep and makes us ramen noodles. I am twelve. We run the streets. Five girls at the shelter at East End playground smoking cigarettes. We carve our names into the picnic table. The Appalachian Mountains surround us, a friendly chokehold. The older guys hold us down. Bra snaps. Dick smacks. It's all in fun. I am thirteen. Happy Birthday. She wakes up from a hundred years of sleep and orders us a pizza. She asks Pink Door to hold a check until the first of the month.

I am angry at the bank. I am angry at the system. But I am also angry at her.

Her father was a gambler too. Red was known around town and down at the factory. He ran the spot sheets. An eccentric, he'd sit at the kitchen table chewing on a cigar trying to figure out how to solve the pattern behind the lottery. Guys would come in and out. He never won enough money to buy a car or to add doors inside the house, so there weren't any barriers between rooms, not even the bathroom. Scrap paper and pieces of brown cardboard were covered with calculations and figures, scores carefully written down from years of college football. He tried to discern patterns, but he couldn't help himself. He always put his money on the underdog.

In our home, we relied on miracles and the government. Deer meat from a family friend, a quarter on the ground at the laundromat, a book of food stamps tucked into the back of an old Christian book from when Mom was in Bible college, a full cigarette unbroken in the bottom of Mom's purse. All of these were moments of divine intervention. Food stamps, manna, government cheese, Catholic charities. Everything bad happens in threes, everything good on the first of the month. The gambler's fallacy fit perfectly into this logic. Deus ex machina, God will provide, Texas Tea, the salvation of the video poker machine.

To Whom It May Concern:
It is not a "courtesy" to provide a client diagnosed with mental illness with bounce protection on her account. I am asking that you waive the courtesy fees and all other overdraft fees. It is obvious that the client was not consciously aware when writing these checks; otherwise she would not have written so many small checks for ten, fifteen, or twenty dollars over such a short period of time. If she were attempting to take advantage of the bank's policy, she would have instead written one large check to avoid the excessive "courtesy fees." The account statement shows an erratic pattern, and it is surprising that the bank did not put a stop on the account or (at the very least) alert the client.

I have less than a week before I have to get back to work. There is no other option. We have to get Mom out.

"I'm trying to talk them into letting me out on Thursday," Mom whispers. "But they want to know that you're going to be there."

"I am her caretaker," I tell the social worker during the family meeting. I don't tell her that I don't live in West Virginia. I don't tell her that I'll be leaving to go back to New York in three days. I don't tell her that Mom is still whispering her delusions to me in secret, asking me if someone put a cross on my head or if my brother knows how to read. This is a risk. We both know we need to get her out. Maybe if she's out, she'll heal.

I am in first grade and I break lots of rules. I talk in class, I never bring my report card back, and the teacher puts my name on the board almost every day. I get in trouble for screaming at the scary parts when we watch the cartoons in class like when Chip almost shoots Dale from a cannon. They put me in the coatroom and I don't get to see the man who brings in the tarantula.

I like the new church. It doesn't have too many rules like school. We get to dance and sing in the aisles. Sometimes I get to shake a tambourine. Sometimes the singing goes on and on and they let me sprawl out in the pews and color pictures of shepherds and lambs and little baby Jesuses.

But sometimes I don't like this church. Like when the grown-ups shout and cry and speak in strange languages. The pastor puts oil on their foreheads and they all fall backward. Sometimes they talk about the blood of the lamb. Sometimes people say they are healed and everybody claps and says, praise Jesus, praise Jesus. Some of them tell scary stories about demons and the Holy Ghost. I'm afraid of the Holy Ghost, but they say he is a good ghost like Casper. I don't like when Mom says askela- ashala- and sings church songs at home. I don't like when she cries and whispers, Jesus, Jesus.

Something is not right. Mom goes to the front, but it's not the time to go to the front. The pastor tells her to sit back down. I can't hear what she is saying but her voice sounds funny. Maybe she is possessed by the Holy Ghost.

   What's wrong with my mom? I ask a lady who pulls me into the nursery.
   You're mommy's just sick, that's all.
   Through the glass window, I watch as they all rush to the front. They hold her down. Maybe they will use the special oil and exorcise the ghost like the stories in the Bible.

Does she have the flu? I ask.
Yes, it's just like the flu.

I seem sensible, normal. They trust me. Just sign here, they say.

"And here are her keys." They hand them to me, the responsible daughter. I don't lie, but I don't tell the whole truth. I'm over thirty years old. I have taken care of the family since I was eight, but I don't know how to drive.

Mom is heavily drugged and giddy when we leave. She breathes in the air, "Freedom," she says and lights a cigarette.

"Don't smoke in the car," I say. "It gives me a headache."

The drive home will not be easy. The stretch of highway is called the narrows, for a reason. On one side is the mountain, on the other the Ohio River and there is very little room to pull over. The goal is get us back without crashing into the rocks or going over the ledge into the water.

"Are you going to be able to get us home alive?"

"God will protect us."

"No, you've got to protect us."

"If you're so worried, you drive."

"Mom, you know I can't drive."

"I'll teach you." She blows a smoke ring.

"This isn't funny. Should we just go back in?"

"No. I'm not going back there."

"Then you need to concentrate."

She wants to listen to K-love, the Christian station, and I don't protest for once. I have to stay in control and to keep things calm and relaxed. But the problem is not her anxiety, it's her lack of anxiety. She's completely unafraid, uninhibited. "Slow down, Mom," I say.

"I'm fine."

We approach some road work. "Mom, be careful."

"I'm fine." She speeds up.

"Do we need to pull over?"

"You're making me nervous, Jodie. You're making it worse. I wish your brother was here." She turns her entire body toward me.

"Keep your eyes on the road." I scream as she sideswipes a barrier.

It is fifth grade
we have to write president reports
I choose Teddy Roosevelt.
I like that his last words are
put out the light.
Mom is in the big hospital now
so much better than
speak softly and carry a big stick
I don't have to remind her
to take her medicine tonight
put out the light
I can't stop laughing
the big hospital is far away
and Teddy Roosevelt
with the pince-nez glasses
and that moustache
it all just makes so much sense

The rearview mirror on the passenger side is busted and dangles from the car. She seems completely unaffected. I take a deep breath.

"Should we pull over?"

"We just got to keep going," she says looking straight ahead.

The house is cold and dark, and I feel a familiar heaviness descend upon me as a I open the door and enter the kitchen, cluttered with bills, receipts, and half empty bottles. For the next three days, I must monitor her sleep-wake cycle and make sure she takes her meds. I try to gauge how she is doing, but she is quiet and withdrawn as she sits at the table and smokes. I try to crack jokes but she doesn't laugh. It's like I'm not there.

The first night, she can't sleep. This is a bad sign. She is worried that a satanic cult has been holding rituals in the basement. I have to go down there to check. It is dark and damp. I pull the string on the single uncovered light bulb.

"See, Mom, there's nothing down here," I say, feigning confidence.

"You don't see an altar?" she asks nervously from the top of the stairs.

"Look back in the corner room."

I open the wooden door. In the middle of the room, there is a pile of burnt paper and ashes and one of my old dolls. "No, nothing down here." I say, casually kicking the doll into the corner. I try not to think about what happened during this delusion.

The second day she gets antsy. "I need to go out," she says.

"Where?"

"Just out."

"Okay, then I'll go with you."

"Just by myself. I just need to go out somewhere."

I stand in front of the door and block her.

"God damn it, I just want to sit in my fucking car."

"Okay, but I get to go too."

"No. Without you." She pushes past me.

I concede. It is her car. She did pay for it with her own Zyprexa settlement. I unlock the door to the driver's seat but refuse to give her the keys. I watch her from the kitchen window.

> *Did you take your medicine, Mom?*
> *I am the agent of biopolitical control*
> *I enforce the status quo*
> *I force my way into her mind*
> *I teach my brother*
> *the pharmacological trade,*
> *one blue pill, one pink,*
> *two yellow capsules,*
> *one white tablet,*
> *fill her pillbox every Sunday night,*
> *or sit with her while she does it.*
> *She won't do it herself.*
> *Make sure she's sleeping at night;*
> *note if she's talking quickly*
> *and if she starts saying stuff about god,*
> *Jesus, blood, the cross, the Holy Spirit,*
> *or withdrawing into her own world.*

these are bad signs
Did you take your medicine, Mom?
Did you take your medicine, Mom?
Did you take your medicine, Mom?

"I took it," she says. "Stop badgering me."

"I just want you to get better."

"God damn it. Why do you keep following me?"

"I'm just worried. We got you out too early. I don't want you to have to go back in."

"I just want to drive around the block."

"Why don't you take a bath?"

"Fine. But you can't come in."

I can't sleep that night. I'm worried that this time, she'll do it. That this time she'll leave us for good, that this time she'll drive off into nowhere.

they say
she's really " far gone" this time
they say
it was a butcher knife
they say
the police shot out her tires
they say
it's a "catatonic state"
they say
they must shock her
they say
it will heal her
they say
if she breaks again
she may never
come back

When she attempts to escape again the next day, I guard the door—better for her to be a prisoner at home than end up back on the ward. When she goes into a rage, I play the Christian radio station to her—over the few days I have even memorized the lyrics to some of the songs.

"Let's paint."

She glares at me. She's been angry before, but never like this toward me. I've always been the one she trusts. The only one. Even in her deepest paranoia, she has always turned to me. But this time it's different. Have I changed? Can I not be trusted anymore? Am I one of them?

"Let's paint," I say to her again.

"Fine." I get out her plastic tote filled with art supplies, acrylic paints, charcoals. We turn on some Christian rock. The only thing I know how to paint is birds. I want to paint a blackbird, but I worry she'll see it as an ominous sign so I paint a bluebird.

"That's nice," she says. She paints birds, a rainbow, a peace sign. She adds her usual artistic signature CAC and the symbol of an anchor. "I think I'll give this one to Dr. H."

She takes two Klonopin and sleeps through the night. On the last day, I help her wash the dishes and we go through the mail together. She is frustrated, but it's now directed at the bureaucracy, not at me. We go to the laundromat and do several loads of laundry. Later that evening, she drives me back to the Greyhound bus station, and she doesn't hit any barriers.

"I wish you could stay longer," she says.

"I don't," I say. "You've been mean to me all week. I thought you were going to run away."

"I hate this illness."

"It's kind of funny though. Not the illness. But how mean you were."

"You know this illness is not who I am, Jodie."

we attempt to predict it
to prophesy
to forecast the
seasons and cycles of time
the meteorology of mom's mind
every time a bell rings
an angel gets its wings

every time grape juice spills
mom gets sick again
step on a crack
psychiatric break
she always breaks
at Easter break
everything happens in threes
after three days
she emerges
from the psych ward
she ascends
after three days
after every funeral
after every break
she rises again

CANARY DIRGE

DALE MARIE PRENATT

American Elegy is coming
Just you wait—
A bestseller will kill you off too
I'm a hillbilly, they plum kill't me
Bulldozed my bones into valley fill
with the other dead canaries
When exxon oil busts up your aquifers
a red state lawyer
will write a bestseller

about your loose bootstraps too
and shove them down your throat
You'll be paying nestlé for your muddy tap
before your bookclub figures out
that our selenium sludge runs
downstream
and we are your headwaters

POET, PRIEST, AND "POOR WHITE TRASH"

ELIZABETH HADAWAY

START WITH ONE VOICE in one wilderness: the wilderness of southern Appalachia in the 1830s, and the voice of a traveling Methodist pastor, Wiley Winton. He forded rivers and field preached, and while some held that pastors should avoid politics or support the state, Winton followed Jesus in proclaiming release for captives. In the antebellum South he advocated for the abolition of slavery. Winton died young, unpopular among many of his contemporaries, and yet others remembered him with such love that in some ways I'm still living out his legacy.

After Harriet Beecher Stowe published *Uncle Tom's Cabin*, defenders of slavery called her a "mere novelist." In reply, in 1853 she published *A Key to Uncle Tom's Cabin: Presenting the Original Facts and Documents upon Which the Story Is Founded*, a collection of her nonfiction sources. Its chapter titled "Poor White Trash" (which Stowe defines as "a class of white people who are, by universal admission, more heathenish, degraded, and miserable [than slaves])" includes accounts of the "committee of vigilance" that lashed a Grayson County, Virginia, man who had said he would free his slaves and, in their efforts at "ferreting out all persons tinctured with abolitionism in the county," offered "a reward of one hundred dollars for the apprehension and delivery of one Jonathan Roberts to any one of the committees of vigilance."[1]

That was a lot of money in those days, and Jonathan Roberts was more than "tinctured" with abolitionism. He had named a son after the notorious abolitionist preacher Wiley Winton. And while Stowe, from her position of privilege in New England, wondered aloud why anyone with abolitionist sympathies didn't simply flee southwestern Virginia, Jonathan Roberts kept on farming there.

Wiley Winton Roberts was twenty when the Civil War finally came. He made his way across the border, fording rivers, enlisting in the Union army, and getting a tattoo of his initials in hopes his body might be returned to southwestern Virginia, to the family graveyard in Roberts Cove.

And so it was—when he died at ninety-six, having spent most of his life farming in Roberts Cove. He visited the 1907 Jamestown Tercentennial celebrations; he spent decades arguing for a pension in light of the war wound that hobbled him; he built a house and opened a post office in it. He was my great-great-grandfather, and had I been a boy I would have been named after him.

As a girl, I was determined to follow Stowe's advice and get out of Appalachia. The Methodism presented to me in the 1980s had, at least at the church and camp I attended, lost touch with Wiley Winton's countercultural hunger for justice and mercy. It seemed content to be a social club. I asked a question about a story in the Apocryphal Infancy Gospel of Thomas, and the pastor not only accused me of *making up* the story, but refused to unlock the church library to let me read the Apocrypha we did have. (The church library was a whole wall of books behind glass doors in the church parlor, where the cohort of twelve- and thirteen-year-olds had confirmation class; our instructors were often late, and while I was pining after books behind glass, reading what I could of their gilded spines, the other kids played spin the bottle.) Shortly after confirmation, we got a new pastor. I was serving as an acolyte, sitting up in a chair behind him, when he said from the pulpit that he did not approve of women's ordination. My mother, sitting in the congregation, thought from the look on my face that I was going to hit him with the candle snuffer.

I didn't commit assault with a liturgical object, but I quit Methodism. This was before even dial-up Internet access: the isolation that came from dropping out of that small-town social club was profound and bracing. For shock value I went around calling myself an atheist, but I was really an aesthete. And while art museums and concert venues were too far away, I had plenty of access to the gray-market book bins at local flea markets. The books themselves had often been stripped of their covers and illegally reported destroyed, then sold. Those were generally too recent to interest me. What I loved were the ones with the gilded spines, the Edwardian editions of Marlowe and Swinburne and Shelley that had taken a century or so to find their way to Appalachia. Not that it was all about the bindings, or the ethereal. Poetry kept me with a sense of the sacred.

That sense—of something wonderful and distant bending close when called, of the communion of poetry saints bridging space and time—carried me along for several years. It carried me away to college, where my accent was mocked (although my own Appalachian relatives found my vocabulary strange) and then to grad school on a poetry fellowship. It was there, while I was earning an MFA, that a professor complained my poetry was "un-American."

Being labeled "un-American" accorded perfectly with my sense of never having been part of mainstream America—when I was an undergraduate another professor had said, "You write like a mountain person," and from him it was a compliment. To be "un-American" in my case was to be a hard-shell formalist, bootlegging sonnets into workshops taught by Boomers who scorned the sonnet form and yet couldn't beat it out of me. Inspiration from this came partly from another legendary ancestor, Great-Uncle Doc. "Doc" was short for Zadok, the biblical "Zadok the Priest" (the one who anoints King Solomon, as in Handel's coronation anthem). According to the story, our Zadok ran moonshine in a car with a fake floor and died trying to get away from a revenue agent. I would write English sonnets and then scuff the line breaks up so they didn't *look* like sonnets. Only the ear could hear them, but they were metrically strict if you bothered to scan the whole poem. (A critic of my book *Fire Baton* would later mis-scan most of it as "rough iambic pentameter," completely oblivious to the point that it was a sampler of meters, often ones that are to be scanned by stanza rather than line alone: Standard Habbie, for example.)

My un-American aesthetic proved too durable to be destroyed by a fashion arbiter's comment. It grew from an entwining. Part of it was rooted in folk ballads, the weird immortal transatlantic ballads, the come-all-ye's and take-warnings I had heard in scraps, despite my grandmother's conviction that stringed instruments, if they led to dancing, were sinful. (The same grandmother responded to my father's observation that King David played the harp and danced with "David did *right many* things he ought not"). Part of it was rooted in English poetry, in beautiful old books that had survived generations to arrive at the flea markets where I-77 crossed I-81. Some of the folk songs would say that the crossroads are where you meet the Devil to sell your soul, but it was through poetry that I first began to love God.

My poetry career went on, farther from Appalachia and all the way to California (where I had won Stanford University's two-year postgraduate Wallace Stegner Fellowship in Poetry, under the name Leigh Palmer). Over the years and miles, John Donne and George Herbert kept growing more and more important to me. Seventeenth-century Anglican poet-priests, passionate and musical—how could I not love them? When, curious about the Anglican Communion, I finally opened the Book of Common Prayer and saw my old friends Donne and Herbert in the Episcopal calendar of saints, it felt as if I finally had a home.

In California, I sought confirmation as an Episcopalian. The priest was delighted that I had questions about the Apocryphal Infancy Gospel of Thomas, and the bishop who confirmed me turned out to be from West Virginia—one more member of the Appalachian diaspora. As a poet who wanted to delight and instruct by writing theologically sound poetry, I applied for yet another fellowship—this time at Virginia Theological Seminary, inside the Washington Beltway in Alexandria, Virginia.

To be housed and fed while I had the privilege of learning Koine Greek and other treasures was a delight, and I loved my two years there. At the end of them I married another seminarian who was already a deacon and scheduled to be ordained to the priesthood shortly after our wedding.

His sponsoring diocese was West Virginia. He was committed to five years of service there after graduation, and he proposed to me by asking if I would come to West Virginia with him. The motto that Virginia Seminary had long ago painted up over the windows behind its altar was Mark 16:15a—"Go ye into all the world and preach the Gospel." I'd worshipped every day for two years looking at that, and "all the world" must include all of Appalachia.

So I agreed. We moved to Parkersburg, West Virginia, for his first assignment as curate at a parish where he was scheduled to have two years of supervised training, and I found an adjunct job teaching rhetoric and composition at the Parkersburg campus of West Virginia University. It was a long way from my friends and from the bookstores and poetry communities I loved—but we had the Internet now! It would be all right.

One thing about Appalachia is that you get used to leaving and being left. You come to expect it. I grew up knowing I was going to leave someday, and I grew up feeling already left behind. On his first day of work, his training rector called him into the office and said, "I've taken a job in another state." Every day of my childhood I heard trains that carried no passengers, only coal. My parents remembered passenger service, remembered being able to catch a train in Rural Retreat and take it to D.C. or Philadelphia or New York. They remembered being connected. But I'd had a whole life of being considered unworthy of passenger service, unprofitable. The coal was worth more to the railroads than we were. I'd had a whole life of feeling discounted, and being reminded of it every time I heard a train.

I loved traveling by rail when I left Appalachia—I'd rarely owned a car and had managed quite well without one from Charlottesville, Virginia, to Palo Alto, California. Train travel allows for sleeping and meeting and stretching your legs. There are lounge cars and restrooms and dinner service. It doesn't require you to be able to navigate eight lanes of speeding traffic or find fuel on a deserted country road. Now I was back in a place with the lonesomeness of trains that carried no passengers, and the leaving was starting all over again.

We stayed in Parkersburg for eighteen months, and when it became clear that there wasn't an appropriate job available for my husband past that curacy, the bishop released him to search elsewhere with the idea that we would come back if something did open here. So we left.

Nine years later, we came back. My husband had been keeping an eye on jobs in West Virginia, wanting to fulfill his original promise, and he came back as rector of a church in Morgantown. By this time I had a collection of my poetry published (*Fire Baton*, University of Arkansas Press, 2006) and was discerning a call to ordained priesthood myself.

"Discerning a call" in this case meant listening to all the people who kept telling me I should be a priest, and my own dreams of being one, of sharing that sense of the sacred in ways that are not limited to poetry. It also meant overcoming the misogynist preachers and congregants of my childhood, and the ones still around.

I had long since learned that the poetry world was not some better, more accepting alternative to the church. Jesus asks his followers to do some difficult things—love our enemies, give our goods to the poor. He never orders us to dance for tips. That's a Bread Loaf Writers' Conference thing. Up-and-coming poets who were deemed worthy of waiting tables there (and it was a competition to get a waitership) arrived in Vermont and then found out we had to learn a choreographed version of Nelly's "Hot in Herre."

And the poetry world includes the same stereotypes about Appalachia that infect the rest of our culture. Even among poets who actively fight stereotyping, it exists. As I was working on an essay for my sponsoring priest during the discernment process, a friend from the poetry world texted that I had "upped my hipster cred" and should take a look at the latest issue of the *Believer*.

There, along with ads for new music from The Mountain Goats and a guest column by Weird Al Yankovic, was Neko Case's interview with Sherman Alexie. Sherman Alexie complimented me! I was overjoyed to see that among "young poets" he was into he named me as "Elizabeth Hadaway, who I really love"—and then he went on, "She's poor and white, from Appalachia."[2]

Which meant I could never show this to my mom. And it meant that he was reading perceptions about Appalachia into my work that I didn't put there. Nothing in *Fire Baton* is about being poor. I've never claimed to be poor; *Fire Baton* is about being from Appalachia and returning to it—but those childhood baton lessons and sequined twirlers' uniforms were luxuries. So was the high school French club trip to Paris and Nice that I write about in that book. So was the education that allowed me to win fellowships to Stanford and to Virginia Seminary. It's true that I didn't have a lot of advantages that someone growing up outside Appalachia might have had, but I also had a much easier time of it than many of my neighbors. Along with the baton lessons I took swimming lessons and piano lessons. Our household subscribed to *Time, Organic Gardening, Jack and Jill, Redbook, Veterans of Foreign Wars Magazine, Vanity Fair, Southern Living, Royal Bank of Canada Monthly Newsletter, Ladies' Home Journal, Highlights for Children, Readers' Digest, National Geographic, Young Miss,* and *Civil War Times Illustrated.*

I don't think Sherman Alexie intended to make a false equivalency between "poor and white" and "from Appalachia," but it *sounds* like an appositive. I don't think it's an insult, coming from him. There's a passage in Alexie's novel *The Absolutely True Diary of a Part-Time Indian* where the protagonist, Junior, considers all his different tribes: in addition to belonging to the Spokane tribe, he lists thirteen others, including "the tribe of American immigrants," "the tribe of small-town kids," "the tribe of poverty."[3] On reflection, I think the comment reflects a shared approach to America from outside its comfortable myths.

Some people do mean that false equivalency as an insult. West Virginia is the only state whose boundaries are entirely within Appalachia, and yet I have heard a native West Virginian, someone who has never lived anywhere else, referring scornfully to "those Appalachian people." She thought that because she had been born into a wealthy family, because she was a lifelong member of a golf club whose dress code was standardized with that of golf clubs elsewhere, because her accent was ground down to the common denominator of network television, because she wore the same name brands and vacationed at the same resorts as people from suburban Denver or Dallas she was "American," not "Appalachian." "Appalachian" didn't mean geography to her: it meant "poor white trash."

Even though Sherman Alexie didn't use the word "trash," it's been lurking behind "poor and white" ever since Harriet Beecher Stowe's "universal" acknowledgment. I would have loved to have been complimented on the structure of a poem, on a particular rhyme or image. Being described by accidents of birth rather than by anything that characterizes my work itself is particularly depressing when the description could have come from the 1850s as easily as the 2010s.

It's even worse, from the perspective of 2017 when I'm writing this, than it was in 2012. Back then we used to have some fun with the image—I remember a parishioner joking that the duct tape over a hole in the rectory front door made us "real West Virginians." When I went back to seminary in 2014–15 most of my fellow students were preparing for General Ordination Exams, a grueling set of essay tests given during one week of January to those about to graduate from seminaries throughout the Episcopal Church. Some dioceses, including mine, used portfolio systems or diocesan written and oral exams on the canonically required subjects. Saying that rather than take the general online tests I was to be dropped on a mountainside with instructions to kill a bear, make parchment with its hide, and write the answers on *that* was just the kind of tall tale no one expected to believe but which gave some enjoyment in the telling. Now that Appalachia is being used as an excuse for the rise of racist and misogynist action in the United States, it isn't funny at all.

As my mother sighed when she found out I had won two years in California, "Bad things happen everywhere, I guess." Even if everyone here had supported Donald Trump—and we didn't—Appalachia alone could not have elected him. Racism and misogyny and the willful ignorance that denies climate change are American evils, not merely Appalachian evils.

Saying from the pulpit that racism and misogyny and willful ignorance are evils did get me pushed out of my first job as a priest. That's to be expected. It's the Wiley Winton tradition. It goes back to Jesus, who tells his followers to prepare to be unwelcomed, to be on the side of the stranger, and to travel without excess baggage.

That excess baggage can include resentment of the way the church itself has treated us. Much as the poetry world failed to be a haven from prejudice, the church outside Appalachia has consistently written its Appalachian members off as a receptacle of charity. We are a convenient destination for "mission trips" in which wealthy parishes send their youth groups a distance from the slums of their own cities to gawk at our rural poverty and maybe paint a porch. If whole parishes were coming to help protest against interstate fracked-gas pipelines and protect our drinking water, they might learn beyond the stereotypes.

They might at least find a conversation topic other than the inevitable snake-handling question.

The inevitable snake-handling question!

At a church conference in Maryland, in a dining room overlooking the Atlantic Ocean, with spray and dune sand blowing against the windows, a priest asked me—a newcomer to the diocese of Maryland, at the conference as a spouse, trying to get acclimated, a stranger—where I was from.

"Southwest Virginia," I said, being too far from my hometown to expect anyone to recognize its name.

"So you grew up with snake-handing?"

No. I did *not* grow up with snake-handling. It's true that not all of my family were Methodists; some were—like St. Augustine of Hippo—suspicious of church music as a temptation to self-indulgence. They became Baptists who used vocal music only. Being brought up with that subtle yet persistent Augustinian influence, I had never even *heard* of snake-handling in church until I was in college. Then an anthropology professor showed a video of snake-handling worship. It seemed to me like another form of self-indulgence. My first reaction was the way I react to applause after music in worship—the gut reaction that applause in such cases is not only theologically inappropriate, it's tacky, because worship is meant to be offered to God, not for self-glorification.

That snake-handling video gets around, though. Episcopalians who brag about their stance on social justice, their open-mindedness, their tolerance hear I'm from Appalachia and the first thing they do is ask about snake-handling.

They have asked me about it at poetry readings in San Francisco and the tray-return line in the seminary refectory.

I spent a school year as a seminarian intern at the Cathedral Church of St. Peter and St. Paul, fitfully rebranded as Washington National Cathedral, although that violates not only the separation of church and state but also the fact that the Episcopal Church is not a national church. Calling one of its cathedrals "National" plays into the same conflation J. D. Vance makes between nominally Christian theology and civil religion throughout *Hillbilly Elegy*. Vance capitalizes "American Dream," his deity. Despite all the Bible reading he describes, the parable he gives as "the wisdom of the book of Mamaw" is not scripture but self-preservation. Vance is not alone in this failure to distinguish between God and country, and I was already leery of this slippery elision. Still, working at Washington Cathedral was astonishing—I loved the music and the soaring architecture and the moon rock on display in a stained glass window. I prepared, joyfully, to answer questions about the cathedral's commemorations of Brother Lawrence (author of *The Practice of the Presence of God*) and Florence Nightingale and Stephen Langton and a host of others. Edith Bolling Wilson is buried there; I'd read her autobiography and had a slew of anecdotes about her. And yet what did the cosmopolitan congregants actually ask me about?

Did I have any experience snake-handling.

Even overseas, at a dinner in Christ Church, Oxford: the snake-handling question. It came from an American Episcopalian who was also there for continuing education, and by that time I had worked out a response that left me with plenty of emotional energy to enjoy the surroundings and the company. But it was still an annoyance to have to deal with that when I could have been basking in the Oxford glow.

Not that being reminded of Appalachia itself is necessarily emotionally exhausting. On another Oxford night, I lay gazing through a skylight at the moon, listening to the music from a pub across Blue Boar Street fill my room. The singer was a Dolly Parton tribute artist. She provided a perfect blending of longing and loneliness and understanding of that loneliness. From the same ground where the moon had kept in sad step with Sir Philip Sidney,[4] it was keeping me company, and the Appalachian words and music articulating it so well made me feel that I belonged in the tribe of those who have known heartbreaking beauty in Oxford, too.[5]

I am probably going to leave Appalachia again. Shaking off the dust of that first pulpit, from which I was pushed, I am already traveling hundreds of miles to preach and preside at the Eucharist in other parishes; I'll leave home and go where that call takes me. That is what I signed up for when I said I'd follow Jesus. And the next time I leave, wherever I go, I'll be stronger for the experience—especially with my (Washington and Oxford tested!) response to the stereotyped question about liturgical snake-handing:

"Do I have any experience handling snakes? I'm doing it right now."

NOTES

1. Harriet Beecher Stowe, *A Key to Uncle Tom's Cabin: Presenting the Original Facts and Documents upon Which the Story Is Founded* (Boston: John P. Jewett, 1853), 184–90.

2. Sherman Alexie, "Sherman Alexie [Writer] in Conversation with Neko Case [Musician]," *Believer*, February 2012, 61.

3. Sherman Alexie, *The Absolutely True Diary of a Part-Time Indian* (New York: Little, Brown, 2009), 217.
4. Philip Sidney, "With How Sad Steps, O Moon, Thou Climb'st the Skies," in *The Selected Poetry and Prose of Sidney* (New York: Signet, 1970), 138.
5. "Heartbreaking" in reference to Oxford from Dorothy L. Sayers, "the heart-breaking beauty of the curved High Street," in *Gaudy Night* (New York: Harper & Row Perennial, 1986), 229.

CONTRIBUTORS

DWIGHT B. BILLINGS is an emeritus professor of sociology and Appalachian studies at the University of Kentucky. He is a past president of the Appalachian Studies Association and past editor of the *Journal of Appalachian Studies*. He is coauthor, with Kathleen Blee, of *The Road to Poverty: The Making of Wealth and Hardship in Appalachia* (Cambridge University Press, 2000) and coeditor (with Gurney Norman and Katherine Ledford) of *Back Talk from Appalachia: Confronting Stereotypes* (University Press of Kentucky, 2000). Other books include *Planters and the Making of a New South* (1980), *Appalachia in the Making* (coedited with Mary Beth Pudup and Altina Waller in 1995), and *Appalachia in Regional Context: Place Matters* (coedited with Ann Kingsolver in 2018).

IVY BRASHEAR is a tenth-generation Appalachian whose family has lived on the Left Fork of Maces Creek in Perry County since before the Civil War. She is the Appalachian transition coordinator at the Mountain Association for Community Economic Development in Berea, Kentucky, and has written for the *Huffington Post*, Spotlight on Poverty and Opportunity, *Yes! Magazine*, and *Next City*.

THERESA L. BURRISS serves as Radford University's chair of Appalachian studies, director of the Appalachian Regional & Rural Studies Center, and director of academic outreach for the Southwest Virginia Higher Education Center in Abingdon. She is the Virginia US delegate for the Appalachian-Carpathian Mountain Initiative. She has published literary criticism on the Affrilachian Writers, including chapters in *An American Vein: Critical*

Readings in Appalachian Literature (Ohio University Press, 2005) and *Appalachia in the Classroom: Teaching the Region* (Ohio University Press, 2013), for which she served as co-editor with Patricia Gantt. Her chapter "Ecofeminist Sensibilities and Rural Land Literacies in the Work of Contemporary Appalachian Novelist Ann Pancake" is included in *Literature and Ecofeminism: Intersectional and International Voices* (Routledge, 2018). Additionally, her chapter "Raven, Woman, Man: A/Religious Ecocritical Reading of Jim Minick's *Fire Is Your Water*" will appear in the WVU Press collection *Appalachian Ecocriticism*.

ELIZABETH CATTE is a public historian and writer from East Tennessee. She holds a PhD in public history and is the author of *What You Are Getting Wrong about Appalachia* (2018). She currently lives in Staunton, Virginia, and is the director of Passel, a historical consulting firm.

JODIE CHILDERS is a writer and documentary filmmaker who is currently pursuing a PhD at the University of Massachusetts Amherst. Her research focuses on Cold War cultural production. Her poetry, fiction, and photography have been published in many literary journals including *Eleven Eleven*, *Feral Feminisms*, *Poetry East*, and the *Portland Review*. Her film work from her current documentary on Pete Seeger has been featured in the *Woody Guthrie Annual* and *In These Times*.

DANIELLE DULKEN is a reproductive justice activist from the mountains of western North Carolina. She is currently pursuing a PhD in American studies at the University of North Carolina at Chapel Hill.

ROBERT GIPE is the author of the novels *Trampoline* and *Weedeater* and is the Appalachian program director at Southeast Kentucky Community & Technical College in Harlan County, Kentucky. He is the former director of educational services at Appalshop, a media arts center in Whitesburg, Kentucky.

CRYSTAL GOOD is an advocate, entrepreneur, and writer poet who uses poetry and performance to explore the landscape of West Virginia/Appalachia as a lens into the multi-universe. She is a member of the Affrilachian Poets and an Irene McKinney Scholar and performs with Heroes Are Gang Leaders, a New York–based Free/Avant-Garde experimental improvisation jazz ensemble. She has performed in five countries and lectured at many universities across America. She is the author of "Valley Girl" and the CEO of Mixxed Media and Good Hemp, an Appalachian small farm natural cosmetics company. For more, see crystalgood.com, @cgoodwoman, #goodforgood.

JESSE GRAVES is the author of three poetry collections, *Tennessee Landscape with Blighted Pine* (2011), *Basin Ghosts* (2014), and *Specter Mountain* (2018). He received the James Still Award for Writing about the Appalachian South from the Fellowship of Southern Writers, two Weatherford Awards for Poetry, and the Philip H. Freund Prize from Cornell University. He teaches as associate professor of English and poet-in-residence at East Tennessee State University.

ROGER GUY is a professor of criminal justice at the State University of New York at Oswego. He is the author of *From Diversity to Unity: Southern and Appalachian Migrants in Uptown Chicago, 1950–1970* (Lexington, 1997) and *When Architecture Meets Activism: The Transformative Effect of Hank Williams Village in the Windy City* (Rowman and Littlefield, 2016). He has published numerous articles on Appalachian migration in *Oral History Review*, the *Journal of Appalachian Studies*, and the *Journal of Urban History*.

ELIZABETH HADAWAY is an Episcopal priest (Virginia Theological Seminary, 2015) ordained in the Diocese of West Virginia. Her first collection of poetry, *Fire Baton* (University of Arkansas Press, 2006), is about returning to Appalachia in an effort to help. She regards *Hillbilly Elegy*'s claim to speak for a people of "deep faith" as an idolatrous conflation of Christianity with nationalism and greed.

RICHARD HAGUE is author of eighteen volumes, most recently *Studied Days: Poems Early & Late in Appalachia* (Dos Madres Press, 2016), and is a frequent presenter at the Appalachian Studies Association's annual conference. He is the winner of the 2003 Appalachian Poetry Book of the Year and the 2012 Weatherford Award in Poetry, and was 1985 Co-Poet of the Year in Ohio. He was the featured writer at the 32nd Emory & Henry Literary Festival, and his life and work was the subject of that year's *Iron Mountain Review*. *Earnest Occupations*, a volume of essays about various local arts, was published by Bottom Dog Press in early spring 2018. Since 2015 he has been writer-in-residence at Thomas More College in Crestview Hills, Kentucky.

ANTHONY HARKINS is professor of history at Western Kentucky University. He is the author of *Hillbilly: A Cultural History of an American Icon* (Oxford University Press, 2004) and "Colonels, Hillbillies and Fightin': Twentieth-Century Kentucky in the National Imagination," *Register of the Kentucky Historical Society* 113 (Spring/Summer 2015), and coeditor, with Douglas Reichert Powell and Katherine Ledford, of the "Media" section of the *Encyclopedia of Appalachia* (University of Tennessee Press, 2006).

KELLI HANSEL HAYWOOD is the mother of three daughters living in the mountains of southeastern Kentucky. She is a writer, spiritual explorer, and avid yogini. She has worked in various capacities with citizen and professional journalism and is currently blogging, teaching yoga, and freelancing.

T. R. C. HUTTON is senior lecturer and university historian in the department of history of the University of Tennessee in Knoxville and the author of *Bloody Breathitt: Politics & Violence in the Appalachian South* (University Press of Kentucky, 2013). His online essays have appeared in the History News Network, the U.S. Intellectual History Blog, and the online version of *Jacobin*.

CHELSEA JACK is a PhD student in the anthropology department at Yale University. She focuses on sociocultural and medical anthropology. She calls the Blue Ridge Mountains home and grew up in Bedford County, Virginia.

ALLEN JOHNSON has lived in rural West Virginia for forty-five years, with extensive work experience including construction, teaching, social work, health care, and librarianship. He holds a BA in biology and a master's in theology. He is cofounder and coordinator of Christians for the Mountains, has been a reservist with Christian Peacemaker Teams, and has written for several publications.

JEREMY B. JONES is the author of *Bearwallow: A Personal History of a Mountain Homeland*, which was named the Appalachian Book of the Year in nonfiction in 2014 and awarded gold in memoir in the Independent Publisher Book Awards in 2015. His essays appear in *Oxford American*, *Brevity*, the *Iowa Review*, and elsewhere. Originally from the mountains of North Carolina, he earned his MFA from the University of Iowa and is associate professor of English at Western Carolina University. He also serves as the series coeditor of In Place, a literary nonfiction book series from West Virginia University Press.

EDWARD KARSHNER was born in Ross County, Ohio. He is proud to represent eight generations of Karshners from the Salt Creek Valley of Southeast Appalachia Ohio. He is an associate professor of English at Robert Morris University and lives in Oberlin, Ohio, with his wife, their two children, and a mixed-breed dog named Carlos.

REBECCA KIGER is a documentary and portrait photographer living in West Virginia. She studied at Shepherd College in West Virginia and finished a degree in photography, education, and antiracism work at Hampshire College. She has a second degree in Spanish and Latin American studies from UMass Amherst. Her work has been published on the Lens blog, *TIME* magazine, Everyday Rural America, Looking at Appalachia, and 100 Days in Appalachia. She earned the 2018 Edward R. Murrow Award for Excellence in Video. She has been selected to be a 2018–19 "Teaching Artist" through the Rural Arts Collaborative (RAC). Her ongoing personal projects are centered around exploring the challenges of living in rural communities in Puerto Rico, central Missouri, and Athens, Ohio.

TRAVIS LINNEMANN teaches in justice studies at Eastern Kentucky University. His writing appears in the journals *Theoretical Criminology, British Journal of Criminology, Crime, Media, Culture, Critical Criminology, Deviant Behavior*, and elsewhere. He is also the author of *Meth Wars: Police, Media, Power* (New York University Press, 2016) and, with Yvonne Jewkes, *Media and Crime in the U.S.* (Sage, 2017). His next book, *The Horror of Police*, is under contract with the University of Minnesota Press.

MICHAEL E. MALONEY is a Cincinnati-based community organizer, social researcher, consultant, and activist who has worked in both rural and urban Appalachian settings. He has taught Appalachian studies at several universities in Ohio and Kentucky and organized community initiatives such as the Urban Appalachian Council in Cincinnati and the Ohio Appalachian Arts Initiative. His publications include *The Social Areas of Cincinnati* (editions 1–5) and, as editor, with Phillip Obermiller, *Appalachia: Social Context Past and Present* (editions 4–5). He grew up in the Three Forks area of eastern Kentucky and was born just a few miles from Jackson in Breathitt County. He came to Cincinnati to go to college and, like many migrants, never made it back home.

JEFF MANN has published five books of poetry, *Bones Washed with Wine, On the Tongue, Ash, A Romantic Mann*, and *Rebels*; two collections of essays, *Edge* and *Binding the God*; a book of poetry and memoir, *Loving Mountains, Loving Men*; six novels, *Fog, Purgatory, Cub, Salvation, Country*, and *Insatiable*; and three volumes of short fiction, *A History of Barbed Wire, Desire and Devour*, and *Consent*. He teaches creative writing at Virginia Tech.

ROGER MAY is an Appalachian American photographer based in his home state of West Virginia. His photographs, essays, and interviews have been published in the *Guardian*, the *New York Times, National Geographic*, the *Atlantic*, and many other publications. In 2014, he started the crowdsourced project Looking at Appalachia. In addition to photographing Appalachia, he writes about place, identity, and visual representation.

MEREDITH MCCARROLL is director of writing and rhetoric at Bowdoin College, where she teaches courses in composition, rhetoric, Southern and American literature, and film. She earned her PhD in English at University of Tennessee. Her essays have been published in *Bitter Southerner*, *Avidly*, *Southern Cultures*, and the *Guardian*. Her scholarship on regional identity, racial construction, voice, and literature has been published in *Appalachian Journal*, *Pluck!*, and *Praxis*. She is the author of *Unwhite: Appalachia, Race, and Film* (University of Georgia Press, 2018). Her work is situated at the intersection of race and regional studies, with a focus on cinematic representations of this intersection.

CORINA MEDLEY teaches in justice studies at Eastern Kentucky University. Her interests include theory, criminology and deviance, culture and media, sexuality and gender, and animal/animality studies.

JIM MINICK is the author of five books, including *Fire Is Your Water*, a debut novel released in 2017. His memoir, *The Blueberry Years*, won the Best Nonfiction Book of the Year from the Southern Independent Booksellers Association. His work has appeared in many publications including *Poets & Writers*, *Oxford American*, *Shenandoah*, *Orion*, the *Bark*, *San Francisco Chronicle*, *Encyclopedia of Appalachia*, *Conversations with Wendell Berry*, *Appalachian Journal*, and the *Sun*. Currently, he is assistant professor at Augusta University and core faculty in Converse College's low-residency MFA program.

ROBERT MORGAN is the author of fifteen books of poems, most recently *Terroir* (2011) and *Dark Energy* (2015). He has published eleven works of fiction, including *Chasing the North Star* (2016) and *As Rain Turns to Snow* (2017). Nonfiction works include *Boone: A Biography* (2007) and *Lions of the West* (2011). A member of the fellowship of Southern Writers, and a native of western North Carolina, he is currently Kappa Alpha Professor of English at Cornell University.

Lou Murrey is a photographer and community organizer from Northwestern, North Carolina. They currently live in East Tennessee and have worked with communities around issues of clean water access, rural broadband expansion, energy efficiency, and building new structures of democracy at the local level through the Knoxville City Council Movement. Lou has nurtured a lifelong love of photography and has used that skill to document a diverse array of experiences in Appalachia. They just recently stepped into the role of interim coordinator for the Stay Together Appalachian Youth Project.

Ricardo Nazario y Colón is one of the cofounders of the Affrilachian Poets and author of the books *Of Jíbaros and Hillbillies* (Plain View Press, 2011) and *The Recital* (Winged City Press, 2011). His work has appeared in *Falling Star Magazine*, *Aphros Review*, *Acentos Review*, the *Round Table*, *Southern Poetry Anthology* vol. 3, *Pine Mountain Sand & Gravel* vol. 14, BlazeVOX, *A Hudson View*, and others. He resides in Waynesville, North Carolina, where he serves as the first chief diversity officer for Western Carolina University. www.lalomadelviento.com.

Kelly Norman Ellis is associate professor of English and director of the MFA in creative writing program at Chicago State University. She is the author of *Tougaloo Blues* and coeditor of *Spaces Between Us: Poetry, Prose and Art on AIDS/HIV*, both from Third World Press. Her work has appeared in *Crab Orchard Review*, *Sou'Wester*, *PMS poemmemoirstory*, *Tidal Basin Review*, *Calyx*, and the *Ringing Ear*. In 2010 *Essence Magazine* voted her one of their forty favorite poets. She is a Cave Canem Poetry Fellow and founding member of the Affrilachian Poets.

Linda Parsons is a poet, playwright, freelance editor, and the reviews editor at *Pine Mountain Sand & Gravel*. She has contributed to the *Georgia Review*, *Iowa Review*, *Prairie Schooner*, *Southern Poetry Review*, *The Chattahoochee Review*, *Shenandoah*, and Ted Kooser's syndicated column *American Life in Poetry*, among many other journals and anthologies. Her most recent poetry collection is *This Shaky Earth*, and her newest endeavor is writing for the Hammer Ensemble, the social justice wing of Flying Anvil Theatre in Knoxville, Tennessee.

DALE MARIE PRENATT is a poet and storyteller from southern West Virginia by way of eastern Kentucky. She earned a bachelor's degree in theatre from Morehead State. Her poems have appeared in *Quarried: Three Decades of Pine Mountain Sand & Gravel* and other publications, and her storytelling has been featured on NPR.

LISA R. PRUITT is Martin Luther King, Jr., Professor of Law at the University of California, Davis. She has written extensively about rurality, whiteness, and class, including "Welfare Queens and White Trash" (2016), "The False Choice between Race and Class" (2015), "The Geography of the Class Culture Wars" (2011), and "Rural Rhetoric" (2006).

KIRSTIN L. SQUINT is associate professor of English at High Point University, where she teaches classes in US multiethnic literatures. She is the author of *LeAnne Howe at the Intersections of Southern and Native American Literature* (LSU Press, 2018) and a coeditor of the in-progress collection *Swamp Souths: Literary and Cultural Ecologies*.

LUKE TRAVIS is a photographer from Pittsburgh, Pennsylvania, who through his camera studies the human species and witnesses their activity in both intimate and public environments.

WILLIAM H. TURNER is senior unit leader of Social Systems and Allied Research, Cooperative Agricultural Research Center in the College of Agriculture and Human Sciences at Prairie View A&M University in Prairie View, Texas. He is coeditor, with Edward R. Cabbell, of *Blacks in Appalachia* (University Press of Kentucky, 1983), author of "The Canaries in Appalachian Coal Mines Were Black," *Now and Then: The Appalachian Magazine* 32, no. 2 (2016), author of the foreword to Thomas Wagner and Phillip Obermiller's *African American Miners and Migrants: The Eastern Kentucky Social Club*

(University of Illinois Press, 2004), and guest editor of "Special Issues on Blacks in Appalachia," *Appalachian Heritage* (1991 and 2011).

DANA WILDSMITH is the author of a novel, *Jumping*, and a book of poems, *One Light* (Texas Review Press, forthcoming). For her environmental memoir, *Back to Abnormal: Surviving with an Old Farm in the New South*, she was finalist for Georgia Author of the Year. She is the author of five collections of poetry, including, most recently, *Christmas in Bethlehem*. She has served as artist-in-residence for Grand Canyon National Park and Everglades National Park and as writer-in-residence for the Island Institute in Sitka, Alaska, and is a fellow of the Hanbidge Center for Creative Arts and Sciences. She teaches English literacy through Lanier Technical College.

KEITH S. WILSON is an Affrilachian Poet, Cave Canem fellow, and graduate of the Callaloo Creative Writing Workshop. He has received three scholarships from Bread Loaf as well as scholarships from MacDowell, the Millay Colony, Poetry by the Sea, Ucross, and the Virginia Center for the Creative Arts. He currently serves as assistant poetry editor at *Four Way Review* and digital media editor at *Obsidian Journal*.

MEG WILSON was born in New Mexico near the foothills of the Sandia Mountains. She has been a shepherdess, a midwife, a nurse, a traveler, and a mother. She has always been a photographer. She shoots with a variety of cameras, including the vintage twin lens film camera that her grandfather used in a small New Mexico town in 1958. She and her husband live on their small farm in Paint Lick, Kentucky. She is a member of the Kentucky Women Photographer's Network, and is a recipient of the 2018 Artist Enrichment Grant from the Kentucky Foundation for Women. Her work is included in the ongoing project Looking at Appalachia, the featured artist section of *Still: The Journal, Appalachian Heritage, National Geographic*, and *New York Times* photography blogs, as well as the *Guardian*. You can see her most recent work on Instagram, @meg__wilson.

RACHEL WISE received her PhD in English from the University of Texas at Austin in 2014. She subsequently spent time as a visiting scholar at the American Academy of Arts and Sciences in Cambridge, Massachusetts. While in residency, she worked on a book-length project, *Losing Appalachia*, which examines Appalachian literature's use of material culture to critique industrial capitalism. Her scholarly work has appeared in *Arizona Quarterly*, *Resources for American Literary Study*, and the forthcoming collection *Timelines of American Literature*. You can find her poetry in *Cave Region Review* and *Chariton Review*. She currently resides in Austin as an independent scholar and full-time grant writer.

SOURCES AND PERMISSIONS

"Hillbilly Elitism" by T. R. C. Hutton first appeared in the online edition of *Jacobin* (2016), https://www.jacobinmag.com/2016/10/hillbilly-elegy-review-jd-vance-national-review-white-working-class-appalachia/, and is republished with permission.

An earlier version of "Keep Your 'Elegy'" by Ivy Brashear first appeared as "Why Media Must Stop Misrepresenting Appalachia," *Huffington Post Blog* (April 20, 2017), https://www.huffingtonpost.com/entry/i-am-appalachian-too-a-response-to-hillbilly-elegy_us_58ebe93ae4b081da6ad006be.

A version of "In Defense of J. D. Vance" by Kelli Hansel Haywood first appeared in *Pine Mountain Sand & Gravel, Vol. 20: Appalachia: Stay or Go?* (Southern Appalachian Writers Cooperative, 2017), and is republished with permission.

"On and On: Appalachian Accent and Academic Power" by Meredith McCarroll first appeared in *Southern Cultures* 22, no. 2 (Summer 2016), southerncultures.org, and is republished with permission.

The photographs *Olivia's Ninth Birthday Party* by Rebecca Kiger, *Watch Children* by Luke Travis, *Aunt Rita along the King Coal Highway* by Roger May, and *Olivia at the Intersection* by Meg Wilson were previously published in Looking at Appalachia, https://lookingatappalachia.org, and are republished with permission.

INDEX

INDEX

Bickerstaff, Bernard, 234
Billings, Dwight, 6, 30, 38, 191
Biloxi (MS), 326
Birth of a Nation (Griffith), 329
blackness, 28, 329
black people. *See* African Americans
Blank, Rebecca, 71
Blow, Charles, 110–11
boarding school, 300–302
bootstrap theory, 5, 23, 32, 106, 162, 189
Bourdieu, Pierre, 116
Bowers, Virginia, 94–95
Bowling Green State University (BGSU), 69–70
Brashear, Della Combs, 157–59, 162, 165, 168
Brashear, Ivy, 7, 46–47, 157, 191
bricolage, 337, 341, 346
Brislin, Chelsea, 67
Brooks, David, 2, 22–23, 32–33, 42–43
Brown, Bill, 339, 347n9
Brown, James, 174, 175
Brown, Karida, 229–31, 232, 242
Brown, Wendy, 45, 47
Browning, Norma Lee, 98–99
Burr, R. Mike, 47
Burriss, Theresa, 9, 80
Burt, Susan, 218

Callaway, Franklin (and family), 235–36
Campbell, Raleigh, 86–87, 88, 103n19
capital, 45, 96
capitalism, 23, 31, 142, 189, 232, 308;
    corporate, 45; industrial, 313, 339;
    materialism and, 333, 343; neoliberal,
    7, 45, 143; oxymoron of, 32; racial, 139;
    whiteness and, 28
capitalist realism, 137, 143–45, 147–50
Catte, Elizabeth, 6, 13, 53
Caudill, Harry, 1, 75–77, 185, 186, 240
Celtic or Scots-Irish culture, 29, 46, 129n26
Centre College (KY), 72
chemical plant (Kingsport, TN), 309–10
Chetty, Raj, 186
Chicago, 6, 88–90, 96, 99, 232, 335
Childers, Jodie, 12, 376
childhood trauma: confronting and exposing,
    202, 223n4; long-term impacts, 203;
    prejudices and stereotypes and, 213–14;
    resiliency and transcendence, 204–5;
    school interventions, 215–18; Vance's, 4,
    38, 119, 201
choice, personal, 48, 55, 196, 242, 283–87;

drug addiction and, 137, 138, 141, 146;
    good and bad, 41, 73, 108, 122, 207, 281;
    neoliberalism and, 46–47; women's, 266
Christmas in Appalachia (1965), 9, 334
Chua, Amy, 5, 22–23, 43, 56n14, 66
church congregations, 183–84, 218–20,
    257–58, 382; Episcopalian, 393, 397–98;
    mission trips, 397
Cincinnati (OH), 90, 173, 256–57, 323,
    325; East/Lower Price Hill and South
    Fairmount, 172, 174, 177
class hierarchy, 337, 342
class migration, 11, 106, 121–22, 124, 131n59;
    academic struggles and, 337, 339
Clinton, Bill, 42, 44, 45, 113, 232
Clinton, Hillary, 48, 52, 66, 111, 113;
    comments on coal miners, 53, 59n45
coal miners, 54, 157; African American,
    231–32, 241–42; Benham (KY), 80, *81*;
    danger and death, 312; depopulation and,
    209; Hillary Clinton's comments on, 53,
    59n45; job loss, 50, 51, 177, 212–13; for
    Kingsport chemical plant, 309–10
Coates, Ta-Nehisi, 42, 65, 76, 106
college campus life, 62, 64–65, 72
colonialism, 261
common reading programs, 62–65, 69–71
community building, 50, 163, 166, 216, 221;
    festivals, 374
conservatism, 22–23, 25–26, 51, 150, 193
Cooke, Grace MacGowan, 339–40, 342, 347n8
cooking narratives, 350–55; baking buckeye,
    265, 267n5; family gatherings, 179. *See
    also* cornbread
corn: planting and harvesting, 357–60, 366;
    sweet and field, 363; winnowing and
    grinding, 362
cornbread: eating, 357, 365; mixes, 362–63;
    opinions, 367; recipe, 363–64
corporate media, 42, 47, 48, 161, 168
cosmovision, 281, 286, 288
Cox, Karen L., 75
Creadick, Anna, 257
cultural decline, 63, 66
culture: adaptive practices, 175; Appalachian,
    98, 191, 212, 286, 332, 374; Arnold's
    description, 339, 347n8; indoctrination,
    64; literary text and, 338, 342; of poverty,
    2, 31, 41, 45, 120, 137, 187; religious, 219;
    shock, 301; social problems and, 195–96;
    term usage, 30–31. *See also* hillbilly culture